A Raid into Dark Corners
and Other Essays

A Raid into Dark Corners
and Other Essays

Benedict Kiely

CORK UNIVERSITY PRESS

First published in 1999 by
Cork University Press
University College
Cork
Ireland

British Library Cataloguing in Publication Data
A CIP catalogue record for this book is available from
the British Library

ISBN 1 85918 235 6

Typeset by Tower Books, Ballincollig, Co. Cork
Printed by MPG Books Ltd, Cornwall

The Arts Council
An Chomhairle Ealaíon

The publishers gratefully acknowledge the
receipt of financial assistance from
the Arts Council / An Comhairle Ealaíon

These meditations I offer to
Douglas Gageby and Jim McGuinness,
good friends and colleagues
for many years

Contents

Acknowledgements

A SPECIAL WORD OF THANKS to Jonathan Williams whose advice and help were worth a lot.

The essays collected here appeared in a variety of sources over the years. The following is a list of publications in which they were first published:

'Ned McKeown's Two Doors: An Approach to the Novel in Ireland', *Ireland and the Arts*, edited by Tim Pat Coogan, *Quartet*

'Land Without Stars; Aodhagán O'Rahilly', *The Capuchin Annual*, 1945–6

'A Raid into Dark Corners: The Poems of Seamus Heaney', *The Hollins Critic*, Oct 1978

'Love and Pain and Parting: The Novels of Kate O'Brien', *The Hollins Critic*, December 1992

'Irish Potato and Attic Salt', *The Irish Bookman*, November 1946

'The Cormorant and the Badger: The Stories of Patrick Boyle', *The Irish Times*, 16 March 1982

'Clay and Gods and Men: The Worlds of James Stephens', *The Irish Bookman*, October 1946

'Praise God for Ireland: The Novels of Francis MacManus', *The Kilkenny Magazine*, Spring/Summer 1970

'Charles Kickham and the Living Mountain', *The Irish Times*

'John Montague: Dancer in a Rough Field', *The Hollins Critic*, December 1978

'The Whores on the Halfdoors: An Image of the Irish Writer', *The Kilkenny Magazine*, Spring/Summer. 1966

'The Coppinger Novels of Bruce Arnold', *The Hollins Critic*, April 1984

'Chronicle by Rushlight: Daniel Corkery's Quiet Desperation', *The Irish Bookman*, January 1948

'Thomas Flanagan: The Lessons of History', *The Hollins Critic*, October 1981

'That Old Triangle: A Memory of Brendan Behan', *The Hollins Critic*

'Liam O'Flaherty: From the Stormswept Rock . . .', *The Month*, II, September 1949

'The Two Masks of Gerald Griffin', *Studies*, Autumn 1972

'Orange Lily in a Green Garden: Shan F. Bullock', *The Irish Times*, 1972

'The Thorn in the Water: The Stories of Michael McLaverty', *Hibernia*, 17 July 1970

'Green Island, Red South', *The Kilkenny Magazine*, Autumn/Winter 1970

~ Preface ~

Behind the Green Curtain

THERE IS A BOOK BY THE FORMER drama critic of the *Manchester Guardian*, C. E. Montague, who may be a distant relative of my own (his father was a priest from Tyrone, his mother a McCabe from Dundalk), called *A Writer's Notes on His Trade*. *A Raid into Dark Corners* is that kind of book; a thoughtful re-examination of the writers who have influenced Ben Kiely's career as a fictioneer for more than fifty years, although he is less concerned with technical niceties than Charles Edward.

Ben Kiely must be one of the most beloved of Irish writers, a smiling Tyrone man, turned eighty. We knew him first as a novelist, *Land without Stars* (1946), which contrasted innocent days in the Donegal Gaeltacht with jagged glimpses of life in an Ulster town, where the gun was not unknown, either in the Army or RUC barracks, or under a brother's pillow. He came often to speak to the fledgeling poets of UCD; red-haired, modest, but devoted both to writing and social drinking. He was the first writer I had met, and an Omagh man at that, my market town.

He earned his living as a journalist on *The (Catholic) Standard* (when will some student exhume those curious files where Kiely, Kavanagh and later myself concealed our passions at the heart of piety?) and then literary editor and factotum of two national dailies. *In a Harbour Green* (1948), his second novel, earned him the only laurels going at the time, those bestowed by the Irish Censorship Board. His vision of life in that Ulster town had become darker; or more truthful?

Call for a Miracle (1950), an attempt to chart a little of the post-Joycean Dublin, also received the hammer; those were not easy years for writers, old or young. So an even darker city appears in *Honey Seems Bitter*, his version of a Graham Greene style 'entertainment'. For those were the days when local critics were yearning for an Irish Catholic novelist, but Kiely's talent was more restless and robust than his friend Francis MacManus, whose *The Fire in the Dust* best fills the Catholic prescription. There is a fine essay here on that forgotten novelist.

Religion in the form of a Jesuit novitiate did appear in *There was an Ancient House*. But I do not think Kiely could be described as having a religious vocation, even as a novelist. Two more early works should be remembered *The Cards of the Gambler*, where, like George Mackay Brown of Orkney, he sought to modernise the folktale and that study of a martinet, *The Captain with the Whiskers*, who made his children drill in the hills of Gortin.

Then, in mid-career, Kiely changed course. He had grown up surrounded by short story writers, mainly from Cork, and had seemed determined to disprove O'Connor's argument that Irish society was not dense enough to sustain a professional novelist. Abruptly, Ben began to write stories himself, at first, affectionate anecdotes of childhood, like 'The White Wild Bronco', then more coiling and curling tales, a voice embroidering its own relaxed song.

For Ben Kiely's true literary godfather was not Graham Greene, or the giant Joyce, with their different burdens of Catholic guilt. Behind him looms the old-fashioned delight in narrative and character of William Carleton, of whom he once wrote a detailed study. It is always important to set a writer in his proper context, and when Kiely's stories are finally collected, their kinship with Carleton's *Traits and Stories of the Irish Peasantry* will be evident. After the man from Clogher comes the man from Omagh.

Carleton spoke of his great work as 'two unpretentious volumes, written by a peasant's son'. There is something unpretentious about Kiely also; he does not present himself as the aloof artist, paring his fingernails, but as almost overcome by the variety of life. His vision of childhood is both more innocent and knowing than Joyce's, but that probably has to do with the moral code of his town and time. The corner boys of a garrison town could give crude hints to Krafft-Ebing, and, through Carleton, Kiely had inherited a pre-Famine sensibility. The pullulating population of pre-Famine Ireland was not noted for its priest-bound piety, and some of that almost Burnsean ribaldry had survived in the hills and glens. A Jesuit uncle of my own wrote (from the safety of Melbourne) that a principal pastime of the Tyrone of his youth was sex, and Kiely's kingdom is tolerant in its eroticism. There is a coarse streak in Irish life which Joyce wrought to greatness; and Kiely never ignores it.

He is also unabashed in his nostalgia, his love of places and the people who love them; I knew the American professor of 'The Dogs in the Great Glen' and the story is so true that it is as moving as one of O'Connor's loneliest pieces, 'Bridal Night'. It is fascinating to re-read an early essay of Kiely's (from the *Capuchin Annual*) on the Kerry poets, especially

O'Rahilly, called 'Land without Stars', like his first novel. Enthusiastic and allusive, it now reads like an oblique commentary on the much later story.

What is striking about this collection of essays is its variety. The largest group of writers is from Munster. We move from O'Rahilly to Francis Sylvester Mahony, 'Father Prout', the Myles of his day, celebrated also in Terry Eagleton's *Crazy John and the Bishop*. Other nineteenth-century figures include the gentle Gerald Griffin, and the patriot Charles Kickham, whose inclusion would have delighted my father, who thought *Knock-nagow, or The Homes of Tipperary*, was the best book ever written (and 'Slievenamon' the best song). I am not sure that he would have approved of a priestly novelist like Canon Sheehan, although he might have applauded his 'simple, ascetic ideal for the Irish people. He wanted a hardy race who lived on milk and oatmeal, came in time for Mass and were content with no money in their pockets.' At times Canon Sheehan sounded like an avatar of Eamon de Valera.

In our own century, Kiely celebrates the bravery of Kate O'Brien, and, of course, the Cork brigade, Daniel Corkery and his two rebel sons, Sean O'Faoláin and Frank O'Connor. I think that the Munster, and indeed Cork, emphasis is because they were the writers best known in Kiely's day, living exemplars of the art of prose writing. He pays back his debts with typical generosity, and does not evade dealing with the harsh climate they lived in, under a censorship that rivalled the Soviet or the Vatican. For Kiely also lived and wrote during those dark times, earning his living as a professional journalist, behind what I would call the Green Curtain, no less implacable for being made not of iron, but slippery green piety, accusing all writers of betraying both country and church.

The principal characteristics of Kiely during those blighted years when de Valera and John Charles McQuaid seemed to be hand in glove, were his courtesy, stamina, and learned curiosity. He did not flinch or complain about this intellectual and moral famine. Young writers gathered around him during his breaks, for soup or drink, from his nocturnal duties at *The Irish Press* or the *Independent*. He sought, and was sought out by the young – Hutchinson, Cronin, Jordan and myself – as an alternative to the stagnant atmosphere of the time. And in his home in Clontarf, at the weekends, there was more time for merriment, with Ben's voice resonating in honey anecdote or song. I remember particularly a night when he sang a poem of MacNeice to the semi-comatose poet himself:

> Then twangling their bibles with wrath in their nostrils
> From Bonehill Fields came Bunyan and Blake;
> 'Laredo the golden is fallen, is fallen;
> Your flame shall not quench nor your thirst shall not slake.'

It would be surprising if there were not some bitterness after such unnecessary constrictions, and essays like 'Ned McKeown's Two Doors' and 'The Whores on the Halfdoors' do address those dreadful days, when the atmosphere of the time was against any honesty in thought or art, and a writer was equated with a streetwalker. But anger is not Kiely's natural element; he prefers his palimpsest of paraphrase and praise, to point us to the pleasures of the works he loves: Ben-evolence is his best critical method.

Ulster plays its part, of course: from the almost forgotten poems of Joseph Campbell, and stories of Patrick Boyle, to poets like myself and Heaney. Always, behind the prose, one hears the rich, reverberating tones of Kiely's Omagh organ voice. Henry James is rightly famous for his exfoliating style, and Kiely is very nearly from the same neck of the Ulster woods: the web of his prose captures his subjects by circling and weaving strands around it. 'The Great Gazebo' is a splendid example of his method at its best, beginning with the West Cork Castletownshend of Somerville and Ross, returning to the Dublin Gothic of Maturin and Sheridan le Fanu, through the North Cork of Elizabeth Bowen, to end with Brendan Behan's hilarious play, *The Big House*. 'Green Island, Red South' is another stunning example of circularity, which brings us from the Boyne Valley, by way of Brinsley MacNamara and Mary Lavin, to the Georgia of Flannery O'Connor. Ben once ran a column in *The Irish Press* under the *nom de plume* of Pat Lagan, and these warm, exuberant meanders through history and literature provide a fascinating gloss on his creative work, and an introduction to the books he loves.

John Montague
Ireland Professor of Poetry

ᴗℯ 1 ℒᴗ

Ned McKeown's Two Doors:
An Approach to the Novel in Ireland

I F YOU ARE IRISH YOU NEED NOT, necessarily, come into the parlour. But if you are Irish and have ever tried to write a novel and then if, long afterwards, you sit down to meditate on the nature of the Irish novel, you may be driven to look back, with sad affection, on your first faltering effort or efforts. Everything, even the great globe itself, has to begin and end somewhere. See Shakespeare and Aristotle. Although there once was a legend about something or somebody that did not have a beginning and would never have an end.

Reared as I was in a provincial town in a river-valley, to all of which I was deeply devoted, it was not surprising that when I first made an effort to write a novel, it should also have been an attempt to celebrate that river-valley.

In a public park on the Camowen river before it reaches the town, a park called the Lovers' Retreat but known by a grosser name to the liberal shepherds, or soldiers in the barracks, I met, one evening in 1936, a young soldier. We became friendly over the next few months. Then he disappeared for a while and when I next encountered him he was being escorted from the railway-station by two members of the Royal Ulster Constabulary. In the relaxed atmosphere of those days, it was possible to stop and ask them what it was all about. It appeared that my pal had deserted from the British army and, while heading for the Border at Strabane, had made love to a few bits of property that did not quite belong to him, like a bicycle, a suit of civilian clothes, and so on. He was, though, quite cheerful about it all and on the best of terms with his captors.

I never saw him again. But I did not forget him and, even if I have forgotten his name, I can still see him laughing his way to jail or somewhere; and away back about the Christmas of 1939 I started to write a

1

novel about him under the title *King's Shilling*. I suppose I could say grandly that my runaway soldier was the symbol of the pilgrim soul and that I was trying to express something very deep about the plight of man on earth. But then I was not trying to make him seem to be anything of the sort, but merely trying to describe the joy I felt as a young fellow in the Strule valley when the grass meadows were going down in late June or July, according to the weather in any year. So I set my soldier running away along that valley. There naturally had to be people in the story or it wouldn't, I thought, have been a story at all, even if I was well aware that the author of *The Wind in the Willows*, and some other authors, had managed without people. But I had genuinely liked the original of that runaway soldier, and the effort of trying to get him down on paper seemed to be well worthwhile. The other people came to mind as easily as the grass grew. They also had grown in that valley. It never occurred to me that those people were any different from myself. Why should it have done so? But grass, and the river, and Bessy Bell Mountain above it were different. People passed, *they* remained.

The only publisher's reader I ever showed the thing to told me that he thought it couldn't succeed because I couldn't make a hero out of a man who was really running away from his duty. He was either being very righteous about the story or very polite to me. He was a quiet, polite sort of man. So I held myself back from protesting that the name of Duty, Stern Daughter of the Voice of God, was no description of what a rookie soldier endured, nor of what he was paid for it, nor of what hopes he had in life.

Then I showed my manuscript to the novelist Francis MacManus, who was becoming a close friend. He read it carefully (he was a careful sort of a man), handed it back to me, said brusquely (he could be a brusque sort of a man): 'It's a long short-story. Cut it to eighteen thousand words'.

So I swallowed my indignation as best I could and the pathetic thing lay gathering dust while I worked on what became my first novel and on a quasi political-cum-historical effort about, God help us all, the partition of our beloved country. Then when Seamus Campbell was editing the *Irish Bookman*, he encouraged me to follow up on the advice of MacManus and shorten my odyssey along the Strule valley to something like publishable length. This I set out manfully to do and it came down to eighteen thousand words. MacManus had an exact eye. What happened to the other thirty-two thousand or what under God they were all about, I do not now recall.

Rereading now, in a venerable copy of the *Irish Bookman*, those eighteen thousand survivors, I feel I am looking at and listening to the ghost of some dear, lost friend from the days of primary school. But the vision of the Strule valley is still bright, and it pleases me as it then appeared to the eyes of the runaway soldier. Let me quote; or try to stop me from quoting:

> He sat on the heather in a sheltered hollow, ate the parcel of food the fat woman had given him, and waited for the day. It came quickly enough in the high place where he was, more slowly below in the long valley. He saw houses and fields and roads and rivers, dimly at first, then clearly as the mists broke and scattered. The red sun came up slowly, and high in the sweet air the larks were singing mad. The last streamer of white mist rose up from the meadows beside the river, broke, and vanished in little white puffs. The wide river came twisting and turning down the valley and a shining metalled road cut straight through the square fields. The valley was new and strange, yet something told him that he had seen that river before, and walked on that road. In a dream, maybe, he had seen the place. It was new and it wasn't new. He was lost.
> He went up with the slope of the moor and, as he went, the light of the sun darkened and a shower went past before the wind, hiding the valley under a white mist. He sheltered behind the piled stones that marked the highest point of that rough land, while the wind went rushing past, herding before it the broken and tattered clouds, and the last of the shower went on up the valley like the trailing white gown of a girl on her wedding morning. From the top of the cairn he saw white farm-houses and green fields and yellow fields, brown bog, dark woods, blue lakes, great straight roads and little twisted roads, three villages and two big towns. But he had no idea as to where exactly he was. He saw great mountains on the other side of the valley, and great mountains far away the way the river was flowing, but he had no notion as to where the Border might be nor which road would lead him to safety.

Just so did I see my native valley with the happy eye of youth, and allow me, now, one glimpse of the hay-meadow when the day's work is done:

> The blade cut down the last clump of standing grass and the whole field was flat under the evening light. The redheaded man and the man with the bowlegs went off together to see to the cattle. The runaway soldier led the team of horses to the stable, down a lane that circled between high, cool, grassy banks, and around a field of potatoes from which he could look down on the roofs of the place.
> Great purple clouds were piled up in the West, crushing down the sun: and in places the light burst up through the clouds, changing the purple to red. A bird on a branch began a song and ended suddenly as if the music had been choked in its throat. The air was hot and quiet, threatening storm.

All that triviality I have written down at some length because, for me, it represents my first close encounter with the Irish novel. For to read a novel is one sort of experience and, at times, a tolerable one; but to try to write a novel, and for the first time, is obviously something else, and the effort may cast a new illumination on the novels that other men and women have provided for you to read.

For instance: as to where they began and, in so far as we can guess, why. Not where and when they first took the pen in the hand and sat down. Flann O'Brien argued most cogently that those two actions were the essential preliminaries to all good writing. (That was said away before word-processors had taken over. Poor old Tolstoy: all those pages and nothing but pen and ink and dip it in that.) No: but what place or person or incident or idea first set the imagination on fire and/or made the novelist think that he, or she, was looking at a life that cried out for expression and that he, or she, felt capable of expressing, felt an urgent need to express.

To take two easy examples from the novels of other countries.

Ireland was, by accident, good to Anthony Trollope both as human being and as novelist but, for obvious reasons, his Irish novels are peripheral to the vast and unified body of his work; which work has two upholding pillars – the soaring spire of Salisbury, the clock-tower of Westminster. He wrote into his autobiography the revelation that came to him in Salisbury. But, in all truth, it was earlier and in Ireland that something happened and set him off into writing novels. Much later on, an Irish novelist is to talk about epiphanies. Since he was not Irish, nor Jesuit-educated, Trollope's waking moments were never harried by epiphanies; or, at any rate, he would never have thought about them under that name. Also: failing in his one attempt to become a member of the Westminster Parliament, although he claimed that his effort had a good side-effect for the cause of reform, Trollope yet created a parliament that seemed more real than the real thing.

Let us cross yet another water.

Is it not high time that we stopped making so much of M. Proust's tea and biscuits? Every one of us has a dozen similar, slight, evanescent memories, but we do need more and more discussion on those twin steeples of Martinville:

> In noticing and registering the shape of their spires, their shifting lines, the sunny warmth of their surfaces, I felt that I was not penetrating to the core of my impression, that something more lay behind that mobility, that luminosity, something which they seemed at once to contain and to conceal.

So, could we say that the Irish novel, in English, begins in Ned McKeown's cottage at the crossroads of Kilrudden? There is, today, a cottage which I, and others, have actually entered, and on the exact site. Does the Irish novel begin there with William Carleton in a cottage at a crossroads in Ulster, or with Maria Edgeworth in a great house in the Midlands? Answer the question to suit yourself. I have an open mind on the matter.

Anyway, William Carleton wrote: 'Ned McKeown's house stood exactly in an angle formed by the crossroads of Kilrudden. It was a long, whitewashed building, well thatched and furnished with the usual appurtenances of yard and offices. Like most Irish houses of the better sort it had two doors, one opening into a garden . . . '

At which point, or door, beginneth the almost two thousand pages of my 1836 edition of the *Traits and Stories of the Irish Peasantry*. At which point, also, it may now be objected to me that we are talking, if we are talking, about the novel. Not about a long series of stories, sketches, novellae.

It has been argued that Carleton did not make much of a success of the novel, although I find it hard to see how such an argument could be upheld against the weight of *Fardorougha the Miser*, *The Black Prophet*, *Valentine M'Clutchy* and, above all, *The Emigrants of Ahadarra*. But the *Traits and Stories* I can accept as one long irregular novel in which the author has done what few Irish novelists have done: given us a vast Balzacian world and brought us into it by way of Ned McKeown's crossroads-cottage and, be it noted, by the folktale that begins with Jack Magennis of the Routing Burn. 'He caught his types,' Shane Leslie wrote, 'before Ireland made the greatest plunge in her history and the Famine had cleaned her to the bone'. The types are valid enough to this day.

As for Maria Edgeworth: she became an Irish novelist, a great novelist, almost, you might say, by a curious sort of accident. Those improving tales she wrote under the guidance of her great and most admirable father are perfect of their European kind and period. They have entitled her to be forgotten in the company of other impeccable female authors. The happy accident that made her forever memorable was that down there at Edgeworthstown she listened a lot to her father's land-steward, John Langan; she borrowed his turn of phrase, transmogrified him into Thady McQuirke, or Quirk, and set him to work to tell the story of Castle Rackrent, discovering, thus, a diction, an idiom, and revealing a society. Otherwise she might never have met the Irish people, even if, in *The Absentee*, she did send the young Lord Colambre to visit Mrs Rafferty, the merchant's wife (Lilith to all Castle Catholics for evermore) in her seaside villa called Tusculum, near Bray, where the drawing-room was 'fine with bad pictures and gaudy gildings', and the windows all shut, and the company, like their betters, playing cards. As she travelled the Irish roads, Maria Edgeworth looked out of the window of her coach and saw their looped and windowed raggednesses begging on the roadside, and was genuinely concerned about their welfare, their lack of education and of the thrifty virtues. But that was not really to know them, certainly not as a novelist should know his or her subject.

William Carleton did say, rather brusquely, that Mrs S.C. Hall and her good husband could never understand the Irish people because they had never been drunk in their company. But you may smell poteen punch from that remark.

In Limerick city, and a little later than Maria Edgeworth, a sensitive young man sat in on a murder trial, was deeply impressed by it and the sad story that led up to it, and also was impressed by some ominous, superstitious circumstances surrounding the execution of the murderer.

From all of which we had Gerald Griffin's novel *The Collegians*, which in many ways, and because of the morbid sensibility of the man who wrote it, is the most contemporary in tone of the early Irish novels. We cannot say: 'of the novels to which the Irish novel owes its origin'. We are part of something larger and cannot lay claim to our own Great Tradition – which may be just as well. Our nineteenth-century Gothic, Maturin and Le Fanu, is as the Gothic was elsewhere. The first few fumbling collectors of folk-tales, Lover, Crofton Croker and, on a much higher level, Patrick Kennedy, did gather something very old, yet new, from the lips of the people. Maxwell and Lever went galloping and soldiering and singing of the girls they left behind them.

Like the nation itself, or whatever we please to call ourselves, the Irish novel sank low in the doldrums or death that followed the middle of the nineteenth century: bravely sustained, perhaps, by a national piety and a most Dickensian national piety that began for Charles Kickham, and others, with the beat of the Knocknagow drum on a Christmas morning. The most interesting novel to look back on that particular period was written by a parliamentarian and eloquent orator, William O'Brien: *When We Were Boys*. It still is of amazing interest. It was written in twelve months or in two periods of six months, each period spent, with some space between, in prison under English beneficence. So that when O'Brien worked on the second portion, he had not the first portion available for consultation. On that occasion, at any rate, Irish art was not the cracked looking-glass of the servant. But in hell or in Ireland, what was it?

The novel in modern Ireland begins, as does the short story, with George Moore. Who, also, in *Hail and Farewell* and 'A Storyteller's Holiday', patented a style as old as Apuleius, certainly as old as Cellini: which style some contemporary writers have debased under the name of faction, a name itself of debased coinage. And Moore begins in a Paris studio, perhaps in the smoke on the platform of the railway station in Stafford, but more certainly by a glimmering lake, haunted by history, in the County of Mayo. He forever maintained that every man had a lake in his heart. As for myself, I go, most humbly, with Edmund Blunden:

> Some love the mountains, some the sea,
> But a river-god is the god for me.

Then a mile or two from Dublin Castle, and in a northside sidestreet, the great Irish novel begins. No, I am not thinking of Eccles Street, but of one of the short stories, those curtain-raisers for *Ulysses*: a story that begins in dullness and reaches out, vainly and tragically, towards Sabian odours and the spicy shores of Araby the Blessed:

> North Richmond Street, being blind, was a quiet street except at the hour when the Christian Brothers' School set the boys free. An uninhabited house of two storeys stood at the blind end, detached from its neighbours in a square ground. The other houses of the street, conscious of decent lives within them, gazed at one another with brown, imperturbable faces.

Now that was also the street along which a refined Quaker lady had walked to pay a visit to a Christian Brother who had once been a novelist, a poet and a playwright, and who had had a gentle platonic fluttering with the Quaker lady; and who, in a fit of flight from the world, had destroyed what remained of his manuscripts and taken to unalloyed religion. When he was told that the Quaker lady, who was, also, blamelessly wedded, was in the parlour to pay him a visit, he gave the matter prayerful thought, sent her a message that he could not see her, and went on being unalloyed.

That crisis of conscience of Gerald Griffin found no place in *Dubliners*, but it is at least of casual interest that it should have taken place in the same street in which the quest for love and Araby began, and ended in a boy's disillusion. Those brown imperturbable faces, behind them the consciousness of decent lives, looked out on that darkness of agony in which man knows himself as 'a creature driven and derided by vanity'.

One door opened on the garden and one on the road and the crowded world.

Obscurely, in that quiet sidestreet, the Ireland we live in had one of its sources.

ᘓ 2 ᘔ

Land Without Stars:
Aodhagán O'Rahilly

IN AUTUMN THE REDS AND BROWNS of the mountains colour the cooling air. You can leave Killarney behind, walk along the road with the grey wall that hides the beauties of Muckross on your right hand, and the moving shoulder of Torc Mountain above you on the left. Up and up: until everything touristed and ticketed is below in the deep valley, until you feel the colour of the mountains soaking into your eyes, your hair, the fragile fabric of skin; until the silence of the high places has seeped into your soul. Then, if you are that sort of person, you can sit down and listen, positively listen to the advance of winter, over and around the mountains, through the high passes, up deep glens as remote as Midrans in the Tyrol where a modern novelist pieced together the terrible story of the miracle boy and the black, mysterious raven.

The secret of winter is in these places: the cold rigid secret blasting and withering all growing green things, stilling the dance and sparkle of lakewater, driving colour and laughter from little fields to shelter in lonely farmhouses until the spell lifts and the sun returns. The secret of the winter of the spirit of man is there in some subtle, elusive allegory, drawn in symbols of high hills, cold winds, withering foliage, desolate swamped fields, lonely homesteads, in mists that filter down through every deep glen, through Glenflesk and around the ruined castle of Killaha, over the bare slope of Scrahanaveal where a poet was born, over the flat sea-sand beyond Castlemaine where the poet listened to the thunder of the great wave and knew that he and his people were among the most desolate of all men.

The mists gather and the leaves fall. The last few lingering tourists, as valiant and as melancholy as the last few lingering leaves, circle obediently on the Ring of Kerry, down the Laune to Killorglin, up the steep street, out

8

over level moorland until the great stretch of Dingle Bay is visible from the high road under the shadow of Drung Hill. The iron discipline of the tour may relax, allowing these last valiant trippers to pray in the church in Cahirciveen which grateful men built to honour God, and as a memorial to the great O'Connell. And, also, allowing them to cross to Valentia Island from the harbour on the mainland, or look into the clear water below the harbour wall at the silver mackerel abandoned, between the boats and the salted, iced packing cases, to the vicious, crawling crabs.

The poet who was born on the slope of Scrahanaveal mentioned that island in one of his stiff, melodious lamentations. He was lamenting the Domhnall MacCarthy More whom an English queen had made Earl of Clancare and Baron of Valentia:

> Dairinis in the West – it has no lord of the noble race.
> Woe is me! In Hamburg is the Lord of the gentle merry heroes.

Only a few of the tourists will be interested in those lines or in the memory of that lamentation. Or in the fact that another poet of those places stood nearly two centuries ago on the height of Coomakesta Pass to sing a Gaelic salutation for the return of the Liberator to the great house at Derrynane: crying out that the great Dan carried his shield before the broken, tattered, barefooted thousands, describing that new democracy in the terms that proud, foolish poets had reserved for eulogies of the wandering Stuarts, crying out that the Hanoverian crown would go down to the dust. These things are memories moving vaguely in mist. And tourists, as a rule, are sensible people who belong to the sun and the untroubled sky.

Bending before the iron will of Killarney hotel-porters, the tourists jolt on sidecars through the Muckross estate, hear jokes and fables prepared for their predecessors in the dawn of tourism, pay their money and view the lakes, pay more money and view the Torc waterfall. The same sidecars, the same jarveys, ponies, and a similar strain of anecdote carry them up the gloomy Gap of Dunloe, abandon them to boats and boatmen and the cool enchantment of the lakes, the excitement of the rapids, the landing under the shadow of Ross Castle. More money and they may climb the tower, uncomfortably conscious of the chill in the wind, the lack of summer light on the wide tossing water, on the great walls of the mountains.

When the last echo of their steps has gone from the dull walls and the twisting stairway, then the darkness, the mists from lake and mountain can thicken around the castle. Darkness, grey mist, grey stone, restless water lulling and deluding the mind, making every noise the rattle of a horsehoof, the slap of a scabbard, every glimmer of lost light on a stone or a wet leaf like the abrupt flash of steel. The wooded places by the lake might be alive with men, presences that have never left the place: Ludlow's Cromwellians, who closed around and captured this castle, trampled on this soil and on these stones, trampled also on a separate civilization, a distinct way of life.

When they rode down towards that lakeshore and saw before them the grey walls of that castle, it was the beginning of a winter that was to last for more than a hundred years.

In the first bite of the wind of that winter, Aodhagán O'Rahilly, the poet from Scrahanaveal, composed his poems: long, stately elegies that litanied the praises of some dead man and the line of gentry to which he belonged, connected the family of this or that castle in south-western Ireland with Greece or Rome or ancient Ireland, or Adam in the Garden. And mirrored the past of his own country, both by the actual historical facts embedded in his elegies and by their revelation of that incredible pride of ancestry that could make a poet glory not in his poetry but in his inherited allegiance to a princely family.

In the small area of Munster in which he lived his life to its miserable end, there was more material for poetry than the fruit that died or dropped off the family trees of the gentry. Or the classical connections of Gaelic genealogy. And because O'Rahilly was a very great poet, he was aware of the existence of that material, and used it exquisitely in lyric and lament. The mountains, the glens, the wooded places, the windy lakes are visible through the careful melodious lines of a handful of those visionary lyrics. If you quote them quietly to yourself anywhere within ten miles of the town of Killarney, you will know immediately that this man understood and interpreted the spirit of the place.

He was not, by any means, a landscape poet. He did not write reliable, detailed accounts of the lives of the common people. Even the descriptions he has given of castle interiors can be as far from social documentary as any fanciful effort of the imagination ever was. But his intuitive power caught in a few sudden lines all the secret of the water, the woods, the great mountains, the beauty of the world and its sorrow, the sunny calm places, the crushing rush of storm. And somehow he has written into all that his own misery, the misery of his people, the horror of his time contrasted with the past as he had imagined it.

The man who has once perfectly expressed the spirit of any place is always alive in that place. The local people may forget that he ever existed. The spot where his body was put in the ground may be forgotten. No man in all the land may name him among his ancestors. The words that he wrote may be read only by a very few. But, at some time or other, men reading those words will understand that he, and he only, gave perfect voice to the beauty that had previously impressed in silence. And that he said the words that described exactly the silences and the wordless sounds, the lights, the shadows, the differing colours.

O'Rahilly's handful of lyrics did all that for the country around Killarney. Down by the lake or under the branches, or on the high mountainy roads, a man can understand what the poet meant when he said that the Brightness of Brightness had met him on his lonely path. From the top of some high hill above Killarney, Aodhagán may have conjured up that vision of Aoibhill and her charming, playful maidens lighting candles on Cnoc Firinne in Limerick, illuminating all the harbours of Ireland to welcome back a king. The vision and the light were transient. The king never returned. The harbours and the shore and the sea were hidden in darkness, out of which the poet cried against the desolate wave, its discordant clamour, its mournful thundering. That was down by Rossbeigh and Castlemaine Harbour, a cycle-run from Killarney.

His life, his misery, his genius are all bound up with that confined tract of country, with Rossbeigh, Glenflesk, Rathmore, Stagmount, Killaha, Killeen. Tradition allows him a journey over the mountains to the town of Cork, and to Ballyvourney to the school of poets. Common sense must allow him occasional excursions to the great houses of the men he eulogized, over whom he preached the conventional poetic panegyric.

Compared with Eoghan Rua Ó Súilleabháin, the rake, the wastrel, the schoolmaster, spalpeen, soldier, sailor, poet from Meentogues, which is next door to Scrahanaveal, O'Rahilly was an untravelled man. His life was confined to a few townlands where his very nature made it inevitable that the popular traditions concerning him should be few, nebulous, contradictory.

Today in Killarney it is possible to find men who, in common with the majority of their fellow-countrymen, have lost touch with the poetry of the ragged men from Sliabh Luachra, with the language in which that poetry was written. But most of those men could tell some story about Eoghan the Wanderer, while even the scholars and the folklorists are troubled to put together the scattered pieces of the story of the man who stayed at home.

To discover the truth behind that paradox is not very difficult. But to try to discover the presence of the poet in those townlands is as wearisome as elbowing one's way through milling, trampling, shouting crowds, looking for one lost and scarcely recognizable human being. The past and the present come together confusedly in that one particular crowd in which this poet has been lost: the people of Killarney, Kerry, Munster, of all Ireland; the visitors who have gone to that place to look at the scenery, to play golf, to fish; the shawled women in the queue outside the cinema in Killarney; the jarveys with the stereotyped jokes. Only an ingenious specimen of screen-montage could do justice to the ironic complications and contradictions of that crowd.

Alfred Lord Tennyson sits to write his poem and the bugles obediently blow. Pugin supervises the building of a cathedral. The author of the Waverley novels pays a platitudinous compliment to the beauty of the

Upper Lake, and writers of guidebooks go on transcribing that compliment to the end of time. Lord Macaulay and Thackeray follow up with appropriate platitudes. Wordsworth and Alfred Austin go striding with faces of doom before generations of tourists. A noted filmstar praises the lakes and the gardaí in identical terms.

Charles James Fox goes swimming round the Devil's Punch Bowl. And in the same circular motion, as regular as the nitrogen cycle, the lesser tourists, condemned to read and repeat the remarks made by the more notable tourists, go up the Gap and down the lakes, up the estate and down the road below Torc, round and round and round, whirling faster and faster, encircling the bewildered shade of the man who really was the poet of the place, to whose voice the echoes replied.

In 1653 the Cromwellian men hanged Piaras Ferriter in Killarney town, on a hill called the Hill of the Sheep. They hanged a gentleman and a gallant soldier. And that was nothing out of character for Cromwellian men. They killed a poet who was great enough to lament the misery that the wars had brought on his people, rich and poor, in a line that recalls the great thought from Donne so elaborately used by Ernest Hemingway: 'Is biogdhghadh bais liom bas mo chomharsan'. His death was symbolical, like the smashing of statues or stained glass. And the corpse of a gentleman-poet of the Gaelic order swinging in the wind on a gallows is a fitting introduction to two centuries in which gentlemen and poets of the Gaelic order were to wither from the face of the earth. His death makes Killarney of supreme importance in the story of those two centuries.

On the Hill of the Sheep today, since the power of the Cromwellians is only a sad memory, there is a Franciscan friary. The road to Mallow comes up the slope out of the little streets of Killarney. Across the road from the friary a statue stands to the memory of the four great Kerry poets. Behind the patch of green ground on which the statue stands are the comings and goings of a railway station; beyond the station a cinema, a hotel, a Protestant church, a shop for curios and souvenirs, the new town hall, the office for the agent of the Kenmare estate. Then the walled estate goes down to the edge of the water, and beyond that there are the mountains.

That was one cross-section of Killarney and it left out much of what is of supreme importance in the modern town: the cathedral, the colleges and convents, the shops and the streets, the little lanes, not unlike the lanes of Kilkenny, except in so far as they did not seem then to me to have preserved the very whisperings and gossip of the past. Yet that cross-section cuts not only through the town of the present day but through two centuries of the story of the place.

In the quietness of the byway that goes round the grey wall that delimits the grounds of the friary, the soft earth dotted with fallen leaves of

Spanish chestnut, an imaginative visitor could feel the past coming painfully to life: the poet on the gallows, the solemn troopers 'bibles in their boots', the cowed and scattered people. An old man digging potatoes in a garden beyond the hedge on the other side of the byway might symbolize Ó Bruadair, or wandering Eoghan, or Aodhagán himself, bitterly turning the heavy brown soil. But today the man at work is sheltered from the wind by the friendly wall of the friary. O'Rahilly, the poet, was overshadowed and shut out by the towering wall of the estate.

It is not now too easy to realize how tall and terrifying the estate-wall must have appeared, for its real height was in the suggestion that it made to the spirit. O'Rahilly may never have laid eyes on the wall that goes out from Killarney, past the cathedral, along the road to Killorglin. He may never have been greatly grieved by the fact that the people had been shut out from the lives of their lords and owners of their land, except in so far as the people could be of use to the lords. But it was bitterness and forever bitterness to know that the new lords had no use for poets, that only the despised and rejected people still treasured and remembered the things that the Gaelic poet had to give.

For us it is not easy to assess in our own standards the value of the order that the poet lamented, the civic or real social importance that belonged to the men of that order. The great castle of the O'Donoghue who lived by the lake, the tall castle of the O'Donoghue who lived in the glen, the halls of the O'Mahonys and the MacCarthys are cold ruins, well preserved or poorly preserved. But O'Rahilly found much to lament in the passing of that order.

Today the wall of the estate that is associated with the name of Valentine Browne is no great barrier against anything: least of all against Tourism which is among the most democratic of human institutions. When the family is not at home, sixpence at the gate will open to you the beauty of the flat green places by the margin of Loch Lein. And you get the feeling that if your accent had been genuine Killarney, nobody would have bothered to ask for the sixpence.

You can see the long house where the present representative of the family of Valentine Browne lives. That particular house was once a stables. But when the great mansion was accidentally burned down in the early years of the twentieth century, efficiency emergency measures converted the stables into a dwelling-place for a lord. You can see the burned-out body of the great mansion with its splendid view over flat grass and woods and lakewater. Across the flat grass a path twists, crosses a small stream, forks right to Reen Point and left to Ross Castle, names that come together in some obscure connection when we think of the poet's deathbed lament:

> The hero of the Rinn, of Kill, and of the land of Eoghanacht –
> Wasted is his strength by want and injustice!
> The hawk who possesses all these and their rentals,
> Does not give favour to a man though he be his kinsman.

The hero may have been Eoghanacht O'Donoghue. The hawk was, in all probability, that Valentine Browne, the inaccessibility of whose purse had already been bewailed by the poet. Walking around the shell of the old mansion or over the flat ground to the lake, a man may realize how dead the hero is, how the hawk has passed off into the blue air. And with them have gone all the passion and agony of that time of complicated transition. Personally, I saw there only the quiet grazing cattle, and a few men sawing wood, and two barefooted boys with a tiny handcart.

When I go to see an estate-agent, I hopefully expect to come up against something like Carleton's Valentine M'Clutchy. And, naturally, in these blessedly civilized days, almost half-a-century after the final collapse of the old system of land-tenure, that childishly morbid expectation meets inevitably with disappointment.

A polite secretary introduced me into the office of the present agent of the Kenmare estate: an affable man, a polite man patient with an intruder, a scholarly man interested in the past of the Kenmare family, interested in any connection that could have existed between the members of that family and this voice from the lost Gaelic civilization. The bulk of the Kenmare papers had already been edited by a scholar and there is in them little or nothing to throw light on the life of the poet.

So our talk was on incidentals and generalities: about Reen townland that had once been mostly bogland, but has been drained and cut away. Farms on the estate had, at one time, been let on condition that the tenant should build a good slated house and assist at the draining of bogland. How many heroes of the Reen had toiled usung at that job of drainage? The agent, Mr Roulston, himself lived in that townland. We talked of the middlemen who had kept their own separate records, with the result that many details about tenants had been lost. We discussed Murtagh Griffin, who drew from O'Rahilly the type of blasting and withering abuse that the world associates with the name of Rabelais. Except that in O'Rahilly's weird elegy on that turncoat and ruffian, there is a note of sharp and intimate bitterness that is not to be found in Pantagruel:

> For ever, O rude stone, bind down with zeal
> The wandering rake by whom the country has been woefully
>   despoiled,
> Lest he might return to us suddenly from Acheron
> Press the villain tightly, bruise his heart.

Yet the last will and testament of that same wandering rake recalls in all the conventional legal phrases such piety towards his Maker and genuine affection towards his beloved wife . . .

Well, perhaps, the bitter poet could have been mistaken.

And, mistaken or not, it is at least edifying to observe the sense of the fitness of things that legally bequeathed the soul to God, while the poor body, bound down zealously by the rude stone, awaited resurrection and judgment.

We discussed the conduct of the modern estate: a purely commercial business of managing property and involving no gale-days. We talked of the scarred shell of the great nineteenth-century mansion. The family mansion had had other sites: one somewhere between the agent's office and the present-day house. But in none of those places had any traces been left.

The Kenmares came originally from a spot seven or eight miles away on the road to Tralee, claiming their land both by conquest and by a mortgage over the MacCarthy Mór. I looked at the office-walls lined with finely bound volumes rescued from the old mansion, wondered vaguely what the ragged and miserable poet would have done with the contents of those shelves, waited vaguely for the past to recreate itself. After all, he had been the incarnation of the spirit of the place. He had tramped to Cork City and there got himself a book. And if he were to be found at all in that place, he would be found among books.

But the typewriter click-clacking derisively in the outer office as I made my way to the street told me plainly what my own world and my own time would think of such imaginings. For the sun has risen over this country, and a lost poet may have liberty to wander through the night that my own time would say he created out of his own dismal lamentations. His night was without hope. His land lacked even the cold light of the stars. We, walking in the sun, know our own minds, see with our own eyes our own familiar landmarks, leave desolation and unbelief to the other nations of the earth.

That was why I didn't look for the lost poet in the town hall, a most elegant town hall. Nor in the busy little streets, nor in the busy shops, nor in the Presentation convent, nor in the cathedral. For the very existence of all those things – the tall beauty of the spire, the busy nuns in the school-room – are plainly visible evidence that the sun has risen, that the night without stars is only a very bitter memory.

The descendants of Valentine Brown helped the nuns to make their home there in days when the energy and charity of the Sisters was the one wall between the people and utter desolation. Today the desolation has passed, the children of the people learn their lace-making and miscellaneous lessons under the shadow of the spire that Pugin conceived. Across the road is the grey wall of the estate, the rattle of a small stream, the wind moving in the tops of tall trees. Trees standing erect, not felled to the ground as the trees were when the anonymous poet lamented the rape of the woods of Kilcash. Trees strong and beautiful, a part of the sunrise and the brightening land. A nation growing, instead of felling, trees is a nation that has at least taken the right road.

O'Rahilly united Kilcash and Killarney in the beautiful epithalamium he wrote to celebrate the wedding of Valentine Brown, third Viscount Kenmare, to Honora Butler of Kilcash. That was in 1720. Ten years later the lady died of smallpox. The poet lived to satirize the bridegroom. Yet not even those desolating facts can take away from the biblical beauty of the verses:

> The languid are becoming vigorous and the great hills are strong.
> In Winter every tree puts forth blossoms,
> Since Kilcash has been united lovingly in bonds
> With the Prince of Killarney, our Champion.

The man who saw the winter-trees put forth blossoms was at least temporarily capable of seeing the sun by day and the stars by night. But not incapable of foreseeing satire and smallpox, and the woods bare and desolate.

Past the convent and the cathedral the road runs to many places: to Dunloe, Killorglin and the Kerry Ring, Castlemaine and Aghadoe, to the thunder of the sea at Rossbeigh. It passes by the house of a man, Joseph O'Connor, a retired inspector of schools, who has devoted his retirement to the examination of Gaelic manuscripts collected here and there in mountainy places in the course of a lifetime.

Yellowing paper, beautiful elaborate handwriting done with effort in a noble attempt to preserve songs, stories, blessings, salutations, lore of the weather and of herbs, all the rich and intricate ideas whose creation and presentation give a divine courage to the souls of men.

'Anything of O'Rahilly there?'

'No, nothing. Not even another manuscript of something already discovered by Dinneen. That's the fate of a man who goes out of his way to follow the gentry'.

'Stories about Eoghan Rua?'

'Certainly. Stories by the dozen'.

I had a vision of smoky hiding-places behind the hearth, cavities in the rafters, corners in a hundred dressers yielding up their golden secrets.

'But there is a story about the last two descendants of Murtagh Griffin who held land at Lisnagawn – that's Headford – in Aodhagán's time. The last of that family were two single men, renowned for hard drinking and hard spending. One day in the market they spent their last penny, came home. In the house one of them struck a match to light his pipe, was chided by his brother for the wanton extravagance that would waste a match while a fire burned on the hearth'.

I saw the match burn down in the fingers of one old man, heard the chiding of his brother, saw the flame die into the darkness in which Murtagh, who had once been administrator to Helen the mother of Valentine Brown, willed his soul to God, and Kilman and Kilmacudd to his 'beloved wife, Jane Griffin also Archbold'. In the same darkness the poet cursed him, saw him in a moment of fiendish imagination drifting bound and helpless into the darkness of Styx.

I left the man of the manuscripts and walked meditatively back to Killarney. He wished me luck, even to the point of discovering the manuscript of a hitherto unknown poem of O'Rahilly. What greater joy could a scholar wish to his fellowman?

In the hotel the commercials sitting around the fire discussed the world, the peoples and nations of the world, the universe, the life to come, the prospects of peace and improved business. The rain whipped at the tall windows. The hotel-porter said it would be foolish to venture out, smiled a resigned Kerry smile when his advice was disregarded.

The road to Glenflesk and Killaha Castle went up into the cloudy mountains, up into the recurring rain, until the castle stood up tall and grey and overgrown with ivy: and overlooking the tops of the highest trees, the wet slopes of the valley, the Flesk river, swollen and thundering down towards Loch Lein. Under the shelter of that high grey wall, poetry and learning had lived stubbornly for years after the fall of Ross Castle, for years after the calamitous transactions around the walls of Limerick.

The rapparees sheltered the poets and the schools of the poets, for the rapparees and robbers and persons of the Romish religion included among their number the last representatives of an aristocratic order that may have had a thousand faults but that did certainly reserve a fireside chair for the poet. It was possibly Domhnall O'Donoghue Dubh, father of Fineen O'Donoghue, who presented the poet with a pair of boots. O'Rahilly did not, like independent Samuel Johnson, fling from him the gift that implied his inability to stand erect in his own footwear. He accepted the boots. He possibly needed them more around Killarney than Johnson, the student, would have needed them for sliding on the ice in Christchurch Meadow. And in return for the gift of leather, O'Rahilly wrote an exquisite classical fantasy, lauding the beauty of the gift, the generosity of the giver, making the deserted walls of Killaha beautiful forever to the man who loves the precious things of the mind.

> The leather had come from distant Barbary, transported over the sea by the fleet of Philip of Spain. The shoes would protect his feet on great hills and in rough meadows, in encounters with foemen. They would be an adornment in public places. Phoebus had loved the white cow whose hide had gone to their making. No rain would soften and no sun would

harden the leather. The awl that pierced it was made of steel tempered for seven hundred years by demons with the craft of Vulcan. Darius, Alexander and Caesar had worn them. And Lir and Lughaidh, Bodhbh Dearg, the Balar of the Blows, Osgar and Goll Mac Morna, Cuchulainn and Connall Cearnach. And Dunlaing had worn them on the field of Clontarf.

Possibly that was only the conventional classicism of the period. John Milton assembled as many mythical personalities from the legends of Greece and Rome into his lament for the dead Lycidas. But the point is that this gift and the poem in praise of the gift and the giver, and some very essential part of Aodhagán O'Rahilly, the poet, gathered around the high castle in that lonely glen. And remained there forever, like a cloud of light or a vision made permanent.

Perhaps the poet was, as somebody suggested, trying to forget his own beggarly humiliation in this classical tap-dancing. That would only add the essential pathos to a vision of the past that is, at one and the same time, always alive and utterly dead: gone, without power to return.

The wind moved the desolate ivy. The rain fell steadily into the empty, roofless ruin, into the small muddy space that must once have served as a sort of guard-room opening to the bottom of the spiral stairway and the entrance to the main hall of the castle. A few fragments of the stairway remained. The great main hall was now a large muddy space with a wide fireplace, and with the wind whistling about the tall chimney. Under the shelter of the great ivy-grown walls was an enclosed garden.

To the dwelling of the Flesk of the slender women the poet wished one and forty welcomes from a hundred druids to that flower of warriors, Fineen O'Donoghue of the Glen. Fineen came up that slope, up from the noise of the turbulent Flesk, up higher than the tops of the trees that grew in the valley, to something very different from those desolate walls and rain-sodden earth, and that continuous whistle of wind about the high stones.

Men today can argue bitterly enough as to what exactly Fineen did return to when the poet greeted him with that song of praise. And from modern bickerings we may at least understand that the poets possibly did a lot of their description in lavish technicolour. Yet it is also possible that a red hearth and a rush-covered floor, food and drink and the good company of men and women may have meant as much to a poet of that time as a Hollywood version of an Arabian tale may now mean to the population of an industrial city.

If O'Rahilly, describing the hall of a patron, wrote down magnificent things, they had real existence somewhere in his soul whether or not they existed in reality. His classic description is in the lines detailing the way of life at what had once been the home of O'Callaghan of Clonmeen: the musical, princely mansion, the speckled silks and garments of satin, the whetting of swords, the warriors playing chess, the drinking of wines, the viands on spits, the music of harps, the reading of genealogies (which could hardly provide entertainment even for the most aristocratic modern), the blazing waxlights, fresh casks being opened for the multitude, horses racing, foot-soldiers contending, beer in goblets of wrought silver. With the exception of that single depressing little item about the public declamation of family-trees, we have there the elements of a very entertaining evening. And since the O'Callaghans at Clonmeen had at one time about fifty thousand acres of Munster, it is quite probable that the account contained little exaggeration. It is also more than probable that when all the fresh casks had been opened, the multitude did not return to electrically heated, semi-detached houses.

Would they have had any relationship, I wonder, with the rude rabblement of Edmund Spenser's Raskall Many?

O'Rahilly's own birthplace was no great distance away from the castle of Killaha: over the Flesk river, over the stream that is now known as the Quagmire. In all his poetry there is no hint as to what the house in which he first saw the light may have resembled. There is no hint as to who or what his parents may have been, except in the one proud cry that they and their parents and grandparents, and ancestors back before the death of Christ, were subject to the same chieftain.

It was not the poetic convention to remember, remember the house where the poet was born. And it is only in Eoghan Rua's defence of bachelors, or his advertisement for setting up a school that we come on an intimate localized note, quite remote from the lamenting waves or the vocal rivers of O'Rahilly or of Spenser. But O'Rahilly remembered and praised the great houses where he had had welcome and hospitality. And while his elegies and eulogies may have been written as obviously from poet to patron as much that came out of eighteenth-century Grub Street, it is obvious that the places where those houses stood were the only places where he ever saw the sun shine.

He saw it shine here at Killaha Castle on the hill above the perpetual tumult of the river. And, in spite of the low sky and the rain and the empty walls, I could hear music and the sound of happy voices, the patter of that pair of magical boots, the chant of welcome greeting the return of Fineen 'from the home of the guilty, niggardly Saxon'.

The parochial house stands now on the same hill as that towering, significant ruin. I talked with a young priest who remembered from his college days only a few lines of the poet. But from his experience in living in that place confessed some respect for the strategic genius of the poet's patron, the chieftain of Killaha. A great place for a rapparee to live, he said to me. Why even today, when the river comes out on the road a force of infantry would have a nasty time tramping up from Killarney. What it was like more than two hundred years ago anyone who tries hard may imagine.

I walked on down the slope thinking of Aodhagán's connections with the clergy: about the poem on the complaint of Aongus, the priest who bought a cock of high pedigree for the price of fifty shillings and had it stolen by a sprite of druidical power. Then I recalled the elegy on the death of Father John MacInery:

> Withered is the fragrant lovely apple,
> Withered is the tree and blossoming plant,
> Withered is the gentle, fair, loving vine,
> Withered is the palm-bough from beauteous Paradise.

For the priests and the poets came together in the common misery that the long winter of the eighteenth century brought them. The most author-itative book on that particular aspect of that period mentions the number of notable men who were both priests and poets, mentions the words of sorrow spoken by a priest when he heard of the death of the vagabond Eoghan. On the way down I thought of those things. And thought irrele-vantly of a wicked fragment from Aenghus O'Daly, employed by Sir George Carew in the opening years of the seventeenth century to lampoon the Irish chieftains. Men believed strongly then in the power of the poet. And that particular poet saw in Glenflesk the crime of fratricide, and the criminal niggardliness that would give a man nothing more intoxicating to drink than stale buttermilk.

But as I looked back down the glen and up the slopes at the grey walls, the clouds were broken and a shaft of sunlight lay across Killaha, the ruined castle and the priest's house. I turned from the bribed bitterness of one poet to the lyrical gratitude of another. For whether O'Rahilly exag-gerated or imagined or flattered, no amount of debunking could disprove the truth that once on that high place there had been something of happi-ness, and a great deal of security for a way of life that wars and robbery had driven backwards from flat fertile places and from the neighbourhood of crowded towns.

When I reached Lisnagawn, the sunlight had departed and the clouds had closed in darkness over the corner of flat land running abruptly to the roots of stiff rocky hills. Tourists who go, not to Killarney but to Parknasilla, will be familiar with the place under the name of Headford. In the life of O'Rahilly and in the poems that he wrote, the name of Lisnagawn is alive with a sinewy hate that has defied and survived the centuries. It is not too easy to make out of the sparse and scattered details, left by the passing of more than two hundred years, a continuous narrative of the struggle that Eoghan, son of Cormac MacCarthy Riabach, made for the right to live at peace on that land. It happened in the opening decade of the eighteenth century. And much of the complicated bitterness of the time is compressed into it, and expressed in a small way.

It was not, by any means, a struggle in which the survivors of the Old Order battled against the more powerful invading forces of the New. The time cannot in that way be simplified into a clearly marked design in black and white. But it can be said of that period, as of all periods, that wherever there was the possibility of profit, honest or dishonest, there also were tricksters, robbers and racketeers. The racket then was land. The land at Lisnagawn attracted Hussey and Griffin, the Griffin in question being one Edmund Griffin, who lived at Killarney and was kinsman and executor to the notorious Murtagh. O'Rahilly's benison on the dead and departed Murtagh has already been mentioned. With Murtagh he connects Tadhg Dubh Cronin. O'Donovan mentions poor black Thady as an industrious farmer, and refers to O'Rahilly's tribute to his memory as an outrageous lampoon. And as in the case of the last will and testament of the bold Murtagh, it is not easy to reconcile O'Rahilly's abuse with fair opinion put forward by enlightened scholarship.

We can only say for certain that the enlightened scholarship of later days had no contact in the flesh with the men whom the poet scarified for some pervasive reasons of his own. Eoghan MacCarthy was banished after a scuffle that involved the death of two men. The poet's lamentation over that banishment runs to two hundred and fifty lines of melodiously hard Gaelic. He gives to Eoghan the conventional virtues and ancestors that must have been among the stock-in-trade of the elegiac poets of his school. And he then cries out:

> It is pitiful that sheepmongers should have thy land
> Which fell to them without payment, without an eiric,
> A portion of it under his elbow held by Muiris of the frieze,
> An unfortunate portion of it from Muiris held by Eamonn.

One can never be quite certain whether to approve or deprecate the purpose of the poet's scorn. For it is seldom certain whether he is whipping a rogue and a scoundrel, or merely some poor man. But if it is possible to view scorn, with some artistic detachment, as a weapon used for a purpose, then there is no denying the merit of the variety in which O'Rahilly dealt. Sheepmongers and Cromwellians, dealers in frieze and jobbers in land, new gentry who did not appreciate poets, merchants from Bristol and Dover who had sunk as low as slave-traffic, all kinds of new men, rich and poor, good and evil, came under the stiff lash of his verse.

It may be that he merely knew what was good for himself. But it is also possible that he may have known very well what was good for his people. It is convenient to think of this defensive bitterness of his concentrated around that last green corner between the hard mountains and the small stream where, at a place now called Oldbridge, there was a tucking-mill: possibly the only machine mentioned in his poems. For in that obscure, half-forgotten dispute there was on one side a MacCarthy. And he had boasted that his forefathers had been under that name for more than two thousand years. On the other side were new men and exploiters, and behind them the soldiers of Cromwell and William, and a code of penal law.

From Killeen mountain, behind Lisnagawn and between the valley of the Owenreagh and the rounded summits of the Paps, his imagination traversed all Ireland in his elegy for Diarmuid O'Leary. Captain O'Leary had fought under James Stuart, possibly, according to Dinneen's note, in Boiselau's regiment of infantry. And the family of O'Leary in the land of Iveleary, from Macroom to Inchigeela and the long water of Lough Allua was for O'Rahilly one of the really significant things in God's universe. In the lamentation for O'Leary of Killeen, he did, as I have said, survey all Ireland. He saw the Munstermen in sorrow, from Inis Finn to the royal house of Mór, from the shore of the Shannon to Leim Con Duibhe and to Baoi of the Ships. He saw the West making its moan, the mist on the meads and the mountains, the sun weeping and the moon under a cloud.

Now it may be just the mania of our time to blame O'Rahilly for not keeping his eyes open when he made one of those surveys of the unfortunate island on which he lived. That fine picture of women bewailing and children, unborn, bewailing the passing of a man to whom Diana gave a ring of gold, Mars a spear and Jupiter a suit of satin, who was kin to all the heroic blood of Erin back to Curi, Oscar and Conall, is as splendidly classical as a picture on an ancient vase. But it is not a picture of the Ireland in which Aodhagán O'Rahilly wrote his elegy nor in which O'Leary of Killeen died: Ireland after the Boyne and Aughrim and Limerick, an Ireland spinning for a moment in the whirl of the marching and fighting of Europe, held for a moment like an object on a speeding disc, then pitched into darkness and putrid isolation.

There is little point in blaming the poet for not writing about these things. If he had understood them down to the roots, and if he had been able to intervene and check their course, he would have had in him something of O'Connell, or Davis, or Mitchel from Ulster, or Davitt with the one arm. But he would not have been O'Rahilly, the last and possibly the greatest of the poets of a dying order. He was the last great eulogist of a system that was very much misunderstood both by those who coloured it rose-red with glory, and by those who saw it as something from which we had, praised be God, escaped.

Yet even if it may be unfair, it is still very human to wish that O'Rahilly had really written not about genealogies or gifts from the gods, or weeping rivers or lamenting waves, but about the Ireland of the cabins on which his eyes opened in the place now called Stagmount.

You see Stagmount to your left hand when you have passed the cross-roads at Barraduff on the road from Killarney to Rathmore. Nothing so distinctive as a hill, just a long smooth rise of land. The map colours it brown, and numbers it as 541 feet above sea level, which is not very much for Kerry. If you are a wise man, you will continue along the road to Rathmore, past the convent and the children coming home from school and estimating all distances and directions by east and west, up to the long house on a windy hill where the Melleray monks made their first Irish home.

Down in Killarney the Presentation nuns say that the monks walked from Rathmore to Killarney to build the wall around the Presentation convent, for which the nuns provided some corporal sustenance and the benison of their prayers. A splendid example of Christian co-operation.

The present resident of that long house is the parish priest of Rathmore, and a five minutes' talk with him among his books would convince any man that O'Rahilly is nearer to Rathmore than to the fields of Stagmount. For the knowledge of Aodhagán, said the parish priest (and who could speak with more authority?) had gone early out of that valley when the road and the railway came and the Gaelic died. Not quite dead though! There was still in the parish – where Dinneen, the scholar, had learned to love the language – in which Aodhagán, the poet, had been born one man who spoke Gaelic learned in the cradle. His name, of all names, was O'Leary and he lived . . .

At Gneeveguilla, where I found him a few hours later.

Gneeveguilla is a very interesting place. The road that brings you there turns to the right-hand of the Rathmore-to-Killarney road, and it may be either of two straight ways made, once upon a time, by order of the Browns, to give access to a stone-quarry. On one of those roads I over-took a man who was a butcher. He was also a next-door neighbour to Charles O'Leary of Gneeveguilla – a man, he said, that, herding the cattle in fine weather, had a book in his hand, a man who loved poetry and talking about poets.

There was something vaguely familiar about that description, some-thing heard somewhere or read in a book. And the irritating sense of half-recognition followed me up that road, in the wind and under the low sky and through the scattered little showers of cold rain, to the sloping field where I found Charles O'Leary keeping an eye on the cattle. He had no book. The day was not fine, and no lover of books would risk his library on that bare slope in broken weather.

Below us in the valley was the Quagmire River (Abhann Uí Chriadh).

Beyond the river, its higher outlines hidden in rain-mist, was the district of Sliabh Luachra and its memories of poets and schools of poets. Across the river in Scrahanaveal, O'Rahilly was born. Here, in Gneeveguilla, Eoghan Rua opened his first school. Beyond the river in those days had been Kenmare land. Gneeveguilla on the west of the Quagmire had been part of the land still belonging to the MacCarthy Mór. Poor scholars came into that country 'for nowhere else in Ireland were so many sweet singers gathered together: the south-west corner of Munster was the Attica of Irish Ireland and Sliabh Luachra its Hymettus'.

Two hundred years later, there was only one man watching his cattle from the sheltery side of a ditch, two girls gossiping at a well in the middle of the flat fields and surveying the stranger with good-natured curiosity. The man was not a very old man. And he wisely pointed out that remembering the past had more to do with your temperament than with your age in years. He said: 'There are older men than myself in the parish who don't remember one of these things. It must be in the twang of your temperament'.

Certainly he remembered Aodhagán. Wasn't Aodhagán born within sight of this spot where we sheltered behind the hedge? Hadn't he lived for a while in Stagmount, a short distance closer to Killarney? There was a rumour, though, that the poet had been reared in the County Cork. And, as for Stagmount, there was no certainty about where the actual site of the dwelling had been. Or the site of the well that Father Dinneen had mentioned as Aodhagán's Well. A man had once suggested a possible site at a place called the Top of the Meadows. Anyway, it was somewhere over there beyond the slope of Scrahanaveal. The Kenmare papers did not tell us much about O'Rahilly. He had read them very carefully. But then it was difficult to get any information about him. Like chasing a ghost.

Consider! Even the man's name was in doubt. Was he O'Rahilly or O'Reilly?

From what he had been told, that Kerry farmer concluded that the people up there in Cavan had never even heard of Aodhagán. Was the name a double-barrelled name or was he really just Owen O'Rahilly? Aodhagán had been proud of the name, very proud. Hadn't he told the story of the trout that spoke to him when he was fording a stream? The trout had said: 'Don't trample heavily on me, Aodhagán O'Rahilly'.

Was he as fine a poet as Eoghan Rua, or the O'Scannells, or Geoffrey O'Donohue of the Glen? That was a debatable question. And with wary academic precision that Kerry farmer debated the point, turned his arguments this way and that way, until once again I was troubled by that vague feeling of half-recognition. Fineen O'Scannell had written a song to the tune of 'The Palatine's Daughter', a fine song and well written, the lilt filled out with melodious words. And Father Dinneen? He remembered him well, tramping these very fields, collecting the songs, poems, stories, the great words read and recited among these hills.

Some happy whim of the gods had given to a locality that had so much untouched treasure an industrious scholar who understood the value of those things. Or was it that the spirit of the place gave birth in a man's soul to the knowledge of their worth and the desire to guard and preserve them?

A young man crossed the field to the well, swinging a white bucket, whistling cheerily. And I realized that the dusk had crept up from the flat-land and the little river, hiding the slopes where a poet had been born, leaving us isolated on the slopes where another poet had opened a school. That cold, misty half-light was the time for fantasy. And I had a feeling that the man who spoke to me of books and poems might, at any moment, prove true to his townland by telling me in lyrical Gaelic verse the story of some obscure, symbolic vision. Then I understood that feeling of half-recognition. And I understood for a moment the stories of the time two centuries ago with learned spalpeens and poetic ploughboys, with a broken people holding fiercely to their ancient learning and their ancient faith, and making for themselves, in the middle of desolation, a Hymettus and an Arcadia.

I shook hands with Charles O'Leary, the last native-speaker of Gaelic in that lost Hymettus.

He said: 'In Tyrone now, in Dungannon, is the castle of the Great O'Neill still there'.

I described that town as well as a man from Omagh could. He said: 'I always wanted to see that place. O'Neill was a great man'.

I went down the wet road past Meentogues school, wondering what would be the fate of Eoghan Rua today, either as scholar or schoolmaster. All about me the land faded backwards into the shadows, the low hills, the moors, the mountains, the fields with the black cattle, backwards over long centuries to the awful day when the great O'Neill from Dungannon failed and fell back in those southern places. For on that day began the scatter-ment and desolation of the chieftains and their poets. Perhaps it was the best thing that ever happened to the country. Perhaps it was the worst. Perhaps it could have been avoided. Perhaps it was as inevitable as are most great tragedies.

At any rate it sent Aodhagán O'Rahilly wandering in his land without dry weather, without a stream, without a star: lamenting the passing of an order and a scheme of things as one might lament the end of the world and the overthrow of Creation. Nowhere in the collapse did he see the material that men might use for rebuilding and remaking. He was not, by any means, a prophet. He foresaw nothing of the Ireland to come. He certainly did not foresee the commercial men around the fire in the hotel-lounge, talking of Upton Sinclair and Flann O'Brien, or listening to a

Nelson Eddy recording being broadcast from some radio station, listening also to the pop-popping of a ping-pong ball in the dining-room, the sound of dance music across the street, the footsteps of Killarney people going down to the cinema.

Up in the hills a man drove his cattle home through the dusk and along a wet lane, sat later by his fire, turned the pages of a book and was back more than two hundred years with the poet whom the trout had spoken to. Or the vagabond poet who founded a school. Or the poet whose dead body swung in the wind on a Cromwellian gallows in Killarney town.

In one small district of one part of Munster he lived his life and wrote his poems, lamenting the wounds of the land of Fodhla, the ruin that befell the great families of Erin. And, as he saw it, the wounds were one and the same thing with the ruin. Through the shadowy land of his lamentation, the spouse of Brian rode on horseback telling of the day when the merchant's son would return to her. And she lived on in loneliness, and without a lover, because the merchant's son did not return.

The bright vision, which he saw somewhere on a lonely path, faded, and along that path rode a wicked, croaking, yellow clown and his black companions. Aodhagán wrote the wedding-song for the son of one of the last of the great houses, and when that son, for some good reasons of his own, closed his door on the poet, the reaction was channelled into a poem in which he concentrated and expressed his own melancholy bitterness. For the great houses were going and taking with them into an eternity of shadows the peculiar rights of the poets of the Gaelic order. The mansion of Tadhg an Duna at Castle Tochar, the tall castle of Fineen O'Donoghue, and the castle of John O'Mahony, the Freckled, in Dunloe: these were isolated, islanded places in a land swamped by three waves of conquest. It is possible that he journeyed outside his own district to houses such as those; for every elegy or wedding-song or poem of pure praise would imply an inducement or a reward, payment or hospitality.

He crossed into Clare to enjoy the hospitality of O'Callaghan. At Ballykennedy he found a vision of goodness and beauty that could not be described fully or properly on parchment, in a female phoenix of the Geraldine blood, a cousin of the children of Milesius. At Ballyseedy, in Kerry, John Blennerhasset died, a hero and a warrior who had, apparently, understood the poet well enough to merit one hundred and twenty elegiac lines. The shoes given to the poet in Glenflesk might have carried him as far as Kilcash when the Butlers and the Browns made that happy union. At Ballyvourney the other poets heard his voice as he came through the night to recite and contend among his soul's equals. And a man called Murphy bespoke for the power and wit of Aodhagán a hundred welcomes.

Somewhere off the Kerry coast he saw a ship wrecked, the crew screaming as they went down under the bulk of the waves. And around the tragedy he wrote a poem of which the wrecking passage of the years has left one quatrain. At Castleisland he saw a fair and a faction fight, and he preserved for us in a few resonant phrases the very noises of that forgotten conflict.

From isolated references, from knowledge almost accidentally conveyed, from sparse traditions and apocryphal stories of a supposedly simple lad driving hard bargains at country fairs, it might be possible to map out the few short journeys of that untravelled man. Possibly that one journey to the lovely place where the Lee meets the ocean was made by way of the castle in Glenflesk, and the O'Leary country: down from the mountains and over the rolling green hills to the city of Cork.

We do not know what he thought of the biggest city he ever visited. There is no written record of that journey. Nothing, except the story of the classical volume acquired by a trick from a city bookseller. He would possibly have known the details of the quarrel and lawsuit between Tadhg Dubh Cronin and Sir Matthew Deans of Dromore. And how Deans had put upon Cronin the inconvenience of arrest. North of Cork at Whitechurch there was a school of the poets. And more than a century later a few of the last lingering Gaelic poets died in the vicinity of the city. But we do not know the name of any man whom Aodhagán spoke to in those streets, nor of any house he entered, except the bookshop where the man behind the counter pitied his tatters and jokingly offered him a book if he could read the Greek that covered its pages.

According to the story, the voice of suffering and neglected learning spoke in the battered poet, read the lines, dumbfounded the bookseller and gained a book.

The booksellers in present-day Cork do not do business in that way. For when some mystic sense of a pilgrim's obligations sent me book-buying there, the girl in the shop offered no sporting bargain. The book I bought was Smollett's *Humphrey Clinker* and it may have been that the girl did not consider the ability to read English uncommon enough to justify the risk of a wager. So I paid my money and walked the bright curves of Patrick Street with *Humphrey Clinker* safe in my pocket. Then up the sunny Mardyke to lean on a bridge over black water with the Cork College of the National University above me on the hill. The night without stars had ended and the day had come: a bright, lively day in Cork City with traffic going up and down the Mardyke, and students cycling down the hill from the college, and everything standing out virile and distinct in the bright sunshine.

I forgot the tattered poet, found myself wondering about the students, calculating the advantages or disadvantages of going to college in Cork instead of in Dublin. Then I forgot the students, remembered *Humphrey Clinker*, old Bramble and his pills, Aunt Tabitha Bramble and her suitors down to the great Lismahago, Lydia Melford and her fashionable tendency to swoon at the sight of anyone resembling her vanished lover, their adventures at Bath and in London and on the long journey into Scotland. I read from one of the letters of the lovely Lydia: 'Sir Ulic Mackilligut recommended his nephew, Captain O'Donaghan, to me as a partner; but Jery excused himself by saying I had got the headache'.

Well, that was going on in England roughly about the time the poet from Kerry got himself a book in Cork. And Sir Ulic was Ireland as the novelist Smollett saw it. But Smollett viewed the contemporary scene on the larger island on which he lived, put his observations into his novels, left them as a lasting comment on a period. O'Rahilly took his book with him and went back into the mountains to a life that is to us, for the most part, a mystery. He was not writing in English and shaping a literary form for the future. He was making poems in a language that was to come very close to extinction. All around him the ragged thousands lived on in the gloom that followed the death and banishment of their leaders. And he did not know that with them was the secret of the bright city by the Lee, and the busy streets in which I would buy the volume of Smollett, and the churches, and the houses going up above the river, the students going up the hill to the college with the step of the sons and daughters of free men.

He took his book with him, and all that it told him of Greece and Rome, and went back into the mountains, to the thunder of the wave in the dark night, to the cataract crying like an animal in the woods, to a grave between grey walls where holy men had prayed for centuries. Possibly there is in those two great poems of lamentation more of the man, and his understanding of his own time, than in anything else he composed. They reveal the man because they are terrible, with an intensity of bitterness and pride that denotes sincere and genuine utterance; just as the last few sonnets of Hopkins betray the torture of the soul of a very different man in a very different time. They reveal the time, because, with just that agony of bitterness and pride, the soul and body of Gaelic Ireland came apart. Not as in decent and honourable death, but in a trance and torpor that left a half-decayed body tormented with whispers and visions of something that had been and now was not.

The long wave gathered power from the wide waters of Dingle Bay, advanced and swelled and crashed against the rocks of Rossbeigh, and died in a pitiful whisper along the flat sands. Somewhere in the night, in a miserable hut, the poet heard the voice of the wave, and spoke to it in answer. He had no cattle, no wealth, no sheep, no horned cows. In his poverty he lived on dog fish and periwinkles. If the great MacCarthy of the

Laune were only alive, neither the poet nor his children would suffer in this destitution and misery. But the MacCarthys were gone from the Laune, the Lein and the Lee, gone from Kanturk, from all the land between Cashel and the wave of Cliodhna, and across to Thomond. For the poet and his children there was left only a miserable hovel on the shore. And outside the darkness, the rain, the storm, the bellowing of the relentless wave:

> Thou wave below, of great repute, loud-voiced,
> The senses of my head are overpowered with thy bellowing.
> Were help to come again to fair Erin,
> I would thrust thy discordant clamour down thy throat.

Fair Erin remained without help. And from that poem to the other great lament, written on his deathbed, there is no change of note, except that pride has hardened into defiance of all the miserable chances that can happen to man. Into a belief in a life beyond this life, in which the chieftains, whose line went back before the death of Christ, would have their rightful place; and he have his rightful place in relation to them:

> I will not cry for help until I am put in the narrow coffin . . .

> I will follow the beloved among heroes to the grave . . .

That made, you might say, a very appropriate deathbed statement from a poet who had consistently used his power to praise such men as that beloved among heroes, to lament the end of the world to which those men belonged. When he lay back on his bed and died, that world had ended with a finality that even Aodhagán the poet, who knew his own merit, would have found it difficult to appreciate. For he was the last great voice that spoke authentically for the vanished order, that superseded scheme of things. The first three decades of the eighteenth century had come to an end. For more than seventy years the poor people in the cabins stumbled through darkness as deep as that in which he replied to the bellow and lament of the waves. They had poets who understood them better than Aodhagán ever cared to understand them. They had no leaders. And the poets looked over the seas to a king who was not their king, who had never been a leader, who had never even been a satisfying legend.

But never again, after the death of O'Rahilly, did any poet see, except in transient and imagined glimpses, the fabulous hospitality of Clonmeen or Killeen or Killaha. Never again did they see the lords of the Laune, the Lein and the Lee walk in majesty before a worshipping people. For practical purposes, that was just as well. The new king, who was to make a new people, came also out of those mountains and fashioned his people in a way that would have wiped out forever the majesty of those men. The transient and imagined glimpses passed on from popular poets to the people who heard them, projected themselves into the vision given by the new king, left us today with an irritatingly insecure hold on the secret on which Aodhagán O'Rahilly closed his lips, and died.

They buried him at Muckross between the lake and the mountains, between grey walls that holy men had built and Cromwellian men had desecrated, under the sanctuary of trees that holy men had planted.

In 1840 someone read and interpreted the inscription on the tombstone as: 'This tomb belongs to the race of Daniel son of Morgan Rahilly from Raheen'.

Today a plain plaque on the wall honours the three great poets that the mountainy places of Kerry gave to Ireland for all time. In the cloister a few yards away is the great yew tree on which, according to an old story, Aodhagán saw the son of a rapacious settler swing, his young neck accidentally caught between two of the ancient branches. The bitter poet praised the tree for its pleasant fruit, prayed that every branch on that tree, and every branch on every tree in the land would bear like fruit.

Now there is peace around the grey ruin, and under the great trees, and on the wide lake. And under the mountain where there is only the cry of the white cataract leaping from rock to rock. Aodhagán O'Rahilly, in his misery, also heard that cry:

> No tune comes near me, as I weep on the roads,
> But the squeal of the hog which cannot be wounded by sticking.

Today the screaming hog is ticketed and guarded in the interests of the great democracy of Tourism. You pay your money and walk right up a carefully arranged path parallel to the white descent of the water. When I last made that ascent, I did it in the company of a man from America whose people had left this land a century ago. We walked back to Killarney through a dusk coming spasmodically alive with the glimmer and movement of stars. He talked, as only Americans can talk, of all the things Americans find to talk about.

Not far away on our left hand, and under the stars, the body of Aodhagán O'Rahilly, the poet from Scrahanaveal, had returned to the dust.

∼ 3 ∼

The Great Gazebo

ASTLETOWNSHEND, IN THE WILD west of the County of Cork, is a curious and interesting village set in that wilderness of tentacle headlands that seem as if they were struggling out to the south-west to entrap the passing ships. An extremely hilly and ancient street descends to the small harbour; and as you descend with it, carefully circling around a monstrous tree that manages to block even the little traffic there is, you get the feeling that the village knows it should be somewhere else: more than likely on the coasts of Devon or Cornwall.

That feeling is probably the stronger because to arrive at Castletownshend you have passed through another small village, Union Hall. And the very sound of the name suggests an Ireland rigidly under the control of the True Blue Bands; such institutions, for instance, as the Moyallow Loyal Protestant Society to which an ancestor of the novelist Elizabeth Bowen, in another part of County Cork, once belonged.

The most interesting house in Castletownshend is on your right hand before you really enter the village and swing left to go down to the sea. It is a small, unpretentious place with a tasteful doorway, gables overcoated with mellowing slates. There are gravelled walks, good gardens. And the woman who once lived there, continuing to write, communing with the spirit of a dead cousin who still remained, she believed, her literary collaborator, looked down from that house, and over the village to the sea, and described what she saw:

> From the high place where the house stood one could look down across the tops of the trees to the narrow harbour. On the farther shore a few lights were coming out, here and there like stars on a cloudy night. The thin turf smoke lay like a film over the houses. The open sea beyond the harbour was pale with the last reflected light from the West. A fishing

31

snack lay at anchor off the whitewashed coastguard station. The young moon hung over her mast like the crescent on a Turkish flagship. A fishing sloop was putting forth for her night's work. Her brown sails were idle, only the throb of her little engine faintly shook the air.

From the high place where the house stood, Edith Somerville, in her time, could ride out to study the 'instinct of secrecy' so deeply implanted in a peasant people long kept in subjection. We must search for the feeling in days of land-war and agitation. She felt it and wrote about it: 'the instinct that makes men turn their backs on a stranger, that sends the women in their villages to hide within their doors, like wild animals in their holes'.

That is a most interesting reflection, and the more so if you balance it against what that other woman novelist of the Irish landed-classes, Elizabeth Bowen, had to say about her own people as they found themselves when the Irish eighteenth century, advancing towards its high moment at the Dungannon Convention, and the absorbing power of the land, and its past and its people, had affected even the Cromwellians:

> This new wish in the new Irish to see Ireland autonomous was in more than the head and the conscious will. Ireland had worked on them, through their senses, their nerves, their loves. They had come to share with the people round them, sentiments, memories, interests, affinities. The grafting-on had been, at least where *they* were concerned, complete. If Ireland did not accept them, they did not know it – and it is in that unawareness of final rejection, unawareness of being looked at from some secretive, opposed life, that the Anglo-Irish naive dignity and even, tragedy seems to me to stand. Themselves, they felt Irish and even acted as Irishmen.

That whisper from the past, or from the Great Beyond, which came to Edith Somerville in the house at Castletownshend, went back to a letter her cousin Martin Ross had written in March 1912. Martin Ross had told how on St Patrick's Day she had driven to see a great cutstone house of three storeys, and of the strange tale she had heard of the family that used to live there. Three or four generations of that family had lived and rioted in the place, living with countrywomen, occasionally marrying them, all illegitimate four times over:

> About one hundred and fifty years ago a very grand lady married the head of the family and lived there, and was so corroded with pride that she would not allow her two daughters to associate with the neighbours of their own class. She lived to see them marry two of the men in the yard. Yesterday, as we left, an old spinster, daughter of the last owner, was at the door in a little donkey-trap. She lives near in an old castle, and since her people died she will not go into the House, or into the enormous yard, or the beautiful old garden. She was a strange mixture of distinction and commonness, like her breeding, and it was very sad to see her at the door of that great house. If we dared to write up that subject – Yours Ever (and let us add, through Death) – Martin.

That letter had its full development in the novel *The Big House of Inver*, which, along with *The Real Charlotte*, several serious authorities, Irish, English and American, have considered as of much more importance than the galloping reminiscences of the Irish R.M. The matter is arguable and contingent on your mood and humour.

Those two novels are certainly less liable than the R.M. and Flurry Knox and Slipper are to set one laughing. And it seems that Edith Somerville surveying from horseback the racing land, and Edith Somerville considering the fate of a family and their Big House, could be two very different people. When she rode out to hounds, disproving forever the pretty heavy dictum of George Henry Moore, the father of the novelist, that ladies were no judges of horses, she could find herself with the fascinating Mrs Knox of Aussolas Castle, where the dining-room was one of the many rooms in Ireland in which Oliver Cromwell was said to have stabled his horse and 'probably no one would have objected less than Mrs Knox had she been consulted in the matter'.

Mrs Knox's nephew, Flurry, said that there wasn't a day in the year that you wouldn't get feeding for a hen and chickens on the floor.

Major Sinclair Yeates, the Englishman who became the Irish R.M., considered that the horse was obsolete as a means of locomotion. Yet the horse brought him on hectic journeys, even through weather in which 'only a snipe or a dispensary doctor' would be out of doors, even halfways to Lisheen Races to hear Slipper talk, in tones that were to develop into those of Michael James Flaherty, of how the horse-rider, Driscoll, was rolled over and killed. And then Driscoll, making straight the way for the father of Christy Mahon, turns up alive at the end of the narration.

Not the only prevision of *The Playboy* that was to come to be found in the *Experiences of the Irish R.M.* Owneen the Sprat could be an elder brother of that Christian man but weakly lover, Shawneen Keogh. And Catherine O'Donovan of Skeagh, writing her list of damages for dead fowl ('five turkies and their mother, five ducks and the drake, five hins and the cock'), to be presented to the errant Master of the Skebawn Foxhounds, could have been providing a stylistic model for Margaret Flaherty, writing for the six yards of stuff for to make a yellow gown, a pair of lace boots with lengthy heels on them and brassy eyes, a hat is suited for a wedding day, a fine-tooth comb, to be sent with three barrels of porter in Jimmy Farrell's creel cart, on the evening of the coming Fair, to Michael James Flaherty.

Or, visiting the Big House that had been bought from previous owners by old McRory, a rich and retired Dublin coal-merchant, Major Yeates could meditate, as did later a more famous namesake (almost!), on riches driving out rank, as he walked in the roomy shade of splendid beech trees: 'Servants of the old regime, preserving their dignity through the vicissitudes of the new'.

Reflections of that sort, such as they are, kept running through my head when, in an August in the early 1960s, I visited the house at Castletown-shend. There I was privileged to talk to Edith's nephew, a retired, high-ranking British officer, and to hear him say that he was convinced that Edith had continued to work in collaboration with the spirit of her dead cousin. Then I thought of the gentle ghost whom Elizabeth Bowen wrote about in her book on the history of her family and their house, *Bowen's Court*. That ghost was a little Miss Prittie, or Pretty as she was called, a niece of the Bowen family, who, staying for a while with an aunt and uncle, persuaded two beech saplings to grow together and planted a garden around them; and left the garden and the Siamese-twin trees and her own enchanted, ghostly memory to trouble the imagination of a young girl growing up in that house to become a most notable novelist:

> Our shadows rove the garden gravel still,
> The living seem more shadowy than they . . .

To the restrained music of those lines I walked back down the avenue at Castletownshend to the fine gateway and entrance where, not so many years before, the aged Admiral Somerville had been murdered, for no particularly noticeable reason, except that the Irish people had not yet learned to trust each other. Will they ever? And I thought then of a story, 'A Broken World' by Sean O'Faoláin, in which an old priest, whom the narrator encounters in a railway-train has this to say: '. . . they in their octagon and we in our lighted cabins, I mean to say, it was two halves of a world . . .

And later in the story, when the train in which they are travelling comes into Dublin, the narrator wonders about the few people he can see abroad in the wintry streets:

> What image, I wondered, as I passed through them, could warm them as the Wicklow priest had warmed us for a few minutes in that carriage now chugging around the edge of the city to the sea? What image of life that would fire and fuse us all, what music bursting like the spring, what triumph, what engendering love, so that those breasting mountains that now looked cold should appear brilliant and gay, the white land that seemed to sleep should appear to smile, and these people who huddled over the embers of their lives should become like the peasants who held the hand of Faust with their singing one Easter morning.

Elizabeth Bowen's account of her home, and of the generations of her people who had built and lived there, was published in 1942. So that during the worst years of World War II she was thinking her way back along centuries of a family history symbolized by the 'Roman urbane strongness' of Bowen's Court. She saw that great house as the negation of mystical Ireland, rebutting with bald walls the surrounding, disturbing light. It had been built by rulers of the people in their ruling tradition and imposed upon a land once taken by the Cromwellian sword. Yet she was also proudly conscious that the house belonged where it was, that it had been built from the local rock. She said: 'I am ruled by a continuity that I cannot see'.

The young girl, Lois, in Elizabeth's novel *The Last September*, said that she liked to be part of a pattern, to be related, to be compelled to be what she was because mere unrelated being was intransitive and lonely. With that Roman solidity of the Big House, with bald walls outstaring the disturbing light of a local mysticism, a house with no haunted rooms, and with strong foundations, cut by the sword and unshaken by later wars. And with the wish to be part of a pattern and with a fear of intransitive loneliness, Elizabeth Bowen's development as a writer began. But by the time she came to write *The Heat of the Day*, so many things had fallen apart that she had found her way to a place and time of chaos, with the world's strongest city and the world's widest empire sorely shaken, and with simple words like traitor and lover losing most of their meaning. And the novelist, the daughter of Cromwellian conquerors, had discovered in that novel a sort of man born with defeat in his heart.

In *The Last September* she indicates the exact moment at which she first noticed that the world was not as stable as the history and the living presence of Bowen's Court seemed to suggest. Her ancestor Henry Bowen IV must have had a similar feeling when the house was first attacked in 1798 and he realized that the house built by Henry Bowen III, 'to stand open to friends of all sorts, had had to repel foes.'

That house casts its square shadow over all the houses in *The Last September*, all houses threatened by a peculiarly illogical guerrilla war going in the surrounding woods and the neighbouring mountains. Lois, prowling alone in the wet shrubbery near her home, surprises life, as Elizabeth Bowen did in so many subtle stories, at a 'significant angle' when she sees an armed man shortcutting secretly across the demesne, and she decides that Ireland is the cause of his haste. Here, certainly, is one of the first unsettling flashes of illumination, showing that something is going on that has nothing to do with stability, something in which, Lois quickly realizes, she cannot share:

> She could not conceive of her country emotionally: it was a way of living, an abstract of several landscapes, or an oblique frayed island, moored at the North but with an air of being detached and washed out West from the British coast.

Yet Elizabeth saw Bowen's Court, and the country around it, as possibly the only place in her world where it was still possible to feel related, to feel that one was part of a pattern. On Sundays she watched the country people going to Mass: horses and traps turning out of impossibly narrow lanes, cyclists free-wheeling down from mountainy farms, dark Sunday-fied figures balancing on stepping stones, or crossing stiles, or following paths through plantations'.

A ruling class may have planted the house on a virgin, anonymous countryside. But since they had built it from the native rock, it was not unrelated to the mountain above; nor to the country's ancient ruins:

> Lordly or humble, military or domestic, standing up with furious gaunt-ness like Kilcolman, or shelving weakly into the soil, ruins feature the landscape – uplands or river valleys – and make a ghostly extra quarter to towns. They give clearings in woods, reaches of mountain or sudden turns of a road, a meaning and pre-inhabited air.

At Christmas time when she lived there at Bowen's Court, by Kildor-rery in County Cork, she burned, in a window of the great house, a Christmas candle, the gift of a neighbour in Farrahey. And in the cottages of Farrahey and Kildorrery the fellows of that candle, she said, were alight.

That would merely have been the wishful thinking of a person who felt that there must somewhere exist for everybody a country of the heart where patterns are not torn, where the interdependence of the various parts is still recognized. It contrasts most interestingly with that other world in her novels *The Death of the Heart* and *The Heat of the Day*, where the heart dies by betrayal and stability is shaken into functional anarchy. It contrasts, also, with that celebrated passage in which Turgenev makes Bazarov reprove his betters because they do not belong to the people. Or with a great deal of what Padraic Colum had to say in his novel *Castle Conquer*. Or with the O'Faoláin story, 'A Broken World'. Or with Daniel Corkery writing about rebels in *The Hounds of Banba*.

The man whom Lois, in *The Last September*, saw shortcutting through Lady Nayler's shrubbery could have been one of Corkery's mystical young men. Or one of Frank O'Connor's running young fellows, in some of O'Connor's early stories, happy in the possession of a gun. (In the 1990s it does not seem all that happy.)

Yet it might have been O'Faoláin's Frankie Hannafey, on his way to American exile in the novel *Come Back to Erin*, or the young man in O'Faoláin's story 'Midsummer Night Madness', cycling out from Cork City to organize revolution and to find in a broken house the halves of a broken world coming together in a sombre mockery of sexual union between a daft old gentleman and a skivy or servant maid.

We are back here with the ruin of the Big House of Inver; we are back even at Castle Rackrent, and with those images of doom that for a century seemed to possess the nightmares of some of the people of the Big Houses: visions of falling walls, of the Great Gazebo in flames, of the lead melting from roofs and running down like rainwater. Those nightmares, as we know, were to prove tragically prophetic. When the houses were built, the conquered land had been stamped and claimed. When the houses, like the woods of an earlier time, were down, an almost unique society had had its day.

It was only to be expected that a writer with the sense of Gothic doom of Charles Robert Maturin should have been one of the first, in the Irish nineteenth century, to describe in its full glory, or complete desolation, a falling house. And to invest that falling with a sense of the supernatural that was quite different from what Maria Edgeworth displayed when she considered, with her calm reason, the fall of the House of Rackrent. The house to which in the novel *Melmoth the Wanderer*, John Melmoth, a student of Trinity College, Dublin, came to find the dread secret of his family, was fit matter for any nightmare even if, while the master lay dying upstairs, there was a hooley going on in the kitchen. The gate-lodge was in ruins, and a barefooted boy from an adjacent cabin ran to lift on a single hinge what had once been a gate.

Then, by the dim light of an autumnal evening, John slowly trod the miry road towards the House and looked at all the signs that showed how penury had been aggravated into downright misery.

On the lawn there was neither tree nor shrub, and the lawn itself had been turned into pasture-ground. And a few sheep picked scanty food amid pebblestones, thistles and hard mould. And to the bare house itself there were neither wings, nor offices, nor shrubbery, nor tree to shade or support it. The steps were grass-grown, the windows were boarded, there wasn't even a knocker on the door.

The colours of the picture are deepened to provide a fitting introduction to a tale of horror. But Sheridan Le Fanu, who was six years of age when *Melmoth the Wanderer* was published, and who followed Maturin along that same dark road, became obsessed with that image of a falling house. E.F. Bleiler pointed out, in the introduction to his selection of Le Fanu, that the author of *Carmilla* and of *Uncle Silas* seems to have recognized 'a parallel between his own life-situation and the world that was dying about him. He was born into a society that was being fragmented by emergent nationalism and was beginning to collapse; he lived in a culture that had great nostalgia for the past – a very unusual trait for the present-centred Victorians. It is recorded in Le Fanu's later days, when his health began to fail, that he suffered from a repetitive dream of a house that threatened to collapse on him. When he was found dead, his doctor mused: 'At last, the house has fallen'.

One could play about with that rare piece of William Carleton, 'The Black Baronet'; or with the more serious moments of Charles Lever. Or, for light relief, with that hilarious moment when Samuel Lover's Handy Andy is tricked into serving the writ on the barricaded and infuriated Squire. But it is, perhaps, more useful to bring the image of the falling, burning house back almost to our own time, to George Moore, and to think of the eyeless, burnt-out skeleton that now stands (that is, if it still stands and is not completely smothered by the efforts of the Forestry Department) where Moore Hall was once raised on Muckloon above Lough Carra. Or back, indeed, to that other burnt-out skeleton above the river Nore at Inistioge, in the County Kilkenny, where the Tighe family once flourished, and produced, among many notable people, a lady poet who was a friend of Charles Lever. She may even have influenced John Keats. And, on her passing, she was melodiously mourned by Thomas Moore and Felicia Hemans:

> Our shadows roam the garden gravel still,
> The living seem more shadowy than they . . .

In the *jacquerie* of the 1920s we know that some houses were burned out for politics, some for loot and some, human nature being what it is, for insurance.

From the house of Tom Ruttledge, George Moore's land-agent and old friend, in Westport, County Mayo, where a Lord Sligo had once had built one of the most beautiful towns in Ireland, George Moore walked forth to meet, he would have us believe, the storyteller Alec Trusselby. And thus to gather the material for his joyous, bawdy book *A Story-Teller's Holiday*. In the end Alec says: 'Faith, I give in to your honour, the shanachie of London has pounded the shanachie of Westport'.

That was a pleasant way, for Moore, of playing about, in his best later style, with two parts of his eccentric personality. And all the time he was aware that his own home was not far away. And, for a while, he ceased from storytelling so as to go to see that home. Going back in the train to Dublin he thought:

Outside of the circle of your own life you are unconcerned with the fate of Moore Hall, my agent's ghost insisted as the train passed by Maynooth, and I answered to the ghost: That is not so, for I would prolong the life of Moore Hall beyond my life if it were possible. What is Moore Hall but one of the thousands of other houses built in the eighteenth century, he replied. The Nineveh into which Jonah marched [I feel certain that neither Tom Ruttledge nor the ghost of Tom Ruttledge ever talked like that. B.K.] for three days before he began to preach, passed away so rapidly that the shepherds who fed their flocks among the ruins could not tell Xenophon the name of the bygone city. Why then, said the ghostly voice, should you trouble about Moore Hall? Nobody will live there again. It is true, I answered him, time overtakes the most enduring monuments, but one continues to build, for we are created with that intention, and every day we strain against death. Why then should it be very foolish of me to dream of Moore Hall as a hostel for parsons and curates when I am among the gone? The Irish Church is very dear to me and Moore Hall

might serve as a token of my admiration for a Protestantism that has
given Ireland all our great men and our Anglo-Irish literature.

To suggest that a colony of Protestant parsons should be set upon the
shores of Lough Carra where there would be little for them to do but fish
or, perhaps, pray, was to fire the last shot in the sad or silly religious war
he had carried on with his brother, Colonel Maurice. It is amusing to think
that had Moore Hall survived the last malicious fires of the Civil War, it
would, possibly, like other great houses, have passed over to the nuns
who, some of them, might have been delighted because of *Sister Teresa*,
and *A Story-Tellers Holiday*, so as to get their own back on George Moore.
If, that is, they had read those books and survived.

But Moore Hall was his 'dreaming house.'

He noted, when he was discovering Walter Peter, that Marius the
Epicurean had lived in an old family mansion, one which he was soon to
leave to go to Rome: drawn thither by literature, as the young George
Moore had been drawn to Paris by the desire to paint. Or so he said. How
delighted he was to reflect that for Marius a literary career had become
necessary through the extravagance of an ancestor. And that Moore Hall, a
Georgian mansion standing on a hilltop amid branching woods, was also
neglected. Like the house of Marius, Moore Hall had fallen into the 'lag
end of its fortunes and he wandered round the ruined stables in which had
stood a hundred horses, and through the abandoned gardens on whose
high walls a peacock, the last of a long race, screamed for a mate.'

Because it remained his dreaming house, he had it in his heart, as he
had the beauty of Lough Carra and as Everyman had, he said, a lake in his
heart. When the burning of the great houses began, he said that he feared
his house was in danger because his brother, the colonel, was in politics as
a Senator of the Irish Free State. But it is more than possible that Moore's
fear for the house was an ancestral thing: that underground fear that had
affected Le Fanu and had, long previously, touched Moore when he had
been reading Balzac on the revolt of the peasants. It was the fear that
Society as it was could not continue to stand.

There was, as Mother Ireland knows, no national or political reason
why the home of the Moores of Moore Hall should not have been safe
from any *jacquerie*. The plaque to the hapless John Moore, first and short-
lived president of the republic of Connacht when Humbert, the
Frenchman, landed, that plaque fastened to the wall of a house, burned out
a century later, allegedly by the republicans of Connacht, is a mournful
commentary on the twisted ways of Ireland.

But we must note that long before the end came, George Moore, in
London, had had his dream of the falling house. He said that, roused from
his bed by a fetch-light, he flung himself across the hearthrug and broke

his wrist in a dream, that 'on seeing a flame shoot up I had leaped forward to quench a burning house. A burning house! they said, but what house? I answered that I did not know, nor was it till the burning of our houses began that I connected my dream with the burning of Moore Hall'.

Elizabeth Bowen said that the troubles of the Bowens began with the building of Bowen's Court. It is much more certain that the troubles of the Moores of Moore Hall began in 1798 with John Moore, the first president of a republic that never existed, and ended, in 1923, when a raiding-party, presumed to be Irish republicans, burned down the house of a family that had, to coin a phrase, a distinguished national record.

In the town of Westport (and just across the road from the gates of the lord's demesne) in which the great house is now a stately home open to viewers, and proud of its memories of Grace O'Malley, the late John Kelly, a master-joiner and a man who had known George Moore well and gave a fine account of him, told me (back in the 1950s) how he had witnessed the burning. And had wept to see the lead from the gutters running down the fine cut stone. He said: 'And the Moores of Moore Hall could never stand the sight of concrete'. Thus echoing the belief of the father of a friend of mine that the two things that had ruined Ireland were concrete and Sinn Féin. George Moore also detested plate-glass as one of the ugliest things from a century of ugliness.

That John Kelly, by the way, was almost certainly, from something he said to me, a connection of an old retainer at Moore Hall. She was a Bridget Kelly whose hands were so hardy that, to the wonderment of the colonel's two sons, she could pick live coals from the fire. She was a native speaker of Irish but was of no help when the colonel and George wished for the boys to learn the language. For she thought, J.M. Hone said, that it was extremely ridiculous for the gentry to be wanting to know Irish.

Moore Hall, the mansion, went up in flames and down in ruin. The young Wiseman had visited there. So had Maria Edgeworth: and had displayed for years a tender interest in the family.

An ancestor, Old George, a recluse historian, had meditated there on the French Revolution that, from a long remove, had destroyed poor President John. Old George had also considered that if the whole bundle of Irish manuscripts, histories and traditions were finally to perish, abundant good would be done to the country: 'They only serve to nourish and foster vacuity, idleness and habits pernicious to industry'.

That desired perishing was, for good or ill, not to happen. George Henry Moore, the father of George, the novelist, had received French revolutionaries as guests in that house. There was even a legend or a rumour, or something, that he might have taken the Fenian oath. In that house, also, George Henry finely reflected, when passing on to his people five hundred pounds he had won on the turf, that his horses would run better with the blessings of the poor.

When George Henry was absent in London, as a Member of Parliament on the business of Ireland, his mother and his wife sat, in the evenings, talking or reading Walter Scott to each other until they had by heart pages of the Wizard of the North. It is a picture that goes well with the light of evening at Lissadell and great windows open to the south. Of all that, nothing remains but a burned-out fragment shrouded in new forestry. And words. And memories.

After the burning of Moore Hall, James Reilly, the land-steward, wrote: 'There is absolutely nothing left but the walls, not a vestige of glass, timber, or even plaster, from the ground floor up, such wholesale destruction in a few hours it is difficult to understand . . .

'. . . fearing that the outoffices would catch, I let out all the livestock, and stood by to see the last, and felt as one does when standing by the open grave of a very dear friend'.

It is commonly accepted that Moore Hall was burned, so as to speak, neat, and that nothing was taken away. George Moore seems to have thought so. But John Kelly, and other people of that part, hinted darkly to me that there were houses in three towns where furnishings that had once graced Moore Hall could be recognized. An interesting subject, I thought, for scholarly research: with the aid of the Garda Síochána.

To old George Moore, the historian and grandfather of George, the novelist Maria Edgeworth had written, reminding him that Edgeworthstown was on his road to Dublin, and that the Edgeworths were always obliged by friends who could make it 'convenient to themselves to give us a day or two, or even an hour, upon their journeys.' The home of the Edgeworths is now a hospital in the care of a religious order. National, or linguistic, fervour has altered the name of the town to Mostrim: a musical name, indeed, even if it may not be much used by the people. Yet it seemed a pity that any effort should have been made to wipe out the name of such a notable family. And I always did feel that a compromise, say Mostrim-Edgeworth, would be in order.

For one of the most interesting chapters in the story of the Big House could be written about the relations between Moore Hall and the house on the road to Dublin, in which house Maria Edgeworth wrote the story of the Rackrents and of old Thady Quirke, who for so long was so loyal, as he claimed and as he may have seen it, to a feckless family. Years after she had written the story of Thady, as she allowed him to tell it, it must have given the grand old lady of Edgeworthstown some grim amusement to come across such a reflection of Thady as that William Mullowney who worked for the Moores of Moore Hall. Even Mullowney's epistolary style reads like a comic parody of the style Maria Edgeworth gave to, or borrowed from, the original of Thady to tell the tale of the Rackrents. Excusing himself for something or other, and aware that bad reports of him had gone abroad, Mullowney wrote to the Mrs Moore of the time, who was at that moment in London:

> I will send you a full copy of my book since the day you went off. I will first send you list and amount of cash received for them and to whom I sold and the wool in itself all in one and then the balance of the May rent that was due before you went off that in itself and then the November – also in self – and Threadsmen and Housekeeping and everything that you may see plainly as I did not lose a day and calling on William Molloy . . . and still the weather is as bad that we can work and in two days after you receive this you shall have the other so that I hope in God it will be to your satisfaction the coppy of the whole account and to a show that you may dout me in what a gentleman told you there is a good many of them by name but very little to be chosen. If I was very liberal and good to gentlemen when they come to Moore Hall I might have a good name but I must take the will for the deed. Our great God carried his cross and it is a poor and dreadful thing to meddle with a servant is earning his bread night and day that I thank my God I have respect for my situation . . .

Somewhere on the soft, green Shannonside land, between Moore Hall and Edgeworthstown (Mostrim), his honest pathetic voice fades into the past. And I am left remembering a stately figure who led a friend and myself through deep woods in the County Laois to the small and secret Grantstown Lough. That tall man had been gamekeeper and close friend to Lord Castletown, the Gaelic peer, who roundabout the beginning of the nineteenth century had been friend to Douglas Hyde and Canon Sheehan and others. He displayed proudly to us the leather belt, with pouches for ammunition and for first-aid equipment, that Douglas Hyde had tied around his waist when the two of them went duck-shooting around that enchanted lough, commemorated by John Keegan, the Laois poet. He talked of the last days of another great house, and said sternly: 'The people always wanted the land. Now they have it'.

He, and what he had to say, would be part of any story of the Big House and our literature. As would Lady Morgan, with the Hamiltons at Baronscourt. Or Jane Barlow, the daughter of the Vice-Provost of Trinity College, Dublin, walking the then narrow roads of north County Dublin and meditating on such poor pelting villages as Lisconnel and Ballyhoy. Which latter, no longer a village, is now known as Dollymount.

Or William Carleton, walking from The Sheds at Clontarf to visit Sir Benjamin Lee Guinness in his great house at St Anne's. Or Francis MacManus, writing in his novel *This House Was Mine* of the downfall of a house of strong farmers in the County Kilkenny. Or John Synge, brooding in that huge house by the Devil's Glen in Wicklow. Or William Yeats, walking in the woods of Coole. Or Edward Martyn, praying in his organ loft at Tulira, or crossing over to the stony places of Clare to talk with the Count de Basterot. Or Hugh Lane, desiring his ideal House of Art, set like a Venetian bridge across the Liffey. Or Hugh Lane's aunt Augusta Gregory, seeing her ideal house as a theatre. Or Patrick Pearse, crying out for the house that he had built in his heart, the noble house of his thought.

It is a wide and varied subject.

I shall leave the last word to Brendan Behan. In his autobiographical *Borstal Boy*, he told how his father, Stephen, during a Dublin strike, brought Brendan out with him to help farm an acre of land on ground once associated with Dean Swift, at Glasnevin. And how Stephen dug with 'great function', but not for long. For talking being always more palatable than digging, Stephen leaned on his spade and told the son that if he kept digging long enough he might uncover relics of Swift or Vanessa or Stella or Mrs Delaney. I like to think of those two rare comedians digging in the ghostly shadow of the Big House of which Brendan was very much aware. For the hilarious brothel in his play *The Hostage* is a noble old house that has held so many heroes and has, in the end, been turned into a knocking-shop. It is romantic, idealistic Ireland fallen on sordid, materialistic days.

In his one-act play *The Big House*, useful on radio but no stage-success, the Baldcocks waken up in the night in Tonesollock House (I need not comment on the subtlety of the names) to the sound of exploding civil war. While they think it just as well that the Irish should be kept occupied in 'killing each other rather than in killing us', they still decide to leave for a while for England. For the Hoggitts, the Blood-Gores, the Ramsbottoms, the Pug-Footes, the Grimeses, all the aristocratic names, 'all the grace and splendour of civilized living that the very syllables of those noble names recall', are gone away.

Off they go to London. And, in their absence and without their permission, the knackers are in and, before the Baldcocks return, the house is in ruins.

The comic vanishing of Tonesollock House is a brutal commentary on the tragic ruin that overtook Lady Gregory's Coole, and Douglas Hyde's house at Frenchpark, and Moore Hall and others.

Whether Brendan Behan ever read *Castle Rackrent* I cannot now remember. But, of a surety, O'Looney, faithful retainer to the Baldcocks, is a shadow of Thady Quirke stumbling forever into the darkness. Ananias Baldcock says of him: 'Dionysius O'Looney is a loyal old soul. They have been butlers here since the house was built. For three hundred years, as long as the Baldcocks have lived here, there has always been a Looney in Tonesollock House'.

And O'Looney says of himself: 'I am a Looney, sir, and descended from a long line of Looneys. I got a medal from the Royal Dublin Society at the Horse Show'.

And Chuckles, one of the house-wreckers, asks him: 'What as . . . a prize-goat?' O'Looney answers grandly: 'For fifty years service to the one family'.

From Maria Edgeworth and Thady McQuirke to Brendan Behan and Dionysius O'Looney the wheel has come full circle.

Or something!

﹏ 4 ﹏

A Raid into Dark Corners:
The Poems of Seamus Heaney

SEAMUS HEANEY'S NATIVE COUNTRY, the country of his early years which has stamped several clear images on his poetry, begins not in Belfast but at the Bridge of Toome. That's where the lower Bann, a deep slow river, goes northwards through water meadows out of Lough Neagh, the largest lake in Britain or Ireland.

Rody McCorley, the patriot boy renowned in balladry, was hanged at the Bridge of Toome in 1798 and was attended on the scaffold by a priest called Devlin, which is a great name in those parts. Seamus Heaney married a girl called Devlin from further south on the Tyrone side of the loughshore, from a place called Ardboe where there was an ancient monastic settlement and where there still stands a stone carven cross that is all of a thousand years of age. Another girl called Devlin, Bernadette from the nearby town of Cookstown, became the first student protester to be elected to any legislative assembly, and the Mother of Parliaments at that: elected as a socialist by the votes mostly of the descendants of men who would have given their allegiance to the Great O'Neill in his wars against Elizabeth the First.

That should be enough to show that this is an old twisted land. It has a deceptively quiet, slumbrous face, but it is a land as thrawn as the tough slow spoken men it breeds. They cultivate small farms, deal in cattle, fish the lough, with baited lines often ten miles long, for the rich harvest of eels for the market in Billingsgate, London. They carry on their own war with the company who work the eel-weir at Toome Bridge, and that war goes regularly to violence and the law-courts. For you might say that the claim to the ownership of the eels has been in dispute since the defeat of the Great O'Neill at the Battle of Kinsale.

To the west of the loughshore are the Sperrin mountains to which O'Neill withdrew between Kinsale and his final flight to Europe.

45

Glanconkyne, where he stayed for a while, has a complicated mythology associated with the autumn festival of Lugh, the father, in the mythologies, of Cuchulain. The mountains are plentifully marked by pre-Celtic standing stones and stone circles.

North of the loughshore is the hump of Slemish mountain where, it is said, a slaveboy, who was afterwards to become Patrick the Christian apostle of Ireland, herded sheep.

By tradition, enamelled in the words of Thomas Moore, Lough Neagh is a place for reflections and sunken shadowy images:

> On Lough Neagh's banks, as the fisherman strays
> In the clear, cool eve declining,
> He sees the round towers of other days
> In the waves beneath him shining.

The past has been profuse with images. But the coming and going of the eels, the dark secrecy of their lives, their nocturnal journeys from pond to river over wet grass, provide the poet with a symbol of the relentless continuity of life, even, for all we know of eternity. It is a long way from the round-tower, as Moore saw it, and the romantic wild harp of Erin to the dark, echoing wells, rat-haunted barns and early Christian oratories, oppressive and cold with ancient stone, which Heaney comes to in his search for meanings. Poetry, he has said, is a kind of raid into dark corners. He remembers himself as a boy searching on the top of the dresser, and in other corners of the farmhouse and its buildings, for those oddments of life that are priceless gold to the young imagination. He remembers his grandfather in the peatbog cutting deeper and deeper with the sleán, or loy, for the sods that would burn brightest on the farmhouse hearth. Poetry is down deep. Truth is at the bottom of a well. He looks out a window and sees his father who - like the men of his family before him - had always taken more kindly to the hectoring and colourful life of the cattle-fairs and the cattle-dealing than to the clay-digging in a flower garden.

> The cold smell of potato mould, the squelch and slap
> Of soggy peat, the curt cuts of an edge
> Through living roots awaken in my head.
> But I've no spade to follow men like them.
>
> Between my finger and my thumb
> The squat pen rests.
> I'll dig with it.

The seven poems, 'A Lough Neagh Sequence', are to be found in his second collection: *Door into the Dark*. They have also been published separately by the Phoenix Pamphlet Poets Press, and to that separate publication he prefixes two interesting quotations from Francis Day's *The Fishes of Great Britain and Ireland*, published in London in the 1880s.

This is the first:

> At an early period in the summer it is an interesting sight (at the Cutts
> near Coleraine, on the lower Bann) to mark the thousands of young eels
> then ascending the stream. Hay ropes are suspended over rocky parts to
> aid them in overcoming such obstructions. At these places the river is
> black with the multitudes of young eels, about three or four inches long,
> all acting under that mysterious impulse that prompts them to push their
> course onward to the lake.

The poet's eels are not simply eels. John Clare's harried and slaughtered
badger was not just a badger.

The sequence moves from the myths of the lake, the virtue of the water
that will harden wood into stone, the legend of the 'town sunk beneath its
water', the fable that the vast cavity or crater holding that water is a 'scar
left by the Isle of Man' when some Titan tossed his two-hands-full of earth
against a foe and formed a new island: moves to the doom of the eels
hooked on baited lines as long as eternity, or to a more modern and less
dignified doom at the weirs where five hundred stone of eels can be lifted
out in one go; moves to the fatalism of the men who fish for them and
never learn to swim:

> The lough will claim a victim every year.

In one poem, 'Beyond Sargasso', that has the glistening muscular unity
of the eel's body, the poet brings him, a hungering gland, from the utmost
deeps to the belly of the familiar lake. By pointed lamplight in the
loughshore fields, the fishermen pluck the worms, 'Innocent ventilators
of the ground', for bait. Then, with the gulls above them, an 'umbrella' of
'responsive acolytes', the fishermen conceal in the worms the murderous
bouquet 'of small hooks coiled in the stern'. The lake is a hungry goddess
that demands a life a year. The whole process is somewhere outside time,
set going by something in the dark infinity beyond Sargasso:

> And when did this begin?
> This morning, last year, when the lough first spawned?
> The crews will answer, 'Once the season's in'.

Quoting again from Francis Day:

> Aristotle thought they [the eels] spring from mud . . . while Helmont
> gives the following curious recipe – 'Cut up two turfs covered with May
> dew, and lay one upon the other, the grassy sides inwards, and then
> expose them to the heat of the sun; in a few hours there will spring up an
> infinite quantity of eels'.
>   Horse-hair from the tail of a stallion was asserted to be a never-failing
> source of young eels.

A common experiment with children in that part of the world: steeping
a hair from a horse's tail in water overnight and hoping it would turn into

an eel. Once, of a morning, my own research was rewarded with the sight of an elver, nimble in a baking-bowl of water where I had sunk the hair from the horse's tail. It was some time before I found out there was a practical joker, or an atheist, in the vicinity.

What were once the speculations of wise men groping for meanings remain as the fantasies of children which, in turn, shadow forth images of the life of the grown man. The little boy is told that unless his hair is fine-combed, the lice will coagulate and make a rope and drag him down to the water. Years afterwards, and in the seventh poem of the sequence, the grown man watches by night the mysterious movement of eels over wet grass, as Francis Day watched them on the hayropes at the Cutts near Coleraine, and sees there that inexorable continuity of life:

> To stand
> In one place as the field flowed
> Past, a jellied road,
> To watch the eels crossing land
>
> Re-wound his world's live girdle.
> Phosphorescent, sinewed slime
> Continued at his feet. Time
> Confirmed the horrid cable.

On the title-page of my copy of his first book, *Death of a Naturalist*, Seamus Heaney has written: 'Our poesy is as a gum which oozes from whence 'tis nourished'. Poetry begins in the search in dark corners, by old well-sides, in the hammering forge with the smell of fire and old iron, in the love-bed. Poetry goes out to the world by way of the next door neighbour: in this case, and in Belfast, a veteran of the Battle of Passchendaele, who will march in Heaney's next book. 'The metal and material of the outside world has to ring on the inner anvils of the brain'.

Poetry begins in the childhood country with pastoral sights and sounds, the dead summer smells of hay, pouring of milk in the milker's pail, water hens on the mossholes, the carpenter in his shop making a joint as the poet makes a rhyme; with the thatcher following his ancient and scarcely surviving craft and coming to give new golden life to the farmhouse roof.

He sees the thatcher as a musician, a fiddler testing the strings:

> Next, the bundled rods: hazel and willow
> Were flicked for weight, twisted in case they'd snap.
> It seems he spent the morning warming up . . .

He sees the thatcher as artist: writer, poet, storyteller, 'pinning down his world, handful by handful'. He sees him, in the end of all, as a magician, turning old straw to new gold: 'And left them gaping at his Midas touch'.

There's a whole rural culture, as old as measurement, in the poem, and an ancient magic.

Farther on along the roadway from the farmhouse where he had watched the thatcher at work is the village of Castledawson where there was a man who once upon a time kept a bull who, like Squire Shandy's bull, went about his business with a solemn face, but without the compulsory licence and permission of the Department, or Ministry, of Agriculture. The poet has written a poem about the bull, lawless love on four solid feet, and called the poem and the bull 'The Outlaw'.

> The door, unbolted, whacked back against the wall.
> The illegal sire fumbled from his stall
>
> Unhurried as an old steam engine shunting.
> He circled, snored and nosed. No hectic panting,
>
> Just the unfussy ease of a good tradesman;
> Then an awkward, unexpected jump, and
>
> His knobbled forelegs straddling her flank,
> He slammed life home, impassive as a tank . . .

The act of life has been performed by Europa's lover. Then, 'in his own time', the snorting god who has just broken the laws of man resumes 'the dark, the straw'. A poem to set a man wondering whether the Castledawson bull didn't actually know that his love-making was unlicensed, unblessed; and wondering, too, about other laws, licences, and blessings. 'The Outlaw' brings back to my mind a vision of the big bulls, terrifying as trumpeting elephants, I saw some years ago in the big breeding-station attached to Mitchelstown Creamery in the County Cork. They were chained giants led, literally, by the nose, contributors to the process of artificial insemination and, by appearances, most irritably aware that civilization had played a trick on them. For them, cloistered involuntarily and without vows, no blazing hearth would burn nor busy housewife ply her evening care, nor would the children know their sire from the brown bull of Cooley. Modern life has tampered with the god and chained him by the nose.

The outlaw of Lough Neagh in Heaney's poem had a happier time. There is here an amiable bawdy acceptance of life, but also a knowledge of the conflict between law and love that is dealt with compassionately, tragically (as we shall see) in the poem about the unlicensed mother drowning her unwanted child in the saltwater where the River Erne meets the sea.

Not so long ago, when I was travelling with the poet on beyond Castledawson, on the road to a new house on a hill where his people now live, we overtook and gave a lift to a neighbour woman walking home from the village; on along narrowing country lane to her house, with a clump of bushes to one side of it, and hidden in the bushes a fine example of an old windlass well - which Heaney was most anxious to show to me and to talk about. You could say that he has a thing about wells.

> As a child, they could not keep me from wells
> And old pumps with buckets and windlasses.
> I loved the dark drop, the trapped sky, the smells
> Of waterweed, fungus and dank moss.
>
> One, in a brickyard, with a rotted board top.
> I savoured the rich crash when a bucket
> Plummeted down at the end of a rope.
> So deep you saw no reflection in it.
>
> A shallow one under a dry stone ditch
> Fructified like any aquarium.
> When you dragged out long roots from the soft mulch
> A white lace hovered over the bottom.
>
> Others had echoes, gave back your own call
> With a clean new music in it. And one
> Was scaresome for there, out of ferns and tall
> Foxgloves, a rat slapped across my reflection.
>
> Now, to pry into roots, to finger slime,
> To stare big-eyed Narcissus, into some spring
> Is beneath all adult dignity. I rhyme
> To see myself, to set the darkness echoing.

He called the poem 'Personal Helicon' and dedicated it to a fellow-poet in Belfast, Michael Longley. Weed-grown well, the spade cutting the ground are transformed into living images. But the new house on the hill has all the windy freedom of the cattle-fairs that his father and his father's people followed – and much preferred to any close grappling and wrestling with the clay. They turned from the dark earth to bright airy places. The great fairs are gone, with the saga of the brown bull, into the past. He speaks to his father:

> And watched you sadden when the fairs were stopped.
> No room for dealers if the farmers shopped
> Like housewives at an auction ring. Your stick
> Was parked behind the door and stands there stil.

The cattle-dealer's stick was his lance, his sabre, his staff of office. Civilization, law, has disarmed him, deprived him. Just as the law and modern laboratory methods now lead the roaring god by the nose. The open markets, with dung and the din of bargaining, and hand-slapping, and drink to clinch the bargain have been replaced by roofed-in marts where matters are conducted in an orderly fashion by one auctioneer.

Seamus Heaney says that the first poet who ever really spoke to him was Robert Frost, a strong voice speaking from the land north of Boston to a young Irish poet north of Bannfoot, a tiny place where the upper Bann empties itself into the southern shore of the big lake. Frost's wall, menaced by an undefined Something, may show up again in Heaney's poem 'Scaffolding'. Masons spend so much time on the building of a scaffolding, so much care in testing it to see is it secure, but when the wall is built 'of sure and solid stone' the scaffolding is taken down:

> So if, my dear, there sometimes seem to be
> Old bridges breaking between you and me
>
> Never fear. We may let the scaffolds fall
> Confident that we have built our wall.

That is the confident note of the young dealer in love, walking out in the bright airy market. But on his first great love-journey, his honeymoon after other 'Mushroom loves already. Had puffed and burst in hate', he has, incidentally, the dark vision of the God that can be both builder and wrecker of walls.

Far from the flat loughshore and on the mountainous Dingle peninsula, which is one of those long arms that reach out from south-western Ireland into the Atlantic, he walks into the early Christian stone oratory of Gallarus. The experience seems to have meant a lot to him and its significance will increase, I feel, as his poetry, and the years, advance. It has linked itself with other moments of epiphany; with the smith or the poet hammering in the dark smithy, the forge red, the anvil horned like a unicorn, and the world on soft wheels passing at his door; with the bright laughing girls, defying the edict of the dark bishop, and coming like Aphrodite out of the Galway sea; with the lovers isolated on an island where rock and sea are eternally wedded in conflict. This is the poem 'In Gallarus Oratory':

> You can still feel the community pack
> This place: it's like going into a turfstack,
> A core of old dark walled up with stone
> A yard thick. When you're in it alone
> You might have dropped, a reduced creature
> To the heart of the globe. No worshipper
> Would leap up to his God off this floor.
>
> Founded there like heroes in a barrow
> They sought themselves in the eye of their King
> Under the black weight of their own breathing.
> And how he smiled on them as out they came,
> The sea a censer, and the grass a flame.

On a television talk, broadcast both from Belfast and Dublin, Heaney made his own interesting and revealing statement about the Gallarus experience, how he felt that if all churches were like this one, 'congregations would feel the sense of God much more forcefully'. That would seem to be an odd idea to such latter-day saints as prefer to worship God in the open air, but Heaney does remember that the ancient Irish monks wrote some of the brightest, most observant and most delightful of the world's nature poetry; and his poem notes how, when the monks stepped out of the contemplative darkness, their God smiled on them in the swinging sea and the burning blades of grass. George Russell (AE) wrote: 'I begin through the grass once again to be bound to the lord'. The ancient Gaelic bardic poets, by the rules of their rigorous schools, found their theme and brooded on it, and in their minds made lines upon it, all in the darkness of their stone or wooden sleeping-cells. The Wordsworthian tranquility, another after-dinner use for Cowper's sofa, seems a middle-class compromise, yet Wordsworth had the same idea as ancient monks and bards. Heaney sees the monks emerging from their 'hutch of holiness', experiencing the shock of daylight after the 'compression and constriction' of such oratories: 'Their vision was rinsed and renewed by their retreat out of the light'.

An image closer to his own time and his own home place is the smith in the roadside smithy, outside the door of which old axles and iron hoops, discarded remnants of his craft, lie rusting. The door leads 'into the dark' in which the hammer rings 'short-pitched' on the anvil that is horned like the white, virgin, mythical animal and also solid like an altar on its black iron base. Off and on the smith leans out of the door, looks at the roadway, remembers that hooves once clattered there where traffic now goes 'flashing in rows'. For his image of the poet, Heaney has not yet gone as far as Byzantium but to the smithy of his boyhood and to an Atlantic headland and, in time, back for fifteen hundred years.

Since the time of the monks, he notes, the 'circumstances have changed and writing is usually born today out of the dark active inner centre of the imagination. The metal and material of the ouside world has to ring on the inner anvils of the brain: good writing, like good smithy work, is a compound of energy and artifice'.

He says: 'I think this notion of the dark centre, the blurred and irrational storehouse of insight and instincts, the hidden core of the self – this notion is the foundation of what viewpoint I might articulate for myself as a poet'. He talks about the cloud of unknowing, about what Patrick Kavanagh, an older Irish poet, called the fog, 'the fecund fog of unconsciousness'. Kavanagh said that we have to shut our eyes to see our way to heaven. 'What is faith, indeed, but a trust in the fog; who is God but the King of the Dark?'

What is acceptable in aesthetics may be a little off-putting in theology, if, that is, one at all desires a theology, and Heaney here may be a conscious victim of an Irish obsession which he can describe so well. For his childhood and adolescence, the equivalent of the dark Gallarus was the confessional, the Irish Catholic sense of sin, 'a negative dark that presides in the Irish Christian consciousness', and 'the gloom, the constriction, the sense of guilt, the self-abasement'. Every creed has its own creepy methods and for Irish writers, as witness O'Connor and O'Faoláin, the confessional, for facetious and other purposes, has, so to speak, paid its way. 'Penance,' says Heaney, 'indeed was a sacrament that rinsed and renewed – you came out light-footed and alert as those monks – but although it did give a momentary release from guilt, it kept this sense of sin as inseparable from one's life as one's shadow'.

Waking or sleeping that King of the Dark would be just as uneasy a companion, or a master, as the capricious Something that Alexander Kuprin sensed at work, a spirit neither of good nor of evil, just an irresponsible and sometimes nasty Sense of Humour, writing at its worst moments Newman's scroll of lamentation. In a poem, 'Against Blinking', Heaney meditates on the folk-belief that an ill-disposed person could, merely by looking at it, 'blink' a cow so that its milk would yield no butter. Is God the Blinker Kuprin's law of logical absurdity?

Of all this, as I have indicated, Heaney is perfectly aware with the strong, balanced, humorous mind that he displays in poetry, in talk and in comment. The rat that slapped across his image reflected in the scaresome well, the grain-bags with lugs that took rat-forms in the shadowy barn and added a terror to childhood, that dark oratory of past ages, become as pitiful if not as endearing as any sleekit, cowerin', timorous beastie when the poet, in his advancement of learning, walks the embankment path, and sees the poor fellow in a drain, and stares him out of countenance. Brother Rat? Just so the ancient monks had stepped out into a Franciscan brightness to see the glory of the world; and the law of logical absurdity could also result in beauty and pity. The sad unlicensed mother drowning her unwanted child may be the fearful obverse to the picture of the bawdy lawless bull, yet horror is mitigated by human compassion. There are also the lovers on the island, the laughing girls by the Galway sea.

Seeing labourers at the potato-digging he sees 'Heads bow, trunks bend, hands fumble towards the black Mother'. They are slaves at prayer before the god of famine of 1847. But the god of famine can also be the god of fertility. The lovers on the island on a night of storm:

> We just sit tight while wind dives
> And strafes invisibly. Space is a salvo,
> We are bombarded by the empty air.
> Strange, it is a huge nothing that we fear.

In another poem, 'Icon', he sits, perhaps kneels, in a church and looks at the conventional pious statue of St Patrick, in full regimentals and complete with crozier, herding the chagrined serpents out of Ireland.

There goes any thundering censoring Irish bishop. The unfortunate snakes could be the embodiment of all evil. The crozier could also be the spade digging for the sowing of the sense of sin:

> Here is Patrick
> Banishing the serpents,
> The gold nostrils flared
> On his crozier.
>
> He has staked a cluster
> One of which slithers
> Its head up the staff.
> Still from low swamps
>
> And secret drains,
> the drenched grasslands,
> Luxuriant growths
> Beside dunghills and wells
>
> Their sphincters quietly
> Rippling, snakes point
> and pass to the sea.
> Crusty with sand
>
> They dirty and fatten
> The lip of the wave.
> The whole island
> Writhes at the edges.
>
> Here is Patrick
> Ridding the country,
> A celtic worm-clot
> Paralysed round his staff.

'Certain life forces,' he comments, 'have been paralysed,' and he reflects comically that because of the profound implications of this statue, there are people in Ireland who will never eat eels.

5

Love & Pain & Parting:
The Novels of Kate O'Brien

FIFTY OR SO YEARS AGO I WROTE something about the novels of Kate O'Brien and, about the same time, was privileged to meet and, as an immediate consequence, to admire that remarkable woman: as everybody who is interested in such things must admire her novels. Now I try to see her as she was then: a handsome, well-built woman with a mannish hair-style and a direct, if courteous, way of speaking; and she put you on your toes and kept you there because you knew she was listening attentively to everything you said. You also knew that as well as being in the presence of a great novelist, you were in the presence of a great lady, with something else added. It was not until I heard her talk of Teresa of Avila, about whom she wrote a book, and about Spain, about which she wrote several books, that I realized what that something else was. It was a touch of the Reverend Mother, but the Reverend Mother in Extraordinary: a Reverend Mother who, like Teresa herself, was capable of great impulses: the poet Crashaw had written of the young Teresa that she was for the East and martyrdom; and a Reverend Mother capable also not only of expressing the profoundest thoughts on life and death, love and pain and parting, but on the nature of God and man.

Then in her book *Farewell Spain*, which appeared in 1937, I came across this remarkable passage. As one among a crowd of tourists, although she had never been a tourist anywhere, she is leaving the caves of Altamira and their neolithic drawings, and returning to the moving present and the lighted world. That simple act acquires for her an eschatological significance. She writes: 'But the sentimentalist – I speak for myself – always comes out of that cave in a condition of broody inertness, a condition bordering on pain of some kind. Feeling unsociable like a homeless, evicted troglodyte. Pondering the accidents and blisses of initiative and genius, and the arrogant irresponsibility of the processes of life and time'.

We must remember that she called one of her novels *Pray for the Wanderer*. It was a novel of protest, an exact and forceful one, against the then prevailing Irish puritanism. The title, as we all know, came from a hymn much heard in Irish Catholic churches in her and my childhood, and, naturally enough, written by an Englishman: and by the same Englishman, Father Faber of the Oratory, who also wrote 'Faith of Our Fathers,' thunderously sung or rendered, not only in Irish churches but on the Gaelic playing-pitch at Croke Park. But the use of the title *Pray for the Wanderer* may have implied more than just a wandering from a Catholic childhood and upbringing; the most worldwide of all wanderers is man, the evicted troglodyte whose name could easily be Adam.

Turning now to a partial re-reading of Kate O'Brien I open first *The Ante-Room*, simply because it was the novel that she seemed, at times, to prefer to her other novels, insofar as any novelist is ever quite certain of such things. Her first novel was the highly successful *Without My Cloak*, published in 1931, a chronicle of the prosperous Considine family in the solid provincial town of Mellick; and few novelists have understood as well as Kate O'Brien did the meaning of a prosperous house, a solid middle class family, of a town not tumultuous enough to be a city yet escaping smalltown stagnancy. That was one theme in her work, yet it was related so closely, if subordinated, to other themes, death, departure, and the slow comprehending of the soul, that her town of Mellick, for which we may read Limerick, and the Considine household are of the first importance.

She delighted in finding her material in such houses and families; not the Big Houses of the Irish novel from Edgeworth to Somerville and Ross, nor the cabins as from Carleton to one aspect of Liam O'Flaherty, but the solemn homes that years of trading enabled a provincial mercantile class to build, or even the better-type convent-school to which the prosperous merchants would send their children. The Considine fortunes that provide the background for the novel *Without My Cloak* start in a sidestreet in Mellick with a canny forage merchant, a trade built directly on the land. From those roots the family-tree grows to produce, in the end, Caroline who has in her a touch of Emma Bovary; or Denis, who has an artist's soul; or his uncle, who, in London, lives the life of a gay bachelor.

When the novel opens, the father of Denis has just built for himself outside the town and away from the dusty pallor that two or three flour-mills give to some of the streets, the house of his heart's desire: a visible symbol of the transition inevitable in such families when the members, still conscious of the hard gnarled roots of their being, are also shortly to become aware of the unaccustomed and exotic. The meaning may be that it takes several generations of hard men of business to produce in the end one son capable of being a poet.

But when three years later *The Ante-Room* was published, Kate O'Brien had moved on to matters much deeper than even the most faithful observation of social matters. The ante-room of the title is not a place where the bourgeoisie suffer for a time before becoming poets but the dread hall of silence and pain where body and soul embrace for the last time before the final parting: and death and departure, suffering and sin, exile, love satisfied and yet never satisfied have been predominant themes in Kate O'Brien's novels, balanced, though, by humour and a great human tolerance. She was a humorous and tolerant woman, and although she had a great feeling for the saint who had longed for the East and martyrdom, she also knew that it was the same saint who could remark wryly that haste was the enemy of devotion. There was no morbidity about Kate O'Brien.

The entire action of *The Ante-Room* happens in and around a great house of the Mellick middle class. This is how it is introduced to us:

> By eight o'clock the last day of October was as well-lighted as it would be. Tenuous sunshine, swathed in river mist, outlined the blocks and spires of Mellick, but broke into no highlights on the landscape or in the sky. It was to be a muted day.
>
> Roseholm, the white house where the Mulqueens lived, stood amid trees and lawns on the west side of the river. Viewed from the town in fine weather, it could often seem to blaze like a small sun but it lay this morning as blurred as its surroundings. It neither received nor wanted noise or light, for its preoccupation now was to keep these two subdued. And this morning that was easy; there was no wind about to rattle doors or tear through dying leaves, but only an air that moved elegiacally and carried a shroud of mist.
>
> Agnes Mulqueen slept with her curtains open, so that at eight o'clock, though still almost asleep, she was aware of movement and light. She turned in her bed and the weak sun fell upon her face though her eyelids still resisted it.
>
> One by one the Mass bells ceased to ring in Mellick, and as their last note dropped away the clock in the hall at Roseholm, always slow, boomed out its cautious strokes. Agnes stieered and sighed. Once, when every whisper in the house had seemed to aggravate her mother's suffering, Agnes had suggested silencing that clock. But Teresa, her mother, would not have it. 'When I can't hear it any more,' she said, 'I'll know I'm at the Judgement Seat.'

Teresa Mulqueen is dying of cancer. Grouped around her last agony, which happens over the Eve and Feast of All Saints and the Feast of All Souls are that daughter, Agnes, in her middle-twenties; her sister, Marie-Rose, two years older; the husband of Marie-Rose, Vincent, in his late twenties; an aged and pious nursing nun and a pretty young nurse who is by no means a nun; Teresa's son, Reggie, broken and uglified by ten years of syphilis and mercury treatment; an efficient young doctor called William Curran, who is in love with Agnes; the husband of Teresa, a decent, worried man; and others. Put in such summary, everything seems banal, but the intricacy of the relations between these people, the intensity of their moral problems, the muted yet explosive atmosphere of that house of death submit to no summary. Agnes, hopelessly in love with her beloved sister's husband, and he tragically with her, sits at the dinner-table and reflects:

> She, seated opposite her father at one end of the dining-table, with Vincent at her right side and William Curran at her left, with Marie-Rose glittering and curvetting on the young doctor's other side, and Reggie, next to Vincent, brooding happily, almost dreamily, above his burgundy glass – contemplating detachedly this softly-lighted group, had felt a cold amazement stir in her that a house ostensibly surrendered to one sorrow should all at once give roof to so many unmentionable, intense and contradictory emotions. Her mother lay upstairs, waiting for God to reprieve a sentence which He would not reprieve – and because of her and her approaching death, this scene – so exciting, so reviving, so passionately alive – was set. Teresa, dying, was the reason, too, of Dr William Curran. And she would die, but the maze they were treading tonight in her honour, one might say, and because she had forbidden them celebrate the Eve of All Saints – when would they who were caught in it have learnt and forgotten, forsaken its intricacies.

The dance of life goes on around the central, final verity of death. Dr Curran feels a cold sense of the futility of that life, its brevity and sadness, and thinks: 'We are helpless, ignorant and helpless. And it isn't the final impassivity of heaven that matters, though that's like a caul enclosing the world. That's unavoidable. But our worst helplessness has only to do with the affairs of this immediate life – and we'll never correct it, because we'll never find a way to learn the workings of each other. This uniqueness, this isolation – oh God, it makes the simplest day unbearable'.

Discovering that the chaste and religious woman he loves is in love with her sister's husband, he walks away from the house in darkness and agony, and knows that nothing is too silly or wasteful to be a fact, nothing too destructive to be true. Even the beautiful but not too brainy Marie-Rose realizes how shocking a thing transience was which sounded gradual and gentle. She and her husband in the early days of a marriage that has now turned sour, existed in such a marvellous sea of passion that for a while it surrounded and disguised their chill islands of self-assertion. The time of the novel is 1880, and without the strict Catholic and social morality that binds them all, the struggles of their souls and bodies would be, if not meaningless, at least otherwise and less agonizing. To release them from such social and religious clamps would be false, in art and in history.

In her novel *Mary Lavelle*, as later in Maura Laverty's novel *No More Than Human*, a young Irish girl goes out as a governess to Spain. Both novelists in their time had done exactly that. It was one way of seeing the world and learning languages. It was also another Irish way of going into exile. The world in those days, before the Atlantic could be crossed in four or five hours, still retained something of its ancient, poignant meaning: as valid a way of going into exile, say, as that of Frankie Hannafey in Sean O'Faoláin's novel *Come Back to Erin*, when he fled for refuge to New York; or that of Patrick MacGill when he went picking potatoes or shovelling red-hot cinders with the migratory labourers in Scotland.

But Mary Lavelle, and Kate O'Brien who wrote her story, did not lose Ireland in order to find Spain and, all through Kate O'Brien's work it was clear that her adoption of Spain had not in any way weakened the grip of the roots that held her to her own country. There is nothing of the exile's traditional nostalgia in the way in which Mary Lavelle, after six weeks in Spain, can compare Irish faces and Spanish faces, finding that the faces of Irishmen are expressive and mobile, that the faces of Spanish men are, with their arresting and reserved gravity of eye, perpetually wearing masks. But Kate O'Brien adopted only one country and not the whole world, and was preserved from becoming merely a cosmopolitan writer by that deep sense of the mystical meaning of arrival and departure, of death, which is the final departure and the prelude to the last arrival. Spain influenced her so powerfully not only because she happened to go there when she was young, but because the cast of her mind had something naturally akin to the land of Teresa and John of the Cross, and even of that odd man, Philip the great King. To this I shall return later.

But it occurs to me now that there is here an interesting parallel, or contrast, between the novel *Mary Lavelle* and a later novel, *The Last of Summer*, published in 1943. *Mary Lavelle* was the first of her novels to get Kate O'Brien into trouble with the ludicrous Irish censorship of the period. For Mary, alas, had herself seduced in Spain, romantically and beautifully seduced but still seduced; and that didn't happen to Irish girls in Spain or anywhere else and, even if it did, other Irish girls were by no means supposed to say so. Nor Irish boys!

In passing it may be worth commenting on how apt Kate O'Brien could be at picking splendid quotation titles: *Without My Cloak*, *The Land of Spices*, *The Last of Summer*, *Pray for the Wanderer*, *As Music and Splendour*. Oratory was not lost in the world she lived in.

To return: the novel *Mary Lavelle* sent a young Irish girl to Europe. But in *The Last of Summer* a young woman, daughter of an Irish father and a French mother, comes back to the County Clare, uninvited and as a consequence unexpected, to search for the house and the places of which she had heard her father speak so often. He had become estranged from his people for marrying not only a foreign woman but a minor actress. He is dead and so is his wife: but some homing instinct or some pietas draws his daughter back to the places of his boyhood. Since she is unexpected, she leaves her bag at the station on the fringe of the small town and sets off walking towards some of her father's people, his home, her home. She meets a number of children on the way and smiles at them ingratiatingly; and one big, bright-eyed girl looks at her with unexpected animosity and says with a sneer: 'What happened to your lips?' Now this was in the days when lipstick and the marks of it were as uncommon in rural Ireland as women in tight trousers:

> The other children looked alarmed but they giggled. Angéle hurried past them along the empty road. She was shaking, dared not speak or look back. She felt tears of fury in her eyes. What a fool she was. Surely she knew yokeldom by now, in many countries, and was accustomed to being a stranger in places where strangers are targets. But in this shaft, sped by a rude little girl – no novelty – she felt without reason a greater force than could have been intended; she felt an accidental expression of something which had vaguely oppressed and surprised her, these ten days, in the Irish air – an arrogance of austerity, contempt for personal feeling, coldness and, perhaps, fear of idiosyncracy.
>
> In this most voluptuously beautiful and unusual land. She could not help the tears in her eyes. She hated the rudeness, and she heard the insult to her reddened mouth symbolically – so self-conscious was she. She heard it as an ignoble warning from the people of her father. If I could only stop being so idiotically self-conscious! If I could give up responding to every dotty little nothingness that blows my way!
>
> The tears did not fall. She laughed outright. At herself and at the rude little girl. What happened your lips? Well, of all the nerve! I've a jolly good mind to go back and give her the thrashing of her life.
>
> She laughed delightedly and leaned on the low mossy wall of a bridge. Divine Olympian river. Of an entirely other character than the sweet English streams or the winding waters of France. And how familiar it was to her from father's description. If it *was* your river you would know it always across years of absence.

Pray for the Wanderer: and the wanderer, or at any rate the wanderer's daughter, returns to encounter that semi-comic insult and censure. There is in that passage a sharp and true analysis of our Irish character. Of course nowadays no little rural Irish colleen is likely to pass remark on a lady wearing lipstick, or anything or nothing else. In fact the little rural Irish cáilín is herself liable to be wearing the oddest garments.

It seems a long time since the old parish priest in a Kerry seaside resort said from the pulpit, and in the height of the holiday season, that he saw a lot of strange women going around in trousers; and it would be much more pleasing to God if they went around without them. And in the 1940s there was a character in Myles na Gopaleen who said gloomily that there was nothing but trousers in Russia.

Howandever: as a symbol of our Irish censorious instinct, the balefulness behind the laughing Irish eyes, the devil, not little and not dancing, that sneering little child will do very well. She learned the art from her elders.

The Last of Summer is one of the easiest of Kate O'Brien's novels, yet it is filled with wonders, among them a splendid description of the Cliffs of Moher:

> It was a hot clear day with, even here, only a gentle breeze . . . the cliffs, declining, exposed an open sea, quiet and luminous, yet hardly bluer than the blue sky. The land shelved downward to the east in a composed, stripped pattern of green turf, grey walls and little houses, painted white, or pink or blue. There were no trees in sight. A few sheep grazed, and gulls and curlews cried; an empty road twisted between the fields like a slack white ribbon.
>
> Angéle considered all of this with wondering pleasure. Sharply outlined, clear, immaculate, and seeming on this day to overflow with light, the scene, dramatically balancing austerity with passion, surprised her very much and made her unwilling to cry out in hasty praise. Yet though so individual, so.unlike other recollected scenes of beauty, it struck at her heart nostalgically, she felt. Something it held of innocence, of positive goodness, familiarized at the first encounter to emotional memory.
>
> The water lay cold and still, very far below, profoundly shadowed by the great uneven wall of rock which stretched to left and right. There was no sound now, either of bird or wave; little frills of foam came and went on the quiet tide, a lonely, black canoe, seeming absurdly small and with three tiny shapes of men in it, moved outward, escaping from the shadow of the cliffs into blue water.

Moher has never been so well described, but the importance of the passage is not even in the fine landscape or seascape painting but in the suggestion that such a vision may also be part of ancestral memory. Yet Kate O'Brien, a rational woman, was not as far as I know (and, perhaps, in spite of her own words, quoted earlier) much given to any sentimental nostalgia; or, if she was at all affected by it, it would be for the study-hall in a convent school, for candles burning for benediction on a flower-laden altar, for gentle voices singing slightly sentimental hymns. The only pain of parting that Kate O'Brien seems to have seen as merely a human affair was the pain in a schoolgirl's heart when schooldays are over and familiar and loved places must be abandoned forever.

Yet in what is possibly her greatest novel, *The Land of Spices*, even that simple emotion is raised to a different level, or seen from a different angle, when the reverend mother who is the central character in that novel leaves the Irish convent to return to the Continent to take over control of the entire Order: 'Her heart was sad. Sad that a return often dreamt of would be at last to graves and empty places; sad that a departure which once she had most bitterly desired should seem at its coming so inconsistently a sacrifice. And indeed, twisting about in her soul against her undisciplined pain, she marvelled how emotionalists endured their lives at all, since she who hardly tolerated feeling found its touch intolerable'.

Kate O'Brien found her title for that novel in the sonnet in which George Herbert, with a magnificent recurrence, names and renames the hope and miracle of prayer. It may have been one of her favourite poems: I do remember her pleasure one day when, with considerable effort for it is an intricate poem, I managed to quote it word-perfect up to the last two splendid lines:

> Church-bells beyond the stars heard; the soul's
> blood, The land of spices, something understood.

The mood of the novel borrowed something from the mood of the great sonnet. But, alas, when the novel was published in 1941 it fell foul of the deplorable censors, who may not have read George Herbert. All this may now seem to people, say under thirty-five, a long time ago: but the case was so ludicrous or scandalous, or both, that it may still be worth reflecting on. Perhaps the censors thought that spices had something to do with spicy, and it would obviously be wrong to write a spicy novel about a convent. To me, it may be the best of the three great sombre, meditative novels she has written – the other two are *The Ante-Room* and *That Lady* – because in *The Land of Spices* she is dealing, as it were, at source with the values she applied in other novels dealing with life outside the convent walls; with the strength and weakness of human love, with life as a series of departures leading to that final and inevitable departure. But because in one brief passage the sexual nature of her father, whom the reverend mother remembers with love, yet whose fault, as she saw it, drove her away from human love, is mentioned, the book was banned, under the terms of the Act, as being in general tendency indecent or obscene. In so far as I ever heard or could make out, this was the relevant passage:

> Her father's study was at the back of the house, above the kitchen. It had a long wide balcony of wrought iron which ran full across the wall and ended in an iron staircase to the garden. This balcony made a pleasant, deep shade over the flagged space by the kitchen door, where *Marie-Jeanne* often sat to prepare vegetables, or to have a sleep. Traffic was free up and down those stairs, and [her father] was not formal about access to his study, even when he was working, even when he was having a silent and solitary mood.
> Helen . . . ran up the iron stairs and along the balcony to the open window of her father's study.
> She looked into the room.
> Two people were there. But neither saw her; neither felt her shadow as it froze across the sun.
> She turned and descended the stairs. She left the garden and went on down the curve of *Rue Saint Isidore*.
> She had no objective and no knowledge of what she was doing. She did not see external things. She saw *Etienne* and her father in the embrace of love.

As we have seen, Kate O'Brien began her novel-writing with that long chronicle of the Considine family, going back a century to find the origins of the people she wrote about and tracing their growth almost up to the present. But her most deliberate use of history as a framework to support her telling of death and departure and families, and sin, was made possible not by Irish but by Spanish history. In the foreword to, *That Lady*, she was careful to point out that she was not writing an historical novel but an invention arising from reflection on the curious external story of Anna de Mendoza and Philip II, of Spain:

> Historians cannot explain the episode, and the attempt is not made in a work of fiction. All the personages in this book lived and I have retained the historical outline of events in which they played a part; but every-thing which they say and write in my pages is invented and – naturally – also are their thoughts and emotions. And in order to retain unity of invention I have refrained from grafting into my fiction any part of their recorded letters or observations.

It is a most interesting approach. For since she has clearly disavowed any intention of writing a straight historical novel (from which, as a general rule, the Lord preserve us), and since she has called the book an invention, any discussion on its truth to the period can be dispensed with, and the novel seen for what it is: a protracted case of conscience discussing with insight the problems of a good woman who has sinned, of a libertine, Antonio Perez, who has fallen in love, of a scrupulous king resenting the ability of the less scrupulous to commit the sin he shrinks from; in the exact sense of the phrase, a classical situation.

As her three great novels bear witness, Kate O'Brien was as fond of a case of conscience as any zealous Jesuit could be. Anna de Mendoza is the widow of a man who has been counsellor and close friend of Philip the king. Vulgar rumour has it that she has also been Philip's mistress. Actually she is, in friendship, very close to the king and he, valuing her friendship, does probably in some obscure corner of his death-possessed soul pride himself in possessing, in vulgar rumour, something that for complex moral reasons, at least, he does not possess. Anna, in her widowhood, her wealth, her family pride, her close friendship with the king, becomes the mistress of Antonio Perez, a married libertine who is also a counsellor of the king. A grand affair begins, is discovered and horribly punished by a king who, like most righteous people doing horrible things, is probably not at all clear about his actual motives. Nevertheless, the novelist makes it quite clear that Philip is not the villain of the story as she writes it. The quotation from George Meredith's *Modern Love* seems here inevitable:

> The wrong is mixed. In tragic life, God wot,
> No villain need be! Passions spin the plot;
> We are betrayed by what is false within.

But there is in *That Lady*, as in *The Ante-Room* and *The Land of Spices*, the power of feeling bursting like a shell among a group of devoted people, devoted, once again, in the exact classical sense of the word. Mary Lavelle in Spain loses her heart and her virginity, returns to Ireland with tears in her eyes and the first seeds of experience sown in her soul. The young man in *The Ante-Room*, loves his wife's sister with a hopeless love and ends it, romantically and sentimentally, by looking down the barrel of a gun and thinking of his childhood: 'He remembered leaning on a gun in the garden at home on a sunny day, leaning like this and talking to his mother. It was summer and she was sewing. She had said: "Don't lean on it, Vin. It will mark your face". Darling mother. She smiled. He could see every detail of her smile. Darling mother. He pulled the trigger, his thoughts far off in boyhood'.

In *The Land of Spices* the memory of the fearful moment when her father's secret, left-handed love had been revealed to her could not black out in the nun's mind the many memories of an endearing civilized man who loved the poetry of Traherne, and Herbert and Crashaw.

But in *That Lady*, Kate O'Brien deliberately sacrificed every human consolation and saw her people and their plight, or sin, against the background of a greater reality, or God. An illicit love-affair in the Upper Reaches of society offers to the romantic and the sentimentalist, or the merely curious, the opportunity for a lot of fun. To the rigid moralist it opens the gate for thundering judgments about scandal and the inevitability of punishment. Kate O'Brien followed her own path, saw the beauty and the pity of the doomed passion, the doubt of the sinner, the complexities of repentance, the instability of the ground on which the king stands when he, playing a sour God, contrives judgment and punishment. Ana, with her lover in her arms and fearful scruples in her mind, thinks: 'Is my poor scruple greater than what I give this man and take from him? Am I to set my little private sense of sin above his claim on me and his unhappiness? Am I cheating because I want him and have grown tired of the unimportant fuss of my immortal soul? Am I pretending to be generous simply to escape again into his power?'

Those questions leave little room for romantic illusions but they open the door to pity; not the destructive pity that obsesses Graham Greene, but a tired, welcoming pity that could be a shadow of God's mercy. Towards the end of the novel Anna talks to her friend the Cardinal Quiroga about her problems, and the novelist removes the last illusion by seeming to say that even mercy can be presumed on. Anna accepts her guilt:

> And I have repented long ago in that clear-cut sense and returned to the usual religious practices. And I accept these years and all this empty loneliness and forsakenness as a part perhaps of my purgatory. But as this purgatory was forced on me, I cannot seek to derive merit from it in

heaven – and, in general, I can't, with any honesty, turn to God, as holy people say. Because, while accepting His ruling, I shall always be glad of Antonio.

The heart, and the novelist, have reasons that slip between the rigid lines of the theologian's textbook. But, and this is where Kate O'Brien shows that in an earlier century she might have been not a novelist but one of those valiant women learned in the science of God, the cardinal says: 'God doesn't ask the impossible of you, you conceited woman'.

The nun in *The Land of Spices* saw the truth after much experience and much lonely suffering: 'Free in her meditations on God's will and His hopes for humanity she admitted that human love must almost always offend the heavenly lover by its fatuous egotism. To stand still and eventually understand was, she saw, an elementary duty of love. To run away, to take cover, to hate in blindness, and luxuriously to seek vengeance in an unexplained cutting-off, in a seizure upon high and proud antithesis – that was stupidity masquerading offensively before the good God'.

She meditates on the future of the girl, another Anna, reared in this upper class convent, as indeed Kate herself was, her parents having died when she was young:

> And now all was done that age may do for childhood. Anna's school-days were closed and there was no appeal against the advance of life and the flight of innocence. She had been taught to be good and to under-stand the law of God. Also, she had been set free to be herself. Her wings were grown and she was for the world. In poverty, in struggle, in indeci-siveness – but for some these were good beginnings. Good for Anna, Reverend Mother thought, and was glad to know that it was forward to them she was going. Prayer would follow her, prayer always could. It would have been happy to have been at hand, a little longer, to have heard something of the first flights and first returns. But such a wish was nothing. All that could be done was done. Anna was for life now, to make what she could of it. Prayer could go with her, making no weight – and whether or not she remembered the days of the poems an ageing nun would remember them. How sweet is the shepherd's sweet lot, from the morn to the evening he strays. Reverend Mother passed by the bright opening of the elm-trees and looked over the lawns to the blue lake.

✑ 6 ✑

Irish Potato and Attic Salt

O NE OF THE MANY PECULIAR tramps, or men with no homes to call their own, whom you meet, or have met, in the writings of Maxim Gorki, had among his many peculiarities a love for tomorrow: his own and only his own tomorrow.

He rejoiced recklessly because he never knew today what tomorrow was going to be like and, for the love of that hilarious unsettlement and ecstatic uncertainty, he had abandoned a life of respectability and culture and ease, was content to be regarded as a drunkard, a debauchee, and an outcast. 'It is not I who have been rejected,' he said. 'It is I who have rejected others'.

Now, regarded casually, that passion for an unknown tomorrow can seem as unimportant as the conventional distaste for monotony known and experienced by all men. But the casual regard sees only the outline of an object and, frequently, sees that outline only from one angle. Contained within the outline there can be infinite and intricate complications, different causes producing different results, different surrounding circumstances making each man, to a certain extent, a peculiar tramp. But making tramp differ from tramp as man differs from man, and place from place, until monotony itself is only another name for the infinite variety of human existence.

Francis Sylvester Mahony was born in Cork in 1804 and, all during his life and ever since his death, he has remained a Corkman. Corkmen are a distinctive sort of people. And it is quite possible that when all the protean parts of the man (the regrettable pun, Proutean, was actually used when he was still alive) are utterly forgotten, and no longer even available in eye-withering small print, men in a certain Irish city will still go on proudly singing, 'with deep affection and recollection', the wonderful song that rhymes Moscow with Kiosk, O and Shandon with grand on.

And why in hell, or in Cork, not?

But once the indisputable, and immutable, Corkonian part of Mahony has been taken for granted, it becomes obvious that the rest of him was as fluid, and as brilliant, as quicksilver, as multicoloured as shot silk. Possibly because he was a Corkman all the time he refused to be, consistently, any other variety of man. Like Gorki's tramp, he rejected, before he was rejected by, the solid monochrome mass of permanent people with stable, permanent lives.

At the age of twelve Mahony left Cork and went, or was sent, to study in the Jesuit College of Saint Acheul at Amiens. His respect for the Jesuits and his love of continental places stayed with him for the rest of his life. Later on, when he desired to be, or thought he could be, a priest, the Jesuits wisely advised him against a way of life for which, they considered, he was not suited. If he was pig-headed enough to reject that advice, he was also reasonable enough to admit, in the end, that the Jesuits had been right all the time.

He studied in Paris and in Rome, in Jesuit houses, and, in the late summer of 1830 the patient Jesuits sent him to teach at Clongowes Wood College in the County Kildare, where his Ignatian vocation vanished in the fumes of whiskey drunk at a dinner in Celbridge. But his long connection with the Jesuits, his recurrent bursts of admiration for their methods and merits, did once give a Gallic enemy the opportunity of writing him down as one of the terrible brigade of sombre, Jesuitical conspirators.

'Born in Ireland,' wrote the Abbé Martial Marest de la Roche-Arnand, (obviously to peasants like you and me, one of the best people), and he with the long name wrote this or that in a work called *Les Jesuites Modernes*:

> I know not if O'Mahoni is descended from the Count of that name, but to the spirit, to the prejudices, to the system of the Count, he adds the fanaticism, the dissimulation, the intrigue, and the chicane of a thorough Jesuit . . . Irish and Scotch Catholics have about them a smack of the Spanish Catholics. They love to sniff the reek wafted from the funeral pyres of the doomed wretches who have declined to hear Mass. The Society designs to place O'Mahoni, later on, as the head either of Colleges or of congregations. Having taught him to stifle all natural sentiment under the morality of the devout life, they hope that, docile to the teachings of his instructors, the young O'Mahoni will become still more insensible and still more cruel than the most pitiless inquisitors of Valence and Saragossa.

The general reliability of the writer of that extraordinary passage can be judged readily enough by the consideration that what the Society of Jesus was really trying to do with Mahony was get rid of him. The Jesuits were also trying gently to dissuade him from becoming a priest, inside or outside the Society. For by whatever extraordinary conduct he had, at the age of twenty-two, made himself sufficiently notorious as to merit the attentions of the author of *Les Jesuites Modernes*, it was scarcely by stifling 'all natural sentiment under the morality of the devout life.'

Not that there was anything vicious in the man's nature, but he was one of those odd people who show acute mental appreciation of the benefits of the religious life while being at the same time utterly unable to adapt their temperaments to the restraints that make those benefits possible. He showed that mental appreciation by writing: 'There is not, perhaps, a more instructive and interesting subject of inquiry in the history of the human mind than the origin, progress and workings of what are called "monastic institutions".' But when he praised the Jesuits and the Benedictines, to the utter exclusion of all other religious orders, he did something that would have made him acceptable neither to Benedict nor to Ignatius. He wrote: 'The system of *mendicancy* adopted by each holy brotherhood as the groundwork of its operations did not strike Loyola as much calculated to give dignity or manliness to the human character; hence he left his elder brethren in quiet possession of that interesting department'. But Saint Ignatius or any good Ignatian could have quietly reminded Mahony of the third degree of humility, and of the possibility that man might not exist merely to be dignified and manly.

The particular type of dignity required by the Ignatian rule could, anyway, not exist in too close a proximity to whiskey punch.

When Mahony had been a few months in Clongowes, he was asked to lead a crowd of students on a routine outing that was to include, as a special treat, dinner at the home, in Celbridge village or just outside it, of the parents of one of the students. When the students and their conductor returned to Clongowes, battered both by good whiskey and bad weather, the Jesuits decided they had had enough. The push they gave Mahony was determined and final, sending him ultimately back to the Continent where, in spite of all the advice given by the Jesuits, he became a priest.

What he actually did become was a scholar, a man of letters, a Corkman completely at home in continental places. He was ordained at Lucca. He said Mass frequently in France and Italy and later in London. Yet although he always carried his breviary, preferring it, according to Charles Kent, to either Horace or Béranger, although he was never suspended, or silenced, and remained in his theological opinions as orthodox as many another, and died in an edifyingly submissive manner, he early on ceased to perform the duties of a priest and, possibly, ceased to take any part in Catholic ritual. Like Constantin Guys, that artist so much admired by Baudelaire, he wanted to be a man of the world, in the best sense of that much misused description: a cultivated and classical mind understanding the movement and pageantry of life, but still remaining apart, detached, integral. Stephen, where are you?

Europe opened out before him. He wrote: 'I have lived among the French in the freshest dawn of early youth, in the meridian hour of manhood's maturity, my lot was cast and my lines fell on the pleasant places of that once happy land. Full gladly have I strayed among her gay hamlets and her hospitable chateaux, anon breaking the brown loaf of the peasant, and anon seated at the board of her noblemen and her pontiffs, I have mixed industriously with every rank and every denomination of her people, tracing as I went along the peculiar indications of the Celt and the Frank, the Norman and the Breton, the *langue d'oui* and the *langue d'oc*; not at the same time overlooking the endemic features of unrivalled Gascony'.

That, by St Finbarr, the well-known patron of Cork, was fine talk.

And introducing his series of articles on 'The Songs of Italy' were these rhymes describing the wanderings of Father Prout:

> Starting from France, across Mount Cenis,
> Prout visits Mantua and Venice;
> Through many a tuneful province strolls,
> "Smit with the love" of barcarolles.
> Petrarca's ghost he conjures up,
> And with old Dante quaffs a cup;
> Next, from her jar Etruscan, he
> Uncorks the muse of Tuscany.

Towards the end of his life, when his short period of brilliantly eccentric writing had trailed off into the hackwork of foreign correspondent for some London newspapers, he went wandering irresponsibly down through the Balkans, through Asia Minor and into Egypt, returning eventually to the south of France. Appropriately he settled down in Paris in the character of a 'scholarly *flâneur*, loitering though life by preference in continental cities; with quips and cranks galore for every one he encountered; gladdened by the chance, whenever he was lucky enough to stumble across one, of foregathering with an old friend from whom he had long drifted apart, and from this time forward, until the very end giving up his pen exclusively to the rough and ready labours of the journalist.'

Appropriately, too, he died in Paris, for where other than in Cork, which gave him life, or in Rome, which to him was the centre of the world of the spirit, could a scholarly *flâneur* better return to the dust. He had written:

O Rome! how much better and more profitable I feel it is to dwell, though but in spirit, amid the glorious ruins of thy monumental soil, than corporeally to reside in the most brilliant and frivolous of modern capitals. *Quanto minus est cum reliquis versari quam tui meminisse.*

But Francis Mahony's privilege or problem was that he had in his heart and head something of three, or four, European cities. Paris of gaiety and wit and intellectual civilization. Rome, solemn with the crushing weight of the monuments of the centuries, the grave of the apostles. And a small place called Cork built by the mouth of a lovely river in Europe's last western island. When he wrote the pleasantly chiming song by which he is best remembered, he heard, clearer and sweeter than all the bells of all the cities of Europe, the bells of Shandon ringing across the pleasant waters of the Lee: There was also London which gave him good companions and a livelihood.

When *Fraser's Magazine* was founded in 1830, and Francis Sylvester Mahony entered the company of the Fraserians, along with his fellow Corkman Maginn, and the notables Coleridge, Thackeray, Lockhart, Southey, D'Orsay and Daniel Maclise, Mahony looked around, in the fashion of the time, for a pen-name, and a person and place behind which to conceal his own identity. The place was Watergrasshill, an upland parish in County Cork. The name was Father Prout, the name of an old and, most likely unliterary, parish priest whom Mahony may have known in his boyhood. But the person was the invention of his own active mind, pressed down and flowing over with classicality: so perfectly at home with the literature of Greece and Rome, and France and Italy and England, that he could play the fool with them as few other men have ever managed to do.

For the purpose of introducing Father Prout to the readers of *Fraser's*, Mahony invented a young barrister called Frank Cresswell, nephew of Lady Cresswell of Watergrasshill. The good lady on her deathbed left her 'lands and perishable riches' to her nephew, on condition that he should in one respect live as a Catholic by strictly observing the Lenten fast. Now, as the nephew saw it, 'no junior member of the bar would not hold a good rental by so easy a tenure', and in the presence of Father Prout and the aunt, 'whose grave is in Rathcooney and whose soul is in heaven', he solemnly bound himself to eat fish during Lent.

'During my short stay at Watergrasshill', Cresswell wrote or, rather, Mahony wrote for him, 'a wild and romantic district of which every brake and fell, every bog and quagmire, is well known to Crofton Croker – for it is the very Arcadia of his fictions, I formed an intimacy with this Father Andrew Prout . . . He was one of that race of priests now unfortunately extinct, or very nearly so, like the old breed of wolf-dogs, in the island: I allude to those of his order who were educated abroad, before the French revolution, and had imbibed, from associating with the polished and high-born clergy of the Gallican church, a loftier range of thought, and a superior delicacy of sentiment'.

There was sardonic humour in that and, also, a little Corkonian snob-bery, for if Father Prout were to be an adequate vehicle for the thoughts, feelings and experiences of Francis Sylvester Mahony, he had obviously to be a man of lofty thought and delicate sentiment. Mahony's capricious wit was never transferred to the stooge that he had created, for the nature of the fiction made it possible for Father Prout, with all solemnity, to utter outrages. In the paper entitled 'Dean Swift's Madness: A Tale of a Churn' the priest from Watergrasshill could prove to everybody's satisfaction that his mother was Stella and his father was Swift. The careful reader would naturally see the implied connection between the wit of 'A Tale of a Churn', and the withering whatever-it-was of Swift's *A Modest Proposal*. Foolish people had, in the eighteenth century, been sadly misled by Swift's modest proposal for the cooking and eating of the undesired babies of the multitudes of the poor. The reader of Francis Sylvester Mahony has still to tread cautiously from the moments when Father Prout is being serious and Mahony, maliciously, has his tongue in his cheek, to those other moments when Mahony's sentences mean what they say, and the identity of Prout is taken up into the bosom of his creator.

Cresswell, the young barrister, troubled in soul and body about his Lenten necessity of abandoning flesh-meat and consuming only fish, brought his problem to Father Prout, who poured from his lips the torrent of classical learning in defence of fish that was the first of Mahony's writ-ings to be published in *Fraser's Magazine*. After that, Cresswell was free to fade backwards and be no more, and Father Prout could die peacefully, provided he left behind him a chest stuffed with learning and literary crit-icism, and charitable fun about Walter Scott and uncharitable fun about Tom Moore, and spiteful asides about Lady Morgan and Daniel O'Con-nell, and parodies and practical jokes remarkable for the brilliance and mock solemnity of the codology.

'The Apology for Lent' appeared in April 1834, and the fifth part or decade of 'The Songs of Horace' in December 1836. In between those dates were 'Dean Swift's Madness: A Tale of a Churn', 'The Rogueries of Tom Moore', Father Prout's 'Plea for Pilgrimages' and his subsequent 'Carousal' in the select company of Sir Walter Scott and a few Corkonians, all returning from kissing the Blarney stone.

Then there were two papers on the Songs of Italy and four on the Songs of France under the four separate titles 'Wine and War', 'Women and Wooden Shoes', 'Philosophy', 'Frogs and Free Trade'.

There was a paper on Victor Hugo's lyrics, a paper on Erasmus, and one on James Barry, the painter, in the Vatican. There were three papers on modern Latin poets: on Vida's 'Silkworm', on Sarbiewsky, Sannazar and Fracastor, on Beza, Vaniere and Buchanan. Finally there were the five papers on Horace.

That's the bulk of Mahony's work and all together the Fraserian papers fill a book of about five hundred closely printed pages: *The Works of Father Prout* (The Rev. Francis Mahony), edited with biographical introduction and notes by Charles Kent, barrister-at-law, author of *Aletheia, Corona Catholica*, etc., London, George Routledge & Sons.

Pages of learning and pages of fun, pages in which learning and fun mingle and assist each other, and sometimes leave the reader a little confused with the Corkonian and continental quick-wittedness.

For instance: Father Prout defending Lenten customs and a fish-diet, reduces the religious revolution of the sixteenth century to a matter of gastronomy or a matter of taste, as simple as the quarrel on tea and coffee between Molly my sister and me.

> The Hollanders, the Swedes, the Saxons, the Prussians, and in Germany those circles in which the Gothic blood ran heaviest and most stagnant, hailed Luther as the deliverer from salt fish. The fatted calf was killed, bumpers of ale went round and Popery went to the dogs. Half Europe followed the impetus given to free opinions, and the congenial impulse of the gastric juice; joining in reform, not because they loved Rome less, but because they loved substantial fare more . . . The Dutch, dull and opaque as their own Zuydersee, growled defiance at the Vatican when their food was to be controlled; the Belgians, being a shade nearer to the Celtic family, submitted to the fast. While Hamburg clung to its *beef*, and Westphalia preserved her *hams*, Munich and Bavaria adhered to the Pope and to sour-crout with desperate fidelity. As to the Cossacks and all that set of northern marauders, they never kept Lent at any time; and it would be arrant folly to expect that the horsemen of the River Don, and the Esquimaux of the polar latitudes, would think of restricting their ravenous propensities in a Christian fashion; the very system of cookery adopted by these terrible hordes would, I fear, have given Dr Kitchiner (an authority of the time on dietetics) a fit of cholera.
>
> The apparatus is graphically described (in 'Hudibras') by Samuel Butler. I will indulge you with part of the quotation:
>
>> For like their countrymen, the Huns
>> They cook their meat . . .
>> All day on horses' backs they straddle,
>> Then every man eats up his saddle.
>
> A strange process, no doubt: but not without some sort of precedent in classical records; for the Latin poet introduces young Iulus at a picnic in the Aeneid, exclaiming:
> 'Heu! etiam-mensos consumimus.'

That lengthy specimen of what Mahony would have called indulging in quotation may be worthwhile, may be the only way, short of reading everything he wrote, of seeing or showing the amount of classical learning the man had at his disposal, either for serious purposes or for mockery and folly. When he wanted to be serious, he could be sound and accurate and penetrating. His appeciation of Erasmus is as good, in most places and in so far as I know, as anything that has been said about the man who, according to Alexander Pope, was, at the same time, the glory and the shame of the priesthood.

Mahony was, naturally, interested in the delicate compromise Erasmus had made between the clerical life and the literary life.

When Mahony turned his back on what he called 'upsetting' a poem from one language into another, he could translate verse with feeling for the movement and meaning and spirit of the original.

But a steady inspection of his portrait will show clearly enough why he preferred the red wine of tomfoolery to all the white water of seriousness: those lines and twists about the mouth, the hard, shrewd eyes looking out over small spectacles, the hair receding wildly and leaving the wide forehead high and round, like a dome.

Those eyes might be laughing quietly at the fun of transmogrifying Father Prout from his quiet, rural original and sending him capering like a wild horse among the people and places and classical past of Europe. And in the imagination that worked behind that round forehead, the high moment must have been when he brought Prout and Walter Scott together at the Blarney Stone, poking fun at the eminent novelist's visit to Miss Edgeworth, tumbling classical references and allusions and parallels about them as a child tosses down toy bricks or a clown uproariously smashes delph.

'We read with interest,' wrote Mahony, 'in the historian Polybius, the account of hannibal's interview with Scipio on the plains of Zama; and often have we, in our schoolboy days of unsophisticated feeling, sympathized with Ovid when he told us that he only got a glimpse of Birgil; but Scott basked for a whole summer's day in the blaze of Prout's wit, and witnessed the coruscations of his learning. The great Marius is said never to have appeared to such advantage as when seated on the ruins of Carthage: with equal dignity Prout sat on the Blarney Stone, amid ruins of kindred glory. Zeno taught in the Porch; Plato loved to muse alone on the bold, jutting promontory of Cape Sunium; Socrates, bent on finding truth, *in silvis Academi querere verum*, sought her among the bowers of Academus; Prout courted the same coy nymph, and wooed her in the Groves of Blarney'.

The solemn fun of the dialogue between Prout and Scott, and a few characters from Cork assembled in the sacred neighbourhood of the Blarney Stone, was quiet and charitable, and was more than balanced by elaborate and obviously genuine tributes to the genius of the Scottish novelist. 'What a host of personages does his name conjure up,' Prout exclaimed. 'What mighty shades mingle in the throng of attendant heroes that await his bidding, and form his appropriate retinue! Cromwell, Claverhouse, and Montrose, Saladin, Front de Boeuf, and Coeur de Lion; Rob Roy, Robin Hood and Marmion; those who fell at Culloden and Flodden Field, and those who won the day at Bannockburn – all start up at the presence of the Enchanter'.

But the fun that, applied to one person, was charitably flavoured with compliment, could when applied to another person be spiteful and malicious. Nor is it possible to find any real reason for the spite and malice, outside Mahony's personal character and his instinctive likes and dislikes. He despised Lady Morgan, he hated Daniel O'Connell, he abominated Tom Moore. Yet there is no record of any unfortunate contact that could explain why his nerves seemed to be on edge when their names were mentioned, no indication that he could have disliked anything beyond the simple cut of their jibs. Their very existence irritated him.

At the famous dinner at Celbridge that had finally decided the Jesuits about his lack of vocation, he made his first declaration against O'Connell, entering into furious argument with Father Dan Callinan, the parish priest of Celbridge, who had made an after-dinner speech in praise of the rising glory of the Liberator. Perhaps the reason for the row was simply the fact that Father Dan was being the life and soul of the party, or, even more simply, the fact that Mahony came from Cork and that Dan, the Liberator, came from Kerry. But all through the Prout papers any and every chance of writing in an insulting aside at O'Connell was eagerly taken.

Politics alone could not explain that eagerness, for Mahony could change from being a little Conservative to being a little Liberal with an ease that showed clearly that, for him, Conservatism and Liberalism were on the same level of folly.

Terry O'Callaghan, who was pound-keeper, grave-digger, notary-public and parish-piper in Watergrasshill, used also to collect the coppers on Sunday morning at the door of the church and 'like the dragon of the Hesperides keep[s] watch over the box with untameable fierceness, never having allowed a rap to be subtracted for the O'Connell tribute, or any other humbug, to the great pecuniary detriment of the Derrynane dynasty. In the palace at Iveragh, where a geographical chart is displayed on the wall, showing at a glance the topography of the Rint and exhibiting all those districts from Dan to Beersheba where the coppermines are most productive, the parish of Watergrasshill is marked: All Barren.'

The gibe about O'Connell's coppers is recurrent and utterly unreasonable. Mahony makes poor Prout talk of the 'all-absorbing Charybdis, the breeches-pocket of our glorious Dan'. Into the middle of his translation of 'Vert-Vert, the Parrot: a poem by the Jesuit, Gresset', he forced these lines:

> And since we lost Sir Joseph Yorke
> We've got great Feargus fresh from Cork:
> A fellow honest, droll and funny,
> Who would not sell, for love or money,
> His native land, nor, like vile Daniel
> Fawn on Lord Althorp like a Spaniel,
> Flatter the mob, while the old fox
> Keeps an eye to the begging-box . . .
>
> But Kerrymen will e'er be apter
> At the conclusion of the chapter,
> While others bear the battle's brunt,
> To reap the spoil and fob the blunt.

Never at a loss for a classical parallel, he wrote in 'Father Prout's Self-Examination':

> To bend the bow of Ulysses, to wield the gridiron of Cobbett, to revive the sacred pigeon of Mahomet, to reinflate the bagpipe of Ossian, to reproduce the meal-tub of Titus Oates, or (when Dan goes to his long account) to get up a begging-box, must necessarily be hopeless speculations.

The language of political or of literary criticism was not, at that time, bound by any hard-and-fast rules of etiquette or much restrained by the law of libel. Mahony's references to O'Connell return always to zany accusations of something like petty larceny. They are interesting because they are expressed with a neatness not common in the actual heat of political controversy, a neatness that did not characterize the Liberator himself when he opened his mouth to vilify and confound his opponents. But Mahony's comments do not display him as any variety of a politician any more than his references to the Wild Irish Girl (Lady Morgan) display him as any variety of a gentleman.

Writing of 'The Songs of Italy' he wrote also of the invasions of Italy:

> It has been the misfortune of that beautiful peninsula, ever since the decline and fall of the Roman empire, to have been invaded by a succession of barbarians from the North. Langobards and Ostrogoth, Alaric and Genseric, Sam Rogers and Frederick Barbarossa, Attila, King of the Huns, and Leigh Hunt, King of the Cockneys . . . but the vilest and most unjustifiable invasion of Italy has been perpetrated by Lady Morgan. We know not to what extent impunity may be claimed by the Sex for running riot and playing the devil with places and things consecrated by the recollections of all that is noble in our nature and exalted in the history of mankind; but we suppose that her Irish ladyship is privileged to carry on her literary orgies in the face of the public, like her fair countrywoman, Lady Barrymore of smashing notoriety . . .
>
> She continues to besprinkle her pages with Italian, of which she knows about as much as the language of the Celestial Empire . . . however

acquainted she may possibly be with the Cruiskeen Lawn she has but a
very slight intimacy with the Vocabulario della Crusca.

So Dan O'Connell was a beggar and a thief, Lady Morgan was a skirted
nuisance, Tom Moore was a rogue; and a great deal of Mahony's time and
energy and malicious ingenuity was devoted to proving, for the fun of the
thing, that the rogue was also a forger. The reason given for the production of the paper 'The Rogueries of Tom Moore' was that a decent, poor
scholar had written to argue that the round towers of Ireland were not
fortifications nor towers of refuge but phallic symbols, and that Moore,
unsympathetic to the theory, had dealt meanly, in a review, with the
scholar. But it is much more likely that Mahony, aware that he possessed
an unusual talent for transferring songs backward and forward from one
language to another, looked around for a victim on whom that talent
could be exercised and picked on Tom Moore.

He had already, in 'A Plea for Pilgrimages', produced a polyglot version
of the song 'The Groves of Blarney', giving passable versions in Latin,
Greek and Norman French, and relegating the original to the status of a
translation. He produced, also, a fragment of a Celtic version, claiming that
it had been copied from an ancient manuscript in the King's library in
Copenhagen; and his final assault on Millikin's song took the form of an
Italian version, 'I Boschi di Blarnea', which he merrily said had been sung
by Garibaldi in the woods near Lake Como.

Later still he displayed this peculiar talent and his peculiar weakness, or
strength, for kicking up his heels in the middle of a serious discussion, by
breaking into his papers on the Songs of France with a French version of
'The Night Before Larry was Stretched', designed, he said, to initiate his
Gallic readers 'into the workings of an Irish mind unfettered by conscien-
tious scruples on the threshold of eternity.'

The original went or, as we all know, goes:

> When he came to the nubbling chit,
>   He was tucked up so neat and so pretty,
> The rumbler jugged off from his feet,
>   And he died with his face to the city.

Which became in Mahony's French:

> Quand fut au bout de son voyage
> Le gibet fut pret en un clin,
> Mourant il tourna le visage
> Vers la bonne ville de Dublin.
> Il dansa la carmagnole . . .

But what he did once for Burrowes and once for Burns in a Latin original,
he said, of 'John Anderson, my Jo, John', and once for Millikin, he did again
and again for Thomas Moore, accompanying his libellous liberties with

equally libellous compliments for Moore's passability as a translator, and with non-stop offensiveness about Moore's talents as poet, historian and writer of polemic. Moore, appealing to somebody to go where glory waits thee, was, Mahony said, really playing pirate on a love-song of François de Foix, Comtesse de Chateaubriand, an abandoned favourite of Francis the First. The song to gentle, bashful Nora Creina, which opened with a line about Lesbia's beaming eye, was copied, said Mahony, from a Latin song made by Prout when he was a schoolboy smitten by the charms of an Irish milkmaid who frequently passed by the hedge school he attended and distracted his attention from Corderius and the Colloquies of Erasmus.

From these and other alleged examples of the predatory instincts of the Minstrel Boy, Mahony concluded that Moore 'could eke out a tolerably fair translation of any given ballad; and, indeed, to translate properly, retaining all the fire and spirit of the original is a merit not to be sneezed at – it is the next best thing to having a genius of one's own'.

For those who, at that time, disliked the linked sweetness, long-drawn-out, of Thomas Moore, or who thought, as some still do, that Moore had made free with the melodies collected by Bunting, and turned the Wild Harp of Erin into a musical snuff-box (William Hazlitt), all that must have made satisfying reading.

Thomas Moore died in 1852, 'fading peacefully out of life', and according to L.A.G. Strong's comment on Brodie's consolatory and even cheering reflection, 'far from fearing death, Moore did not know when it came to him'. It is just possible that Moore, for a similar reason, seldom feared life.

Francis Sylvester Mahony died in Paris in 1866, a lonely pathetic death, given additional pathos by the final submission to the Church that brought this Irish 'peculiar tramp' into line with all men who fear tomorrow because tomorrow is eternity and tomorrow is mystery, and tomorrow may or may not be happiness in the bosom of God. The popular and melodious singer is remembered for his songs, and occasionally for his polemic and his friends and his lifelong love and his happy disposition. The literary oddity is remembered, with an accidental irony that he would have been quick to appreciate, because he wrote a song about the Bells of Shandon and then jocosely proceeded to prove that the popular singer had copied the Shandon song when writing another song about bells.

Perhaps he would prefer that gentle remembrance, all bitterness forgotten, all gibes lost in the silence of death.

Of the genius of his fictionary Father Prout, Mahony wrote that it was a 'rare combination of the Teian lyre and the Irish bagpipe; of the Ionian dialect blending harmoniously with the Cork brogue; and Irish potato seasoned with Attic salt'.

Of the death of Father Prout, Mahony wrote: 'By the philosophic seclusion of his old age he fittingly wound up the adventurous period of his rambles over the continent. After such a fluctuating existence final repose was natural and desirable . . . His views were fixed on loftier objects than the pursuits of ordinary men . . . his musings were those of a priest, priestly. In his intercourse with the Nine Sisters he taught them not to imitate the foolish virgins in the gospel . . . and the waters of Siloa's brook mingled in his cup with those of the classic Aganippe'.

Somewhere between that serio-comic description of a genius who was all contradictions, and that quiet description of days ending and all contradictions reconciled, there is the cry of the heart of the wanderer for final and unalterable peace.

7

The Cormorant and the Badger:
The Stories of Patrick Boyle

AS A YOUNG BANK OFFICIAL, Patrick Boyle had been stationed, or garrisoned, in my native town of Omagh. At his funeral, in 1982, I talked with a man who had been in the bank with him then and who had married into the distinguished Macmillan family in that town. The friendship between Pat Boyle and that man had lasted for the best part of sixty years.

Some of Boyle's stories reflect the mood of that town, and the name is mentioned when, in the story called simply 'Sally', Aunt Mary threatens to send her holidaying nephew back to Omagh if he can't settle down and enjoy himself in the village of Drumkeel.

It was interesting that a man who had worked so long in the bank should come, somewhat late, to the writing of notable fiction. Interesting, but too much has been made of that. For the first stories of his that I read did not, by any means, reveal an amateur taking time off from granting or withholding overdrafts. It was obvious that he had a gift for the short story, that he knew how to select his material from what, over a pretty rich experience, he had seen and heard and felt. It was clear, too, that he was not just content with his gift. Any raconteur in a pub might, hit or miss, have that. But this writer had been working hard at the techniques of his trade. Those brusque, offhand openings that, in a few sentences, drag the reader deep into the story are not the gift of the gods to the gifted writer. They were well planned and worked over.

Yet it was not until I read the story 'The Betrayers' that I stopped in my stride and raised the hat and touched the forelock with something in the nature of awe. 'No other writer', I said, 'short of Turgenev, could have written this.'

That's the sort of remark that a frustrated reviewer might, and

79

frequently does, make. As I well know. But what I was thinking of was the Turgenev who wrote 'First Love', and I could think of no higher praise to give a writer of the story. That was many years ago and, since then, I have had no cause to alter my opinion.

What were the qualities that got me about 'The Betrayers' The confrontation between youth and age, once again between a nephew and an aunt, and in an old house by MacGilligan Strand to the east of Lough Foyle. Then: the primal innocence in which the simple farmer buys the circus pony to train her, he hopes, for domestic uses, and in which he also falls in love with the maidservant in the house of the young boy's aunt and tries to woo her, symbolically, through the training of the pony. Then: the shattering intrusion into that idyllic world of the brute-beast in the shape of a lecherous constable, the destruction and degradation of innocence and of a young boy's dream: and, above all, the unending regret that is a prelude to death.

There may be in every writer a story, a poem or a novel that has a sort of root at the centre of things, and out of that root tendrils may grow in all directions. In the case of Patrick Boyle that root could, perhaps, be found in 'The Betrayers'. It could be recommended as an introduction to his novel *Like Any Other Man*, and to his three collections of short stories. At the time of his death there was another novel ready to go.

The sea had a lot to say in his stories: the sea by the flatness of Benowen Strand in 'The Betrayers'; the sea by the rocks of Donegal in a most ironic love-story, 'Three Is Company'; the eastern sea at Portmarnock (where Pat Boyle died) in another ironic love-story, 'The Rule of Three'. Like Flann O'Brien, he seems to have been fascinated by triads and trinities. Here is a demonstrative passage from 'Three Is Company':

> The sun was low over Hawk Head. Already the lengthening shadows of the cliffs reached out, turning the sea to a pool of molten moss. On the horizon, the Island was still steeped in sunshine, the heat haze lingering over it so that to Frank it looked like a reptile drowsing in the steaming mud of some tropical swamp. Hawk Head and Glen Head, on either side of him, dozed too, their massive muzzles tucked between outstretched paws. Sounds had become muted to the whisper of the surf and the distant wailing of the gulls.
>
> The sea stretched around them in an oily calm with shifting whorls of colour – green, red, purple, grey – moving over its surface. It had a curious soothing effect as though the swimming colours were cast upon eyelids closed against the glare of the sun. At the same time, there was a nagging compulsion to seek out and clothe in words – perhaps in a single line of poetry – the exact descriptions of those coloured spirals, dappling the surface of the sea like huge, myopic, staring eyes.

A man and woman have been swimming in that sea. As they leave the water, a cormorant surfaces with a fish in its beak: the bird juggling deftly with its dinner, then swallowing it in one gulp, then fanning its wings across its breast 'as though beating warmth into its body'. It flies away, gaining height, towards the open sea and, 'with wings outspread in heraldic attitude', perches on the peak of a rock guarding the entrance to the cove.

The sea may be a sunshot, idyllic swimming-pool for a couple who are half in love, but its very beauty afflicts the writer with the nagging feeling that he should find words to describe it. The sea may be beautiful, but in it, unceasingly and as elsewhere, life preys upon life. That heraldic cormorant, perched on the rock, digesting his catch, is also a relation of the guillemot, befouled by an oil-slick, washed up helpless on Portmarnock Strand in the story 'The Rule of Three'. When the narrator in that story tries to rescue the doomed bird, it turns on him savagely. Destroyed by the activities of man, it cannot, in its blind savage heart, accept the approach of the man who would aid it.

Boyle, in that tale, was not writing only about the creatures of the wild.

In Patrick Boyle's stories idyllicism gets short shrift. Life motivates some of the time, but the struggle for survival is never easy. The threat to life begins, as most of us should know and as he reminds us, with disillusion and the destruction of youthful dreams. He dealt delicately and comically with that matter in the story 'Sally', in which Jim, a young fellow from the select Campsie Avenue in Omagh, is holidaying in the village of Drum-keel with his Aunt Mary. There he meets Sally McGahan, a shopkeeper's daughter, home on holiday from her convent school. They play tennis. Sally is very good and, although he is too, he finds it as much as he can do to assert his male mastery. She invites him to the home of her parents, who are prim and proper and who object to dancehalls and pop-music and the like. Jim and Sally play the piano upstairs while her parents sit down-stairs. Sally is very good at the proper sort of music and played in the proper style she has been taught at school. They play duets in that proper sort of music. The incongruities in the whole set-up display Boyle at his best as a comic writer.

After that secret, hilarious, musical wooing, the couple conspire to get together to a dance in Bundoran and, on the dance floor, Jim discovers the oddity in Sally's character: that being a domineering sort of girl, and never having danced except in the convent-school, she has always been accus-tomed to play the man and lead. For a genuine two-fisted male to take the floor with her reduces the happy business to the level of a wrestling bout. So Jim flies from her and practically wills her into the arms of his randy, disreputable friend, only, afterwards, to watch them enviously as they glide around the floor like happy skaters, and to hear his friend whisper to him, as they circle past, that Sally is, in the liveliest sense of the work, 'Deadly'.

It is all excellent comedy, yet the sense of loss and disillusionment is complete, and there are depths below the simplicities of disillusionment. There is never anything about Boyle's irony which cannot be, now and again, as genial as a May morning. But he is in control of the sort of contrast that makes for effective irony and, at times, he can be brutal about it.

One of the appallingly memorable details about the policman in the story 'The Betrayers' is that he has a hairy backlike the back of a badger; and the badger himself makes a ceremonial appearance under his Latin name in the story 'Meles Vulgaris'. A man, abed with his wife, and on the verge of making love, cannot wipe out of his mind the day in his boyhood when he saw a badger done to death by the dogs: a bloody end for the badger, a bloody victory for the dogs. The man lies on his bed and remembers, and reads a book about the life and nature of the badger: about the cry of the badger which, some naturalists hold, may have sexual origins. Or may have some connection with the funeral rites of that strange animal. But that cry is still in his ears: '. . . the wild defiant shout of an animal ringed about with enemies'.

The man knows that his life has been one retreat after another, in comparison with the bayed-about, desperate bravery of the badger. As he takes his wife in his arms, love and betrayal and loneliness are all one and the same thing, and he sees only 'a mangled body, mired and misshapen, bloodied muzzle grinning senselessly at a senseless sky', hears only 'the scream of agony that death alone could arrest'.

For another husband, cowering with a hangover in the story 'At Night All Cats are Grey', the domestic cat, clawing on the crinkling eiderdown, is the denial of everything that the doomed, brave badger stands for. The cat is second-rate contentment, which is to be avoided by all means, and, also, soapy, good health and sanity and main drainage, and all the other Christian virtues. Wondering who in hell's wife he had made a pass at the night before, the errant husband experiences a comic desire for the lawless, for a world of tip-and-run delight.

For the old farmer in the story 'Go Away, Old Man, Go Away', the ironic contrast is everything but comic. His young wife despises him and he suspects that she has interests elsewhere: a folk-theme as old as the rocks. Once, on a hot day in the farmyard, he feels that she is relenting towards him, but he is rejected again, and with an obscene remark; and in the final passage of that story, land and sea and the white bird of the air join with her rank youth in mocking his agèd, arid person.

Death can only arrest the ultimate agony but is also the ultimate disillusion, the ultimate betrayal. In the sad, lyrical story 'Rise Up, My Love, and Come Away', the spirit of a distracted woman who has taken her own life contemplates her gravestone, and her life and death. Death can be sad, awkward, ordinary. Death can be a gulpin of a card-player, as in the story 'Oh, Death, Where Is Thy Sting-aling-aling'. In the story 'All Looks Yellow to the Jaundiced Eye', death, totally destructive, takes over the whole scheme of things, another old man on the land, and in the high heat of summer, goes crazy, slaughters a few rabbits and the domestic fowl and his own dog, murders his wife and, before he destroys himself, hears 'the intolerable cry – the howl of a wild beast, harried and starving, whom only the hunter can release from its torments'.

Death is the hunter.

It is a vision from which one turns away with a certain relief to find that humanity, even with difficulty, still survives: and that the pages of Patrick Boyle are also crowded with comic, loveable, hopeful and hopeless, but still striving, human beings.

There was that drunken bank manager, kicking at the ledgers in the strongroom, in a morning frenzy, in the novel *Like Any Other Man*. It was jocosely said to me in a Dublin pub that to write such a novel about an Irish parish-priest would have been bad enough; but to write it about a bank manager showed that there was no religion left in the bloody country.

Then there was Shaybo, the curator of a Dublin City Corporation-comfort-station, who acquired philosophy of a sort from observing men not quite at their noblest. Pat Boyle once said to me that he thought for a long time that there must be some class of a man about whom nobody had ever written a story. Quite rightly, in so far as I know, he came up with Shaybo. The first paragraph is a reasonable, comic judgment on a lot of life:

> You'd be right in thinking that an underground jakes is a poor place for a smoke and a chat. The more so when the sun is knocking the sparks off the glass roof and stirring up a stink that would bloody near talk to you. But when you haven't the price of a packet of fags and when Shaybo Gallagher, the Corporation attendant, is a country-man of your own, a bit of hardship is neither here nor there.

A bit of hardship is neither here nor there. A profound acceptance of life.

ᴖ 8 ᴖ

Clay and Gods and Men:
The Worlds of James Stephens

THE PHILOSOPHER FROM COILLA Doraca, or the Dark Wood, wandering the world in search of Angus Óg, a sort of Irish Apollo or Sun-God, met on the road two men and one woman, and the two men were quarrelling to find out which of them should marry the woman. So the woman, wise in her own way, decided to solve the problem by marrying the Philosopher, greatly to the consternation of the Philosopher, who, long before the stealing of the crock of gold from the leprechauns of Gort na Cloca Móra, of the Ploughed Field of the Big Stones, and long before the elopement of Meehaul MacMurrachus's daughter with the God Pan, had been solidly and securely married to the Thin Woman of Inis Magrath.

In the extremity of his embarrassment, the wandering Philosopher lectured and lessoned the importunate strange woman on the meaning of wisdom. Wisdom, as he saw it, was not to mind about the world, not to care whether or not you were hungry, and 'not to live in the world at all but only in your own head, for the world is a tyrannous place'. Life was slavery and Nature drove men with whips of appetite and weariness. But men had declared war on Nature and would win in the end because Nature, being a female, was bound to give in when challenged.

'It's good talk,', said the woman, 'but it's foolishness. Women never give in uness they get what they want, and where's the harm to them then?'.

And confronting the straight, dry wisdom of the philosopher with the round, rich wisdom of a woman, she said: 'What is Nature at all but a word that learned men have made to talk about. There's clay and gods and men, and they are good friends enough'.

The words of the woman are worth remembering in relation to the man who wrote *The Crock of Gold*: clay and gods and men, and men, undeniably, more complex than clay and, perhaps, more complex than the gods, but all three mingling together in friendship and poetry.

There was a day in Dublin when James Stephens, man, poet and philosopher, friend of the Good People and acquaintance of the ancient gods, stood near the Shelbourne Hotel and looked through railings and over a hastily built barricade into the park called St Stephen's Green. 'There were only the trees to be seen,' he said, 'and through them small green vistas of sward'.

Now a poet who had written of three centaurs playing upon a hill, stamping the ground in their power and pride and lust, and written of a wicked satyr creeping through a wood, and of meditative goats quietly following crooked paths through the furze, could have seen wonderful things on green vistas under the trees. He might have seen the gods. What he did see was a man walking across the street, directly towards the barricade, and attempting to pull out of that awkward structure a piece of his property. Then suddenly the park was living, not with centaurs or satyrs but with young men carrying guns: threatening and warning that lonely, indignant reclaimer of confiscated property, shooting him down on the street when warnings and threats had failed to make the poor man realize that he was opposing himself to a revolution.

James Stephens and some other people ran to the man's assistance, 'while a woman screamed unmeaningly, all on one strident note. The man was picked up and carried to a hospital beside the Arts' Club. There was a hole in the top of his head and one does not know how ugly blood can look until it has been seen clothed in hair'.

The ugliness of clotted blood, the horror of an unmeaning scream, might stand symbolically for one aspect of the violent thing that burst into the streets of Dublin wherein James Stephens and a dozen others had fed gloriously on verse and legend and high heroic stories. But the violent thing, at that half-heroic time, was never utterly divorced from the suggestion of another world of poetry and colour. Somewhere else, during the week of fighting that followed Easter 1916, Stephens saw a boy with a revolver, doing his routine revolutionary duty from a determination implanted previously on his imagination, but in a way that showed plainly how completely his mind was then separated from the mechanical actions of his body:

> Continually his eyes went searching widely, looking for spaces, scanning hastily the clouds, the vistas of the streets, looking for something that did not hinder him, looking away for a moment from the immediacies and rigours which were impressed where his mind had been.

The men and women in the world in which James Stephens, in his formative years, lived and, consequently, in the world that he built up in his prose and poetry, move always and have their being on the edge of something more tense and radiant, and more full of movement, than ordinary life. They are never gone completely into the country of the gods, never completely into the world of the Good People. As a result, they are never above human faults, never lost in statuesque and terrifyingly tranquil dreams. But, on the other hand, they never rest in the 'warm tenderness and the acceptance of what is' that Francis MacManus once commented on when writing of Padraic Colum.

Colum's ultimate allegiance to the world of mortal men and women was never in doubt for a single moment. When he twisted and turned a few ancient tales to make the book called *The King of Ireland's Son*, he most decisively brought giants and heroes and magic people into the warm circle of the hearth, making his characters at home with his listeners, and his listeners equally at home with his characters.

Dorothy M. Hoare in her book on Morris and Yeats in relation, respectively, to the sagas of Iceland and the sagas of Ireland, considered Stephens, justly, as a corrective to the mutually dehumanizing influence that poets from the modern world and stories from the ancient world exerted on each other. Yet the reader of Stephens will again and again find himself far from the hearth, in a house like the house in which Tuan MacCairill barricaded himself, 'shuttered his windows, and in a gloom of indignation and protest continued the practices of ten thousand years and would not hearken to Finnian calling at the window or to Time knocking at his doors'.

For the contrast between the woman and the philosopher, between the body of the young man in revolution and the mind of the young man high in the clouds, between the ancient gods of Tuan MacCairill and the new God for whose sake Finnian, Abbot of Moville, sat patient and immobile on Tuan's doorstep, 'wrapped in a meditation that was timeless and unconcerned', are all part of some basic contradiction that can trouble the mind in search through the printed page for the mind of James Stephens.

John Millington Synge could quite simply, in a randy ballad, bid adieu to Sweet Aengus, Maeve and Fand and the plumed, yet skinny, Shee, for the sake of drinking in Tubber Fair, or stretching in Red Dan Sally's ditch, or poaching with Red Dan Philly's bitch for the badger and the hare. A character in that odd play *The Bending of the Bough* could say that the land of Ireland was the birthplace 'of our anterior selves; at once ourselves and our gods. Our gods have never perished; they have but retired to the lonely hills'.

It scarcely needed the added explanation that by 'our gods' we were to understand our ancient ideals, to give us to understand that the character speaking did not mean anything in particular.

But James Stephens on a lonely hill seemed always alive to a real conflict, possibly between God and the gods, possibly between warm, round, comical humanity and the cold realities of wind and water and air. He might go out to the hill in response to a stray couplet from an old Irish song, calling to his love to come with him under his coat, to drink with him wine or the milk of the white goat, naming his new poem in English after the Cúlfhionn. But once out under the stars, he could forget the warmth of love, could look up to cry:

> I may have been a star one day,
> One of the rebel host that fell,
> And they are nodding down to say,
> 'Come back to us from hell'.

Life in at least two worlds has always been possible in Ireland. The possibilities can be terrifying and the results can be both very beautiful and very ugly. A man would go farther than Dante ever dreamt of going, through the world of men, through hell and the World of the Shee, for the pleasure of hearing the beauty of women described as the old physician described that luxurious and complicated matter when the Dagda, the Father of the gods, was displaying to his son, or to one of them, Aengus, a vision of the women of the two worlds of Ireland. That description, for several reasons, deserves full quotation. It is, in its own line, as good a poem as James Stephens ever wrote. It is satisfyingly coloured with beauty and it is touched, also, with the humour that Stephens brought to, and found in, the ancient stories:

> 'I perceive,' said the physician, 'that you have begun with the plump women, and I perceive also that of all created beings a well-rounded woman overtops all others, for she can set the heart at ease and fill the mind with fancy'.
> 'There is,' he said later, 'much to be said of slender women. They have a grace and movement that is infinitely satisfying. They curve and flow'.
> 'How agile the thin maidens are,' he murmured thoughtfully. 'How deep is the appeal of their willowy youth'.
> 'But,' he said again, 'golden-haired is the one colour for women: only with gold are they adequately crowned'.
> 'And yet,' he murmured, 'how winsome brown hair can be. What a sly sparkle lies in the braided tress, and how tenderly it finds the heart'.
> 'Noble,' he asserted, 'noble is the darkness piled above the dawn. Majestic are the black-haired heroines. Full of frolic and loveliness are they of the fragrant locks'.
> 'To the red-haired queens I give the palm,' he cried. 'They warm the world. They are the true honey of delight'.

In that mood the poet looked on all the worlds and found them good, on all the colours and shapes that beauty took in women and found them desirable.

But the complications of the Irish past casting shadows on the Irish present did not end, simply and decisively, when the old gods went back defeated to the lonely mountains and the secret places under the hills. The centuries that followed added to the story of battles never properly won, never utterly lost. To a certain extent something similar could be written of any country or any people carrying the accumulation of memories that we refer to, vaguely, as history. But in Ireland the man attempting to shape the present by looking back into, or listening attentively to, the past becomes the victim of a perpetual meeting and agreement and disagreement of opposites, hears one voice telling of death, one voice shouting in joy and another voice creaking in bitterness.

The poet who looked back and saw, through the love-wounded eyes of young Aengus, the beauty of the women of the two worlds of Ireland, saw also the agony of mortality and the transiency of all beauty in the person of Deirdre. He wrote in 'Deirdre' from *Songs from the Clay*:

> The time comes when our hearts sink utterly;
> When we remember Deirdre, and her tale,
> And that her lips are dust.

> Once she did tread the earth: men took her hand;
> They looked into her eyes and said their say,
> And she replied to them.

> More than two thousand years it is since she
> Was beautiful.

And Etáin, over the sick-bed of the boy Ailill, thought wearily, not knowing of her immortality or the death of all things:

> The men, she thought, and the beasts and the trees, they will all die! They are all dying now! and in every part and parcel of earth all that is living is dying by slow inches, and will be gone in a little while, and be never again remembered.

Raptures about beauty and meditations on death may be the common property of all poets in all places. But putting his ear to the long whispering arch of the centuries James Stephens could absolve himself from any sin against art in putting those chill thoughts of death into the mind of one so young and beautiful and doubly desired as Etáin. He heard the poet, Ó Rathaile, in his deepest misery, shouting out that, under certain conditions, he would choke the long wave with its own lamentation. Or that other poet, Ó Bruadair, cursing and begging and lamenting, and invoking the Triune God to send to Ireland, when Ireland was worthy of it, a better singer than the calloused and broken Ó Bruadair. Or he heard Keating, the priest, desiring, and repulsing, the advances of terrifying beauty: or Blind Raftery, with the vivid, inward eye, helping men for a hundred years to the vision of the loveliness of Mary Hynes.

Stephens retold the story of Deirdre more successfully than Synge or Yeats or AE managed to retell it, putting as much of himself into the retelling as they did, but finding in himself something that was also in the old story. Now, comparisons of that sort can almost always be exceptionally foolish; and any attempt to find standards of comparison between a tragedy written for the stage by Synge and something resembling a romantic novel, written by Stephens, could end up at the bottom of an abyss of asininity. But there is a certain validity and a certain value in making comparisons between the qualities that the story of Deirdre drew from such diverse characters as Synge and Yeats and AE and Stephens: for, in spite of their diversities, they belonged approximately to the same movement and shared variously in the same impulse.

Sean O'Faoláin, writing an introduction for his anthology of ancient Irish verse, *The Silver Branch*, described what that impulse was. He quoted Yeats when Yeats was writing in admiration of 'the breadth and stability of the old poetry'. Yeats had said:

> Elaborate modern psychology sounds egotistical when it speaks in the first person, but not those simple emotions which resemble the more, the more powerful they are, everybody's emotion, and I was soon to write many poems where an always personal emotion was woven into a general pattern of myth and symbol.

O'Faoláin commented that the old Gaelic lyricists did exactly that, and that Irish balladists keep on doing it:

> It is racial. A personal emotion woven into a 'general pattern' – it is the note of Irish literature in every age. Those old Irish lyrics gain all their power, and much of their charm, from that mingling of personal and general, individual and racial, the moment of the man compressing the time of man into a verse.

The story of Deirdre has provided a very attractive 'general pattern'. Dorothy M. Hoare pointed out how AE had made Lavarcham, Deirdre's nurse, a druidess, seeing with 'subtle eyes the shining light'. But AE was, I might risk saying, temperamentally incapable of reproducing the speed and action of the original tale, and so was Yeats, even in spite of his admiration for the decisive and active ancestor who leaped overboard after his hat in the boiling Bay of Biscay. Anyway, leaping after hats into boiling seas or murdering a lover and his two brothers are not actions that can be performed convincingly on the legitimate stage. Even if Synge did bring onto the stage the Deirdre who had been spoken of in the glow of every hearth, he brought also his own understandable sense of imminent death and the grave, already opened, of men and women growing weary of love and abandoning life almost without a battle. Possibly the most valuable thing that Deirdre did for Synge was, again to quote O'Faoláin, to help him to sense the self-consciousness of his race when he made her 'something of a player-queen, aware of the drama of her own fate', crying out, 'there will be a story told of a ruined city and a raving King and a woman will be young forever . . . a thing will be a joy and triumph to the ends of life and time'.

But James Stephens, free of the limitations of the traffic of the stage, told the story with the blending of elaboration and breathless speed with which stories are told in the red place between the fire and wall. He could pause to analyse the character of Conachur: 'That clever, energetic man could not exist without a tame mate. A mere bodily satisfaction he, sated in such satisfactions, would have exhausted in a week . . . for he was diabolically clever, and so not wise, and so not great. Only the great escape slavery and he was slave to his ego and would be whipped'.

Casually one might think that to beget that analysis of the soul of a legendary kKing, Stephens had crossed something out of Theodore Dreiser with something else out of Bradley's *Shakespearean Tragedy*. But a closer reading will show nothing fundamentally out of keeping with the mind and manner of the traditional storyteller: just as there is nothing out of keeping in his lingering with and ornamenting the story of the lost childhood of Deirdre or, in his *Irish Fairy Tales*, the lost boyhood of Fionn.

Childhood in a sort of enchanted solitude always seemed to fascinate Stephens. Alone in the great city, Mary Makebelieve, the charwoman's daughter, saw the tall policeman at the street-corner first as a demigod and finally as an ogre, saw the lake in St Stephen's Green like an enchanted mirror laid down in the centre of fairyland. In *The Crock of Gold*, the philosopher's children playing in the wood have no company but shadow and sunlight, the tall trees and the green leprechauns. Séamus Beg, in the poems, saw a giant, with a club in his hand, searching for a princess by the orchard wall, and the devil walking down the lane behind the house and a soul struggling in the bag on his back, and a weird woman, who might have been a witch from foreign lands, and a man running and panting like a horse and gripping a knife.

The fantasies of childhood in the present met and mingled with the fantasies of childhood in the past. Deirdre, beckoning across uncounted centuries to the charwoman's daughter, would 'look on her arms as they hung helplessly in the grass, and wonder that they were so unoccupied and wonder that they were so empty. And an oppression came to her heart, gentle enough, but without end, as though something stirred there that could not stir, as though something sought to weep and could not weep: so that she must weep for it, and be of a tenderness to that unknown beyond all the tenderness that she had sensed about her'.

Young Fionn, watching the great robber Fiacuil MacCona chase and kill the band of wandering poets, was experiencing the full horror of a Séamus

Beg fantasy: 'He chopped them up and chopped them down. He did not leave one poeteen of them all'.

But when the robber with the black mouth, 'with the red tongue squirming in it, like a fish', heard that Fionn was the son of Uail, son of Baiscne, then 'the robber ceased to be a robber, the murderer disappeared, the black-rimmed chasm, packed with red fish and precipices, changed to something else, and the red eyes that had been popping out of their sockets and trying to bite, changed also. There remained a laughing and crying and loving servant who wanted to tie himself into knots if that would please the son of his great captain'.

To die in that way was a poor end for a school of poets. But the poet with his ear to the grey stone that held the whispers of the centuries could look out through the hard archway of 'general pattern' and see the present alive and colourful. For Stephens, the present so joined with the past that gods and men moved easily over the same fruitful clay, and the giant called Time became a good-natured servant, and the real danced with the unreal, and the life that the philosopher from Coilla Dorca lived in his own dry mind blended forever with the life in which a philosopher might lean forward, without scruple, to kiss a fat woman, meditatively, on the eye.

Looking out through that archway, James Stephens saw the two worlds of Ireland meeting comically, when the leprechauns in *The Crock of Gold* attacked the policeman, ponderous with the phrases peculiar, always and at all times to policemen, but the especial property of the Royal Irish Constabulary, which has found its own place in the mythological background to the mind of Ireland.

Writing about three plays, Michéal macLiammoir's *Ill Met By Moonlight*, Francis Stuart's *Strange Guest*, and Mervyn Wall's *Alarm among the Clerks*, Roger McHugh, a most percipient man, said, back in the 1940s, that:

> Good blends of the strange and the real seem to have a particular attraction for the Irish creative mind in literature. One remembers James Stephens' angels sitting down with tinkers and discussing the nutritive value of grass; or Cuchulain joining a tennis club in Drumcondra in Eimar O'Duffy's King *Goshawk and the Birds*; or the poker game between Mad Sweeney, three cowboys, a Pooka and a fairy in Flann O'Brien's *At Swim-Two-Birds*; or the dream-sequences in O'Casey and Joyce.

When Stephens dedicated a 'Theme and Variations' to Stephen MacKenna in thanksgiving for a copy of MacKenna's translation of Plotinus, he humbly denied that he was in any way adequate to read or to return thanks for the gift of the thoughts of the philosopher whom Yeats had, for a moment, mocked in the same breath in which he had defied

Plato. Stephens wrote:

> So, when great Plotinus came
> He found me playing at my game,
> Moving the will, the mind, the pen,
> To moods that lie beyond the ken
> Of poet or Philosopher.

Just such a mood might have brought the angels down to the campfire of Patsy McCann, the tinker, and his daughter, Mary, and to wander the roads of Ireland meeting Eileen Ní Cooley and Brien O'Brien. Niall Ó Dómhnaill excellently translating *The Demigods* into the Gaelic to which it already partially belonged gave the story the title *Seachrán na n-Aingeal* – the Wandering of the Angels. He could also have called it the Fall of the Angels, for if the descent was by no means irrevocable, neither was the wandering utterly without a plan or a definite objective. All the little heedless roads that the angels and tinkers travelled together led back to the place where the celestial garments of Caeltia and Finaun and Art had been hidden so that they could, for a time, appear like men in the world of men. It was some part of the idea of this mingling of heaven and earth that angels without those clothes and dressed as men, could pass for men, and that men, wearing those clothes of heaven, might possibly masquerade as angels. It was in complete keeping with that idea when Art turned his back on the high places, tore his wings and scattered the plumes on the wind, and went down among men with Mary, the tinker's daughter.

For James Stephens something had to follow the Fall. In the Christian theory of things, mercy and sacrifice and redemption followed the Fall of Man, but in one very strange poem James Stephens redeemed the devil. He extended to the world of angels, good and bad, the pity felt for a withered leaf blown far from the sun and the swinging branch and into a Dublin hallway; into, in truth, the hallway of the Royal College of Surgeons in St Stephen's Green:

> As I stood in the hall, sheltered out of the wind,
> Something blew in that I scarcely could find.
> I searched and I searched and I searched till I found
> A dry withered leaf lying down on the ground.

Or the pity felt for a snared rabbit crying its pain on the frightened air, making everything afraid. Or for a decrepit cab-horse symbolizing all the pitiful 'people and beasts who have never a friend'.

In the volume of stories and sketches *Here Are Ladies*, Stephens wrote of Brien O'Brien and the threepenny piece that was stolen by the seraph, Cuchulain, of the verdict of Rhadamanthus that sent the two of them whirling through space, through deep unending quietude, past Saturn and Orion and Venus, to strike the earth and stand stark naked in the neighbourhood of Donnybrook. It might have been an impish parody on a certain notable passage in *Paradise Lost*. But when, later, the story of Brien and Cuchulain found its appropriate background in *The Demi-Gods*, it was obvious enough, whatever the intention may have been, that the primal tragedy of the Fall of the Angels had been seen as an event with humorous possibilities.

To begin with: the seraph, Cuchulain, knew the misery, the utter misery, of being guardian angel and higher self to a contemptible mortal miser, so contemptible that the seraph's little mistake about the three-penny piece was actualy traceable to the infectious avarice of his charge. And when the miser, reformed into Billy the Music, told the tinkers, and Caeltia and Finaun and Art, how Cuchulain had treated him and of the words the seraph had, with all the pardonable vexation of a demoted angel, used to him, he said: 'The queer thing is that I believed every word the man said. I didn't know what he was talking about, but I did know that he was talking about something that was real although it was beyond me. And there was the way he said it too, for he spoke like a bishop, with fine, shouting words . . '.

In Ireland what better could a seraph do?

Anyway, James Stephens, like many another, left Ireland and went to live over the seas. In 'Independence' from *Songs from the Clay* he wrote:

> I will rise, I will go
> To the land of my foe;
> For his scowl is the sun
> That shall cause me to grow.

And playing a variation on an old jingle, he wrote in 'In the Red' from *Kings and the Moon* what was possibly a later impression of the lot of the poet in exile: when he was young he had had no sense, no pence, no fiddle, and finally:

> There was no tune
> That I could play
>   Now I'm older
> None play I:
>
> But, over the hills,
> And far away!
> – Now I'm older
> There am I.

Now there is no reason why a poet should not, if he wants to, live over the hills and far away. There have been, and are, frequently good reasons for an Irish writer to live far away from the fair hills of Ireland. The difficulty was that James Stephens left behind him the gods and the demigods and the wandering angels, and no man or woman in Ireland today knows the little roads that lead to the lonely hills where they live.

Also in *Kings and the Moon* in a poem called 'Envying Tobias', he wrote:

> No more do we
> Of angels talk. . .

But the sad thing was that life in the land of the foe, over the hills and far away, could have reduced James Stephens to the level of envying Tobias, whose acquaintance with the angels was, after all, strictly limited.

Apart from clay and gods and men, there may only be machines. The Irish mood for a while was prepared to see Irish writers as realistic people down from the high places of heroism and romance to the realities of clay. The mood was possibly as false to what we really look like from the outside as any other mood that has tormented us in the past. For we might hope that we may never be so realistic as to praise machines above clay, and clay can be as exquisitely clear as crystal, and cattle can be as friendly as fat women. Praising clay, we must also praise the gods, who are always alive, not only on the lonely mountains but in lonely places in the minds of men; and men walk on clay, and work in clay, and were fashioned out of clay by the God to whom the gods are only shafts of sunlight, or winds blowing in green places, or movements in the red hearts and grey heads of men.

❧ 9 ❧

Praise God for Ireland:
The Novels of Francis MacManus

T HE YEAR IS, OR WAS, 1966, AND I am far away in Oregon and
hearing of the death of a good friend.

By the rivers of Oregon . . .

I mean the Willamette and the Mackenzie that leap and tumble down
from the snows and forests of the high Cascades, and join with a shout at
the city of Eugene, and go on across flat land of wonderful fertility to join
the mighty Columbia.

By the rivers of Oregon I sit and read and remember thee, O Kilkenny,
and the enchanting Nore.

The book I read is *The Fire in the Dust*, and I think how fine it would be
to walk and talk here by the Willamette with Francis MacManus as we
often talked of the Nore from Castletown to Thomastown, or of the
wonderland along the Barrow's towing-path from Graiguenamanagh to
the holy place of St Moling, or even about my own northern rivers: the
Strule, the Mourne, the spreading estuary of the Foyle.

'That summer,' I read, 'the trees were puffed out in clouds of light
green foliage, and the weeds and grasses grew extravagantly tall, thick
and odorously juicy out of the deposited muck of the floods. The surface
of the river was dark, gelatinous, under an elastic skin that wrinkled
under the feet of swimming flies and rippled out in symmetrical creases
from the movement of the boats. It was a good time for boating, for
driving the prow like a knife into the new reeds and grasses and the over-
hanging bushes, for finding ducks' nests and fishing out water-logged
baulks of timber, and for sweating with lashing oars in mad spurts up the
river towards Green's Bridge'.

MacManus had a great eye for rivers. He loved the smell of sun-
warmed Norman stone.

In *The Fire in the Dust* he poised two worlds against each other on the banks of the Nore and in the ancient Norman city of Kilkenny. There is the dried-up repository world of Miss Dreelin, the dust in which a fire could be only abnormal, destructive, and, also, of the coarse-tongued boys who talk dirty but are still afraid of what would be said to them in the secrecy of the confessional if they had it to tell that they had looked on the picture of Aphrodite rising naked (how else?) from the foam, or Maria Golden skinny-dipping in the Nore.

Then there is that other world, the suggestion of which Stevie Golden brings back with him from South America: a Madonna and Child of carved wood, 'smothered with the fadings of opulent gilt, blinding blues and reds, a squat Madonna with slit eyes'.

That was as foreign to the religious imagery Larry Hackett knew of as a pagan idol would be on a side-altar in the cathedral. The furnishings the Goldens had brought with them looked so bizarre against the solid, polished mahogany in the house they had rented from Miss Dreelin. They had flamboyantly coloured mats, hand-beaten silverware, those queer images carved from hardwood, and the pictures, of which the central one was Aphrodite. They made the respectable mahogany look like an incongruous, dull intruder.

Even the old Norman city seems to change as Maria, Stevie's sister, paints it, for she gives to it in her paintings the prodigal colours of her own clothes – and tropic glimpses of a town that never would stain the air with running dyes.

Because of that destructive fire, the more destructive because so long smothered, and because of the withering dust, the colours of Maria, the clear-eyed, outspoken honesty of Stevie are lost, in tragedy to the old city of darkened brick and sober, ancient stone. It does not seem necessary to point the parable. It made itself abundantly clear to eight or nine students who were studying the novel in a class in Oregon in 1966. It was always painfully obvious to us in Ireland.

One of those students to whom I had passed on some copies of *The Irish Times* put me in a tangle by asking me what the paragraph meant about the banning of Edna O'Brien's latest novel. (This, we must remember, was a quarter of a century ago in an almost pre-television era.) It wasn't, at that time, easy to explain. For one thing: the Oregonian student looked up to me, it was in the era of revolting, excuse the adjective, students, as a man from a land of rebels, from a small, indomitable island that had fought the greatest of all empires and produced, on the side, Yeats, Shaw, Synge, O'Casey and some others.

Brendan Behan once had a parallel difficulty making his explanations to a French visitor to Dublin who saw the Total Abstinence Pioneers marching to Croke Park and thought the parade was in memory of the heroic dead slain on some blazing barricade. When the truth, after much talking, had filtered through to the Gallic mind, the visitor said wearily: 'Oui, Brendan, I understand. They do not drink. But why do they not stay at home and not drink at home?'

With the student in Oregon the matter of explanation was simpler: merely to return to *The Fire in the Dust* and to point out that, at that time, Miss Dreelin was very much with us in Ireland and that she lived in the office of the Censorship of Publications. The old lady with the repository mind was then still saying 'No'. Francis MacManus himself may never have fallen foul of her whims, but with the courage and honesty that always marked him, he drew an exact portrait of her in *The Fire in the Dust*.

MacManus, when *The Fire in the Dust* was published, had four more books to write: two novels, a life of Columbanus, and a travel book about the United States. That book, in the native Irish, was first sketched out in a series of articles he wrote for James Pearse McGuinness and myself, when, as editor and literary-editor, we were associated with a Dublin daily newspaper. Those articles were the first writings I ever read that gave me any idea of what the United States actually looked like. They came back to me, sadly, and long ago, in that riverine American place so far, indeed, from the Suir, the Nore and the Barrow. To have had the following essay at that time reprinted, by grace of James Delahunty, in *The Kilkenny Magazine* was my poor tribute to the memory of a man who meant so much to all of us, and who for twenty-five years was to me close friend and another brother.

In Ireland once upon a time it took a certain amount of courage mixed with a certain amount of discretion for a schoolmaster to write a novel about a bishop. Francis MacManus, who was for part of his life a schoolmaster, in *The Greatest of These* wrote one of the best of modern Irish novels and certainly the best novel ever inspired or provoked by the Irish hierarchy in their relations with the Irish clergy and the Irish people. It was not, I may add, an attack on the Irish hierarchy. It was a vision of the virtue of charity blossoming in the soul of an old man as 'the long borders of tulips, yellow, lemon, crimson, and wine-coloured, blossomed in the sheltered, episcopal garden'.

In another novel, *Flow on Lovely River*, MacManus allowed a country schoolmaster, John Lee of the village of Drombridge in County Kilkenny, to tell the story of his own thwarted love for the daughter of the village drunkard and, by allegory, the story of his thwarted love for his own people. In the case of John Lee, the green leaf withered on the thorn and the bud of charity did not blossom. John Lee wrote, according to Francis MacManus:

> There was sunshine all this cold, dry day. It was flashing off the windows of Drombridge as I strolled through in the afternoon. Nobody ever seems to wash the few flagstones that compose a pavement on one

side of the street, and nobody ever seems to sweep up the refuse and dead leaves from the cobbled channels, and yet the place is always clean like a sacristy. The Quakers must have resided in Drombridge at some time, for they appear to have left their lust for physical cleanliness and their passion for inner virtuousness on the people. They left a taste for the old woman's peace of Sunday, too. Shea, the publican, Hynes, Hayden and Murphy, the jacks of all provisions; the cobbler, the newsagent, and the bullseye merchant; the old doctor wheezing through his treacle-brown moustache, and all the other worthy folk who would look so well in a gross, wine-red grotesque, fleshy, carbuncular oil-painting, are reposing on their buttocks before warm fires and clasping their hands affectionately on well-fed tummies to doze off roast mutton and beef and boiled bacon and cabbage. I love them all.

There is something grim about that love, just as there is something grim about the cleanliness of Quakerism, reflected, as in a cold mirror, in the clean street of Drombridge. That clean street, where the only pig is the boiled pig already going through the machinery of digestion, might have been to certain readers, who had too strictly limited their reading, a novelty in Irish literature. A far greater novelty: the writer as clean and clear of sentiment as the street is of dead leaves, so clear of sentiment that the reader finds it necessary to keep telling himself that the truest love is not feeling but knowledge. John Lee's love for his people is at times so devoid of any of the tenderness of feeling that it is possible to suspect him of a perversity that might express itself more readily in cuffs than in caresses. But if he, or Francis MacManus, had written 'I know them all', instead of 'I love them all', no man or his mother could have smelled out a contradiction in the passage I have just quoted. That contradiction is only on the surface, for, once again, the truest love is true knowledge and, after that, the preservation of patience.

John Lee is loved by the good daughter of a strong farmer, and expected by the farmer's relatives to marry the girl whose love he tolerates. But a man who possesses a three-volume Dante and who is cursed with a certain power for seeing himself, and others, at a distance, is unlikely to accept finally and return fully the devotion of the obvious girl.

The great river flows down by the village: 'sliding between clay banks and the thick, marshalled spears of the reeds and rushes. Spray leaped in delight from the boiling whirl in the arrow-pointed weirs, flecking the waters and dissolving again, momentarily refreshed, into the broad humdrum sweep that moved along by mills, houses, towns, Kilkenny, Bennettsbridge, Thomastown, Inistioge, to open out free at last for the inrolling surge, salt and redeeming and cold: poor human folk muttering their own fragments of a vast story on their short, broken, inevitable journey to the sea'.

That passage would have made sense to the poet Edmund Spenser, who knew about the souls of rivers and who numbered the Suir, the Nore and the Barrow among his own particular friends. But the coloured love-sonnets that Spenser gathered together under the title 'Amoretti', or even his song of fulfilment in the 'Epithalamion', would never have entered the head of the schoolmaster John Lee, leaning on a bridge and watching the Nore flowing down to the sea. John Lee's creator did not anywhere in his novels see love either fulfilled in the flesh or frustrated in the spirit. Fulfilment or frustration do not seem to be all that important. What matters is that the river flows to the sea and that Time flows on into Eternity.

The lines that the schoolmaster, meditating on the river, mutters to himself are lines that, six years after the writing of *Flow on Lovely River*, followed Francis MacManus into the concluding pages of his study of Boccaccio. They are lines from the poet whom Boccaccio, and many another, acknowledged as The Master:

> *En la sua volontate e nostra pace:*
> *ella e quel mare, al qual tutto si move*
> *cio ch'ella crea e che natura face.*

To see human love, either sexual love for a woman, or benevolent love for all men, against the white light of those lines may be something that only saints could do, or artists, or men as hard as rocks. Francis MacManus only once, in *The Greatest of These*, wrote about a saint; nor, unlike Giovanni Papini, he did not believe that only saints and great artists were worth writing about. It seems to follow that in his hard, compressed English he wrote mostly about hard men.

MacManus's first novel, *Stand and Give Challenge*, was the first of a trilogy written around the fragments of the life-story of the eighteenth-century Gaelic poet Donnacha Rua MacConmara. The trilogy was continued and completed with *Candle for the Proud* and *Men Withering*; and, disclaiming all intention of writing history, biography or literary criticism, MacManus said that the first volume and, by inference, the entire trilogy was 'an attempt to present the lives of a few people, as I have conceived them, of the hidden Ireland. You or I, had we been alive and Irish and troubled with song, might have been such a person as the chief character who lived when a dark nightmare was on this nation'.

The young rebellious poet in the early pages of the trilogy may or may not be historical. He undoubtedly is a twentieth-century democrat's projection of himself into another century when a broken people had accepted helotry, and their poets gave them coloured dreams about a Stuart king. The red-headed poet's meditations on his people, as he walks from the Samhain fair at Cappoquin, could scarcely have burdened the minds of many of that school of poets spinning fancies about wandering hawks and Caesars over the sea. But they would leap like light from the soul of a free man contemplating the spectacle of slavery anywhere and at any time in history:

> A rift in the clouds, the moon sailed across the bared patch of sky, and there beneath the light were the ridged beloved hills, the plume-like trees – and slimy, damp, lice-infested cabins. Inside those novels the people would be gathered on this holy night of All Souls, while the wandering spirits of the dead drifted before the purgatorial winds. They would tell stories about the dead, about Fionn and the Fianna, about the heroes and gods and philosophers of Greece, about saints and kings and princes and lovely ladies, as if no care or worry ever touched them, and on the morrow or the day afterwards they would pay their last rents and go home to live in want or to die of starvation. Why did they yield? Why did they not fight?

The poet of the trilogy loves this broken people, possibly, because he belongs to them: and the novelist who wrote the trilogy made things hard for his own heart by looking for a long time at his own people as they were in their deepest degradation. His sentences are always hard, like bricks built around a tomb, never soft like the sweep of a garment around a graceful body. He spares neither himself, nor the people, nor the poet whose soul for a time is hardened by apostasy and pride. Nor does he spare his reader. There are moments when it is not easy to look at this people without a shudder, when, for instance, they crowd into the landlord's presence to ask for mercy:

> The men had instinctively removed their caps and hats in the presence of their masters. They were terribly silent, save for their laboured breathing. Moisture dripped from their clothes and spotted the floor. Their trousers, skirts and soiled coats gaped with rents and tears, and these tatters of clothing clung damply to their bodies. Two or three wore wooden-soled clogs, but the rest were barefooted, and Sir John noted with disgust how streaks of slime ran down their legs and ankles and clotted between their bare toes on the immaculate carpet.

Writing three novels about a poet, whose shadowy odyssey began in the first half of the eighteenth century and came down to days when mysterious strangers whispered news of a new gospel in France, was as good a way as any other for a novelist to learn discipline in style. Steady and continuous contemplation of a degraded people could be the best possible discipline for the emotions. One result of that discipline, as far as an Irish writer was concerned, was that it became possible to accept Ireland without being sentimental about Ireland; and there was less softness of feeling in the acceptance displayed by Francis MacManus than in the rejection made classical by James Joyce, and so subtly analysed, and sensed like a burning in the bowels, in, say, Sean O'Faoláin's novel *Come Back to Erin*. Another result of that discipline can be felt at moments when the reader is not certain whether the novelist is giving the characters the benefit of his own hard objectivity, or the characters are infecting the novelist with their own hardness of heart. The same problem arises in reading some of the stories of Prosper Merimée and makes clear what Stendhal meant when he wrote of Merimée: 'I am not too sure of his heart, but I am sure of his talents'.

The doubt about the heart implies, in this case, not viciousness but the absence of softness that can make a man wise, just as softness of the head can make him foolish. The emotions are disciplined but they are never deadened: and Donnacha Rua, walking the roads, can shorten his journey and lighten the burden on his heart in the company of spalpeens and tinkers, beggars and pedlars: 'Whenever he wearied of voices and faces he drank deeply of the loveliness of the land about him. At times he spoke aloud the beginning of his new song, and added lines to it; and then he moved as in a sleep'.

There is no softness, no sentiment. But there is the complete acceptance that marked MacManus's work, whether writing of poets in the eighteenth century or of priests or hard farmers in our own time.

All this calls for some comment, because acceptance, unless accompanied by other feelings that sweeten the bitterness of saying yes, was not customary among Irish novelists. The school of Lever and of Somerville and Ross, and somebody at the back of the hall may have heckled that 'school' is not the exact word, accepted Ireland as a polo-player accepts the spinning, bouncing, ball: on the earth while he is in the saddle . . .

The years that have passed since I first wrote that down, possibly under the influence of Corkery, have persuaded me how outrageously wrong I was about Lever, wrong, even, about the Grand Old Lady of Drishane and her cousin, living, or passed-on, but still writing.

But to proceed . . .

William Carleton accepted his own people at the price of a dozen denials that, in his worst writing, completely separated him from his own people. James Joyce denied them, horse, foot and artillery, and then experienced and defined the agony of the man who has torn up everything except the roots in his own soul. Sean O'Faoláin did, with understanding, comment on the wisdom of Joyce who, at the age of nineteen, could write in his pamphlet *The Day of the Rabblement* that the artist freed from servitude 'inherits a will broken by doubt, and a soul that yields up all its hate to a caress, and the most seeming-independent are those who are first to resume their bonds'.

Sean O'Faoláin's own formula for acceptance made allowance for the way a castaway feels about his coral island; while Frank O'Connor could be as outrageously at home with his people as a country parish-priest skelping the courting couples out of the hedges. That was one of the ironies of Ireland and of Irish fiction at that time; and of Frank O'Connor.

But MacManus accepted his people without any reservation; without the nationalist enthusiasm that, for Daniel Corkery, could transform louts into mystics; without O'Faoláin's stipulation that the people would be more acceptable if they were more continental. MacManus took them as he found them, and if it is clear that in *The Greatest of These* he found them with charity blossoming in their souls, it is equally clear that in *This House Was Mine* he found them as mean as dirt, as mean as the dirt that the land-hungry and the worldly-wise can pride themselves on possessing.

The land-hunger of the dispossessed is understandable and most pardonable, if pardon is needed or asked for. In the period covered by the MacConmara trilogy, it led men to apostatize; and MacManus touched gently on that apostasy, as men living in days of peace should treat gently the apostasy of men who failed in days of trial. In *Stand and Give Challenge*, he analysed acutely, and with as much mercy as can ever go with analysis, the position of a man who had denied his soul in order to retain his land:

> His love for the land, the last thing left him in the tumbled down world was too urgent to be unsatisfied. The faith in which he was born and reared was gone from him like a puff of smoke, denied under duress, and then forgotten under the perpetual conflict with the law of the Gaill. It were better for the sake of ease not to think of the day when he renounced the Faith in the neat cold Church of the heretical creed. And he had a paltry thing in its stead. In place of the warm Mass he had now a minister before a lectern, or an altar that was as empty as a naked mountain. All he had now were the fields. The sword defended them once. The sword was broken. What remained? the spirit, twisted and hurt and troublesome and crying like a woman bereft of her spouse.

The denial of the spirit for the sake of the body will always provide a theme for novelists who see man against a background that suggests something more than the visible, material world. The little people in the *Manhattan Transfer* of John Dos Passos are mostly as busy making dollars as bees are busy making honey, but their souls are no more discernible than that souls of bees in a hive. The hard farmers in Gottfried Keller's story 'A Village Romeo and Juliet' are so greedy for the patch of dirt that means wealth, and so headstrong in their possessiveness and their antagonisms, that they lose all their wealth and destroy the love that has flowed between their children. But what Keller never makes clear is that the chief thing that greed kills is neither commonsense nor passionate love, but the soul's hope of God. The Irish eighteenth century should, among other disservices, have done Ireland the service of making a clear distinction between God and Mammon, between retaining possession of a farm and maintaining belief in a creed. MacManus, in the passage just quoted, sketched that distinction as it might have existed and been realized in the soul of an apostate Irish Catholic in the eighteenth century. But in the novel *This House Was Mine* he showed how greed, exemplified in the land-hunger of the hard Hickeys, can calcify the soul as effectively as fifty recantations.

The novel *This House Was Mine* is awesome with the silences of the countryside. Martin Hickey, returning to view the ruins of the house where his people had once been powerful, steps from the sleepy little railway halt and walks into a silence that is of the confessional, or of all moments when man, believing, may feel that he is alone with God:

> The train drew out to Kilkenny, the crossing-gates were opened and a motor-car passed through, and in a minute I could hear nothing. The things I saw were dragging me back into times I thought dead and forgotten. There was no sign of a change on the village and still it looked smaller. Maybe it's because I've lived so long amongst the high streets of Waterford that Drombridge seems shrunken. There wasn't a man, woman or child in sight. They were having their dinner, I suppose, or were out at the hay in the good weather. I couldn't hear a voice or a stir. And when I lifted my eyes beyond the little houses, beyond the chapel, and saw Camp Hill that had been ours, the world seemed at a standstill and nobody was alive but myself and God Almighty.

Martin Hickey's story, as he walks back through his memories, has certain resemblances to, and one fundamental difference from, Cela's sun-maddened story of Pascal Duarte and his abominable family. The difference is that Martin Hickey is never maniacal as Pascal Duarte is, both in his sins and in his repentance. But the Spanish story and the Irish story are told in the same hard words, accompanied by the same stiff gestures, and Martin Hickey's memories are compressed to the unyielding hardness of the tombstones on which the names of his ancestors are cut:

> The shadow of the Chapel fell broad across my road and, as I walked through the coolness of it, I began to come to life, slowly and with great pain. In that chapel I was christened, confirmed and married, and there I saw my son, *my* son, being given his name. Over in the graveyard behind the painted, iron railings that weren't there in my time, is the ground where they put my father and mother, my wife, my father's people, and many and many a body of ours. Their names are all cut there on the slabs and the crosses with the dates of their deaths, the Hickeys of Camp House, the house that they raised up, stone on stone, with their own hands and sweat, the house that grew with the family and went of a sudden like a tree dead at the roots.

His journey along the sunny road from the station to the blackened ruins of Camp House is a symbolic journey backward through Time. He looks at the stones and the nettles, he remembers the house as it once was, and he cries out: 'No other remembering is like this. A generation and more is lived in me. I could sweat blood'.

It is for Martin Hickey a moment of 'terrible revelation'. For the reader it is a moment that reveals a lot about the novelist; so much of his work was remembering, not the personal remembering that has, gently or sadly or comically or bitterly, filled so many novels, but the hard racial remembering that can draw the generations together and squeeze blood out through the pores.

But remembering is, at least, the beginning of the novelist's business.

Even the little girl in the novella *The Wild Garden* remembers more than her experience would account for, because her mind is, at one moment, bright with memories of a sun-steeped village that might be heaven, at another moment dark with the shadows of a damp, decaying garden that might be a sort of hell. In the shadowy moments, the child is as much alone with God as Martin Hickey is in his repentant desolation. It is not the God that children are told about, but a God imagined by her tortured childhood as always ready to reveal His Godhead terrifyingly:

> It was a sickening thing to sit in the room at the top of the house, without anybody to talk to, and to draw with pencils and crayons that were aimless, or to get into bed knowing that in the morning, when sleep was over, another day would begin to drag across the world like a dying dog going home. God was like a storm somewhere all right, if you could only reach Him. He was just beyond your head, but when you wheeled suddenly, He, like your own shadow, was still out of reach.

The Wild Garden could scarcely be, for that reason, called a light novel. In it the novelist's touch was indeed more delicate than anywhere else in his writings. But his one attempt, in *Statue for a Square*, at a light novel which he called a diversion was, I feel, a failure because MacManus was trying to write like Brinsley MacNamara and no man can write successfully with another man's pen. Yet *The Wild Garden* deserves a place with such studies of childhood as the *Madame Thérèse* of Erckmann-Chatrian, or the *Mon Oncle et Mon Curé* of Jean de la Brète. The books with which one automatically classifies it seem all to belong to France, and the French, or so it appears to me, can see childhood normal or abnormal, in a clear light that has nothing to do either with Wordsworth's clouds of glory or with the pimples of awakening sex.

In that clear light MacManus saw Margaret Kane, the little girl of *The Wild Garden* – her father dead, her weak stepmother dominated in a most unwholesome fashion by a precise and sadistic lover – surrounded by unhealthiness, as rank as the abandoned and neglected garden. Attached to the house, she remains healthy, desiring the happiness she feels she will find with her uncle Ignatius Kane, making his name and the name of his village into the sort of rhyme that happy children love: Ignatius Kane of Kilfinane.

Only in this short novel and in *Watergate* did MacManus touch on the twisted and the abnormal: and the sadistic lover of Margaret Kane's stepmother, and the gipsy woman with the imbecilic child, who dominates the farmhouse at Watergate, would have made a timid enough showing in any gallery of characters from Graham Greene. The concern of MacManus was with the things, good or bad, that happen on the highways of the human soul (Marsilio Ficino), because it is the happenings on the highways that save a man or damn a man. The poor people lost in tortuous byways are, even by man's partial wisdom and unfeeling justice, sent not to the scaffold but to the mental home.

From the twisted man and the wild garden Margaret Kane flies, bringing with her the frightened stepmother, to the normality of Ignatius Kane, a man fond of serenity. He says: 'I like smooth-flowing rivers and steady sunlight on old walls where moss has been creeping patiently from cranny to cranny. Rushes and storms I hate. They're not worth it'.

Margaret Kane's flight to normality and Ignatius Kane's preference for serenity are worth remembering. They indicate preferences in the novelist responsible for Margaret Kane and Ignatius Kane. They indicate, also, his belief that the normality and serenity he preferred can be found in quiet Irish places and among Irish people who may sometimes be as hard as tombstones, and sometimes as raw as rocks, but who are seldom completely twisted out of all resemblance to normal, responsible human beings. The emphasis on the hardness, the rawness, the meanness could give rise to the impression that MacManus was not really feeling with the characters he created, yet, when his people go in search of the fullness of peace, they go not away from, but towards, their origins.

Margaret Kane runs from horror to her father's brother, who loves serenity in a sunny village. Donnacha Rua MacConmara goes over roads, where strange men talk of revolution in France, to die in peace among his own people. Alice Lennon, returning to Watergate from the great American city that had changed her from a soft girl into a hard, blonde woman, looks out of the window of her compartment in the train and sees the serenity she desires:

> Ireland sliding under a clear sea-depth of sunlight. Thin smoke coiled upward slowly like stirred chalk-ooze above trees petrified in the stillness. The hedges were ridges of brilliant, white hawthorn. Along a road a cart drifted, moving at an imperceptible gait that would lodge it finally in some deeper, sundrowned valley among lime-washed, lost houses. Her restlessness was dissolved. It was so good to be home again.

Significantly, before she can make all that peace finally her own, she has to fight and conquer the usurping gipsy woman and all the abnormality for which that strange sad woman stands.

John Lee, the schoolmaster who lost his love, found as much peace as he could ever find in watching the river flowing to the sea and remembering a few lines in which Dante saw God as the sea towards which all created things move. The thin face of Lee appears again, like the face of an ascetic in a Spanish painting, in the novel *Watergate*, seen this time at a distance and misjudged, by a beholder, as an unlovable and loveless person. But the internal evidence of *Flow on Lovely River* shows Lee, not only loving, as foolishly as any man ever loved an unattainable woman, but, also knowing his people for what they are, knowing his people in himself, and himself in his people, and still saying, truthfully and deliberately, 'I love them all'.

The old embittered priest in *The Greatest of These* comes down from his mountain solitude and finds his peace when walking between the flowers, and with the bishop, in the bishop's garden. Above them the air is restless with the bells of the cathedral city, and for the bishop the bells are Europe and the story of Christianity, and he remembers the Sabbath music of the Low Countries:

> The Flemish bells, sweet and civil in his mind, sweeter than any birds in the morning, called up, as over an horizon, all the bells of the cities and towns in which he had set foot and said Mass: Rome, Milan, Paris, Lourdes, Jerusalem, London, Chartres, places of pilgrimage, miracles, deserted quietness, bitter debates between rebels and authority, and proud, immemorial beauty.

Along the street outside the bishop's garden, feet moving on the pavement as the bells move in the air, the people walk to Mass:

> . . . shoes and boots clapping the concrete and flagstones, new fashionable shoes daintily seeking for Sunday morning notice, shining respectable boots, old bent shoes with worn heels, and heavy, gaping boots dragging shamefully: they would echo and re-echo in the tiled aisles of the churches, boom and batter on the pews and in the organ-lofts, and at last come to quietness, a shifty quietness that settled into momentary, absolute silence at the tinkle of Consecration bells.

The old bishop, whose charity was strong enough to bring peace to an abnormally proud, rebellious and embittered priest, naturally accepted and loved his people. He saw them as they were and was content that they should be as they were but, because he was a wiser man than John Lee, he said not 'I love them all', but 'God love them'.

For if acceptance is to go beyond a stoical suffering of fools, it must become praise, it must become gratitude. The creative artist must be grateful even for the existence of evil. In one of the handful of poems, collected, with some essays and stories, into the book *Pedlar's Pack*, Francis MacManus wrote:

> Ireland's a rock that men scoop out for their bread.
> Ireland's a door where the living collogue with the dead.
> Ireland's a river, a valley, a young nation, an old,
> A house guarded by heroes, a fair where heroes are sold.
> Ireland's a priest with a chalice, a scourge and a bell,
> A monk who prays prone on the stony floor of his cell,
> A singer's regret, a dream of an exile who makes
> A hovel a castle, and princes of randy old rakes. . . .

And so on for a rich load of descriptions and definitions.

And the first four words of the poem were: 'Praise God for Ireland'.

ꙮ 10 ꙮ

Charles Kickham and the
Living Mountain

THE PICTURE OF CHARLES J. KICKHAM that I prefer to think of is of the man happy among his own people, by the banks of the little river that he named in his songs, within sight of the mountain he had in his heart. Just as George Moore, who was born by the beauty of Lough Carra in the County of Mayo, said that every man had a lake in his heart.

In 1869 Kickham wrote one of those idyllic descriptions of happiness in those surroundings that deserves a high place in any anthology praising rural peace and entitled, say 'The Sabine Farm':

> I breathe my native air in the midst of scenes from which nothing could tempt me to stray, but a call, the neglect of which would have made my life unsupportable, I am at home. Opposite my window is an old ruin, whether castle or abbey no one seems to know. But the head of a United Irishman was impaled upon it in '98, and it has, almost from my infancy, possessed a strange fascination for me.
>
> Beyond I have a glimpse of the hills, every foot of which is as familiar to me as the street below. I move my chair and the chapel cross looks in upon me, and seems to point at once tot he graves below and the sky above. My sister's children, whom I see at play in the garden among the budding shrubs and the Spring flowers, recall to me the loving hearts still around me. Wherever I turn I am greeted with something more deep and touching than mere popularity, something that would be too great for all the sacrifice that mortal man could make, and of which I will try to be more worthy if God spares my life. It is a dream too blissful for earth.

That is a touchingly beautiful passage and to the history of Kickham's country, which he had absorbed from the very rocks and trees and streams, and to the place which he and his writings have held for the best part of a century, it is also a significant passage. He could find unalloyed happiness

107

among his own people, in and around the village under the shadow of the great mountain, around the hearths of the homes of Tipperary.

But the broken wall with its grisly memory of 1798 was always there to remind him of a 'call, the neglect of which would have made life insupportable'. So, loving his peace and his people, he still found himself following that call, and all the way to the cold blackness of English prisons as the Fenians knew them. That was a cold and a blackness that weighed ten times as heavily on a man whose sight and hearing had been injured by an accident in his boyhood. His desire for rural peace, for the simple ways of loveable people, his ability to picture faithfully that peace and those ways, even to echoing the words when he sat down to write, gained for his books, and have held ever since, that 'reception more deep and touching than mere popularity'.

The young fellow, who loved the mountain and the hunt, was drying gunpowder before the fire when it exploded and caused the injury that was to add to the suffering in a life that had more than its share of suffering. But the heart of the boy remained uninjured. And it is of that boyish love of mountain and stream, and reckless adventure, that I think of when I turn to Kickham's tale of 1798, *The Eagle of Garryroe*. It is a boy's adventure story even if, in time, it is placed in the year when laws of death and transportation were served like banquets through the nation. Even if, in that early symbolism of the chained eagle and the ancient tower, and the black charger of the wise woman, and of the mighty blacksmith, a genuine Vulcan, Kickham might seem to have been playing a sophisticated game.

Sophistication, particularly literary sophistication, was, to put it mildly, no part of his make-up. But with a fresh imagination he took the images his land offered and they proved to be most effective in the opening pages of *The Eagle of Garryroe*. There is a rich excitement of anticipation in the moment when the agèd eagle comes from his wooden house on the roof of the castle, and slowly spreads his wings to their full extent, and cries in hunger to the evening. And the parson's black hunter, which in the course of the story is to be ridden by a rebel, rears in terror.

But in the story that follows there is little to live up to the awesome impressiveness of that moment. And even when the hero is in the dungeon with the gallows in store for him, one cannot be seriously worried about his fate. We know that true love in the end will be united and requited, and noble speeches are ten a penny, and Ellie MacManus can turn from her painting to give tongue to the best that ever came out of Boucicault:

> The fate of poor old Ireland is trembling in the balance and God forbid the patriot's chosen bride should prove unworthy of him. She suppressed a sob that swelled to her throat. She wiped the tears from her pale cheek. 'And No,' she added, 'Ellie MacManus will be worthy of Ireland and of the love of Fergus O'Carroll'.

When you have read that, you have read the weakest, perhaps, of Kickham as a writer of fiction and you are free to go on to a contemplation of his golden merits. And even the tearful heroics and melodramatics must be reckoned as part of his period, and must be seen, too, against the background of the iron courage of the man who lay so long in a dungeon and stayed unbroken. Or who, imprisoned for life by that defect of eyes and ears, sat patient but proud while a friend tapped signals on his knee to interpret for him the conditions under which the archbishop would allow him to practise his religion.

A man who carried those marks in his soul or body could be pardoned or, rather, greatly praised if his imagination set off around his own valley on a schoolboyish adventure in which a flogging yeoman was not the sort of monster that, in harsh history, Lieutenant Hempenstall, the walking gallows, actually was.

And in which a fat yeoman sergeant who, by accident, had his breast-plate sewn into the seat of his pants was hotly pursued by Vulcan, or Shaun Foddha, the smith, and stabbed by the smith's pike in his impregnable tail-end, and sent sailing (to the natural wonder of the smith) over a double ditch to land in the soft mud of a dyke.

For Kickham's world had not encountered the full horror of mechanized violence, and even the enemy must be let down easy. And Sergeant Bullfinch, resting thankfully in the mud, decides to have done with soldiering and to follow from that out the calling his paunch fits him for. He decides to be the cook at Garryroe Castle. It will be a great day for the world when all men of violence make similar or parallel decisions.

For the five tales contained in Kickham's *Tales of Tipperary* I find I have a particularly deep affection. They were the first of Kickham I read, reading them even before *Knocknagow*, and reading them in a Tyrone boyhood when, partly because of family origins in Kickham country and partly because of that music-hall song that had become a marching song, Tipperary seemed a faraway romantic place.

Years afterwards I find that they stand up well to rereading, bringing me into the homes of Tipperary that gave his greatest work its subtitle, and under the shadow of the mountain that dominated him, his work, and his people. For Kickham is a writer to whom, for good or ill, you must have a personal reaction, and a sentimental reaction. And you cannot have him if you do not accept his myth and his mystique of the mountain. It is in *Tales of Tipperary* that he wrote his most sustained passage of praise for the person, almost the deified person, of Slievenamon:

> Old Slieve-na-Mon (Sliabh na mBan) did we ever indulge in daydreams of which you were not part and parcel? Its sweetest draught was to contemplate the happy homes round thy base, freed forever from the despoiler.

Was the dream of Love? It was to thy azure outline the beloved one turned her eyes to hide the blush and the tear called up by the impassioned avowal. And when the trembling hand was at length yielded and the pure heart wooed and won – you, old mountain, peeped in through woodbines and sweetbriar upon a home scene, the like of which, alas, is but too seldom to be found save in the visions of a dreamer.

And when the time for such visions was gone by, and despair crept in where hope had been – when the cup of sorrow was drained to the dregs – was it not to Thee we fled like a child to its mother's lap – and Thou has heard the groan, which torture on the rack would fail to wring in the hearing of human ear?

And when every earthly hope had withered, save one – what was it? To sleep, the last, long, peaceful sleep beneath thy shadow. And saddest thought of all, is this too but a dream, destined never to be fulfilled? We do not wonder at the reply of the United Irishman when asked, after a life-long exile, why he returned to a land where there was not a single friend or acquaintance left to bid him welcome. 'I came back,' said the exile, 'to see the mountains'.

That is a curious passage, beginning with that image of positively simpering lovers straight out of some Victorian print called, perhaps, 'The Question'; going on to touch movingly on pain and loneliness, and on the man exiled in his prison cell for whom the vision of the mountain was luminous; and ending with that splendid story of the returning exile of Erin, for whom the mountains were still living though his friends were long dead; and remembering all the homes at the foot of the mountain and the people in them, and the unjust laws that battered at all their hopes of permanent happiness.

It was Kickham's natural bent to be a writer of rural and village idylls; and *Sally Cavanagh* and *Knocknagow* have in plenty those glowing pictures of a simple people contented with little. Like Carleton's people in *The Emigrants of Ahadarra*, they wanted only to live. But Kickham's revolutionary impulse meant that he could not, like Patrick Kennedy, the Wexford folklorist, confine himself to the idyllic things, to simple observation of the habits and ways of the people when they were left at peace.

For Kickham, the harsh realities kept breaking through: of poverty, rack-renting, the emigrant ship. His sweetest song about the nut-brown maiden from the banks of the Anner and the foot of Slievenamon ended up with the maiden dying of consumption in a foreign city. His great ballad about the strong young glensman, Patrick Sheehan, went by way of Sebastopol's trenches to leave the glensman a poor blind mendicant in Dublin's dreary jail. His fine song of love and the sheltering mountain, and the maiden met in the valley near Slievenamon is first sung by Susan Maher in the story 'Never Give Up' in *Tales of Tipperary*. It became, by the nature of the case, a song of revolution. Nor is it possible his true love to enfold unless the flag of revolution is also unrolled.

Kickham could become as melodramatic as any writer of tracts about the fate in store for Irish girls in the hovels of London or Chicago. But then, in all truth, the facts were melodramatic enough, and Kickham's ideal was a high, chivalrous and remote one, a little too high for the world he lived in and very nearly incomprehensible in ours. Yet it will always be a wonder to me how a man with his physical disabilities saw and heard his people so well, unless it was that he saw and heard them with his heart, that his very handicap increased his attentiveness and attachment. And the pages of *Tales of Tipperary* come to life with such vivid twists of speech and character:

> 'I was there myself the same day, Shemus,' said Joe Wholohan (talking of the faction fight), 'and the divil a harm we had in it only just to puck away at one another. I never seen fairer fightin' whatever made Father Ned get so savage about it, barrin' it was because Tim Mooney died of the fracture he got'.

And the man Thomson, who had got a shiner in the pub scrimmage from which 'that fool, Joe Wholohan, was obliged to be sent home on a car', meets the hunchback, Shemus Beg, next morning and, alluding to the deformity, says with splendid rural charity: 'How early you're loaded'. And Shemus not at all nonplussed says: 'It must be early seein' that you have only one of your shutters open yet'.

Those fragments, alone, display a man who had no illusions about his people. And I submit that he knew his people for now as well as for his own time. How sweetly, too, are the relations between ourselves and our neighbours studied in the evidence the British soldier gave against wild Paddy:

> 'Your worship, Bill Stumps, as was on guard last night, your worship, and this wild Irish fellow walks up to Bill and offers to box him, your worship, and when Bill charged him with the bayonet, the Irishman ups and knocks Bill down. He then lifts the sentry box into his cart and lifts Bill Stumps into the sentry-box and drives away home, your worship'.
>   'Ask him, your Honour, did I trate him dacent in my own house or not?'
>   At which Bill Stumps, grinning, honestly admits that Paddy is a right good fellow.

That sketch from Clonmel in bygone days is a fair introduction to some of the richest of the humour in *Knocknagow*. Just as the great stone-throwing contest in the story of 'Annie O'Brien' is a fine prelude for the epic contest between Matt Donovan and the Major that is at the heart of his finest book.

Any consideration of Kickham as a writer must inevitably be influenced by his nobility as a man and by the fact, too, that he is a national piety. But he who is still, I should hope and trust, so close to the heart of his people, observed and understood them with all the exactitude and intensity of the ideal Jamesian novelist, on whom nothing is lost. And at his best he wrote about them as only the best have written. It is something also that if we must number a novelist among our national pieties he should be one who has spoken and suffered for that liberty and equality of all Irishmen which still provide the principal problems we have to solve.

The road back to Knocknagow is a well-worn and a long one, back to that Cnoicin-na-Gabha near Cashel of Munster, on which, according to the living record of Humphrey O'Sullivan of Callan, 'heavy hail and snow fell in the July of 1835 and continued falling with a west wind until it ruined the potatoes'.

We'll break the bitter journey for a look at the novel *Sally Cavanagh, or the Untenanted Graves,* on my edition of which the teetotal publisher's blurb consists of this inanity: 'Though not so famous as *Knocknagow* many critics think that this novel is a finer literary work'. Even the syntax is at sea there and we are wisely not told who the many critics are.

Thackeray, or somebody, said about *The Vicar of Wakefield* that endearing and loveable as it was, and everybody in it, it was probably the most ill-constructed fable ever written. *Sally Cavanagh* runs it a close second, may even surpass it in that dubious distinction; and one of the odd things about the book is that it scarcely seems to be about Sally Cavanagh at all. Indeed, Kickham appears to be as seldom concerned with her in fiction as her neighbours are concerned to keep her out of the poor house. And the best that Brian Purcell, the young patriotic gentleman, can think of doing is to give Sally and her children a breakfast and a lift to that same poorhouse. He, also, in a fit of frenzy, slaughters his greyhounds because they eat too much: an action that nowadays we might call counterproductive.

Later, when it is all too late, the Cavanagh household is restored and we can only think that because Kickham wanted to write about the evils of the poorhouse – and why not? – he had to get Sally and her children there by hook or by crook.

The symbolism of the Untenanted Graves, the green mounds under which the dead children are not, is good, but it is so slightly treated as almost to be thrown away. Yet Kickham does many interesting things in that shapeless novel. My friend John Wilson Foster, in his book *Forces and Themes in Ulster Fiction,* wrote in relation to Michael McLaverty's first novel, *Call My Brother Back,* of the painful beauty of a first novel wrenched from deep feeling. *Sally Cavanagh* has something of that quality, and in it Kickham sets his themes, or the themes his time and place dictated to him; which could be the way with any worthwhile novelist. For instance: even from the misery of the poorhouse, Sally Cavanagh looks out and sees the mountain:

> She looked distractedly about her until her eyes rested on a blue moun-
> tain, ten miles away. She bent a long piercing gaze upon the mountain.

And then, uttering a wild shriek that rung through every corner of the palace of poverty . . . the broken-hearted woman rushed through the gate, her hands stretched out towards the mountain.

It is highly melodramatic in the style of many of the novelists of the period. Yet we must also remember that Irish society, with Famine always on the doorstep, with rackrenting and eviction and mass emigration, did drive the man who portrayed it towards melodrama. Carleton wrote the blood-red story of 'Wildgoose Lodge'. The Banins wrote the almost equally horrific story of Crohoore of the Billhook. Maria Edgeworth escaped melodrama because she was well protected by the walls of the Big House. She could at her ease write those tales of fashionable life which Balzac said reminded him of nothing.

Kickham in *Sally Cavanagh* saw the cars laden with the outcast children of Erin as they toiled wearily up the hill, through the gap, and he heard the wail of agony as if hearts were rent asunder as friend after friend turned back after bidding a last farewell. He described Mick Dunphy's miserable cabin, and four famishing children watching the pot, and the father on his knees trying with his breath to kindle the scraws. But Kickham also saw and described happy homes. And he revealed his wonderful ability to see into and describe the odd and comic activities of children. He observed the social pattern and faithfully described our multiple snobberies as they were, and as many of them still are.

In the story of Sean Gow, the smith, and his wife, who had holy war over whether a bird was a blackbird or a thrush, he handled well a piece of crude, comic folk-literature. And he did write, in that same story, one of the best descriptions of an Irish hunt, and the very best account of the fox that got away. So that there is, on the credit side, much to be said for *Sally Cavanagh*. What it lacks, in relation to his great work *Knocknagow*, is concerted movement and organization, that sense of the joys and sorrows of a whole community. In *Knocknagow* Kickham, as we say, took off. It is not a faultless book, no more than life itself is, but it is unique as every life is, or should be.

To begin with, the title is a fine resonant one and it is not possible to exaggerate the importance of the subtitle, *The Homes of Tipperary*. That was exactly what he intended to, and did, write about. He was a man for the hearth and the domestic felicities, provided always that the vision of the mountain could be seen from the window. And the novel opens well, clearly and crisply, and inviting you to read on, as the best books should:

It is Christmas Day. Mr Henry Lowe has just opened his eyes, and is debating with himself whether it is the grey dawn, or only the light of the young moon he sees, struggling through the two round holes in the window-shutters of his room.

We are told that he has on the previous day travelled eighty miles on the outside of the mailcoach from Dublin to a town which we may assume to have been Clonmel, then a dozen miles in a gig to the house in which he is now a guest; that he knows little of Ireland, having spent most of his life in what is oddly described as the 'Sister Country' that he is the nephew of Sir Garret Butler, the landlord; that he is the guest of his uncle's principal tenant, Maurice Kearney; that he is aware that he is a land-agent in embryo; that Ireland is not a safe place for land-agents; and that his room is on the ground floor. Then:

> He was beginning to succeed pretty well in calling up a vision of a blun-
> derbuss loaded to the muzzle with slugs, and two tall figures in frieze
> coats and knee-breeches with crape over their faces, when a tremendous
> report – as if the blunderbuss had gone off and burst – made him start to
> a sitting posture.

But it is only Mat Donovan, the Thrasher, thundering on the Knock-nagow Drum to lead the people to seven o'clock Mass. And the boom of the drum is as effective an opening for the novel as the great gong to which the curtain used to rise in the old Abbey Theatre.

The Englishman, preferably young, discovering Ireland, had since the time Lady Morgan wrote *The Wild Irish Girl* and Maria Edgeworth wrote *The Absentee* been a stock-in-trade of the Irish nineteenth-century novelist and playwright. Bernard Shaw, even, used it, but with a new ironic perception in *John Bull's Other Island*. With earlier writers it was part of a wish to do what they called delineate the characteristics of the Irish people, so that other peoples, particularly the English, should learn to know, respect and even love them. William Carleton, who was perhaps the most considerable Irish novelist of that century, put the matter clearly and with a good deal of pride. And a long time later James Joyce was to make a parallel and more startling declaration.

Kickham was also consciously delineating: he wanted to display the best about his people to everyone who read English. And it was tempting to try to display a young man of the English, or the very anglified Anglo-Irish being captured by easy Irish ways. But the trouble about Mr Lowe is that he is a woodener when compared with the real living people in the book, and Kickham, it might seem, forgets or ignores him in the crowd. Kickham knew more about English prisons than he did about polite, young, anglified or English gentlemen: he had had more experience of the prisons. Captain French, who throws the hammer against Mat the Thrasher, and Bob Lloyd, the amiable Protestant landlord, are real in a way in which Mr Lowe never succeeds in becoming.

He wanders about, vaguely and hopelessly admiring the two lovely ladies, Mary Kearney and Grace Kiely, who are, for a while, sharing the one roof with him; and, in the end, he and Richard Kearney, the doctor, and Captain French are off somewhere in India hunting a tiger. There are the makings of a model Castle Cawtholic in Richard Kearney. You feel that if Mr Lowe is going to find out anything about Kickham's people and the homes of Tipperary, he will have to step out of the pages and read Kickham for himself: like a character in Flann O'Brien's *At Swim-Two-Birds*.

But when the Knocknagow drum sounded in my ears (on a recent rereading) to set the people moving on that Christmas morning, and when I was prepared to relax, as it is so easy to do, into the warm world of Knocknagow, I postponed that relaxation for a time so as to cross-examine a few friends of mine on their attitude towards Kickham's novel. Quite frankly I was looking for (although I did not say so) adverse criticism, for I felt that my own attitude was one of too-easy acceptance. *Knocknagow*, for me, is crowded with all sorts of nostalgias: Tipperary and Tyrone, to find your own surname in a novel, the only one novel in which it occurs. For me *Knocknagow* may not be the greatest novel of the Irish nineteenth century nor the novel of that period that has most relevance to our own times, but it is certainly the most loveable, the one with least pretension, presenting easily to us a whole community of people who become precious to us because the warm heart of the novelist considered them to be precious.

The first friend I queried on the matter reacted much as I did myself, but that may have been because his name was Ryan and his father came from Bansha. Such circumstances would dispense with the need for any academic criticism. From other people I had some provocative statements that, I feel, are worth considering.

One man, and a pretty reputable one, said that he regarded Kickham – and that, from internal evidence, it seemed that Kickham regarded himself – as a poor man's Dickens. It is easy enough to see how that criticism originated; it might have been better put by saying an Irishman's Dickens, for Charles Dickens regarded himself as a poor man's Dickens. But any novelist then writing in English who wrote a long novel crowded with characters, moving easily from humour to pathos to tragedy to melodrama, and then round the ring again, and who allowed the novel to begin on a Christmas Day, was more than liable to be regarded as under the shadow of the great English master who did all those things so superbly.

Dickens was, after all, the mountain among the novelists of the time. Yet I can only think of one specifically Dickensian passage in anything I have read, or reread, of Kickham's. It occurs somewhere in *Sally Cavanagh*, and it happens to be very good and well worth the space it takes up. There is, also, in *Knocknagow* a passage that echoes Sydney Smith, whom Kickham had read and admired sufficiently to refer to him glowingly elsewhere in that novel. It is a passage of excellent political satire and well worth its space; nor on account of it would my friend think of referring to Kickham as a poor man's Sydney Smith.

It must also be remembered that earlier Irish novelists writing in English struggled to some extent under the shadow of Walter Scott who, in his turn, claimed to have drawn inspiration from Maria Edgeworth. William Carleton, when he wrote a book, not a good one, about Redmond Count O'Hanlon, was very conscious that he was putting himself into invidious comparison with the Wizard of the North writing about Rob Roy. But Carleton liberated himself from the shadow when he kept his eyes steadily on his own people; and when he adopted, as he easily did, the method and style of the Seanachie.

This gives rise to another and, I think, unjustified criticism of Kickham: that while he observed and well described the ordinary people and the strong farmers and half-gentry, he was not too closely akin, either in song or in story, with the Gaelic modes that were still well within reach of him; and that practically the only piece of Gaelic mythology in *Knocknagow* comes from Bessy Morris, the old rebel's grand-daughter, when she tells the well-known tale of how the mountain got its name, and how the women raced on the mountain for the love of the hero.

But that criticism is merely to say that Kickham lived long before the Gaelic League was thought necessary, longer before the League became propagandist, longer still before it became political. He was ahead of his time in many ways. To fault him for his being ahead of his time in every way is to make historical judgements through the wrong end of the tele-scope. William Carleton was a native speaker, yet his attitude towards Irish is always sentimental, never preservationist, not to speak of propa-gandist. It is, for him, the language of the heart, the language in which his father told stories and his mother sang songs; never the language of the new utilitarian ethic which then seemed to dominate the world and had, as its dark side of the moon, Irish famine, a few hours' journey from the hub of Empire in London: and had in London itself, and in Manchester and Birmingham, hovels of misery and slums described so fearfully by Eliza-beth Gaskell in her novel *Mary Barton*. The conditions she wrote about were to be studied with stupendous results by Engels and Marx. After all, Britain provided the first great exemplar of industrial capitalism – greed is a simpler word and an older one – in action.

The sternest criticism of all that I encountered was that, while Kickham was prepared to give up his life for an idealized Ireland, he might not have been prepared to give up his social position. This can be a strong argu-ment, or can be made to seem so when stated at first. Yet I honestly feel that it is a meeting-ground for multiple misunderstandings.

First of all: if a man gives up his life he, *ipso facto* and for all practical purposes, gives up his social position. The criticism is based on the unde-niable truth that the novelist who wrote *Knocknagow* was very aware of the social distinction in the society he was writing about: the Big House and the Lord, and the landlord, the rascally agent and his more rascally son.

Then there was Bob Lloyd, the good but somewhat feckless landlord, and his man-made sister with the elegant notions. There was the strong farmer, Maurice Kearney, with a son a doctor and a daughter who never seemed to do anything but be good and beautiful, and play the piano and visit the poor. There were the farmer with a lease, the farmer without a lease, the tradesman, the cattle-jobber, all very conscious that they had an independence denied to the small farmer. Then on the bottom rung, and always excepting the tramp on the road or the pauper in the poorhouse, there was the labouring man or servant-boy, never supposed to look above his station to marriage with the daughter of a strong farmer.

Yet in *Knocknagow* it is the labouring man who, in the person of Mat Donovan, the Thrasher, who is the noblest figure in the book, even if his English is not the best. And the author's sympathy and the dictates of the sentimental novel of the time make him emerge triumphant in the end.

It has been objected to me, incidentally, that Mary Kearney, daughter of the strong farmer, and Grace Kiely, daughter of the patriotic but apolitical doctor, never wet a hand in the course of the whole book. They walk about, they talk, they visit poor Norah Leahy, dying in a decline, and sentimentalize over her without killing themselves to find out what the state of her health actually is. They carry on prim Victorian communications with young men; they play the piano and sing the sentimental songs of the time, and the recurrent sentimental reference to 'The Coolin' only makes it more clear how far they are away from the real thing. It is, though, once recorded in the novel that Mary Kearney prepares the dinner while her mother is otherwise engaged.

Yet surely the point is that Kickham was not writing *Knocknagow* as the revolutionary and political propagandist that he was, but as the novelist that he also was. Somebody said that Disraeli's politics were romantic and his romances (or novels) were political. For myself, and many others, his politics and novels are equally at fault through sheer falsity and contrivance.

Kickham was wiser. He wasn't James Connolly, Michael Davitt or Fintan Lalor, but he was aware of much that was and was to be important to them. And as a novelist, his concern was to write it down as it was, to record the people he knew and their social usages. Which does not mean that he accepted those social usages, any more than he approved of all the people. Although, indeed, his natural sympathies were very wide.

He wrote much against the evils of emigration. But as an observer of his time, he had to accept the fact that an American dollar could be beneficial: Bessy Morris's father and Tommy Fahy prospered in the New World. No man was more aware of the evils of the Irish land-system. But, as a novelist, he made use of the possibility, as indeed Goldsmith did in *The Vicar of Wakefield*, that a good, if eccentric, landlord could also do good because he had the power. That the origins and basis of such power were evil did not alter the story.

Kickham had the iron courage to face up to the English prisons of the time which were not exactly convalescent homes. Yet, because he was a nineteenth-century novelist writing according to a sentimental mode, Grace Kiely swoons when she discovers that Hugh Kearney has all that time been preserving a lock of her hair. She is the only Kiely woman I ever heard of who swooned under those, or any, circumstances.

The small amount of intrusion the propagandist actually makes into the novel may not please propagandists, but it makes for a better novel. His concern was to describe the homes, the hearths, the people, the land and the little river, the mountain above. The one Dickensian thing he did do was to create, or rather to preserve, a whole world, and for our benefit. Shane Leslie said of William Carleton that he caught his types 'before Ireland made the greatest plunge in her history and the Famine had cleaned her to the bone. For the hardiest of the race rose up and went away into the West of which their storytellers had been telling them for a thousand years'.

Kickham, in a melancholy mood, lamented that that same flight to the West meant that we might be a doomed race. Mary Kearney thanked God that there were happy homes still in Tipperary, but then said sadly that Knocknagow was gone. Mat Donovan met his great opponent, Captain French, on his way back from the wars, and with one arm only, so that never again would he throw the hammer. And when the Captain asked Mat about the hurlers, he was told that the hurlers were gone.

The landlords, and their agents, and the men of the crowbar may have destroyed most of Knocknagow and banished its people. Yet Kickham gave them a life that will last as long as our literature. And if we have clear eyes we may see ourselves in our ancestors and hope even for a better and peaceful future.

❦ 11 ❧

John Montague: Dancer
in a Rough Field

IF I WERE, AS I AM, BEGINNING a rereading of John Montague, or if I were advising others where to begin reading him, I would go, and send those others, to the heart of his collection *Tides*, which had the Poetry Book Society Recommendation in 1970. And to two works there, one of them a quite horrifying prose-poem entitled, with a cold irony that is typical of Montague, 'The Huntsman's Apology'. As you will see, it is not likely to be used as an argument for the defence by the unspeakable who pursue the inedible, or by those genial knee-booted Kerrymen who know by the inner voice that little hunted hares really love the chase. This is it:

> You think I am brutal and without pity but at least I execute cleanly because, like any true killer, I wish to spare the victim. There are worse deaths. I have seen the wounded bird trail her wing, and attract only the scavenger. 'Help me' he croaks as he hops near. One dart of her beak would settle him, for he is only a pale disciple of Death, whom he follows at a distance. But she needs sympathy and when he calls 'I am more unhappy than you' her womanly heart revives and she takes him under her broken wing. Her eyesight is poor and her senses dulled but she feels an echo of lost happiness as he stirs against her breast. She does not realize that he is quietly settling down to his favourite meal of dying flesh, happily enveloped in the smell of incipient putrefaction. The pain grows and spreads through her entire body until she cries aloud but it is too late to shake off his implanted beak. He grinds contentedly on and, as she falls aside, his bony head shoots up, like a scaldy out of a nest. His eye is alert, his veins coursing with another's blood, and for a brief moment, as he steps across the plain without looking back, his tread is as firm as a conqueror's.

The second work is brief, called 'A Meeting', and is from the ninth-century Irish:

The son of the King of the Moy
met a girl in green woods a mid-summer's day:
she gave him black fruit from thorns
& the full of his arms
of strawberries, where they lay.

The startling thing is that both are poems about varieties of love, or about love at different stages of development or decay. They come at the heart of a book that holds other fine love-poems and in which the blurb, with perhaps an echo of the poet's voice, says with a great deal of justification that the directness and passion of Montague's love-poems have been admired, and his feeling for people and landscape, and claims that in *Tides* all these are seen as a part of a larger struggle where life and death are interwoven like the rhythms of the sea. Love in green woods at midsummer has its black fruit from thorns and a plenteousness of strawberries. Love can also be a rasping and cankerous death.

He has a nightmare in which he lies 'Strapped in dream helplessness' and some hand unseen, unknown, is cutting up the body of the beloved, till the rhythm of the blade rising, descending, 'Seems the final meaning of life'. Released from the dreadful dream, he lies in a narrow room, 'Low-ceilinged as a coffin', while outside the Liffey knocks against the quay walls and the gulls 'curve and scream' over the Four Courts: Gandon's great domed building, the flower of the eighteenth century, the heart in Ireland of unalterable law. There is much agony in these love-poems, a something not allowed for when, in one of the most celebrated passages of raving about love, Shakespeare allows Berowne to take off for seventy or so lines, and a lover's eye will gaze an eagle blind, a lover's ear will hear the lowest sound, a lover's feeling is more soft and sensible than are the tender horns of cockled snails; but Berowne had not at that moment, and as Shakespeare well knew, arrived at consummation, not to speak of satiation. Montague, lean and sharp and soft and sensible, as Berowne uses the word, sees his lovers absurdly balanced on the springs of a bed, shadows swooping, quarrelling liked winged bats, bodies turning like fish 'in obedience to the pull & tug of your great tides'. A wind-swept holiday resort on the shore of the North Sea becomes a perfect setting for the monster of unhappiness, 'an old horror movie come true', to crawl out of the moving deeps and threaten love. The hiss of seed into a mawlike womb is the whimper of death being born; and lovers whirl and turn in their bubble of blood and sperm before, from limitless space, the gravities of earth claim them. Back from the business of loving, resuming workaday habits with the putting-on of clothes, the lover finds himself, comically driving through late traffic, and changing gears with the same gesture that a while ago had eased the 'snowbound heart and flesh' of the beloved. It is a bitter sort of comedy.

It is scarcely then by accident that Montague places in the middle of all these love-poems the best rendering, from the Irish of the ninth century, of the love-dirge, or bitter memory of past loves and bitter consciousness of bodily decay, of the *Cailleach Beara*, the Hag or Old Woman of Beare, which is the south-western peninsula between Bantry Bay and Kenmare Bay, the land of the O'Sullivans. The Cailleach, a formidable ancient, overburdened with all knowledge and weariness and, sometimes, all wickedness, is a recurring figure in Celtic mythologies and shows her face, on occasions and on various bodies, in Montague's poetry.

A one-eyed hag, she – or the poet who interpreted her, as Montague does eleven centuries later – reckons that her right eye has been taken as a down-payment on her claim to heaven; a ray in the left eye has been spared to her that she may grope her way to heaven's gate. Her life has come to be a retreating sea with no tidal return. Gaunt with poverty, she, who once wore fine petticoats, now hunts for rags to cover her body. The great and gener-ous gentlemen who once made love to her have now ridden on into eternity, their places taken by skinflints, well-matched with girls who now think less of love than of money; and she looks at her arms, now bony and thin, that once caressed with skill the limbs of princes. Yet she gives thanks to God that she has lived and loved and feasted royally and misspent her days, even though now, to offer up that gratitude, she prays by candlelight in a darkened oratory and drinks not meat nor wine with kings, but sips whey in a nest of hags: a memory. Never more can she sail youth's sea, she hears the cry of the wave, 'Whipped by the wintry wind', and knows that today no one will visit her, neither nobleman nor slave; and the poem rises to that recurring consideration of life as ebb and flow, and it may be that it was that very image that attracted Montague so strongly to the ancient poem:

> Flood tide
> And the ebb dwindling on the sand!
> What the flood rides ashore
> The ebb snatches from your hand.
>
> Flood tide
> And the sucking ebb to follow!
> Both I have come to know
> Pouring over my body . . .
>
> Man being of all
> Creatures the most miserable
> His flooding pride always seen
> But never his tidal turn.
>
> Happy the island in mid-ocean
> Washed by the returning flood . . .

In this collection, one of the two most striking poems is certainly 'Life Class'. It opens calmly, clinically, a cool detailed survey of the body there to be studied, the hinge of the ankle-bone defining the flat space of a foot, the calf's heavy curve sweeping down against the bony shin, the arm cascading from shoulder-knob to knuckle, shapes as natural, as inanimate almost, as sea-worn caves, as pools, boulders, tree-trunks. This is the artist in the neolithic cavern recording in wonderment the skeleton of the life he sees, an art that may have been as utilitarian as modern engineering. Until the awakening comes to the existence of secret areas: 'hair sprouting crevices, odorous nooks & crannies of love, awaiting the impress of desire'. Thereafter, the frenzy of the desert father tormented by images and visions that drag man down 'to hell's gaping vaginal mouth'. Until the eye and the mind swing the other way and the phantom of delight (Wordsworth did not follow it, neither into the desert nor to hell's mouth – as far as we know, that is) becomes an ordinary housewife earning a few shillings extra, a spirit, good or evil, yet a woman too: and the very soul of the machine blossoms, 'a late flower', into a tired smile over a chilled, cramped body.

The other poem, 'The Wild Dog Rose', follows the woman into more terrible and more holy places. It confronts again the *cailleach*, the ancient enchanted hag who recurs in our mythologies and in Montague's poetry. The image of the *cailleach* in this poem is a figure who haunted his childhood, lived in a cottage, circled by trees and with a retinue of whinging dogs, on a hill-slope in south Tyrone. A grown man, a young poet, he walks to see her and the outside appearance is as it was when she used to terrify his boyhood: the great hooked nose, the cheeks dewlapped with dirt, staring sunken eyes, mottled claws, a moving nest of shawls and rags. But she talks to him gently and sadly about her memories of youth, her own unimportant sorrows: she is kin to the *Cailleach Beara* and in her own *coulisse* in time, and the dogrose shines in the hedge: and there is no sense of horror until she tells him of the night when a drunken oaf staggered into her cottage and attempted to rape her. She prays to the Blessed Virgin for help and after a time she breaks his grip, he sleeps and snores on the floor, then awakes in shame and lurches away across the wet bogland:

> 'The wild Rose
> is the only rose without thorns,'
> she says, holding a wet blossom
> for a second, in a hand knotted
> as the knob of her stick.
> 'Whenever I see it, I remember
> the Holy Mother of God and
> all she suffered'.

That image of the *cailleach* reappears again when, in Montague's poem-sequence *The Rough Field*, he stands squarely facing into the past and present of his own place and people, and meditates also on some of his own personal agonies. He has a regulated passion for retracing his steps, changing and rearranging.

There is much more in the collection *Tides* than I have here indicated: more than love and lust, and woman, young and old, and ancient mythologies. There are, for instance, wise words to and about Beckett, and about Joyce, and a moving farewell to places and parents, and a seagull's view of his own town which misses only history and religion; which Montague is not to miss when later he takes a more than seagull's view of Garvaghey (Garbh Achaidh), 'The Rough Field', from where he comes. The collection, too, is rich, as is his earlier poetry, with the preoccupations of a man who has known, and to the bone, the ways of three countries: Ireland, France and the United States.

He was born in New York in 1929, of Irish parents, who had left Ireland in the confusion following the Troubles of the 1920s. From an early age, as he said to Mary Leland in an interview article in *The Irish Times*, (23 November 1976), he was aware of the confusion of the time through the unhappiness of his parents and had also an 'emerging sense of bi-location', out of which he was to make a theme. As a child he was shipped back to Ireland and grew up on a farm in south Tyrone with his father's unmarried sisters, somewhat isolated from the rest of his family, a situation that has also left its mark on his work.

Something of this I myself was aware of from away back. In my final year in high school, in 1936, a young fellow called Montague, American-born, came into third year and right away became of a group who were attempting to found a school magazine. Several of us then thought that this young man was so bright in a literary way that he was destined, or doomed, to become a writer. As it happened, he became a medical doctor, and it wasn't until the late 1940s that a young man, whose name I was already aware of in the magazines and elsewhere, came into my house in Clontarf with some other college people of the time and said, quietly and confidently, that he would be the writer of the Montagues and that I had, for a while, gone to school with his elder brother.

By his own words, written down two years ago for a revised edition of his first collection, *Poisoned Lands*, he was not at that time as confident as he seemed. In the early 1950s he was 'discovering with awe' that he might possibly 'be able to write something like the kind of modern poetry' he admired. But in the 'acrimony and insult' of the poetic world of Dublin at the time, he found out that the atmosphere was against doing anything of the kind. To explain the subtleties, more social than literary, involved in all that would need an essay five times as long as this one. The easiest way to understanding would be to do as I have done: come to Dublin permanently, say at the age of twenty and in 1940, and live there ever since, seeing it, I hope, steadily and seeing it whole. Voltaire, you'll remember, suggested to somebody who was anxious to do something of the sort that one way to found an enduring religion would be to be crucified and to rise from the dead.

✑ 12 ✑

Sean O'Faoláin:
A Tiller of Ancient Soil

SEAN O'FAOLÁIN'S FIRST BOOK appeared in 1932 when the author was the same age as the century. It was *Midsummer Night Madness*, a most notable collection of short stories, and it immediately placed the author among the Masters in Ireland, or in any country or age you care to think of, a position that he held and steadily fortified over the years, as you may readily see for yourself by consulting the fine three-volume edition of his collected short stories.

Forty-plus years ago when I was attempting, with great impertinence, to write about his short stories, I came up with something like this:

> It is not easy to find an exact description for O'Faoláin's mastery of the short story. There is easiness and grace, and a preference for the significant moment which can frequently be the contemplative moment, and more important for O'Faoláin, or for any other wise man, than the platform called Plot or the unreality called a Central Character. Life, O'Faoláin has always maintained, has no central characters, and life flows through his stories so easily that it is possible to lose sight of the art involved. Humour breaks like coloured bubbles on the smooth flow, a whirling twist of the water reminds us that life can be cruel and terrible and heedless of the results of its own cruelty. There are moments deep with contemplation, silent like some lost valley in Muskerry, yet alive with the life of silent places. There are stories as crowded with jostling characters, and words and ideas, as any lane in the city of Cork. And that city has importance in so much of what O'Faoláin has written. Life began there, and exile begins where life begins. Reading his stories you can get, at times, the feeling that, for him, memory is neither a locked box nor a tidy room with objects on orderly shelves, but a living body still growing and capable of intense pain.
>
> Frankie Hannafey is one of three significant brothers in O'Faoláin's novel of exile – actual exile in the States, spiritual exile in Ireland, and ironically entitled *Come Back to Erin*. Frankie, remembering his childhood,

124

feels 'as if Death works on us by gnawing away the beginning, creeping after us daily, eating away the road over which there is no return, until at the end there is one last day or two left; and then – the pit'.

That was, more or less, what I was trying to say forty-plus years ago.

When the third volume of the collected stories appeared, I found I was still struggling to describe or define that most urbane and learned man who, after William Yeats, has been the greatest encouragement and inspiration to Irish writers of our time. There was also, a voice tells me, a Dubliner by the name of Joyce. And a few others.

Stories, novels, biographies, autobiography, books about travel in Ireland and Italy, criticism, translations from the Irish and even, on the side, a play for the Abbey – the achievement was awesome and, perhaps, even disheartening to those of us who were trying to do our best, even if the example was inspiring. One book I always missed from that list because, for all I know, it was never put together. That would be a collection of, or at least a selection from, the leading articles written when he was editing the literary magazine *The Bell*, and giving most invaluable support to what we may still be bold enough, or antiquated enough, to describe as the cause of civilization in Ireland.

The first time I ever heard O'Faoláin speak in public was at a bookfair in the Mansion House in Dublin, some time in the 1940s. It was a most impressive occasion. He was at the height of what I may call his Bellism – eloquent, provoking to those who provoked, as the old Spaniard might have said in the movie of *For Whom the Bell Tolls*, even provokingly civilized, a state of being that can rattle a lot of people. With his friend and fellow-Corkman Frank O'Connor, he maintained a most reasonable and ultimately effective attack on the absurd literary censorship of the period: a wearisome business and even wearisome to look back on.

He had also about him then the stormy reputation of having upset many accepted ideas on our history and politics by his biographical study *King of the Beggars* of the Liberator, Daniel O'Connell who, Balzac said, incarnated a nation. That notable book appeared in 1938 and had been preceded by a lively study of Constance Markievicz, one of the dear shadows of the poem Yeats wrote about the light of evening and Lissadell: a lady of the gentry who took to the cause of the people and to the streets with a pistol. To the misfortune of one policeman . . .

But O'Faoláin's study of the Great Hugh O'Neill, who had fought the armies of the first Elizabeth, was to follow in 1942 and, later still and perhaps to balance the boat, came a study of John Henry Newman who, like the others, had had some misfortunes in Ireland and who might, by some, be also regarded as a rebel.

O'Faoláin's first novel, *A Nest of Simple Folk*, appeared in 1933. The title was a courtly salute to Turgenev, but that was the only connection, for the novel is very much 'out of' Ireland. At the close of his autobiographical volume, *Vive Moi!* (1965), he said of that novel:

> It was an historical novel, or family chronicle, based on everything I had known, or directly observed in the countryside, of my mother's people, and the city life of my mother and father away back . . . in Cork City. So that, in this book that I am now writing, that novel . . . links these last pages with my earliest pages describing my childhood. It was a child's view of the world brought into relation to a grown man's view of the world. The grown man was, in his cave of Self, explaining to the child he once had been what it really was that he thought he saw as a child. It was a relating of aspirations nourished in innocence to the world experienced in knowledge. While I was working at it a friend might have asked me, 'What are you writing about?', and I might, for short, have said, 'About Limerick and Cork between 1840 and 1916'. But it would not have been true. Just as a critic reading the novel might have said, 'He here describes life in Ireland over three generations,' and it would not have been true. I was writing about dreams . . . I was hearing every time – no matter what I was writing about – the drums of my boyhood dreams.

The novel *Bird Alone* came two years later and the drums of boyhood may have by that time beaten off into the dim distance. For here the novelist is in conflict with himself , and with his country and people. He once said that Henry James writing on Hawthorne did not know the half of it, that a few more conflicts would not have done Henry James any harm, might even have made him as good a writer as Hawthorne, who 'faced so many problems – and kept sweet'. O'Faoláin might have said to Edward Garnett that the real problem for the Irish writer was to keep sweet about his material, not to go sour on it. And Garnett would have roared at him to give Ireland hell; and that he would have had to reply that he did not want to do that because, in his divided heart, he loved his people.

Corney Crone in *Bird Alone* is surrounded and, perhaps, entrapped by the lights, colours, odours and sounds (if there are or should be any) of the sanctuary. Yet he thinks and feels that his tragedy was not that he did not believe in men but that he could not believe in what men believed.

Then, thirty years after the writing of *Bird Alone*, O'Faoláin looked at an old notebook of the years that formed the basis of the novel: 'odd thoughts, wonderings and problems of the soul, and I am not surprised that they all look slightly daft to me now'.

Socrates, looking backwards, must have thought that he had wasted a lot of breath. Yet it seemed to me some years ago, on my fourth reading of *Bird Alone*, a novel I have long admired, that for a man at variance with the ideas on life and history accepted by many of his countrymen, the inevitable place to begin a statement was with the betrayal by bishops and politicians of the Uncrowned King, Charles Stewart Parnell, the man who for a few brief years was even more than the Liberator. Few Irish writers, or few Irishmen who gave serious thought to anything, but were not, over a half-century, affected by that agony.

When Conor Cruise O'Brien first printed his brilliant essay 'The Parnellism of Sean O'Faoláin', I felt that the work in biography of O'Faoláin would not be complete until he had written a study of Parnell. It was, as we know, Conor Cruise O'Brien who was to write that study. He also has meditated much on that classical tragedy.

The agonizing love-story in *Bird Alone* is not, as Cornelius Crone early realizes, simply the surrender of lover to lover, but a war between the two worlds in which they suffer, separate and apart. There was example for it: not in Cork but in fair Verona. Corney, with Parnell in his mind and, even more potently, with the blood of his grandfather, Fenian revolutionary and anti-cleric, in his veins, cannot accept the suffocating, cloistral atmosphere of the house of the beloved. The act of love might seem to be, as I once heard it said of an affair that began in a somewhat similar fashion but did not, fortunately, last long enough for disaster, like tossing the tall candle-holders off the Irish altar.

For a brief moment the living, fighting figure of Parnell helps to hold the young lovers together:

> There were two other places where we used to meet, and one was when, with Christy and my grander, we tore after the warring factions who turned the city into a bedlam at every political meeting. For, however much her father grumbled and disapproved, she loved to watch the stones flying, and the stub-legged police crashing their batons on flesh and bone, and women screaming, and the tar-barrels sending their black smoke into the sky. She and I were mad Parnellites in those days and when we shouted his name as we swayed back and forth in the Mêlée, we felt every shout as a blow for the old cause; it was a triumph for us if we saw old Phil, my grander, up on the wagonette, his badge in his coat, his stick waving down to the surging sea of faces, and behind him in his place the pale face and burning eyes of The Chief.

Then the Chief, the Uncrowned King, is betrayed and dead, and desolation and death follow as the night the day, and Corney is a bird alone, a heron without a mate in an expanse of grass, an exile among his own people. There are echoes of the young Yeats giving a tongue to Aleel, the poet, who must out where wind cries and water cries and curlew cries: 'How does the story go that calls them the three oldest cries in the world?'

In the words, above-quoted, from Frankie Hannafey in the novel *Come Back to Erin*, there was more than the echoing of a phrase to remind one of the Book of Job. Three of O'Faoláin's four novels deal with old men. The fourth and last novel was, as we shall see, a special case. One of those three old men comes, at times, close to the God-permitted sufferings of

Job. Corney Crone in *Bird Alone* acquires Job's patience, although he applies it not in relation to the will of God but in relation to 'those little accidents' that prevent some men 'from taking part in the affairs of their city, or from marrying a little wife and bringing up a family in the fear and love of God' (Thomas Hardy's 'Chance').

It might have seemed that for O'Faoláin, the genuine rebel against the beliefs of other men and his fellowmen, is always an exile. Frankie Hannafey is left, in the nineteen twenties, isolated by the end of a revolution, an exile in New York, an exile when he comes back to Erin. Corney Crone never holds a gun in his hand and never, apart from a journey all the way to Wapping Wall, seems to have left Ireland. But his life ends in exile, brooding upon his first and last and only and rebellious love-affair. The old age of Corney Crone, his old man's love for morning and evening, has a place among the classical stories of exile: the exile of a man from his people, of man's spirit in the world of men:

> For I am become an old man and my friends are few, and that new faith I set out to find I never did find, and because I have sinned all my life long against men, that whisper of God's reproof, who made men, has been my punishment. I have denied life, by defying life, and life has denied me. I have kept my barren freedom, but only *sicut homo sine adjustorio inter mortuous liber* – a freeman among the dead.

The irony, for which we all in Ireland had reason to be grateful, was that the man who wrote so feelingly of exile and alienation had, also, devoted his intellectual life to his country's welfare. To compound that irony, and with a sardonic humour of which only he would have been capable, he published as late as 1979 the novel *And Again*. That was the life story, or the two life stories, of a man who, by a double trick of the gods, finds himself growing backwards, or whatever, into youth and boyhood and worse. When I began to read that novel, I thought, simply, that the novelist could not get away with it, that nobody could, not even the gods themselves. But the novelist was so plausible that once you began to check statistics, the laugh was on you, and you had accepted the monstrous impossibility that provided him with the framework for an amazing, amusing, learned, wise, human book about life.

And talking of the gods, one of the ladies in the double life of that man may be allowed these courageous words:

> My own feeling is that the gods have long since forgotten the whole thing as they so often seem to have forgotten this world they idly made one supernal morning when playing with a handful of Olympian cloud, out of which, boredly, kicked into limitless space, man as through millions of years created every speck of the splendours and miseries of civilized life.

So twelve years ago I was wrestling with that novel *And Again* and this was, more or less, how it affected me:

Only a fool would halt a masque to challenge a fact. That fine statement is not my own. I borrow it from this novel. But since it is to me the best if not the only opening for a consideration of this book, it seemed a shame to disfigure it with quotation marks. Nowadays, anyway, quotation marks always turn up in the wrong places.

So when Bob Younger, the hero (Wow!) of this novel makes such odd statements as the one I am about to quote, you can reach for your ready-reckoner or adding machine, or type it out and send it to your community's computing-centre. But you might be foolishly wasting good time and coming between yourself and much enlightenment and, what is more important, entertainment. You may also find, as I did on the one occasion, when I was fool enough to try or bother, that the statistics check out.

For the novelist is so plausible that once you begin to check statistics, the laugh is on you and you have accepted the monstrous impossibility that provides him with the framework for an amazing, amusing, wise, human book about life, as we call it, and love, as we call it. The monstrous impossibility is that a man could live his life, or something resembling his life, over again, backways, or from the end to the beginning which proves also to be an end.

Sean O'Faoláin once wrote an excellent work of, say, literary history, under the title of *The Vanishing Hero*, and you will see what I am ponderously hinting at when you finish this book. He had written many distinguished books and it should have been no matter for wonder that he offered his novel as he approached his eightieth birthday. A little before that I had the privilege of meeting him and telling him that he looked like twenty-eight; and afterwards, and when this novel appeared, I was sorry that I didn't say to him that he was getting younger.

This is the statement, made by Bob Younger, which I said I was about to quote:

> It is my fourteenth birthday as the world wags, in my hundreth and sixteenth year thanks to the fancy of the gods, fifty one years since I was reborn. I have fourteen more years to live. To live? Consciously to decline into infancy. This March wind in from Dublin Bay is a white hare flying fur-blown under the north-east wind across Rosmeen. How soon shall I start sleeping alone? Last night as she undressed she said . . .

Nana is his mistress or wife, or whatever, for that generation at any rate, and she tell us with, not unnaturally, something of a good woman's wonder: 'Gratefully I gave him my Indian Summer. Gratefully he gave me his boy's body, his Springtime bird-song and nesting-time, daffodils, bursting buds, even though I knew at the back of my bewildered head that all these were the hints and foresigns not of his opening Summer but of the shut time of his life. And where would I be then? A professor of philosophy with fog in her hair . . .'

Nana is, indeed, a professor of philosophy, or a lecturer in philosophy in Trinity College, Dublin. She is the daughter of Anador, who painted strange pictures of disaster and the betrayal of all childish dreams: 'Three small boys in harlequin clothes falling off an elephant, a hooting storm upsetting a merry, youthful picnic, a pair of baby hands in the sky gaily shaking a pepper pot and a salt sprinkler over a baroque cathedral, a gaily-coloured Children's Zoo with all the cage doors open'.

Anador was the daughter of Ana, who was very much a woman of the world; and all of them in their time, each in her own generation, had had the privilege of being beloved by Bob Younger.

Somewhere in the blanks of a mind that the gods have depatterned, mildly though, and not with the style of Dr Ewen Cameron, there is a masked wife and a child in an empty railway-carriage, in or on an empty steppe. Then in the United States which seems, at a certain stage in his development, to be the only place for him (if development is the word I'm searching for) there is a vital young lady who may be his great-grand-daughter. If you feel licked, call in the computer.

How did all this come about? There have been precedents: that tormented man who lived though the shapes of all flesh and fish and fowl. There were Melmoth the Wanderer and the Wandering Jew and others, one of whom I once met in a pub in Crossmolina. Bob Younger got into the line not by making a deal with the gods, for nobody gets away with that one, but by being tricked by the gods into a second life, going into it backways, as they trick us all into one life, short or long, good, bad or middling, or a bollicks at the best of times.

Like the gods themselves, Sean O'Faoláin here cheats a bit or, to be more exact, mocks us, gently though, not as magpies mock cats nor as wanton boys dispose of flies. The questions you ask indignantly from one page, he slyly answers from the next or from a few pages further on. And you can only conclude that he has given much thought to the merest mechanics of growing younger, that he knows a lot more about it, if he were only willing to talk.

For instance: after one hundred pages scrambled on the margin: 'Doesn't anybody ever say to him: You're getting younger. Or better in bed'.

Then I turned the page to find that I had been foxed into so scrawling.

'Middle age has stolen on me. Anador did not notice it until her fifty-fifth birthday when she said crossly one Sunday afternoon from pillow to pillow: "You've changed." So had she. One does at fifty-five. What should I do? Dye my hair white?'

And about his earnest attempts to disguise his advancing youth:

I used to carry a walking stick, limp whenever I remembered to, wear spectacles of plain glass, complain of secret ailments, try to look doomed. A waste of time. All these pensioners around me, bond holders, coupon clippers, rentiers, septuagenarians, octogenarians are as jealous of one another's salubrity as a bevy of old bull fighters, a brood of quondam boxers, voiceless divas, superannuated bishops, throneless kings, jowled movie stars twirling their thumbs, rereading their morning papers, peeping through their lace curtains, studying the oracles of their bowels, contemplating the future of their immortal souls.

As I have said: he has given thought to this matter of growing old, even if it means growing young at the same time.

In style and wisdom and knowledge, this novel was an outstanding performance from one of the most civilized Irishmen of our time, to whom Ireland, and particularly everyman in it who has ever tried to write or keep a clear mind, has reason to be grateful. O'Faoláin talked about everything. Out of that novel alone one could compile: 'A Thought from Sean O'Faoláin for every day in two lifetimes'.

I was about to quote him on Banagher and the bogs around it and on Descartes and/or Dallas. But one lifetime would not be long enough.

O'Faoláin's *Collected Stories* were complete in 1982, in three handsome volumes (from Constable) an ornament to any shelf: one thousand, three hundred and fifteen pages and a good round total of ninety stories.

There was no guarantee, though, at that time that O'Faoláin would not add to the ninety. The third volume contained six previously unpublished stories, written after his eightieth birthday. When about ten years previously a luncheon was given in his honour by the then just-about-surviving Irish Academy of Letters and with the aid of Allied Irish Banks, he said: 'Now that I have retired'. That was generally and quite rightly regarded as the best joke in a most pleasant and humorous performance.

The first time that I heard Sean O'Faoláin speak in public was, as I said, at a bookfair in the Dublin Mansion House sometime in the early 1940s. I recall that it was the year of the publication of Maura Laverty's first novel, *Never No More*, extracts from which had, I think, appeared in *The Bell*. He was then at the height of his Bellism, eloquent, provoking to those who provoked as the old Spaniard said in the movie of *For Whom the Bell Tolls*, even provokingly civilised, a state of being that can rattle a lot of people. He had also about him the reputation of having upset many accepted ideas on history and politics by his study of Daniel O'Connell.

He was wearing then what I take the liberty of calling the second of his three faces: the face reproduced on the dustcover of the second volume of the collected stories. For it was a happy and amusing idea to use three different photographs on the three dustcovers: of the young man, of the middle-aged man, of the octogenarian or patriarch; and particularly since they all represented the novelist who had but recently in the novel *And Again* written about a man growing young again, not the Vanishing Hero about whom he had also written a book but about the hero renewing his youth like the eagle.

At the time of that Bookfair in the Dublin Mansion House, two of his eight separate collections of short stories had appeared: *Midsummer Night Madness* (1932) and *A Purse of Coppers* (1937). So that in the three volumes that were completed by Constable in 1982, we had, and have, more than half a century of what the writer did in the art he favoured most and practised as well as, or better than, any writer in this century; and about which he has theorized with suavity and reason in *The Short Story*.

Even in one of those additional six stories he had, with every right, theorized in a most amusing and instructive fashion. He called the story 'The Wings of the Dove: A Modern Sequel'. He wrote: 'To rewrite a great novel as a short story can only be regarded as an impertinence or an experiment. I have made the experiment with "The Wings of the Dove" to find out what is gained or lost by writing fiction briefly or at length'.

A portion of this story can be regarded as, and is, delightful parody. Particularly when the reader is reminded of the length of time it took Martin Densher to 'pick-up' Kate Croy; and it wasn't even their first meeting. In my edition of the Henry James novel, it takes four pages or about one thousand, five hundred words: the longest and slowest pick-up in love, lust, lechery, literature or loitering with intent.

Such mannerisms did, perhaps, drive E.M. Forster to be caustic about Henry James and made André Gide write, not too wisely, that the people imagined by Henry James were only winged busts from whom all the weight of flesh was absent, that their figures, while lighted from every side lacked 'the cone of inexplicable shadow where the suffering soul lies hidden'.

Yet, to think like that would be to be unaware of the ability of Henry James to pause, and make the flesh creep with the realization that quite ordinary human actions may also result in a sort of evil.

O'Faoláin's experiment seemed, startlingly, to underline that aspect of James. Only a Master could, in that way, take liberties with the work of another Master.

Consider then, for a moment, the ninety stories in those three volumes. Take a look at them at random and state, briefly, what they are about.

Here is one about four people who meet on the *teleferique* on Pibeste mountain, near Lourdes: an old priest, a young priest, a young schoolmistress, a young farmer-cum-butcher – all Irish. Later on, the young woman and the farmer marry. But all her life, she remains in love with the young priest. And he with her.

Then here's another story: about a woman doctor in a mental hospital who falls in love with and marries one of her patients, a remarkable man who had, in his past, tried to be a writer and who had, on his record, two instances of violence – one against a wife, who is now dead, and one against a daughter.

And here is a third story which, for the fun of it, is called 'How to Write a Short Story'. A country doctor, an old man, tells the county librarian, a young man, about a boyhood homosexual experience at a school (Catholic) in England. The librarian would be a writer and he comments, and remakes, as the narration goes on.

Just three stories out of ninety. Yet a full description of the way in which the matter takes form would make up a considerable dissertation on the nature of the short story. It is simpler to read and savour, and reflect with some wonder on O'Faoláin's ceaseless, unresting consideration of the world around him, and on his rearranging of it by his tireless imagination.

The last story of that ninety is called 'A Present from Clonmacnois'. This is how it ends: 'All humanity has but one song to sing, and that written in many forms by life itself. Was that what Paul Valéry meant by his: *La mer, lamer, toujours recomencee?* Life renews itself endlessly. The artist is a mere tiller of ancient soil'.

❧ 13 ❧

The Whores on the Halfdoors:
An Image of the Irish Writer

Knockanure,
Both mane and poor,
A church without a steeple,
And ignorant hoors
On half-dures
Demeaning decent people.

IN A SHOP IN DONNYBROOK, DUBLIN, round about 1975, a dear old lady asked me was I not a writer. Blushingly I mumbled a sort of admission, or apology, or confession. Then she said: 'Nowadays there are a lot of writers. Long ago there used not be so many writers'. She had, clearly, been influenced by chat-shows on television and newspaper interviews, and fine talk of bestsellers and blockbusters and the lucky ladies who write them. On another level, though, the existence of the Arts Council and Aosdána, and bursaries and the Haughey Act, and prizes, and several active and enterprising Irish publishers, has, over the 1980s, altered vastly the lot and the status of the writer in Ireland. The word-processor may also have something to do with it. If Tolstoy had had one of them things he could have disposed of *War and Peace* in a tenth of the time.

But let me look back a bit: say to roundabout 1945, in which year I first saw my name on the title-page of a book.

The first Irish writers whose work I knew much or anything about were, in this order: Andy McLaughlin, Alice Milligan, Peadar O'Donnell, Robert Burns, Patrick MacGill and Jonathan Swift.

Andy McLaughlin was never, except to a select circle, as well known as the others. Chauvinistic Scotsmen may be surprised, if you could surprise

134

them, at finding the Bard of Ayr sandwiched between two Donegal men. But wait.

The most notable things, at first sight, about Andy MacLaughlin were that he was small and squat, and needed badly a haircut and some decent clothes, and that one of his legs was shorter than the other. He was the last bell-ringer or town-crier in Omagh, County Tyrone, and a sort of laureate, too, for he commented (something in the fashion of John Dryden) on passing events. He claimed a poetic licence, much as if he had bought it like a dog-licence or, more aptly, a gun-licence, to call everybody names: and on one occasion when the municipal fathers had passed out a job to a man whom Andy and everybody else, except the municipal fathers and the man himself and his relations at home and in the United States, thought was the wrong man, Andy wrote thus trenchantly:

> Mickey Lynch, you did it dirty
> Have you any eyes to see?
> And, Alec, what's the matter?
> You're our nationalist M.P.
>
> McConville and Frank Cassidy,
> Ye are not the poor man's friend,
> Nor our well-famed bookie,
> W.F. Townshend.

He had, as I said, but little recognition and died, sometime in the 1930s. But on one occasion he said to a friend and myself, and with a dignified gravity at which we were by no means inclined to laugh: 'Burns was the best of us'.

Burns is on my list because Burns was, away back before Dunkirk and television, a folklore figure in rural Ulster, just as Daniel O'Connell, the Liberator, or Eoghan Rua Ó Súilleabhain, the rake of a poet, were in other parts of Ireland. Most of the folklore about Burns indicated that he was a dacent fellow, but dirty. When my mother was bearing her slate and primer to a country schoolhouse, the teacher, a Master Reid, and a relative, presented her with a volume of Burns with heavy black lines pencilled through the poems she was not to read. Then there was a Popular Underground Ulster Burns unknown, as far as I know, even to David Daiches and to such experts in Underground Burns as James Barke and Sydney Goodsir Smith and J. de Lancey Ferguson, or even to Alistair Compsie. And Hamish Henderson.

There was the couplet he spoke to Lord Byron when the semi-Saxon milord walked through a stable that Bobby was sweeping: and the milord haughtily ordered the Scottish groom to lift the broom and let Lord Byron by.

What was Byron doing in that there stable? Or, for that matter, Burns?

There was the quatrain he spoke quick as a shot when he had the girl against the gate and looked over his shoulder and saw a wee fellow watching him, and eating a bun. The subject of the quatrain was the wonder of the works of nature. Full quotation is not advisable but you may, from my adroit hints, get one popular picture, or image, of the poet.

Patrick MacGill, no more than Burns or Dean Swift, I never met. A sort of Irish Gorki, he came out of the Glenties, in the lovely but barren mountains of west Donegal, to write of the plight of the Irish migratory labourer in Scotland, to serve with the London-Irish in the Kaiser war and to write, even on the field, war-sketches in the style of Barbusse: and, as a way of saying goodbye to all that, to write a great comic novel, *Lanty Hanlon*, about life in Donegal. It reads as if Christopher Mahon had played Pirandello on that meditative man John Synge, and written another chapter to tell in his own words of his life as a likely gaffer.

My first of several misadventures with literature and censorship was to be discovered by that incorrigible mother, (Our Mother, Eire, is always young) reading MacGill's *The Rat Pit*, to have the book impounded, to discover that my mother had actually known MacGill and, although it would not have occurred to me at the time, had in her innocence been shaken by the reputation the clergy had given him. And that was that. At the moment of impounding I had been trying to work out the connection, as the London telephone girl said to the Canadian soldier, between a young Scotsman, the son of the boss, going into a shed with a young Irish girl, a potato-picker in the fields of Fife, and somebody in the distance playing Swanee River on the fiddle: and then the girl having a baby and sinking in misery in the gutters of Glasgow. Music, it seemed to me then, at the age of nine of ten, had the oddest charms.

But, it was said all around me and, as I afterwards found out, with the grossest exaggeration, that MacGill had it in for the priests. There was, at any rate, one he mentioned who was potbellied and purple-faced and who squandered more money on a water-closet for his own carnal comfort and convenience than would have housed, bedded and cleaned out three parishes.

Not in the least like our own pastor, the reverend Dr John McShane, a grey, grave monsignor who dressed in threadbare suits, had been to the Irish College in Rome, had met, oddly enough, D'Annunzio, who spoke of Italia Irredenta and Hibernia Irredenta, or the Six Counties of the Northeast, and whose polished and literate sermons my mother quoted to the point of distraction. He was known to have called 'murderer' to the teeth of a prominent and pious Dublin politician whom he abhorred because of his Civil War record. He had also told the enthusiastic and progressive leader of the local drama group, who had yearnings towards the stars, plus the plough, that Sean O'Casey was a dirty dog and that if he wrote the Stations of the Cross, you couldn't say them.

Dean Swift is on my list because of an early reading and rereading of *Gulliver's Travels* and the simultaneously acquired knowledge that the learned author had died in the crazyhouse: a something quite compatible, it seemed, with the state of being an Irish writer.

Alice Milligan, as is only right and proper for a poet who had sung the Fenians of both the old and the new dispensations, and who had walked with the gods, has a very special place on my list. A clergyman of my acquaintance brought me when a young man to her hallowed door: a stern old puritanical man from a part of the Sperrin mountains where there had been a priest in the family in every generation for over three hundred years. – so he said proudly, not boasting. His favourite poet, oddly enough or perhaps not at all oddly, was Robert Burns, and his favourite sliver of Burns was that beautiful passage of moralizing inset to the night-rakings of Tam O'Shanter:

> But pleasures are like poppies spread:
> You seize the flow'r, its bloom is shed;
> Or like the snow falls in the river,
> A moment white – then melts for ever;
> Or like the Borealis race,
> That flit ere you can point their place;
> Or like the rainbow's lovely form
> Evanishing amid the storm.

The aged poetess of 'The Fenians' and the Abbey playwright of 'The Last Feast of the Fianna' was then living among unkempt lawns and shrubbery in the old rectory on the fringe of the mountain village of Mountfield, County Tyrone.

'Not much she ever made,' old Father Paul said, 'hobnobbing with Yeats and that crew. She dresses like Maggy the Rag. If you met her on the road, you'd reach her a penny'. Then he hammered on the front door and called out: 'Alice, where art thou?'

The door opened and the dear lady appeared in wreaths of smoke. There was a jackdaw in the chimney for whose invasion and occupancy she courteously apologized. We sat in the musty drawingroom and listened to her telling us how she had once spent a wonderful day with Miss Gonne and Mr Bulfin (Mr Yeats couldn't make the trip), studying druidic remains in Glencolmcille. The smoke thickened until she could be seen only fitfully, and we were set free to imagine visions of the woman Homer sung of, or of that statuesque thought from Propertius, going with the walk of a queen along that most wonderful of western glens. Yet it was saddening to think that to be poor, lonely, smoke-dried should be the lot of a poet in the end of all.

Later it might have occurred to one that there was some connection between an old woman abandoned in a smoky corner and that cracked looking-glass of the servant mentioned by a bitter young Dubliner as the symbol of Irish art. But that is not to say that the old poetess was ever anybody's servant: even in the smoke she was proud and noble.

To make mystical the number of writers I first knew aught of, there was a seventh: Brinsley MacNamara. His name was a household two words, and long words at that, for horror, and the title of his novel *The Valley of the Squinting Windows* was a handy description for any nest of vipers. Dire tales came through, on the wind, of riot and disorder in the Free State, down in the grasslands and lakelands of Westmeath, where a young man had written this holy-awful book, calling names to everybody in his village, or so some of the people in the village thought and said. To aggravate his villainy, he had been off prancing around the States with that Abbey Theatre gang, disgracing Ireland forever by playacting in a play about a Kerryman who killed his father and was sheltered by the women of Erris and Tyrawley: and it was well known that bloomers had never got further west than Ballina.

People were brawling about his book at street-corners in the village he came from and arguing about it in courts of law, and a copy of the book had been burned on the main street of that village by a butcher: and an old woman (yet another) had been heard to say: 'Thanks be to the Sacred Heart the trouble's over. The book's burnt'.

That same stern priest from the Sperrin mountains did once say to me . . . He was congratulating me on some out-of-the-way brilliant school essay, possibly on the autobiography of an old boot. That was a great theme then, and the roads of these islands must have been littered with discarded talkative boots. But be that as it may, Fr. Paul said to me: 'You'll be a writer some day. See that you never disgrace your country the way Brinsley MacNamara did'. That was a remark that, in years to come and over the course of a friendship which was to last until the day of his death, was to inspire in Brinsley touches of that wry humour with which he surveyed almost everything in this curious world.

But you do get the picture. It was damn nearly to be expected that an Irish writer would disgrace his country, his mother and father, his wife if anybody would ever have him: or his neighbour's wife if he had a hoor's chance. There was precedent for it: back as far as Owen of the Sweet Mouth O'Sullivan and the Gaelic poets of Sliabh Luachra. Why even Maurice Walsh, a Kerryman like Red Eoghan, yet not a spalpeen poet with the lust of the world on him, but a respected an popular novelist then writing, about the Scottish Highlands, novels to warm the heart of Sir J.M Barrie at his window in Thrums: even Maurice Walsh was an authority on whiskey. It was also darkly hinted that he did not practise. It was never necessary to say what it was that he did not practise. To be an authority on whiskey and not to practise were among the salient characteristics of Irish writers.

By other marks, too, you knew them when you met them. Those included poverty, general blackguardism, anti-clericalism, partial lunacy, loneliness, and dreams as crazy as those of Shaw's Father Keegan. There was that tendency towards mocking and demeaning the decent people as displayed by the whores who leaned on the halfdoors in the celebrated village whose church it had no steeple, or had neither church nor steeple: there are variant readings. All this and more of the kind went to make up the image of the Irish writer among, and to, his own people.

If one had not been irrevocably doomed to trying to be a writer, all this might have put one off. Who wants to be regarded in his own country, or anywhere else, as a cut between the village idiot and a tinker who might steal the chickens, or a market-stroller who might steal cherries from maidens or wives from husbands. It seemed odd that this mixture of contempt for, and suspicion of, the writer (an English writer told me it was twenty times worse in Nottingham) should exist in the same place as an ancient respect for poetry, ballads, tales and those who could tell them, for the shadows of Burns in the north-east and of Red Eoghan in the south-west, and of many others in-between. There was mystery here, somewhere.

So, in due course, up with me to Dublin to find out what it was all about. That was many years ago.

In a hilarious book which he described as *A Tourist's Guide to Ireland,* Liam O'Flaherty divided the people into four groups: priests, peasants, publicans, politicians. That might then (1929) have been a fair enough categorization, although if you wish to be nice about it, split the four up into smaller or lesser groups, making, say, the civil servants attendant on the politicians. The new middle-class, of which some years ago we heard a lot, may have been peasants aspiring to be publicans, or publicans aspiring to be politicians. But nowhere, in 1929, did O'Flaherty find a place for writers. Although, later on, it might have been a significant symptom of a thwarted natural function that the young men in the mohair suits in the advertising agencies called themselves writers: as sign-painters in the painting-trade in Dublin had always called themselves.

Like the sign-painters, the modish painters and the sculptors could be fitted in somewhere: as servants to the clergy when those latter were stricken by an attack of Art: or as public performers because they did not use words and did not do much harm to anyone: or because they could, at times, express and fulfil history, or ornament a public square.

But the writer in Ireland then seemed to fit in nowhere except, perhaps, in a pub, talking his guts out and doing no writing: elsewhere he might as well have been a loner and a drifter. There were few Irish publishers to publish him and give him a fighting chance of making his bread. Like every other country in the world, we have a literate minority. Some statistician, or mythological poet, once told me that per head of the population we buy books as or better than they do in Britain. But then what is our population?

So a writer to get his head at all above the surface had, then and as a general rule, to take his wares to London and/or New York: and to be afterwards accused by the Unco Guid of writing for a 'foreign market'. What that hoary accusation really meant was that the Plain People of Ireland thought that the Writer, to line his own pockets, was making a holy show of them before the English. While the writer, driven on by his own personal curse or affliction, was merely trying to express himself, his people and his environment for his own ease of spirit or the satisfying of his demon, for the information or delight or annoyance of all or any who cared to read him.

Yet writers are by nature, or by sheer necessity, a vociferous and clamant people. As the man in Flann O'Brien's *At Swim-Two-Birds*, said about Fionn MacCumhaill: 'Let him talk. It has to come out somewhere'. Nor was M. Proust much different, even if he went about it in a quiet way. Not all the professors, from Plato to the late Professor William Magennis, who was a sort of High Priest of the Censorship of Publications in the 1940s, could totally silence the poet. And poets in the Ireland of the time had, for reasons patriotic, acquired some respect. So many of the men executed in 1916, by General Maxwell, had been poets, and all the Irish poets of that fatal year, with the possible exceptions of Moira O'Neill and Jane Barlow, had approved of and duly mourned the executed poets.

Professor Magennis, by the way, did, at the height of his glory, outline an attitude, prevalent at the time, towards the Writer when he said that he did not want to see a Writer on the Censorship Board because that would be to set Bill Sykes to catch the burglars. He also said of some Irish writers that they were not, nor could not be, novelists but only short-story writers padding out with smut to make their wares more marketable in London. Especially, I think, he had in mind Kate O'Brien, Sean O'Faoláin and Frank O'Connor: and if you have a fondness for irony you can strike a pocket of it by comparing the good professor, God give him peace, on the nature of the novel in Ireland with the odd ideas on the same, expressed by that most amiable of men, Frank O'Connor, in his book *The Lonely Voice*.

All of which has me still floundering around in Dublin in the Fearful Forties.

For the two most clamant voices then in Deserto or in Dublin were the voice of O'Faoláin and O'Connor. Or, to be more exact, O'Faoláin, in a voice both iron and eloquent, was clamanting on behalf of the two-headed Corkonian genius begotten by Daniel Corkery on Mother Eire in a state of revolutionary frenzy: a genius that developed to merit the priestly blessing of William Yeats and that had cousinships with Chekhov, Turgenev, Babel, Daudet, de Maupassant and some others.

O'Faoláin and his generation had been committed men, as he pointed out in an article written for the fiftieth anniversary of Easter 1916; and he wondered, in the same article, if any younger writers were or could be so committed. Well, at least, they could be committed to a considerable admiration for Sean O'Faoláin, both as a great writer and as a man ready and able to protest against a smug, self-satisfied sort of Ireland, an Ireland that, at odd moments and in some odd statements, seemed to think itself better and holier than the 'outside world', a description then in constant use: an Ireland that seemed to have come out of nowhere, to have appeared like a cherubic changeling in a surplice, in place of the free Ireland that the poets and patriots seemed to have promised and hoped for.

The height and depth of that smugness was suggested to me when, as a young journalist, I was approached by a wealthy Dublin merchant to write a publicity sheet for a project that he, and some other godfearing men and merchants, had in mind. It was to build on Howth Head (where the young William Yeats had brooded in the bushes, and where he and Miss Gonne had watched the white birds soaring over the white foam of the sea) a gigantic statue of the Sacred Heart of Jesus, as big, be the holy, as the Christ of the Andes.

My immediate thought, fortunately then unexpressed, was that it was high time Howth redeemed its reputation: for there had been recently around Howth Harbour a most unholy outbreak of buggery that had given rise to a bookful of Dublin jokes. Like the one about the man who dropped the half-crown in Howth and had to kick it all the way to Sutton Cross before he had the nerve to stoop down to pick it up.

But no! The mammoth statue was to stand up on Howth to thank the Sacred Heart and Blessed Oliver Plunket (no mention was made of Eamon de Valera), for keeping Ireland out of World War II. And it was, religiously to be hoped, that all the sailors, including Irish sailors, on all the ships coming into haven from seas a million times at that time, perilous, would see that statue and be inspired by it.

At that moment I demurred to the extent of mumbling that neither the Sacred Heart of Jesus nor Blessed Oliver Plunket would be much inclined to thank us for thanking them. Or might not even think that we, the Irish, were so special. Blessed Oliver, who had been a sort of an agent and had suffered sore for it, might only with difficulty see why Irishmen should hide in the corner from anything. The Sacred Heart, too, had had his own sad experience of power politics and might find it against his principles to associate with a group of well-to-do merchants and money-changers congratulating themselves on their own comfort while the rest of the world, including a lot of their fellow-countrymen, were hip-deep in chaos.

Yet in spite of such revelations of the sadness of the separatist mind, it did take some imaginative effort for writers younger than O'Faoláin and O'Connor to understand the extent of the change, the darkening, the altering of the skies from that dawn in which it was bliss and all that jazz to be alive, to the dreary early afternoons of the 1940s, with flatulence and headache after six raw whiskeys and a soggy lunch.

O'Faoláin could remember so delightfully the days when he, and other young fellows, poured into the mountain valleys of Muskerry to learn the Irish language, and brought happiness and music with them into places that were lonely and silent for the rest of the year. But the story that began with that wistful look backwards ended with the black backview of a cleric whose 'elongated shadow waved behind him like a tail', a decent fellow, and cheerful and respected by all, but, nevertheless, a persecutor, and the man who invented sin.

In the early stories of Frank O'Connor, in the collection *Guests of the Nation*, and even although the title-story is a hard tragedy, and although tragedy recurs throughout the book, the dominant impression left is that the writer is genuinely enjoying his material: enjoying guns, manhunts, ambushes, attacks on barracks, racing and chasing and battling, with the splendid appetite of healthy youth. The revolution, such as it was, did not freeze O'Connor's people into rigid, sombre contemplation as it did Daniel Corkery's people. Instead, it set them moving as a windy day might set a streetful of men chasing their hats. In that mood, and for the love of life and country and poetry and scholarship, O'Connor made himself a Gaelic scholar and, in post-revolutionary times, when the laughing morning wind had died down into a dismal drizzle, he was to know the chagrin of having his translation of Brian Merriman's 'Cúirt a' Mheadhon Oidhche' (The Midnight Court) banned by the Censorship of Publications Board for being 'in general tendency indecent or obscene'. He was to say ruefully, but with a humour and a Munster brogue that never deserted him, that the only compliment his countrymen had ever paid him was to think, some of them, that he was the author of the original poem.

Because he wrote a friendly introduction to a pleasant book, Frank O'Connor's name was involved in the most celebrated case of book-banning, or persecution, in that period. For the censoring mind, as George Moore noted in the London that sent Vizetelly to jail for publishing Zola, is also the persecuting mind. Here follows the illustrative story:

Eric Cross was an English research scientist and mathematician. He was a quiet, saintly man who lived in the West of Ireland in the sort of rural quietude that he had always desired, ever since he discovered in the early 1930s that the work he and some others were engaged in could be used to make the world safe for germ-warfare. So he turned his back on the whole shebang, came to Ireland, got him a horse and caravan and took to the roads. In a quiet valley in the Muskerry mountains he met a man after his own heart, a tailor who did not tail much any more but who lived, with his wife Anstey, in a cabin on a scrap of land, ten shillings a week pension, and the milk of one black cow. A man who thought, or knew, that time did not exist and that the world was well on the way to what he called alabastery. That old man was seventy-seven years of age and walked, albeit with some agility, on a crutch. No formidable enemy, as you might guess, to a nation's morality.

Eric Cross, and he wasn't alone in this, felt the out-of-time enchantment of this old man, his talk, his stories, his wisdom, his humour that had, now and again, a touch of lively rustic bawdry: the story for instance about the sow that ate the eel, or the story about the weakly father of seventeen children who hadn't the price of admission to see the great performing bull, or about what the widower on the way home from his wife's funeral said when he saw the cock treading the hen.

The quiet Englishman, on the run from a world of horror, was happy to sit in the chimney-corner and play Boswell to the talk of the kindly, wise old man of the glen, to write it down in a book and to have it published under the title *The Tailor and Anstey*, with an introduction by Frank O'Connor. For how was Eric Cross or Frank O'Connor, or anybody in their sane senses, to imagine that in Dublin a learned professor and Senator was to say that the book was low, blasphemous and obscene, that it was circulated to gratify the English mind, or eye, by allowing it to see 'what the Irish peasant really is when shown up by one who knows him'. The learned man, who was then chairman of the Board of Censorship of Publications, also spoke of the 'foulness' of the Tailor's mind.

That was in 1943.

Even in that bad year and period, for printed books in Ireland and for a lot of other matters elsewhere, it was possible to wonder if Senator Magennis, and the owners of the owlish voices who spoke with him, were talking of the same book that one had read with some merriment, and with a certain nostalgic longing for the unspoiled and simple life. It was even ordered, with the turn of the screw of idiocy, that the quotations from the book, read out in a Senate debate on censorship, read out in the nation's highest assembly once dignified by the presence of William Yeats, should be struck from the record; lest, perhaps the determined and devoted muckrakers among the Irish should, for the sake of the dirty reading, make a best seller out of the Senate report.

A lady Senator who wrote lives of saints for sub-cerebral religious magazines, said that if Dante came back again and really wanted to put the screw on some of his enemies (she didn't put it exactly like that), then he could find no more effective way of doing so than by forcing them to read this diabolical book.

It was implied that in conversations at rural hearthsides nobody ever mentioned bulls and cows: and it was impossible not to wonder if those senatorial speakers had not been reared like Marie Louise of the Hapsburgs who was married off to Napoleon. In a world where protocol had for centuries taken precedence over commonsense, it was said that she was never allowed to possess a pet animal of the male variety, and that all reference to any difference between the sexes was snipped with scissors out of the books she read. An interesting example of censorship, but a poor preparation for going to bed with Bonaparte.

While all this angry wind was being blown off, on behalf of purity, away down in the Muskerry mountains the desire to persecute had worked itself out in a nasty, backhanded way. Some local hooligans, incited by the newspaper reports, tried to make miserable the last days of the poor old tailor. The big English laboratories were not the only places where men went in for devising methods of germ-warfare. Then one afternoon three priests invaded the old man's house and forced him to go down on his knees at his own hearth and burn the book. Dante could not have thought of a better one than that. Seamus Murphy, the sculptor, who knew and loved the Tailor and immortalized him in red stone, assured me that all that had broken the old man's heart and hastened his death.

That to me, or to anybody with half a heart or one quarter of a sense of decency, was a horror story; but instructive. It was a gruesome interlude in the proceedings, normally merely ludicrous, of the Dublin censorship. That it should have happened in a country which prides itself, with at times some reason, on kindness and tolerance, was a sore smudge on our good name:

> The lovely land that always sent
> Its writers and artists to banishment . . .

All that seems to be, and was, a long time ago. Even twenty-five years later matters were a bit better. For when all the harm was done and the book *The Tailor and Anstey* was unbanned by an Appeal Board that was as comic as the Censorship Board, and when it was reissued about that time, I was reviewing the case for Radio Eireann, at the behest of the novelist Francis MacManus. So I asked MacManus how much he would allow me to say over the air.

'Everything,' he said, 'except, for legal reasons, the names of the three black heroes who, to defend Irish purity, bullied an old man'.

To say as much as I then said over Irish radio would scarcely have been possible in the doldrums of the 1940s. Indeed a little after the time of that broadcast things were looking so lively for a while that on the occasion of a certain swinging folksong and music festival in Mullingar, John Montague, then a young poet, jubilated that Puritan Ireland was dead and gone, a myth of O'Connor and O'Faoláin. And John McGahern, then a young novelist who had just received a money-award from the Arts Council, seemed inclined to think for a while that O'Connor, O'Faoláin and others had been suffering from persecution mania.

But they were at their old tricks yet, and what the Poor Old Woman gave with one fist, she, at that time, grabbed back with the other. McGahern's second novel was banned and there were difficulties about his job as a teacher in a clerically controlled school in the archdiocese of Dublin. For how, in reason, could you have a man teaching in such a school who admitted in a novel that an Irish boy might masturbate, or hinted that between an adult cleric and a youth there might exist a state of disturbed emotional relationship. 'No book,' as a Dublin reviewer once said about a fine, healthy, open-air novel by Walter Macken, 'to put into the hands of a pure-minded boy'. Ever since I read that, and in my own writing, that pure-minded boy has never been absent from my thoughts, and some day, when words have really answered to my call, I hope to get through to him. He didn't go to school with me. But then I was educated, if that's the exact word, in a garrison town, British army; and as Joseph Holloway, the eternal diarist, roared at Seán O'Casey on the first night of *The Plough and the Stars*: 'If there are prostitutes on the streets of Dublin, it was the British army put them there'. He didn't mention poverty or William Martin Murphy.

But, at any rate, there had appeared in the sixties an open and widespread discussion and criticism that just did not exist in the forties. The most amusing things began to get said on television programmes and it was much more generally recognized that the censorship was a cod, or worse. A sign of sick minds, as O'Faoláin had pointed out. A symptom of deplorable Fearthought. In the 1940s when my own second novel, *In a Harbour Green*, a harmless enough piece God knows, received the national literary award for being in general tendency indecent or obscene, the editor of a Dublin daily newspaper for which I then worked told me, more in sorrow than in anger, that he couldn't give the book to his wife to read. In a better time and under, perhaps, more liberal editorship, the same paper came out firmly against the banning of John McGahern's *The Dark*.

The determined persecution of the early novels of Edna O'Brien was a case that called for particular study. Was it caused by a hangover, our Irish timelag, from days before women got the vote, from a feeling that while it was bad and very bad for a man to speak out like that, it was utterly unthinkable that a woman, bringing shame on Erin's fair daughters, should claim any such liberty. Especially a woman who had been educated, as the saying then went, at one of the best convent schools.

It always did strike me as odd that, at that time, some decent men preaching pussyfoot sermons about the dangers of drink seemed to be most deeply concerned that girls educated 'at the best convent schools' should take to swilling cocktails in the lounge bars of Dublin. They never seemed to show any concern about the alcoholic capacity of females who had not had those educational advantages. They wouldn't have had the price of it, I suppose, and couldn't do themselves much damage on half-pints of plain in dockside pubs. Or was the assumption that the daughter of Erin educated at one of the best convent schools had a prescriptive right to a special sort of vestal innocence. Edna O'Brien's early novels were a little severe on that assumption.

In my student-days in University College, Dublin, I listened in on two triduuums preached to such of the students as, out of fervour or curiosity or because they hadn't the money to be anywhere else, cared to sit and listen. The preaching was done in Newman's Church in St Stephen's Green. One decent Jesuit, who wrote a devotional column for the popular press, advised the students that when they went out on picnic parties to the Dublin mountains, they should be gregarious: should, he meant, stay with the herd and not pair off in that exclusively Irish occasion of sin once upon a time denounced as Company-Keeping. On another evening a rattling Redemptorist, one of the sons of thunder and hellfire, said that just as the lapel-pin of the Pioneer Total Abstinence Association was a public declaration of war on the Irish vice of drunkenness, so there should also be a Purity Pin to indicate that the young people of Ireland had declared war on unchastity.

It seems now hard to believe, I know, that two grown men should have talked thus to an audience, or congregation, of young men and women. You will just have to take my word for it that they did, in truth, do so. The possible uses and abuses of the purity pin gave rise, naturally, to much speculation of a light or frivolous nature among students of the male sex. Possibly, also, among the ladies. A friend of mine, a merry Kerryman, once, in my hearing, hailed a well-set-up girl from the cattle-country of Meath by asking her where was her Purity Pin. Whereupon, with a smile as broad as a Boyne Valley pasture, she replied that she was using it to hold up her drawers.

In her own sweet way Edna O'Brien was as brutally direct, and it would have seemed that those moles, the censors, or whoever egged them on to their idiocies were not able to take it. The persecution of her novels at the time had something pathological about it: even if it had nothing of the nastiness of that tale of the Tailor in the Muskerry mountains where Allua of Song rushes forth like an arrow. It did, too, delightfully seem that in Miss O'Brien the staring eunuchs, 'resembling fakirs in their fragile and renunciatory sterility', the holy Joes who hid behind the doors and never wished for their whining and snivelling to be brought out into the light of day, had caught a tartar. That the convent girl with her temper riz might do what the reasonable argument of Sean O'Faoláin had tried to do. Somebody in *Esquire* hailed her, along with Brigid Brophy, as a prophetess of sex. You could never be quite certain what that was supposed to mean. The only other candidates in Irish history for any such title would include, perhaps, the Cailleach Beara, or Queen Gormlaí, or Gráinne of the Ships. Ireland, to do her justice, has made heroines out of them. Lady Morgan, for several reasons, failed to qualify. Lady Blessington was not of the first class.

The poet Paddy Drury walked through Knockanure and elected, on that occasion, to see it as mean and poor and, in some savage memory of ancient days when it was reputed that a poem might kill, saw the people as the whores on the halfdoors sneering at the poets. The people, adroit and nimblefooted, simply switched places. Or so I thought the best part of fifty years ago when, leaning on the portion of the halfdoor allotted to me, I could meditate on where Puritan Ireland, or that portion of it that was, for a while, Puritan, had come from. There were theorists who would have traced it back as far as the early hermits and monks and who argued that a certain sour hatred of life was part of the All that ancient Ireland knew. Most unlikely: for if the story of Curithir and Liadain has restraint and penance in it, beauty and passion are more predominantly there. In his story 'Lovers of the Lake,' Sean O'Faoláin made an ancient tale live again and relate to our own times.

We all heard that argument about Irish priests, educated on the Continent, bringing Jansenism back with them to consummate on Irish soil an unholy union with the respectability of English Protestant Puritanism. But Emmet Larkin pointed out reasonably that what those clerics picked up was not Jansenism but Gallicanism; and that the calamity of the Famine punished so fearfully the body and spirit of the people that the wrath-of-God preachers had a cowed multitude before them. And that their preaching style came not from France but from Italy, the principal preachers being those searing sons of St Alphonsus Liguori, the Redemptorists. Even in my boyhood it was still possible to see and hear, repeat hear, a Redemptorist preaching a mission-sermon, waving the cross of Christ in the air and roaring to the congregation 'Shall I curse the company-keepers?'

Boy meet girl indeed. Today, somebody tells me, etiquette is calmer.

There was, also and once again, the time-lag. Irish novelists in Ireland then faced something of what novelists on the neighbouring offshore island faced when George Moore came back from Paris. Or faced later when James Joyce had his problems with Grant Allen and the moral British printer. It may be some comfort to know that two Irishmen did, in that matter, help the English towards a reasonable liberty.

A diverting specimen of time-lag, or something, was once to be seen and, perhaps, heard in the great stadium of Croke Park, where the strong men of the Gaelic Athletic Association had been known to stand up before a big game and solemnly sing a hymn called 'Faith of Our Fathers'. Which, as we all know, was the work of Father Faber, a devout Italianate-English priest of the Oratory, who wrote many hymns and many volumes of a blossoming and spiritual prose. There were four lines out of 'Faith of Our Fathers' that never rent the air in Pairc An Chrochaigh:

> Faith of Our Fathers, Mary's prayers
> Shall win our country back to Thee.
> And, through the truth that comes from God,
> England shall then again be free.

Wordsworth is reputed to have said that when Faber went over to Rome, England lost a poet. He could never have foreseen that the Gaelic Athletic Association was to gain a cheer-leader. Or, perhaps more simply, he could never have foreseen the Gaelic Athletic Association. Or the almost liturgical preliminaries in Croke Park where there used to be such an introduction to a big game, the ball and all being thrown in by an archbishop, that a friend of mine from the USA (and over there he had been a Jesuit scholastic and had almost made ordination) once asked me were they going to play ball or read the Mass. At that time and in his own unregenerate land, he was accustomed, under such circumstances, not to archbishops but to dancing girls. But then an Irish lady pointed out to him that if the American fashion were followed in Ireland, the pitch might be stormed before the game began. But since then we have had cheer-leaders and drum-majorettes in Croke Park, and on parade on the streets of Dublin, and nothing violent happened. Etiquette grows calmer.

So leaning on what is left of my own personal halfdoor, I lift my eyes from the mean street, and its squinting windows and see, away out there, sunlight on green fields and enticing roads. And, did time and Space permit, it would be fun to walk out there and meditate on the lives of the Half-Doorists of my time: from Padraic Colum, say, on to Thomas Kinsella and by way of Austin Clarke, Donagh MacDonagh, Patrick Kavanagh, Robert Farren, Padraic Fallon; from Liam O'Flaherty and Francis Stuart to Patrick Boyle, Brian Moore, John McGahern, John Broderick; from Elizabeth Bowen and Kate O'Brien to Val Mulkerns and Honor Tracy and Edna

O'Brien; from the philosophic quietude of Arland Ussher and Hubert Butler to the formidable suavity of Conor Cruise O'Brien.

There have been many others, and at the moment (1990) there are many more. Writers, male and female, now proliferate. Or was that the word I was searching for? There have even been what a friend of mine, a man of the Dublin theatre, called the subversive and underground priests.

And out there was the world and all the fun of the fair. If the moles could not appreciate it, well what, anyway, would you expect from moles? The moles, Balor and Mannanan be praised, were in a minority, and Ireland was Ireland through joy and through tears and hope never dies through the long weary years, and each age has seen countless brave hearts pass away, but their spirit still lives on in the men of today.

Which hilarious peroration, so much more worthy of recital in Croke Park, as I then thought, than the works of Father Faber, I cannot alas claim for my own.

⚜ 14 ⚜

The Coppinger Novels
of Bruce Arnold

W HEN I READ THE FIRST OF THE Coppinger novels, as they
have now come to be called, I felt as now and again in a lifetime
a reader feels when he comes unexpectedly on a work, written
perhaps by some writer he may have vaguely heard of or not heard of at
all, and knows he is reading what he might call an isolated masterpiece;
and reads it with illumination and emotion, and remembers it all his life.
The simple truth at the time was that the author was a friend of mine, well
known as an art historian and the owner of an art-gallery, an odd combination, as an astute political commentator for a Dublin daily newspaper.
Not often does an Englishman take such an intelligent, often humorous
interest in Irish politics. Perhaps to be intelligent it has to be humorous, for
most of us find it hard to take ourselves seriously. Since Bruce Arnold is by
now both English and Irish, it would be pointless to say that the English do
this sort of thing well or to mention, as one early reviewer inevitably did,
Anthony Powell or L.P. Hartley.

That first novel, *A Singer at the Wedding*, the first of four, seemed to me
at the time to take its place by unchallengable right with the classical
father-and-son stories, fact or fiction, or fact and fiction, as told by Dickens,
Meredith, Gosse, Samuel Butler, James Joyce and others. In one of its many
moments of exceptional perception, the narrator, who is the son, a grown
man remembering a boyhood Christmas season that, although he did not
know it then, was to shape his life forever, sees inexorable and transfigur-
ing Time working on his father and himself, compelling them, so to speak,
to change places. This moment comes long after that fateful Christmas
season of making and remaking:

> As I walked away from the house to catch the London train – he always
> waited at the gate until the turning in the road shut him from view – I

was struck, vividly, forcefully, and quite without the usual preamble which leads to such thoughts, by the feeling that he had taken on – been forced to take on – precisely those limitations and restraints which, in childhood, are imposed by parents and schools on children. He had become me, and I had become him. That was exactly how I felt. I was the man of affairs, striding away under pressure of business and responsibility; he was the child all over again, yearning for the unattainable, yearning to be other than what he was.

Any man who has watched a father grow old and die will recognize that simple and moving truth, so expertly expressed: and, in the case of the father and son in this novel, the irony is multiplied. The father, at fifty, is a big, handsome ex-naval-officer, clutching on to pathetic little habits of order, perhaps, you might say, part of his pension from the British royal navy but a frail barrier against his innate attraction towards disorder, revolts against rule followed by bouts on the booze, and entanglements, as they used to be poetically called, with women.

When the story really begins, the son is almost fourteen years of age, a thoughtful, sensitive, musical fellow. He sings in the choir at a classy wedding. He is one of the soloists and meets a wonderful girl called Babette and her beautiful mother; and his father has Something going on with Babette's aunt, Ursula, out of which Something, the son vaguely hopes, good may come for Babette and himself.

The son goes to a special sort of school, Coppinger, which has now given its name to the four novels. It is more-or-less designed for boys who have lost one parent or both parents or in whose homes there is some disorder to justify their acceptance into Coppinger:

> ... that gaunt peppering of Victorian school buildings on the rounded top of one of the Cotswolds, 600 feet or so above the sea, with its hardships and its disciplines, had made us all familiar with cold and with waiting.

Philpotts, a senior boy and at the head of his house and a quite memorable chap, says: 'We're different all right. ... We'll be carrying this school on our backs for the rest of our lives. We're different because we're at Coppinger. It means that we've been plucked out from some family background that went wrong, and given the privilege of this place. That's how the trustees see it. That's how other people who know the school see it'.

But it is away from the school and during the Christmas holidays that the patterns of the idyll, which is to be very brief, and of the lifelong memory and regret, are drawn. Babette is beautiful. We have all been almost fourteen and have had a holiday or two. The father is as real as real; and at times the reader feels that the narrator knows the pain so much that he is actually hiding things from us. Bruce Arnold is, in that, a master of subtle suggestion.

All the women in the novel live and breathe. Philpotts is as memorable as Steerforth but with, in so far as we are told, no fatal flaw. All Bruce Arnold's people stay with you long after you have closed the novels and he writes so well that he makes the reader feel civilized. Consider this perfect portrait of a lady, our introduction to Babette's mother:

> And in the wearing of this hat, moreover, she was quite distinct in her appearance from what I understood the fashions in the country as a whole to be at that time, and not just among the wedding guests in that part of the Cotswolds. Yet distinct in a way that made her more attractive, more daring, more beautiful. The visual references by which I might judge her were meagre in the extreme: films, magazine photographs, my own reading – yet they, or some native intuition on my part, invested her now with qualities of romance and beauty. Yet there was in her face a certain sadness, hard to define, which would quite soon become apparent to me in other ways. She looked at me, openly, candidly, without speaking, and I felt radiating from her a relaxed self-assurance which gave depth and definition to her natural beauty.
> 'So you are George's son,' she said.

Most certainly he is George's son, which is what the Coppinger novels are about. The second novel, *The Song of the Nightingale*, brings us, naturally and inevitably, closer to the moment already mentioned when the son has become the man of the world and the father, yearning for the unobtainable, has receded back into childhood. But the narrator is still at that strange school; and the opening chapter, a wonderful achievement in style and atmosphere, tells of an enchanted summer night when the housemaster, Mr Forrest or the Gaffer, and his senior students listen from their dormitory to the singing, in a wood on that Cotswold hillside, of the enchanted bird.

The Gaffer rambles on, telling the boys that they have perhaps been conditioned by literature to think of the song of the nightingale as sad, that: 'That fellow Keats, with his attractive but inaccurate observation about the night being tender, has conditioned us all wrongly'. He is about to say that Keats was thinking of himself, and not of the night nor the nightingale, when the bird interrupts; and the novelist, who knows a lot about music, comes very well out of his description of a song that so many, in prose and poetry, have described or tried to describe.

Nor had the Gaffer the chance to mention, as I feel sure he intended to do, how that solid man, William Wordsworth, exhorted the ethereal minstrel, pilgrim of the sky, to leave to the nightingale her shady woods: and, when the good housemaster is safely abed, the narrator and two of his friends and the housemaster's daughter (the more fortunate among us have known girls like Janet) wander illicitly in those shady woods. It is a moment that sets a consecration on what follows and on what, we may at that moment guess, is still to follow.

But the main business of the novel is far from the shady woods of summer, and birdsong and young love. Out in London is the father, living a sad-enough life as a jobbing gardener, less and less buoyed-up by dubious memories of days when he had been officer-class, and he is now on most uneasy terms with the woman whom he actually married. The mother of his daughter and two sons is dead. Even before her death, they had been separated. Most delicately, Arnold here writes about that ignominy of growing-up against which Yeats raged as, for good value, he did also against decrepit age that had been tied to him as, to a dog's tail, a rattling can. There can be so many ignominies in a man's or a woman's life. And so many rages.

At Coppinger the care given to those young men with unsettled family backgrounds can be most considerate and intensive. As a special bonus, or because of a special plight, one chosen student can become the Porphyry scholar and benefit from something like the fosterfathership of Mr Porphyry, a wealthy City man given to religion.

For the narrator, it is a delicate situation and intriguingly handled by the novelist, who is building up around this growing boy a world with all the shades of the prisonhouse. He tantalizes us with a question that the young fellow, less expertly, asks of himself:

> Occasional faces, angular, raw, unformed, perhaps caught with an odd or awkward expression on them, provoked in me the curious and momentary questioning: how much of what we would all become is prefigured in youthful bone and flesh?

At this point it may be useful to make this dull but, perhaps, necessary annotation, which is that while the four novels add up to one long novel, they can be read separately and you need not necessarily begin with the first but with the first that comes to hand. With any one of them you enter into a distinctive world and you will wish to know how it came to be the way it is and, in it, what afterwards transpired. It is possible, indeed, that in the days of publication by serialization not every reader came on the first part first. Which of us, anyway, ever hears any story right from the start, and we have only one man's word for it that in the beginning was the Word. A memorable sentence, but what, even with the qualification, could it possibly mean?

In the third novel, *The Muted Swan*, the narrator, now eighteen, attempts a reconciliation between a brother and sister, beautifully drawn, and that tragic figure of a father, now given to drink and casual women and dreary occupations and apartments, all frequently changing. These are, perhaps, the most moving pages in the entire tetralogy. That attempt is doomed and the young man thinks of the sister he scarcely knows, for they have been reared separately; and here he meets her but briefly:

> Under what compulsion would she and I, even, retain and pursue the
> meanings of our kindred blood? What was that meaning? Did it reside
> in a common response to poetry, in the recognition within each other's
> eyes and features, hands and gestures, of kinship, or simply in the
> knowledge that our blood was common? Much as all these things
> seemed true at that time, and combined together to convince me, more
> or less completely, that everything would be all right, I was neverthe-
> less a little overwhelmed by the pace and intensity of it all. Our
> encounters were taking on a breathless quality. I felt momentarily that
> we were being carried, at too fast a speed, into a web that had been
> spun by foolish spiders between two vehicles parked together only for
> a night.

The tragedy is intensified to the point at which the father loses almost
completely the adherence of the only child, the narrator, who has been
with him and struggled to love and understand him; and that child goes
back, sadder and wiser, for his last term at Coppinger.

After the 133 pages in which that doomed reunion is described, I felt
uneasily that anything more might be an anti-climax. But no, the return to
Coppinger stands up: to the moment of another and different sort of
tragedy and to the moment when the young man says farewell to the place
and goes out forever into the world; and to the final quest for the father.

Back, and in the fourth novel, *Running to Paradise*, and finally and
forever to the father. That tragic man's devotion to the flowers that bloom
(he is a good gardener), his attachment to the one of his two sons who has
lived and suffered with him, his genuine love for two women out of a
procession of women, for that dead wife and one other, are the happiest
things in a life made up otherwise only of a half-anger against the gods.
Now, in this final novel, the father assumes his full promised stature. His
stumbling feet may be on clay that is brightened only by those flowers,
but his head is among the stars and, aptly, the novel begins:

> That is Betelgeuse, I thought. Dimly there came back to me words my
> father had used when I was a child, and with his drunken finger he had
> stabbed into the visage of the stars, prompting his uncertain memory:
> alpha, beta, gamma, delta, epsilon, wild gestures, uncertain recollection,
> awkward skeins, invisible, between the crystalline glowing spots of
> distant light; and from them he was asking me to imagine the figure of a
> man spread out in the heavens.

But George, the father, is not merely a drunken star-gazer, a man stumbling on the earth and falling, at intervals, more-or-less on his feet. The star
he talks most of is Orion, whom Tennyson saw sloping slowly towards the
West: an image that has always reminded me of a toucher, making a silent
getaway after a successful coup. George, the father, sees Orion with
greater faithfulness to the legend and, perhaps, some relationship to the
story of his own life: as a hunter, the child of Poseidon, god of the sea, who

fell in love with one of the Pleiades:

> And he was punished and blinded, and went to the rising sun to get back his sight. And in the end . . . what happened to him in the end? The Gods killed him, that's what happened. An arrow in the head while he was swimming in the sea. And he drowned.

In one drunken moment he feels that he must atone for the mistakes of his life. Then he talks aloud about the illogicality of the idea of atonement: that if you spend the present in going over the past so as to make the past right, then you are neglecting the present. He says that some of the time you must just live out every day; and, listening to him, his son knows that George is only mechanically repeating the advice of Isobel, one of the truly beloved women, given one day long ago when they had listened to a reverend gentleman preaching on atonement. Isobel, like many others, has gone out of his life. The day the two of them had listened to her, the son had thought:

> Atonement? Redemption? Were they concepts to be applied to him at all? Ever? Surely he belonged to a different tribe of men, that of the wild and brutal hunter in the sky?

Isobel on one sad occasion says to the son that people cannot help it if they fall in love. There is a catch in her voice and he thinks she may cry. He is not sure whether she is talking about herself or about George, but he concludes that she means herself and George and, perhaps, all the other women in his life.

George dies, as we all must. The pages that describe that deathbed are among the most moving I have ever read. After his death his son echoes to the stars his defiant Luciferian cry: 'George, live forever'. And we, the readers, are swept back to that most memorable moment in the first novel:

> As I walked away from the house to catch the London train . . .

This remarkable work ends with a great question mark. As does the life of George; as do the lives of all of us.

❦ 15 ❧

Chronicle by Rushlight:
Daniel Corkery's Quiet Desperation

ONE OF THE MANY INTERESTING things about the rereading of Daniel Corkery is that he sets you to the rereading of Henry David Thoreau. Somewhere in *Synge and Anglo-Irish Literature*, Corkery's carnaptious book on John Millington Synge, and other matters, Corkery quoted with approval: 'Perhaps the facts most astounding and most real are never communicated by man to man. The true harvest of my daily life is somewhere as intangible and indescribable as the tints of morning and evening. It is a little star-dust caught, a segment of the rainbow which I have clutched'.

So, from Thoreau: nor was the elusive moment ever better described than it then was by the part-time hermit of Walden Pond.

It may be fair enough to say, in jest, as an American friend of mine does, that Thoreau might never have survived in his solitude without the knowledge that he could, when he felt like it, go over to Ralph Waldo Emerson's for dinner. But what Thoreau had to say was true, when he said it in 1854; and, in 1900, the state of man in prison to the machine emphasizes that truth.

Emerson blandly said that it cost Thoreau nothing to say No, that he was, by his own choice, and no doubt wisely for himself, the bachelor of thought and of nature. Those words return to one when considering the plight of the tragic bachelors, the clerks of Cork, in Corkery's one novel, *The Threshold of Quiet*.

The one man in that novel who seems hell-bent on matrimony or, at any rate, on really making love and not merely brooding about something undefined and indefinable, is driven out of the house and runs away to sea, and on the way home again is drowned off the Old Head of Kinsale. The novel begins, and ends, with a drowning. But if anyone had ever queried Corkery about that prevalence of virginal bachelors, he could have fairly answered (the novel was published in 1917) that he was writing about an unmarrying, excessively chaste and dying society.

Ned Connell the hurler, a giant of a man, but in pitiful thrall to a tyrant of a boss who is, God help us, a public philanthropist, says: 'But we that stay behind – even to this place we're no use. We know it. We have lost faith in ourselves'. Corkery's comment was: 'Time out of mind, perhaps as far back as the disaster of Kinsale, Ireland has been talking in this hopeless strain. The vigour of the nation seems to be abroad, only the timid at home. Talk drooped for want of spirit'.

That, of course, was more than seventy years ago. Corkery's tragic bachelors became, in time, transmogrified into O'Faoláin's comic bachelors, and one of the three Hannafey brothers in O'Faoláin's novel *Come Back to Erin* dreams of Paris, even if he is never to get there. Another of them gets as far as the United States and matrimony and success; a third to the States and the brother's wife in a way that Stevie Galvin's younger brother in *The Threshold of Quiet* may, perhaps, have dreamed of. But then Stevie wasn't married to the girl and never would be.

From that threshold of quiet, by the still lough above the city, the only way out of Cork seemed to be by sea or by suicide or by way of St Patrick's College, Maynooth – and the ladder of a religious vocation. There was, also, at that time the British army, which Corkery does not mention. But since then the big aeroplanes came and the new factories, and it seemed, and increasingly still so seems, that the comic bachelors and the humble clerks might and may be vanishing breeds.

On the flyleaf of *The Threshold of Quiet* Corkery wrote down, almost lovingly, Thoreau's sombre maxim: 'The mass of men lead lives of quiet desperation'. Boisterous desperation might be more apt for the Irish. But then Corkery was not a drinking man, nor was Martin Cloyne, who, at Frank Bresnan's wake, was noticed to leave his one glass of wine untouched.

In the dusk in the streets of Cork, a newsboy is calling out that a man has been found drowned in the Lee. Frank Bresnan's friends, sitting quietly in a quiet house by the lough on the hill above the city, hear the cry, not, at that moment, knowing that the dead man is their friend:

> It brought the wide and lonely spaces of the night in on top of them. They still listened, as if its repetition could further enlighten them; and while they did so their imaginations were craving to banish the sense of chance out of human affairs, were craving for completeness, for cause and effect, for design. In suicide there is effect, design, completeness – the ending of a tale.

Frank Bresnan, the man whose body had been taken dead and dripping out of the waters of the Lee, had been a commercial traveller with all the stories at his command that commercial travellers garner, develop and redistribute. Corkery allowed us to know little more about him than his good sister, Lily, whom indeed he willed to the convent, might have done: and the travellers' tales that are hinted at, in the novel, could be told in any convent. There was, as far as I recall, only one obscenity in anything Corkery ever wrote; and that was, clearly, inadvertent.

Yet Corkery wrote about Frank Bresnan, with a terrifying illumination, that 'his sorrow of heart increased with his budget of good stories'. You can hear therein the laughter of a hundred hotel smoke-rooms, if such things still exist, mocking the isolation of a man's soul. When I first read or, rather when I first wrote about Corkery, and that was more than fifty years ago, I thought that a storyteller should not feel that way: that a multiplicity of stories, smutty stories or tragic stories, or just funny stories, should make a man not rigid in negation, like Thoreau, but content like Chaucer. Chaucer was a storyteller and Thoreau was not, and even the prayer in which Chaucer begged God to forgive him for writing most of his stories has, it always seemed to me, more genuine content about it than Thoreau found in his woodland solitude.

But then a storyteller, even if he has a lot to be content about, has, or had, a lot to be complicated about, particularly if he was an Irish storyteller reacting sternly against earlier Irish storytellers, who, as he considered them, saw the plain people of Ireland (Mylesian not Milesian) merely as comic relief. And Daniel Corkery reacted in that way against Somerville and Ross, against Lever and Lover and George Birmingham and, I fear, even against Sean O'Casey and Liam O'Flaherty. Although I cannot now remember about what documentary or other proof I had, forty years ago, for adding those two names to Corkery's condemned list. There must have been some or I would not have so added them.

How far Corkery's reaction was justified, every reader must judge for himself. But his conclusion was fair enough: that moral responsibility did not belong to a people playing the part of comic relief; and that the writers who saw the Irish people in that light had to paint them 'as if they were incapable of ever going beyond the teaching of mother-wit'.

The people in Corkery's own stories could be hard people from the mountains or tattered people from the lanes, or young rebels, or chaste and clerkly men, or young women on the way to the convent. In the story 'The Price', Lily Bresnan's eyes were 'wide with staring at the tabernacle door'. In the story 'The Hounds of Banba', Nan Twohig, in the eyes of the people of her place, was 'already a Sister of Charity'.

They have all, certainly, gone a long distance beyond the mere counsels of mother-wit, beyond the remotest possibility of being mistaken for Handy Andy or used as comic relief. They live in places where the shadows of moral responsibility are as bewildering and terrifying as the mists on the stony mountains of Leaca na Naomh.

Suicide along one road and the cloister along the other, and the sad brother who opts for death in the waters of my own lovely Lee had previously told the priest that he would like his sister to be a nun and that he, the priest, should pass the good word along: 'With this thread from out the tomb my dead hand shall tether thee'. Thus is Martin Cloyne left for the rest of his life to spend long evenings in the house by the lough, staring into the fire, the open book spread on his knees. It is a fascinatingly morbid situation.

Martin's best friend, Stevie Galvin, is described as a 'highly-sophisticated bachelor carpenter'. When he is not thinking of ships and the sea, and the younger brother who last wrote from Rio, he is praising the utmost in renunciation. He talks in the style of Alfred Jingle, Esq., though on far different themes, and with a Cork accent:

> The Cistercians are the most blessed of all . . . they know that peace is not to be won except by violence . . . it is all true. I often think of the Tibetan monks . . . they go out into rock-built tombs. Not even the light of day enters . . . food is put to them on a ledge . . . and a skinny hand draws it in . . . one day the food remains untouched . . . and the birds carry it off.

Patriotism brings Corkery's people, or some of them, back to the world of living people and sets them moving as if they, also, were alive. Years ago, when I first thought I had something to say about Corkery, his importance, his undoubted influence on other Irish writers, I called my effort at appreciation 'Chronicle by Rushlight'. That title came from his dedication, in verse, to the young men of Ireland of his collection of stories *The Hounds of Banba*.

> You stride in here, chant your wild songs, and go.
> The chroniclers, with rush-lights, stumble after.
> And oh! to see them blot the sunrise glow
> Of your bright deeds and dreams, your tears and laughter.

But inevitably, or so it seemed to me, the young men with the guns who moved through Corkery's stories borrowed something from the contemplative turn of mind of the storyteller: like a singing procession of fighting men silent for a few moments as they march in the shadow of a convent wall. By contrast, as I say elsewhere, the revolution did not freeze Frank O'Connor's people into any rigid and sombre contemplation. Instead, it set them moving as a windy day might set a streetful of men chasing their hats.

The first passage that came out of Corkery's patriotism reminds me of nothing so much as the immobility of the figures seen in photographs of Easter Island. Or, to cut down on travel-cost: of some stone image or ancient cross half-hidden in wet grass on an Irish hillside. It is a passage that is always worth quoting:

> I saw that every extreme movement in Ireland leaves behind it a remnant
> of its broken army – an old workman in a factory in a city, a cobbler in a
> little shop in a village or . . . a shepherd in a hut on a mountainside –
> great old hearts that preserve to the next generation, even to the second
> next, the spark of fire that they themselves had received in the self-same
> manner from those that long since were gone home into the silence. Old
> embers that seem extinct and grey. Oisins dreaming of the heroic dead
> they have so long outlived . . .

His own stern patriotism involved him, naturally enough, in controversy, in which he was not at his best, round about the time when a very different sort of writer was showing in *An Beal Bocht* that the Irish language was very much alive. But reasonable people will be less likely to reread such a pamphlet as Corkery's *What's This about the Gaelic League?* as they will be to return to the stories in *The Stormy Hills*, or *A Munster Twilight*, or *Earth Out of Earth*. He has his high place among our masters of the short story. He is of interest, too, as a rigid moralist dealing in his special sort of desperation or gloom. Or Christian resignation?

For the record, too, he had, as we know, a clear eye for our own history. Yeats, lost in some sort of nostalgic haze, talked of the people of Burke and of Grattan who gave though free to refuse. All honour to Burke and to Grattan and to some others, and to the men who built the Great Houses. But what people? And what did they give to the people? Corkery wrote more simply and sensibly of the College Green Parliament: 'That noisy sideshow, so bizarre in its lineaments and so tragi-comic in its fate'.

Back in 1964 I found myself in Hollins College, Virginia, where members of the Faculty were accustomed, out of politeness and if unable to muster any zeal, to give, once a year, a chapel-talk to such of the students as frequented the college-chapel. Having no particular moral or religious ground to stand on, I elected to read out loud Corkery's sombre story 'The Ploughing of Leaca na Naomh'. And afterward to have played Seán Ó Riada's arrangement of the solemn music for the great movie 'Miss Eire'.

Some serious students, and only a few even of the serious students, came to chapel, found that Corkery's story was a considerable religious experience, and that the music did, also, help to establish the dim religious light. When I asked one of the students did the story remind him (Hollins College had by 1964 accepted male graduate students) of the Russians, he said no. Not of the Russians, but of Edgar Allan Poe.

It is a point worth brooding about.

‿ 16 ‿

Thomas Flanagan:
The Lessons of History

THOMAS FLANAGAN HAD WRITTEN his critical work *The Irish Novelists: 1800–1850*, before he ever saw Ireland or the County Fermanagh in which his people had their origins. His interest in the history and literature of that Irish period began with an early reading of the great Downey edition of Charles Lever, although, oddly enough, Lever, the author of *Charles O'Malley* and a lot more, was not dealt with in that book. Nor was Samuel Lover, the author of *Handy Andy*, who was novelist, short-story writer, folklorist of a sort, poet, songwriter, singer, miniaturist, Dublin wit. Flanagan's reason for their exclusion was that Lover and Lever (it sounds more gentlemanly, but physically impossible, if you put the names the other way round) had, because in their time they had enjoyed considerable popularity in the neighbouring island, been written about and studied many a time and oft, although it is possible that the good critical estimates have still to be written about them.

So Flanagan dealt with five writers who, you could say, looked at Ireland perhaps more closely, certainly more steadily: Maria Edgeworth, Lady Morgan, John Banim, Gerald Griffin and William Carleton, of whom William Butler Yeats said that he was 'the great novelist of Ireland by right of the most Celtic eyes that ever gazed from under the brow of storyteller'. It is a sound comment, even if it was made by a young Mr Yeats and before the advent of James Joyce.

It is also possible that Lady Morgan's romantic, enthusiastic concern for the affairs of her country was lightweight when compared with Lever's long consideration from many angles.

The Irish Novelists appeared from the Columbia University Press in 1959 and has established itself as one of the best books on the period, and it is to that book that I owe my first contact with the author. The late Francis

MacManus, a fine novelist, was then features editor of Radio Eireann. He passed the book to me for review. Since I was, at the time, literary editor of a Dublin daily newspaper, I passed the book to MacManus for review. A reasonable exchange. MacManus said to me: 'We must watch out for this Flanagan. He sounds like a man of judgment and scholarship'. That turned out to be pretty close to the truth; and the fact that a book I had written on William Carleton was referred to, in complimentary fashion, by Flanagan did not lessen my opinion of his judgment.

On the eve of his departure for his first visit to the land of his fathers, he was in New York with his friend, Kevin Sullivan, author of *Joyce among the Jesuits*. Flanagan was in the glooms and, when asked why, said: 'What's going to happen if I don't like the place?' As it happened he did and, over twenty or so summers, got to know it well; and out of the knowledge thus acquired, and out of his scholarship and a natural gift for such matters, *The Year of the French* has come.

It is customary nowadays, and was not so in the times of Thackeray, Tolstoy or Stendhal, for a writer to say that he, or she, is doing 'research', or 'researching', so as to write a novel. In better times it was assumed that the writer's life was the research. In a radio interview in Dublin, Flanagan said that the only matter he had specially to look up had to so with the French background. The rest, although he didn't say so, was in his life: ancestral origins, long reading and long thought on what he had read.

For those unfamiliar with the place or the period, the best and most easily available general history is Thomas Pakenham's *The Year of Liberty*. The most doctrinaire, more Frenchified Irish rebels of the time referred to the dreadful year of 1798 as The First Year of Liberty. So, with tragic and unconscious irony, they dated their letters.

Thomas Flanagan has George Moore of Moore Hall in the County Mayo writing a letter in 1798 to the Rt. Hon. Edward Barrett, member of parliament at Westminster. This is not, as the date might indicate, George Moore the novelist, but his grandfather, a man in his youth noted for duelling and gallantries in the great world of London. But being also of a philosophical cast of mind, he returned to his native Mayo and devoted his time to writing the history of the Girondins: a work never to be published.

Flanagan's management of the character of George Moore displays at its highest the expertise with which he brings people out of the past and sets them living beside us and relevant to our present, thus transforming his amazing book from what we might call, pejoratively, a historical novel into a profound comment on our time, or on any time that we know of since our modern western civilization took shape. His management of Moore's character is also a prime example of the many subtleties that delight and instruct in *The Year of the French*.

The novelist Flanagan reasonably assumes that George Moore, the novelist, who is very close to us, was not totally unlike George Moore, the philosophic historian. He even attributes to the historian a few of what have come to be known as Flanaganisms. But then, as Flaubert would have been the first to admit, it might be difficult to write a novel of five and a half hundred close pages, to paint a canvas as crowded as MacClise's great rampage around the wedding of Eva and Strongbow, and not allow yourself an occasional, shy, ironical, Hitchcock appearance.

Moore is writing to London on behalf of his brother John, who, following on the landing of General Humbert and his handful of French at Killala, has got himself involved in rebellion against the British crown to the absurd extent of allowing himself to be appointed the first president of the republic of Connacht. Very conscious that he is writing from the wilds of Mayo to what was then the world's most powerful city, or one of the four of them, Moore allows himself a little meditation on the history of his benighted and misgoverned country:

> How many dramas of modern history have chosen for setting this Godforsaken bog, and always without any recompense for my unfortunate countrymen save further misery? What were the rebellions of Desmond and Tyrone but chapters in the struggle between Elizabeth and Spain and thus of Reformation and Counter-reformation? What were the wars of Cromwell here but a sideshow to the English Civil War, in which the divine right of kings was challenged and overthrown? When James and William, the two kings, faced each other at the Boyne, the game was Europe, and Ireland but a board upon which the wagers were placed. The history of Ireland, as written by any of our local savants, reminds me of a learned and bespectacled ant, climbing laboriously across a graven tablet and discovering there deep valleys, towering mountains, broad avenues, which to a grown man contemplating the scene are but the incised names of England, Spain, France. Now the name of France appears a second time upon the tablet.

An elegant, if cynical, point-of-view, yet from what we know of George Moore, the historian, it seems certain that he would have thought and written exactly like that; and his is only one of the many points-of-view that Flanagan uses in a novel elaborately and brilliantly constructed. Nor do his people speak to us out of a history book and about a dead past. They are contemporaries telling us about matters common to us all, and I find that reading this novel I am afflicted with an odd feeling of two things happening at the same time. It is so close to what we know of the history that it seems the author must have come on a hundred old books, not known to anyone else, in which it is all written down exactly as he has it. It is also so close to life as we know it now that he must have taken the liberties with history that could only be taken by a reckless recording angel.

He calls to his aid five narrators who, along with about fifty characters, make up a considerable cast: a large crowd to handle, as the Russian high command might have said at the battle of Stalingrad; and there are also the French, the Irish rebels, and the army of Cornwallis. Yet nowhere – and I have searched the book carefully – can I find any fault in logic or coherence. The simplest reader need nowhere be confused. The professional writer will be (and one might as well confess it) more than a little ill with envy.

The book opens quietly, casually. Four men are in a tavern by Kilcummin Strand, there in all its innocence waiting for the French. They talk of rumours of thousands of rebel men out on the roads of Wexford, of the prophesied army of the Gael marching at last, of English yeomanry and hireling militia beaten and redcoats dead on thick-grassed fields; and of the French upon the sea and sailing to save the Poor Old Woman, Mother Ireland; and of Cooper, a small landlord whose people had come over with Cromwell; and of the Big Lord himself, owner and master of all the land as far as you can see. But the man himself is as far away in London as the Lord Almighty in the high heavens. They talk of and belong to the Whiteboys, nightriders of the long warfare of the peasants against those who owned the land they slaved on. Sometimes on nocturnal exploits they wore long white shirts: a fashion that crossed the ocean, as did the fiery cross of the Scottish Highlanders. But not nightriders exactly. For want of the means and the steeds, they went on foot.

The men are Connacht peasants sunk as low into serfdom as a depressed rural class could be. Among them a wandering Gaelic poet from the province of Munster: Flanagan could easily have been thinking of Eoín Rua Ó Súilleabháin, the eighteenth-century poet. His fictional Munsterman is conscious of the plight of the people he talks with, and of his own plight. He will, in a mood of contempt and cynicism, write for these pitiful people their Whiteboy proclamations; they themselves are unable to do so. He will go, almost like a sleepwalker, with the rabble of peasantry, canon-fodder, in the tail of the French, to the fatal battle of Ballinamuck, and be dragged back to Mayo to the gallows. His head filled with poetry, he is very conscious that in Mayo he is Ovid, 'banished to wild Tomi'.

A wandering Gaelic poet might seem an obvious choice for a character in a novel about the period, but Flanagan makes of him a gigantic tragic figure and places him in a telling relationship with the throng of people he moves through. With the Protestant clergyman Arthur Vincent Broome, M.A. (Oxon), he has a most ironic conversation about the exact meaning of the Irish verse that tells of Troy and Rome and Caesar and Alexander and their passing, and prophetically holds out the hope that the power of England might go the way they went; and Tara, once the halls of the High Kings of Ireland, itself is grass. Broome is conscious of the irony and, writing about it afterwards in a self-mocking effort to be the Edward

Gibbon of the events that happened at Killala, he says: 'How little we will ever know these people, locked as we are in our separate rooms . . . He [the poet] dwelt deep within the world of his people, and theirs is an unpredictable and violent world'.

Yet when Broome looks at the bare white walls and slender windows of his own church, at the two battleflags brought home from the wars of Marlborough, at the memorial plaques to those who fell serving the king on the fields of France and Flanders, he fears that he is less a minister to Christ's people than a 'priest to a military cult, as Mithra was honoured by the legions of Rome'. An instinct bred in the bone, nourished by childhoods of Sundays spent staring at the battleflags, compelled the Protestant gentry of Ireland to send their young men into the British army or the army of the East India Company.

Yet (he thinks) it is also true that the arts and benefits of civilizsation, an orderly existence, security of person and property, education, just laws, true religion and a hopeful view of man's lot on earth, follow the British flag and sword. Many then, and before and since, would dispute the matter with him who would have less quarrel with his conclusion: 'Only here have we failed, in the very first land we entered, for reasons which were in part our fault and in part the fault of the natives. But I think it pernicious to rummage over the past, sorting out wrongs and apportioning guilts'.

It is possible that the novelist's greatest achievement in blending the broodings of his imagination and historical truth so as to create a living reality is in the character, and statements, of this same Arthur Vincent Broome. At the time of the landing of the French, a Protestant Bishop Stock was in residence in Killala. He kept a journal. Some professional historians of my acquaintance have asked petulantly why Flanagan dropped Bishop Stock. Walter Scott could have told them that Flanagan was wise to do so, and to substitute Mr Broome for, shall we say, greater mobility, mental and physical. Bishops can be cumbersome.

Mary Renault has said very well of this novel that in it the ironies of time and the disasters of war are seen with contemporary eyes and to great effect, and that it should not be missed by anyone prepared to learn from history. But Hegal said that we learn from history that men never learn anything from history, and that ironic reflection allows Flanagan to allow Broome some of the profoundest paragraphs in the book. For Broome had once asked a learned and sagacious friend if man learned anything from history, and was told that he did not, but that it was possible to learn from historians. To this matter, while reading the capacious works of Hume and Gibbon, he had given much thought. Then follows a meditation on history in relation to Edward Gibbon, as striking as anything I have ever read on the matter. It is a long passage either to quote or summarize, but since it is, from a certain point-of-view, the core of the book, it is worth much consideration; and brutally and totally to summarise would pay little respect to the style.

Flanagan-Broome or Broome-Flanagan writes:

> Gibbon gives to us the breadth of the classical world, from the Hellespont to the pillars of Hercules, a vast temple with colonnades and recesses, glowing white marble beneath a blazing Mediterranean sun, and displays to us then its hideous and shameful destruction. How firm a sense do we derive of all its constituent parts, of their intricate relationships! How certain is its destruction, with alien creeds subverting its powers and alien races wearing away its far-flung frontiers. Each cause and reason is locked securely into place. And over all the mighty drama presides the awesome authority of Gibbon's splendid language, his unimpassioned rationality. Here, we think, is the chief civil drama of human history, in which tens and hundreds of thousands played their parts, but a drama compelled by the human mind to yield up its uttermost secrets. Great was Rome and catastrophic was its fall, but great too is the energy of the historian's mind, the cool deliberation of his judgment.

But then afterthoughts come to the Rev. Mr Broome, the Gibbon of Killala. Perhaps it had not been at all as Edward Gibbon had described it, perhaps everything had been chaos, chance, ill-luck, or simply the judgment of God – as had, in more pious ages, been believed. Perhaps everything that he had read had been only Gibbon's imagination: 'And the past remains therefore unknowable, shrouded in shadow, an appalling sprawl of buildings, dead men, battles, unconnected, mute, half recorded. Perhaps we learn nothing from history, and the historian teaches us only that we are ignorant'.

Broome sees himself as vain and affected in his own poor narrative; and here Flanagan is being at his most subtly ironic. Broome sees himself, his poor self as he puts it, for he is a genuinely humble man, as a confused clergyman with an indifferent education, a lover of comfort and civility and buttered toast – and so he is made to seem to the reader. But also (and he is not allowed to know it himself) he is a man of gentleness, sensitivity and humanity. In electing to play Gibbon to the events that happened around him, he finds that he has written only about a squabble in a remote province, a ragbag army of peasants, files of yeomen and militia, plough-boys hanged from crossroads gallows.

André Gide telling us that the novel about the novel might be more interesting than the novel itself could not be more astute than Flanagan is on that page.

The hopeless war goes east to the County Longford, to end in defeat and slaughter at Ballinamuck or the Place of the Pig: in Irish *Baile na Mhuiche*. The dire events that are, at some time in the future, to take place in the Valley of the Black Pig are imbedded in ancient Irish legend. But

neither myself nor the *Shell Guide to Ireland* know where that valley is;
and the fatal field of Ballinamuck in 1798 may merely have justified and
fortified a folktale.

Out of the whole tragic story this moment remains most vividly in the
memory of Arthur Vincent Broome. While the Rebels held Killala, and the
French and their ragged allies marched eastwards, Broome had made a
friendship with Ferdy O'Donnell, who kept the Rebels in the town in
order. One late evening they sit together in Broome's kitchen: 'the light is
thin, the far corners of the room are in shadow. Neither of us speaks. Men
are shouting in the street outside. At last he raises his hand, then drops it
again to the table. I have a vivid recollection of the scene, and yet it lacks
significance, a random memory. But what if the mysterious truth is locked
within such moments? Memory urges them upon us, implores us to
ponder them. A hopeless message'.

Albert Camus, living uncomfortably and in ill-health in occupied
France, planned an introduction to an anthology on Insignificance.
Because it would 'practically describe not only the most considerable part
of life, that of small gestures, small thoughts and small moods', and also
our common future; and even great thoughts and actions end up by
becoming insignificant.

The doomed, drunken poet, the dry as dust clergyman who would be an
historian are only two in Flanagan's crowded field of folk. Apart from
Broome, there are four other narrators plus Flanagan himself to help out,
and, as I've said, fifty other characters and a host of bystanders who are
yet not content to stand idly by. His people range from Humbert in the
bogs to Boney in the desert; from Tone and Teeling in Paris and on the sea
with the French, to a half-crazed prophecy-man hanged for shouting out
about the Place of the Pig, or just for existing; from Cornwallis in the field
to the Big Lord in London concerned about the condition of chimney-
sweeps and the abolition of negro-slavery, but with his scrawny withers
unwrung by the woes of his tenants on his lands in Mayo.

For some of the throng Flanagan had copious historical material to work
on, for others less, and some had birth only in his brain. All are alive and
memorable.

The last words, a superb dying-fall or fading echo are left to Seán
MacKenna, a schoolmaster and draper in Castlebar and a close friend of
the poet MacCarthy. When all is over, he goes to Killala to collect some
linen from Johnston of Sligo and writes when he comes home again:

> As I rode past Stoballs Hill in the darkness, I attempted to imagine what
> the great battle there had been like, the drums and bright banners and
> cannonshot and shouting. I could not. I told myself that the battle already
> lay with the Norman keep upon the far shore of that sea which separates

past from present. But that is not true, there is no such sea, it is but a trick of speech. All are bound together under God, mountain and bog, the shattered fortress and the grassy pasturelands of death, the drover's eagle that took wing upon the eve of battle, memory, history, and fable. A trick of speech and of the blackness of night, when we are separated from one another and from the visible world. It is in the brightness of the morning air, as the poet tells us, that hope and memory walk toward us across meadows, radiant as a girl in her first beauty.

July 3. The linen which I have brought back with me from Killala is badly bleached, and I will think carefully before I have further dealings with Johnston of Sligo.

This vast book moves slowly, but with a majesty that the more compels the further you advance. The attempt to write about it afflicts me with a sense of inadequacy. That a book of such quality should join the best sellers is most unusual, but must not be held against the author, who approached with great style a high and universal theme and has singularly triumphed.

Do not mistake me here. There is not a writer in the world (myself included) who would not like for various reasons, money being one of them, to sell good, better or best. But that best-selling should by some people be accepted as a commendatory critical adjective is indeed odd. Herman Melville had stern views on these matters and said bluntly that, looking around him, he would not wish to write the sort of books that were popular. But Herman Melville was stronger-minded than most of us and had, in his own time, his wish.

Thomas Flanagan has written a book that, by a quirk of whatever gods now manage these matters, is selling and will sell so well that many copies of it may still be around, after the great catastrophe, for a new and hope-fully chastened world to meditate on.

~&~ 17 ~&~

That Old Triangle:
A Memory of Brendan Behan

IN THE END OF ALL, THE HOSTAGE, an English boy by the name of Leslie Williams, rose from the dead in full view of the audience (or do I mean spectators?) and mocked the bells of hell that go ting-a-ling-a-ling, and, in a cheery parody of St Paul, asked the grave where was its victory, and death where was its sting-a-ling-a-ling. The victory and the sting were in the sore truth that the bold Brendan, quiet for the first time since he yelled as a newborn babe, had drawn the Glasnevin coverlet over his head and was no longer to be found raising the roof, or entertaining the customers, in any one of the many places of public resort that then lay between the two White Horses, the one in Greenwich Village and the one that Michael O'Connell kept on Burgh Quay by the Liffey.

Brendan was, as we say in Ireland, much missed at his own funeral, for he was always one to bury the dead with sympathy but with a spirit that mocked at mortality, and he would have appreciated the newspaper misprint that made one graveside speaker say that he had had the privilege of being interred with Brendan. What the speaker said was 'interned'; and while the dead man, in his time, had had his reservations about the joys of internment, he would, of a surety, have preferred them to the *nox perpetua* of the grave. Dying as a 'lark', he often said, had no attractions for him. It was a lonely business and he was, even to the detriment of his work and health, the most gregarious of men. The one thing he found most wearisome in prison was to be locked alone in his cell: 'There were noises of key-jangling and door-banging. I hoped they would open my door. Even if they were distributing nothing better than kicks or thumps, I'd prefer not be left out in my cold shroud of solitude. Fighting is better than loneliness'.

Even in prison where, for matters political, Brendan Behan spent eight years of his short life, he did his best to beat off loneliness, and so much of the best of what he really wrote, not talked about into a tape-recorder when he was sick, is that very rare and odd thing: a shout of laughter from the cell. The name of the prison in north Dublin City where his play *The Quare Fellow* was played out to its end in a hanging, was ironic enough to please him: Mountjoy; for yet further irony, abbreviated into 'The Joy'. An ale brewed in that part, his own part, of Dublin, was called by the same name as the prison; and an enticing advertisement, displayed at one end of Russell Street, where he was born, and visible every Sunday to the followers of the Gaelic games in Croke Park which, in 1920, had had its Black-and-Tan Bloody Sunday, said: 'Joy Be With You in the Morning'.

Song erupts from the punishment cells as the curtain rises on *The Quare Fellow*. Brendan adapted that song from a cruder original by another notable prisoner:

> A hungry feeling came o'er me stealing
> And the mice were squealing in my prison cell,
> And that old triangle
> Went jingle jangle,
> Along the banks of the Royal Canal.

Behan understood and could make laughter out of the old lag's perverted pride in his record between stone walls and iron bars. One old prisoner says to a novice: 'Meself and that man sitting there, we done time before you came up. In Kilmainham, and that's where you never were. First fourteen days without a mattress, skilly three times a day. None of your sitting out in the yard like nowadays. I got my toe amputated by one of the old lags so I could get into hospital for a feed'.

Warden Regan says to a prisoner who boasts that he has been in English prisons: 'There's the national inferiority complex for you. Our own Irish cat-o'-nine-tails and the batons of the warders loaded with lead from Carrickmines aren't good enough for him. He has to go Dartmooring and Parkhursting it. It's a wonder you didn't go further when you were at it, to Sing Sing or Devil's Island'.

Brendan's temperament, a comical sight more than that of Lovelace, made light of prison because prison was familiar to his rebel family and his Irish blood and, in prison as outside of it, he had a happy passion for making mockery of authority. For instance in *Borstal Boy* he looks at the Governor of Walton Prison, England, and sees a 'desiccated old-looking man, in tweed clothes and wearing a cap, as befitted his rank of Englishman, and looking as if he'd ride a horse if he had one. He spoke with some effort and if you did not hear what he was saying you'd have thought from his tone, and the sympathetic, loving and adoring looks of the screw, P.O., and Chief, that he was stating some new philosophical truth to save the suffering world from error'.

Dunlavin is the Lord and King of all the old lags in *The Quare Fellow*. It is amusingly possible that the crazy, comic spirit which made Behan laugh even at those patriotic things that were dearest to him, inspired him, if that's the word I'm searching for, to call the man by the name of the Wicklow village famed in the heroism, and suffering, of the rebellion of 1798. He could make a very good effort at singing the ballad of Dunlavin Green.

How and ever: Dunlavin, the old lag, expresses his disgust at having to live cell-by-cell with a sex criminal: 'Dirty Beast! I won't have an hour's luck for the rest of me six months'.

Those who are alive, even though they lie in jail, must accommodate themselves to the conditions of living, and Brendan took his durance vile as a priceless part of his experience, and all the time, and quite naturally and logically, he intended, when he took to the writing, to exploit those prison memories. Once when I complained to him, when things were as they once were, that the soaring cost of living in Dublin would land me in jail for debt, he said with affected horror: 'Don't take from me the one advantage I have in this hard-backed book business'.

His best hard-backed book, superbly done, as the scattered, dictated notebooks were not done, was, too, in the oddest way, a continuation of the considerable library written by Irishmen in English prisons or on the run from English law or justice, as it used to be called. There were Doheny, Davitt, Kickham, Tom Clarke, Darrell Figgis *et alii*. Through his mother's brother, Peadar Cearnaigh, who wrote the lyric, by no means his best, that were to become the Irish national anthem, Behan was very much part of all that. But no accused patriot adding to that holy scripture *Speeches from the Dock*, a paper-backed national piety that was once a bestseller in Ireland, could have permitted himself the humour, the mockery of Behan; and the resonant Carlylean voice of John Mitchel of Young Ireland in 1848, orating rather than writing his classical *Jail Journal*, finds an uproarious *reductio ad absurdum* in Behan's *Borstal Boy*.

The Joy, then, was a fine and private place when compared with The Bog: the long-term Portlaoise Prison (formerly Maryborough Jail) in the heart of the Irish Midlands. The Joy had, because of a kindly governor whose blackthorn stick Behan borrowed and never returned, the reputation of being easy. Easy, that is, until matters went as far as hanging. Then the laughter sourly dies in the cell and the prisoner called Neighbour tells how once, for the reward of two bottles of stout, he took the hood off 'the fellow that was after being topped'. And how he wouldn't do it a second time for a bottle of whiskey, for the 'head was all twisted and his face black, but the two eyes were the worst; like a rabbit's; it was fear that had done it'.

Brendan was in the Joy not, as was his wont, for politics but, like the Bold Thady Quill of the great West Cork ballad, for 'batin' the police' when the last man to be hanged in the Republic of Ireland went to the drop. With two warders, he and the condemned man made a four for handball. He drank the condemned man's daily bottles of stout because the crime for which the unfortunate fellow was doomed to suffer had been done under the influence of that beverage, and he could no longer be convinced that Guinness was good for him. When the pitiful man asked Brendan if hanging would hurt him, Brendan assured him, with his own special type of kindness, that he didn't think so, but then he had never been through it himself nor had he talked with anyone who had.

He was in prison for politics when the original of the Quare Fellow was hanged: a pork-butcher who, alas, had murdered his brother and filleted the corpse, so skilfully that nothing was ever found. It was one of Brendan's more lurid jokes that the murderer had sold his brother as fresh pork to the Jesuits in the House of Studies at Tullabeg, County Offaly. But when I mentioned that aspect of the case to a friend of mine, a Jesuit, who had been resident there at the time, he said that he fervently hoped and prayed that that might not have been the case.

That Brendan Behan, like Lord Byron, woke up to find himself famous overnight, right in the middle of the English debate on capital punishment, was in no small measure due to that hanging; and that was the only good turn a hanging ever did him or anybody else. For people are as interested in hangings now as they were on the night before Larry was stretched in full view of the public, and think of all the long years during which Tyburn was London's greatest theatrical draw, a popular open-air theatre.

The famous drunken appearance (in the company of Malcolm Muggeridge, who was chillingly sober) on BBC television came to the aid of the hangman in the popularization of Brendan, and that was the only good turn drink ever did him. But now that I've raised the question, and since it must be answered, let me say how grossly by some people, and by some newspapers, the drunken legend was exaggerated. It was no news at all that an Irishman could be sober and doing some work. Yet while Brendan did not invite such publicity, he did nothing, by word or deed, to diminish it. He went a long ways further than Samuel Johnson ever did in believing that to be talked about, well or ill, drunk or sober, was the best way for a writer to bring in The Readies – meaning dollars and pounds. It is the way of the vile world. But Henry James and many another might have demurred. It is customary and correct to lament the drinking and the waste, as my friends Irving Wardle, the London critic, and Francis MacManus, the Dublin novelist, did. But it was also a wonder that so much good writing was done in such a short time, not only against the impediment of drink but because Brendan never had any regularly developed habits of work, and being, as I said, the most gregarious of men, he craved company which, in Dublin, frequently leads to drink, unless you care to join the Legion of Mary or the Pioneer Total Abstinence Association, which neither he, myself, nor any of our friends in Dublin ever showed any fanatical signs of doing.

The mornings I was aroused at six or seven, to find Brendan smiling at the foot of my bed with the bright idea that we could start the day well in the early bars in the fruit markets or on the docks!

There was a sweet story that once, when following his first trade of house-painter Brendan was at work on a ceiling in the Land Commission Office in Merrion Street, he had his head out the window for air and for looking at the people. James Sleator, the painter and then President of the Royal Hibernian Academy, was passing by. He invited Brendan round the corner for a 'tincture'. And Brendan went, and never came back, leaving the ceiling half-painted, or whatever, and his kit there for anyone who cared to collect it. He painted the flat of the poet Patrick Kavanagh for free but, for laughs, did it, in the poet's absence, in a complete and total sable. He had, at times, an odd sense of humour.

He was also, we must remember, in his final years, a sick man with an ailment that craved the sweet heat of wine and which the wine only aggravated.

He was, first and before all, a Dublinman from that restricted area of north Dublin City, to which true Dubliners confine the high title of the Northside. The rest of the North City can, by purists, be regarded as suburbia, inhabited, or inflated, by provincials: *Cuiltes*. After that, Brendan was an Irishman and a member of the underground Irish Republican Army at, up to then, its most troublesome period since the bloodshed and burning had eased off in 1923, (That idyllic little bit I wrote in 1965. . .)

By his own definition, Brendan was a 'bad Catholic', or, as Irish euphemism has it, a lapsed or non-practising Catholic.

His IRA activities brought him at an absurdly early age to an English prison and a Borstal institution, gave him the makings of his best book which, either as autobiography or as part of the literature of penology, has established itself as a classic. That time in durance also inspired him for various reasons with a healthy respect and a liking for the English people. Although his first feeling, after two months studying and experiencing the brutalities of the warders in Walton Jail, Liverpool, was that he was most anxious for a truce with the British, that not only was everything he had ever read or heard about them, in history, true but that 'they were bigger and crueller bastards' than he had taken them for because 'with tyrants all over Europe, I had begun to think that maybe they weren't the worst after all but, by Jesus, now I knew they were, and I was not defiant of them, but frightened'.

But later acquaintance with kindlier types . . .

They included, sadly enough, a polite Borstal inmate by the name of Neville Heath, later to be renowned, although Behan, with splendid restraint, did not say so nor fully name him as the sadistic murderer of the two women.

But later acquaintance with kindlier types, as I was about to say, made Behan modify his opinion and he allowed himself that deliberately exquisite understatement 'The British are very nationalistic'. He was, too, always glad and grateful, and rightly so, that London Town gave him such a splendid welcome as a playwright and that, once, when on the way through England, en route to France, he was arrested under a deportation order and the resident authorities deported him not back to Ireland but onwards to Fair France, where he wanted to go anyway. And paid his fare. Fair stood the wind . . . A humorous and decent people, he almost thought.

For all previous sharp statements about the neighbours, he made amends in the drawing of the character of Leslie Williams, the hostage, in the play of that name. The voice of Leslie was, also, a voice from a prison: that of an ordinary young English boy caught fatally and wonderingly in a situation he cannot hope to understand.

The likes of him have been much to be seen, from 1970 onwards, standing or wandering around in the north-east of this island, armed to the bloody teeth and not knowing where they were or are, nor what it is all about.

But in *The Hostage*, Teresa, the sweet, young, Irish country girl – an orphan, as the hostage is – tells him that Monsewer, the daft old owner of the house in which he is held, is an English nobleman: 'he went to college with your king'.

Soldier [i.e. Leslie]: We ain't got one.
Teresa: Maybe he's dead now, but you had one one time, didn't you?
Soldier: We got a duke now. He plays tiddly winks.
Teresa: Anyway, he [i.e. Monsewer] left your lot and came over here and fought for Ireland.
Soldier: Why, was somebody doing something to Ireland?
Teresa: Wasn't England, for hundreds of years?
Soldier: That was donkey's years ago. Everyone was doing something to someone in those days.

It seems, now, unnecessary to say so, but the times have not changed. Anywhere.

Yet, in that dialogue, Caitlin Ní Houlihan and John Bull had never before spoken so simply, so comically nor so wisely to each other; never before, not even with the assistance of Bernard Shaw. And mad Monsewer was, indeed, English: the son of a bishop, and had gone to 'all the biggest colleges in England and slept in the one room with the King of England's son'; until one day when, because his mother was Irish, he discovered he was an Irishman or an Anglo-Irishman which, in Behan's deliberately misleading definition, was a Protestant with a horse. Anglo-Irishmen, he comically argued, only worked at 'riding horses, drinking whisky and reading double-meaning books in Irish at Trinity College'. To become Irish, Monsewer took it 'easy at first, wore a kilt, played Gaelic football on Blackheath . . . took a correspondence course in the Irish language. And when the Rising took place he acted like a true Irish hero'.

But when he lays down his bagpipes, and raises his voice in song, as all Behan's people, including himself, were forever ready to do, his father's bloody British blood proves living and strong:

> In our dreams we see old Harrow,
> And we hear the crow's loud caw,
> At the flower show our big marrow
> Takes the prize from Evelyn Waugh.
> Cups of tea or some dry sherry,
> Vintage cars, these simple things,
> So let's drink up and be merry
> Oh, the Captains and the Kings.

Monsewer has a dual, lunatic significance. The house he owns and in which the young hostage is held, and accidentally killed by his rescuers, is, as Pat, the Caretaker, says a 'noble old house, which housed so many heroes' and is, in the end, 'turned into a knocking-shop'. It is also romantic idealistic Ireland fallen on sordid, materialistic days. And that a madman of that most romantic people, the English, should, in his imagination, lead the last Irish Rebellion, playing the pipes and making heroines out of decent whores, would have seemed, thirty or so years ago, to be a fair enough chapter of our national story. It all seems a long way away from Guildford and the 1990s.

Yet even then, that house was more than heroic Ireland down in the dumps. It was the world in a mess and God gone off his rocker. The very first stage direction says: 'the real owner isn't right in his head'. Monsewer, in sad truth, is one of Behan's visions of God, and as he parades, salutes, plays the pipes and sings of tea and toast and muffin rings, the old ladies with stern faces, and the captains and the kings, he falls into line with images of the Divinity that appear elsewhere in the plays and prose.

The ministers of religion, because of Brendan's experience with prison chaplains, who had to inform him, at that time, that as a member of the IRA he was excommunicate, seldom come well out of the story as he tells it. Yet God is, nevertheless, not to be judged by the deficiences of his servants. Dunlavin, satirizing the Higher Civil Servants in the back snugs of pubs in

Merrion Row, defends the Almighty against their patronization: 'Educated drinking, you know. Even a bit of chat about God at an odd time, so as you'd think God was in another department, but not long off the Bog, and they was doing Him a good turn to be talking well about Him'.

That same turn of phrase, almost, recurs in *The Hostage* when Meg attacks the canting and impossible Mr Mulleady. In a good cause, Brendan was never afraid of repeating himself.

The cynical Meg may say that 'pound notes is the best religion in the world', but the 'chokey bloke' in *Borstal Boy* points out that some men are so miserably constituted that they 'couldn't be 'appy no matter where they were. If they was in the Ritz Hotel with a million nicker and Rita Hayworth they'd find some bloody thing to moan about'.

God could sometimes be faltering, as Monsewer was, in his judgments on people. For Ratface, the altar-server in the prison chapel, looked like a 'real cup-of-tea Englishman with a mind the width of his back-garden that'd skin a black man, providing he'd get another to hold him, and send the skin 'ome to Mum, but Our Lord would be as well pleased with him, if he was in the State of Grace, as He'd be with St Stanislaus Kostka, the Boy Prince of Poland, and race or nationality did not enter into the matter, either one way or another'.

But, regardless, the Maker of All Things had compensatory qualities. Following in a mob (what other way?) the course of the Saviour's Passion around the Stations of the Cross in the prison's R.C. chapel, the prisoners were enabled, in a passage that is pure Hogarth, to fuse and mingle and exchange cigarettes and even fragments of food. The crooked greyhound-men taking the doped dog to the races, in one of the best sketches in *Brendan Behan's Island*, were respectfully pious enough to warn Brendan that it wasn't a lucky thing to mock religion and they going out to 'do a stroke'.

If the law that excommunicated the then IRA had not existed and Brendan had been allowed to go to confession, he would have missed the sight of one of the nastiest of the warders slipping and falling and floundering in a snowdrift, and shaking his fists in anger, and falling again while those of the prisoners who were not at the R.C. devotions were at their cell-windows roaring with laughter. Brendan sat down again at his table and, in the terms of an old Gaelic proverb, thanked God and His Blessed Mother for all that: 'God never closed one door but he opens another and if He takes away with His right hand, He gives it back with His left, and more besides'. Pressed down and flowing over, in fact. And we are back with God as Monsewer, a decent fellow, not quite in control of things, whose actions, even when He doesn't plan them too well, frequently turn out for the best. Even the 'lapsed' Catholic comes out in defence of the Old Faith when he tells Hannen Swaffer, the columnist, who has just announced that he is a spiritualist, that Catholicism keeps a better type of ghost.

Borrowing a sentence from the lingo of beloved Dublin streets, Behan was fond of saying that every cripple has his own way of walking. It is also true, or should be, that every writer has his own way of writing; and I have already pointed out how wonderful it was that so much good writing came out of his gregariousness and chronic restlessness. His great kindly spirit had to express itself in every possible way. And what was writing, if it didn't go on for too long, but another form of movement?

Borstal Boy, The Quare Fellow, The Hostage, and the better portions of the notebooks or sketchbooks are the considerable achievement that he left us, although one stage-direction in *The Hostage,* reading 'What happens next is not very clear', seems to indicate that Behan threw his hat (he never wore one) at the whole business of writing and said: 'Joan Littlewood, the decent girl, will look after that detail, and Blank the Begrudgers'.

Reading your own works, he argued in his sad book on New York, was a sort of mental incest. But as a general rule it is better, at least, to write your own books; and to some New Yorkers who had been disappointed with what he had to say about their stupendous city which, as cities go, he loved next to Dublin, I can only say that his book about what he saw in New York was not so much written as just spoken, and by a sick and weary man, and into a tape recorder.

Yet even in the tired ramblings-on of a man who was coming close to the end, there was flash after flash of the spirit that made him the most entertaining companion I have known, or am ever likely to know. One night in Michael O'Connell's White Horse, on Burgh Quay in Dublin City, I was, and others with me, weak with laughter at his antics. Here were some of them:

1. Toulouse-Lautrec: by walking up and down the floor on his knees, with his knees in his shoes.
2. The Poor Old Woman, Mother Ireland: with the tail of his jacket over his head for a shawl.
3. An aspiring Irish politician, mouthing every platitude ever heard from an Irish platform, and borrowing a few more from the pulpit.
4. Sex in the Abbey Theatre: for which there were no words, but only mime, and the mimic is now forever motionless.

I remember thinking that if he ever got a wider audience he might make a fortune. I can't claim much credit for the prophecy: it came easy. My sadness was to be that that great, kindly, comic man held the stage only for such a brief time. And we were left, as I have said, with the plays, including the one-act *The Big House,* the autobiography, and what was good in the notebooks. Then there was *Richard's Cork Leg,* which, borrowing a title from James Joyce, was to be the meeting of All Ireland around the grave of Honor Bright, an unfortunate girl done to death by gunshot on the Dublin mountains sixty or so years before.

Brendan Behan had a happy, boyish belief that you could find a good man everywhere and, being always, in some ways, a boy, he liked talking about the important people he had met. He liked talking about being invited to the inauguration of President John F. Kennedy. Well who, politics apart, wouldn't have? He liked talking about Gilbert Harding, who was a good man, and about Oona Guinness, who was a great lady, and about John Betjeman who was, anyway, a sort of Irish institution while he was in Dublin. I detected an ironic flicker of the eyelids, even if by then they were very tired eyelids, when he said: 'As Hemingway once remarked to a friend of mine . . '. He was vain, and proud of his success, and eternally talkative, but he was not so much a namedropper as a friend naming friends, and Princess Margaret and Rosie Redmond, a celebrated and lovely lady of the streets of Dublin, were all equally to him just lovely people.

Rosie Redmond we remember from Sean O'Casey's *The Plough and the Stars*, and I feel that Brendan and certainly his father, Stephen, knew stories about her that even O'Casey may not have heard. This is not the place to tell them; yet the mention of her fair name brings me by a most 'commodious vicus of recirculation back to Howth Castle and Environs', to the 'Fort of the Dane, Garrison of the Saxon, Augustan capital of a Gaelic nation', to the city built around the body of the fallen Finnegan, and that more catastrophically fallen giant: Haveth Childers Everywhere.

A city, Brendan said, was a place where you were least likely to get 'a bite of a wild sheep', and the test of a city was the ease with which you could see and talk to other people. And New York, away back all those years ago, was the friendliest city he knew. He was talking, I suspect, about some good pubs. But Dublin was his own town. Not the middle-class Dublin that John Mitchel, in the 1840s, had seen, in Carlylean style, as a city of Bellowing Slaves and Genteel Dastards. Nor yet that city that Patrick Pearse said had to atone in blood for the guilt of allowing to happen the execution of Robert Emmet.

No! Brendan's Dublin was the Dublin of the fighting poor who had been organized by James Larkin in 1913, and the Dublin with the everlast-ing memory of the General Post Office in flames in 1916. It was the Dublin, too, that the prisoners, Neighbour and Dunlavin, fondly dream over in *The Quare Fellow*. Meena La Bloom belonged to it, who, with Dunlavin's help, gave many's the Mickey Finn to a sailor. And the Dublin of May Oblong who debagged the Irish MP on his way to the comic House in Westminster to vote for Home Rule for Ireland. And Meena locked the MP in her room, and neither for the love of her country, or his, would she liberate him until he had slipped a fiver under the door. And there was the patriotic plumber of Dolphin's Barn who swore to let his hair grow until Ireland was free. And there was Lottie l'Estrange, who got had up for pushing the soldier into Spencer Dock.

Lovely people, all of them. They belong in the Nightown seen, or imagined, by a young man by the name of Joyce. Or perhaps on the shadowy streets that Liam O'Flaherty wrote about in *The Informer* and in *Mr Gilhooley*.

Behan's Dublin, too, as the plays show, was as much or more that of Boucicault and the old Queen's Theatre Variety as it was of the Abbey Theatre, except when O'Casey was in possession of the Abbey stage. And his Dublin was my Dublin from 1937 onwards, and with warm brotherliness he once told me that I was one of the few country fuckers he had ever met who had enough in him to make a Dublin Jackeen. For, from an early age, he had what he called a pathological horror of country people. Because to a child in the Dublin in which he was a child, the symbols and exercisers of authority, school-teachers and civic guards, all came from the country, from the provinces. And the jungle began where the Dublin city tram-tracks came to an end.

Yet his heart was too great for one city to contain. It opened out to Ireland, to the Aran Islands, to London, Paris, New York. Although to the end he had his reservations about Toronto and Berlin. As they had about him.

He would have died, and almost did die, for Ireland, but he was cynically conscious of the delirium of the brave in the Robert Emmet pose of the dying hero. It was a fine thing to feel like Cuchulain, guarding the Gap of Ulster, his enemies ringed round him, his back supported by a twisted tree, and he calling on 'the gods of Death and Grandeur to hold him up until his last blood flowed'. But if the only spectators were two Walton jailers, Mr Whitbread and Mr Holmes, clearly Private Compton and Private Carr in later life, and if Mr Holmes was methodically beating you up, then the hot glow went out of the heroism. You could be mangled in an English prison and who would 'give a fish's tit about you over here. At home it would be all right if you were to get the credit for it . . . But the mangling would have to be gone through first'.

Behan was brave from boyhood to death, but there were no false heroics about him and he felt that between mangling and martyrdom there should be some satisfactory, poetic and, preferably, unpainful relationship.

Like Peter Wanderwide (and how Behan would have mocked at me for quoting Belloc), he had 'Ireland in his dubious eyes'. In Irish and English our ballads and classical folksongs were ready to his lips and when he wasn't deliberately roaring his head off, he could sing. At penal work, digging on the Borstal farm, his fork uncovered from English soil a golden apple; and biting it surreptitiously he thought of Blind Raftery, the poet, and of the spring coming, after the feast of Brigid, to the wide plains of Mayo. But in the swift switch of humour that was characteristic of him, he would admit that digging was an activity he wouldn't pick for pleasure, and he would tell how his father brought him out, during a Dublin strike, to help farm an acre of land on ground, at Glasnevin, that had once been associated with Dean Swift. Stephen dug for a bit 'with great function', talked about the land, how his ancestors had come from it, how healthy it was, and how, if they kept at the digging, they might uncover relics of Swift, Vanessa, Stella or Mrs Delaney. But next day, bored, he got a countryman to dig the plot, in exchange for Stephen doing the countryman's strike-picket-duty, down below there on the happy and homely streets of Dublin.

That, to me, is a touching, endearing picture of father and son: two rare comedians.

But Brendan was grateful for the golden apple and the good weather. He was alwasy grateful and pious in good weather, and the day he found the apple was the sort of day that 'you'd know Christ died for you'. A bloody good job, he thought, that he had been born in rainy Ireland and not in the South of France or Miami Beach where he would have been so grateful and holy for the sunshine that St Paul of the Cross would only have been trotting after him, 'skull and crossbones and all'.

As a great swimmer, next to the sunshine he loved the sea: the eastern sea at the Forty Foot, the swimming pool famed in the opening of *Ulysses*. And he loved the laughter of the western sea which, according to the poet Louis MacNeice, juggled with spars and bones, irresponsibly. Brendan did not view it so sombrely. On the Aran Islands and along the Connemara shore, and in Glenties, County Donegal, with my friends and relations, the Boyles and the Harveys, he claimed he could forget all the cruel things of this world. He wrote so pleasantly of the night, after the licensed hours, in a pub in Ballyferriter, County Kerry, when the Civic Guards obligingly sent word that they were going to raid so that the customers could withdraw a little up the mountain slope, taking supplies with them, and drink in peace until the raid was over.

> It was a lovely starlit night and warm, too, and one of my most cherished recollections is of sitting out there on the side of Mount Brandon, looking at the mountain opposite, called the Three Sisters, framed against the clear moonlit sky and the quiet, shimmering Atlantic, a pint of the creamiest Guinness in my hand as I conversed in quiet Irish with a couple of local farmers.

There was a happy Irishman at home in Ireland.

Mount Brandon, as he would say with proprietary pride, was named after his patron saint, Brendan the Navigator, who, the legend says, reached the New World before either Norsemen or Columbus, and who left to all who came after him the promise of the Isle of the Blest that all mariners might one day find.

'And that,' as Brendan said when he finished his sketchbook *Brendan Behan's Island*, about the island of Ireland, 'the end of my story and all I'm going to tell you and thanks for coming along'.

~~e 20 9~

Canon Sheehan:
The Reluctant Novelist

FATHER MATHEW RUSSELL, THE Jesuit priest who made and edited for some considerable time a periodical called *The Irish Monthly*, which lasted right into our time (if you're aged roundabout seventy), wrote in 1902 that the author of the sketches of clerical life entitled *My New Curate* was 'the most literary of Irish priests since the author of *The Prout Papers*'.

To most of us now who are capable of giving any thought to the matter, that would seem an odd way to put it and, even in 1902, Fr Russell could scarcely have made a more striking or more comic comparison and contrast.

Granted the two men came from Cork, and were ordained priests and men of letters. But one of them was the devoted parish-priest of Doneraile, zealous in his duties, a patient, able administrator and educator, friend of the poor and of the children, so scrupulous about the claims his priestly office made on him that he could yield to his natural literary instincts only when he had convinced himself, to the good of his soul but often to the detriment of his books, that he was extending the scope of that office by being a writer.

The other man mentioned was an eccentric Erasmian, stubborn enough to resist the advice of some of Father Russell's Irish Jesuit predecessors when they told him it would be better for the Church and himself if he didn't become a priest. They made certain sure that he wouldn't become a Jesuit. And he was, also, perverse enough when he had become a priest to wish to be nothing else but a man-of-letters. Francis Sylvester Mahony became, as we have seen, an urban wit, one of the *Fraser's Magazine* crowd, fond of travel and good living, the author of witheringly witty attacks on Tom Moore, Daniel O'Connell, Lady Morgan, and, absolutely, no respecter of the feelings of the people he decided deserved wounding. Patrick Augustine (Canon) Sheehan became a rural recluse, an ascetic, a kindly man perplexed by his discovery that it is difficult to write, particularly to write novels, without offending someone.

He wrote to Father Heuser, the editor of the American *Ecclesiastical Review*, who had published *My New Curate*, in the *Review*, who did much to encourage Sheehan, and who enshrined his memory in an authoritative, if dull, biography. Sheehan wrote:

> My great difficulty is to draw from life and yet avoid identifying any character with living persons. And we are so narrow and insular here in Ireland, that it is almost impossible to prevent priests saying: 'That is So-and-So. That is Father — etc'. But I shall steer clear without wounding charity.

Even by the use of the words 'narrow' and 'insular' he was running the risk of wounding the sensitive souls not only of some of his clerical colleagues but even of some of their lay-brothers in the Lord. He was to make that discovery *in tempore opportuno* and that was to add to the perplexities of being, all together, an Irish parish-priest and a sensitive, considerate man endowed by nature with all the instincts and evil impulses of the natural novelist, which are frequently neither sensitive nor considerate.

Canon Sheehan, in fact, was worried at finding himself writing books just as some of his characters, particularly that fantastic fellow, Geoffrey Austin, were worried at finding themselves reading books. Father Henry Liston in *The Blindness of Dr Gray* is reproved by his pastor for his devotion to frivolous and profane literature and, conscience-stricken, he detects suddenly in Heine a blasphemous anger and a leer, and thinks: 'Is it right for me to find pleasure in such things? Am I not a priest, chosen from thousands to be the loyal servant and faithful subject of my King? . . . And am I serving Him whilst my bookshelves are lined with literature, every line of which seems to be a fierce indictment of His Sovereign goodness?'

There, now, was a real predicament, whatever lighter laymen with little conscience to trouble them, or even trendy clergymen in the 1990s, might think; and Sheehan was to devote some of his best writing to an effort to reconcile the claims of theology and of profane literature:

> There has been amidst the myriads but one vast intellect which wedded Poetry to Philosophy and Theology, and entrained Aquinas and Aristotle in the service of the Muses; and that was the poet who stands alone and pre-eminent – Dante. But the man of letters looks up to the lonely watch-tower where the theologian is bending over his oak-bound, brass-clasped folios, and mutters: 'A horned owlet, blinking his bleared eyes and flapping his cut wings by moonlight in a dismantled ruin'; and the

theologian, looking from his lofty eyrie on the 'man of letters', mutters:
'A popinjay with borrowed feathers, chirping some ribald chorus in the
market-place'. No one appears to understand that there is poetry — the
very highest and most supernal poetic inspiration in these musty
medieval folios; and no one appears to understand that underlying the
music and magic of modern poetry there may be hidden some deep
theological truths and untruths which, perhaps, it would not be alto-
gether unwise to learn or unlearn.

In an article that he sent to Father Heuser in 1898, Sheehan said that the
trend of modern writing was towards adopting the novel or the short story
as the best and most attractive vehicle for teaching not only morals and
history but science as well. He believed that if Newman, Buckle, Ruskin
and men of their genius had been, at that moment, in their prime, they
would have chosen fiction as the means of putting forward and populariz-
ing their favourite theories.

He was a truthful man and, almost certainly, he did believe that piece of
nonsense, a complete misunderstanding or, at any rate, misstatement of
the impulse that makes any worthwhile writer write anything. Canon
Sheehan had to find a reason for yielding to the natural man who wanted
to write novels. He had, as I have already said, to make novel-writing a
living branch of the whole vine of his priestly vocation; it was a legitimate
way of speaking to a larger congregation than the one that sat docilely
before him when he stood in the pulpit in Doneraile.

Writing anything for printing and publication, least of all writing
novels, stories about other people, could never be for him a vocation in
itself, neither could it be a pastime as it might have been, and often has
been, in the case of a doctor or lawyer dabbling in literature. By nature
Sheehan was, obviously, no dabbler or dilettante, and his idea of what it
meant to be a priest would have made such waste of time, or eternity,
unthinkable. He had to overcome, too, as his stern old Dr. Gray never
overcame, 'that dread or shyness of print which seems to be the *damnosa
hereditas* of the Irish priesthood'.

His novels would have to be serious affairs, written not because he was
a storyteller by nature or inherited impulse, nor because he was fascinated
by the behaviour of people, including himself, but because he was
preacher and teacher by a higher calling.

Then he had to battle with a Savonarolesque bias against profane literature, a bias forced on him, half against his will, by his narrow education
in St. Patrick's College, Maynooth (much altered over the years), as well as
with an ingrained Victorian contempt for, and suspicion of, the novel as
something that went with young ladies and frivolity. The struggle in him
between the Levite and the man of letters seems to have been agonizing
and, from the evidence that his books provide, it contorted, with anguish
of soul, his student days, and the days of his curacies in Ireland and

England, until he wrote the worst of it out of his system in the turgid pages of his *bildungsroman*, his hallucinative, nightmare memory of *Wilhelm Meister*, or of Keller's *Der Grune Heinrich*, the two connected novels, *Geoffrey Austin: Student* and *The Triumph of a Failure*, that tell of Austin's adolescent priggishness, his inability to get a job, and of his high-falutin' meditations. Those two novels were the work of a young, inexperienced cleric tormented by books which, like the beckoning bathing beauties once providentially provided to tempt anchorites and now provided by the tabloids in an effort to make some of us open our eyes on Sunday mornings, sang to him the Circean praises of a world he had vowed himself to God to fight.

What he meant those two early novels to be was a warning to young men of the dangers to faith of an exclusively secular education. Not surprisingly. Not surprisingly (for how could a cloistered celibate novelist prove his point by life-like examples), he left alone the delicate topic of dangers to morals: and even Geoffrey Austin's scruples about his lost or diminishing faith incline to make less sensitive, less cloistered men than Sheehan wonder what all the fuss was about. An American Catholic critic, Blanche Mary Kelly, once talked of *A Portrait of the Artist as a Young Man* as the classic portrayal of the soul saying no to God. Canon Sheehan, an Irish priest walking nervously among all the poetic, romantic monuments of the Rhineland, was trying to tell young Irishmen how to say yes. The Jesuit Father Darlington, an Englishman like Hopkins, but serving the Lord in Ireland, claimed that Canon Sheehan succeeded and that those two novels were influential among students of Newman's Catholic University in Dublin. But it is one of the many incidental ironies of the relationship between Geoffrey Austin, the student, and other things that were going on in Ireland at the time that the student James Joyce, as learned in Aquinas and Newman as Geoffrey Austin was in Jean Paul Richter, should have uttered in grim seriousness, and with positive literary results, the demonic *Non Serviam* that poor Geoffrey fondly thought he was uttering when, in a moment of worldliness, he preferred Richter to Ephrem of Edessa, who in his time said a ninth beatitude for those who served, praised and were silent in fear.

'To prevent contamination by these pernicious doctrines (of materialistic science), of our Irish youth,' Sheehan wrote, 'must be the proximate and pressing duty of those to whom the faith and morals of the rising generation are largely entrusted'.

With that laudable intention, unimpeachable from a pulpit but cribbing and crippling for a novelist, Sheehan created the absurd character of Geoffrey Austin, sent him to such a civil service college as never was, made him talk more learnedly than seventy savants, but, because some humiliation was clearly necessary to bring him back to a knowledge of the truth, allowed him to fail an elementary examination. Undoubtedly Geoffrey Austin had something in common with that other erudite student, Stephen Dedalus, but it was a pity for the forces of orthodoxy that Joyce wrote a good novel about Dedalus, or about himself, and Canon Sheehan put together around Geoffrey Austin two eccentric bundles of learning, some fine writing on Catholic philosophy, and a series of impossible incidents happening to incredible people.

The doubt and pride of Dedalus strike us as the truth, and the book-learning he has comes naturally from him, because Joyce really understood and shared the doubt and pride and was skilful enough in the art of narration to keep his own learning under control. But the reflections Geoffrey Austin is supposed to make and the learning he lays claim to are always obviously not his but the property of the man who made the book, and Geoffrey's doubts, whatever they are, merely make the normal reader, whoever he or she may be, feel perplexed or impatient. He hints darkly at dark vices. Standing among his polite, astounding friends, who, in a tiny whispering-gallery of a city like Dublin, even more noxious then, because smaller, than it is now, were inexplicably ignorant of the fact that he had been starving for years in ill-paid employment, he reflects:

> If I now were to go on the platform and tell of my experience with the Princes of Darkness and of Doubt . . . what would be the result? I know I should be hunted from that platform as if I were a mad dog, and the hands of the gentlest woman would be raised against me for my profanity and blasphemy.

When a novelist allows a character to talk like that, he should, if he is playing the game according to any ascertainable rules, allow the character to prove to the reader that he or she (the character) was as big and bad as his, or her, words. Otherwise, the novelist, in the next chapter, should have the character certified and taken away.

But Canon Sheehan was not playing the game according to any ascertainable rules. He was exploiting the novel to preach a sermon, through the example of Geoffrey Austin, to the young men of Ireland, who, heaven knew or should have known, got, at that time, enough sermons in the conventional ways from the very conventional pulpit. Even as sermons and exemplary talks, those first two sad novels were dismal failures, forced on Sheehan the natural novelist by the high sense of dedication of Sheehan the priest. Those novels were failures for, surely, neither in Ireland, I hope, nor anywhere else was there ever a young man like Geoffrey: a scholar of vast scope who failed the footiest examination, not, mark you, from lack of work or application to the prescribed texts, but just because the clerical novelist decided it was necessary for the soul of Geoffrey that he should fail.

And Geoffrey was, also, a sinner, or so he said, who could boast without a blush that he had a shrinking from all suggestiveness that made it, for him, a positive torture to hear or say anything gross or impure. That angelic shrinking put him up, Geoffrey had the audacity to claim, with saints who, according to legend, were thrown into insensibility by one obscene word, and raised him to the level, too, of friends of his, people whom, he said, he knew would actually sicken at a question of indelicacy. One is reminded, oddly enough, of the swoon of the young cleric in Zola's *La Faute de l'Abbé Mouret*.

If we are to consider Canon Sheehan as a novelist, and there is little point in considering him as anything else, since his work as a parish priest did not differ from the work of other zealous priests and would not in itself call for a critical consideration . . . then we can see the real triumph of failure in those two novels about Geoffrey Austin. They were a long, hard apprenticeship. When they were ended, he was never again completely blinded by books, neither by their merits nor their moral dangers, and he was better able to look at his people and his scene as a novelist should. Those two novels, ending with the visions seen in a Dublin church before Geoffrey Austin becomes, as one always knew he would, a monk, are the hallucinations not of a man who had prayed and fasted too much but of a young priest who had read too much and been afflicted all the time with the feeling that he shouldn't be reading at all. Yet even in the middle of *The Triumph of a Failure* comes this luminous passage foretelling better things. It is a reflection attributed to the unworthy and absurd Geoffrey:

> The high regions of speculative thought are, like Alpine altitudes, too thin for man to breathe in for long periods of time. There is a craving of the heart for human fellowship, as well as a thirst of the mind for knowledge; and what is said of solitude is true of study – that but an angel or a beast can tolerate its continuances. I confess life was taking on new lights and colours since I became interested in the little drama of human feelings and passions; and whilst I thirsted for the unattainable heaven of pure thought, I felt that the very pricks and stings of human passion give life a zest to which my solitary life had as yet been a stranger. I believed now that the best of all existences here below is a compound of action and thought, a steady practical interest in the welfare of the race, and occasional breathing moments of silent conference with the eternal.

His doubts about moral justification for the novelist, or generally for the writer, were to remain with Sheehan to the end. Old Daddy Dan, in that uneven series of sketches of clerical life, *My New Curate*, more popular with Sheehan's brethren than the searching novel *Luke Delmege*, though the sketches were less competent and had less to say, was far too kind to be any sort of a literary critic. Yet Sheehan, always fatally capable of mutilating a character for the sake of a homily, makes Daddy Dan deliver himself on the novel, attacking it like any Victorian archdeacon as the 'gospel of the world', and seeing married life in Ireland as the most splendid refutation of that gospel.

Geoffrey Austin had, as one might have expected from him, spoken with his usual priggish contempt of the contemporary three-decker novel whose hero thought that the greatest possible achievement in life was the conquest of a married woman, and he devastated a collection of books in a shop by saying that they were the usual French novels by Dumas, the father, and Dumas, the son, and Paul de Kock (sweet angelic spirit of Marion Bloom), and Guy de Maupassant. You stop when reading *My New Curate* to realize with a shock that Daddy Dan was, through the mind of Canon Sheehan, a relation of that awful boy Geoffrey Austin, and to wonder about another of the incidental ironies in relation to the reluctant novelist. Was he or was he not aware, or, if he had been, would he have seen it as comic, that George Moore, who was the sworn enemy of the three-decker novel and the stifling morality that went with it, had written one of his pseudo-confessional passages in *The Confessions of a Young Man* to prove that a young man of feeling could not perturb himself for the sake of any woman unless she was over thirty and married to somebody else?

Neither Geoffrey Austin nor his creator could, naturally, have been aware because both of them lived too early (as a young Mr Joyce said to Mr Yeats) to be influenced by Joyce, of the ironic use that Joyce, in *Ulysses*, would make of the name of one of the French novelists mentioned by Geoffrey Austin, or that the favourite reading of Marion Bloom would be the novel *The Sweets of Sin*.

The stern old Doctor Gray in one of Sheehan's great novels, *The Blindness of Dr Gray*, heard a novel before he ever read one, for he had never read one in his life and when, in his blindness, his niece tried to entertain him by reading one out loud, he said: 'Is there not sorrow and trouble enough in real life without wringing our hearts with pictured misery and desolation?'

That half-American niece, the best woman character, certainly, in the odd collection of women in Sheehan's pages, beloved enough by her parish-priest creator to be allowed to follow her heart and contract that curious Irish cocktail – a 'mixed marriage', could be seen as the warm spirit of life endeavouring to temper the Jansenism of the older Irish clergy. She was percipient enough to desist, to close the novel, and humour the granitic old man by reading the gospel of Saint John in Greek. Quite a girl!

Sheehan himself, when he offered the first few sketches of *My New Curate* to Father Heuser, clearly thought that he was condescending by providing 'popular reading' and by introducing his own ideas and suggestions under 'the sugar-coating of a story'. The secret novelist, hidden behind the white collar and black coat of the pastor of Doneraile, still had to be deprecated, apologized for as an unworthy limb of the Old Adam. Sheehan was affected, naturally, by the fact that the small, inbred country he belonged to was undeniably, and perhaps justly, suspicious of people who wrote novels. The neighbours were never safe from such a man. As late as the 1920s there were those ructions and riots and actions, legal and illegal, around the village of Delvin in County Westmeath, over Brinsley MacNamara's novel *The Valley of the Squinting Windows*. But Sheehan himself shared that suspicion, and in that infinitely wise, gently ironic introduction to another of his great books, *Luke Delmege*, he studies himself, and the problem of creative writing from living models, and lists what he studies among the puzzles that perplexed Luke Delmege. He even hints at the censorship of publications, an absurdity that the future had in store for the novelists of holy Ireland: for, after the death of Luke, the old priest who had been his friend challenges the right of the narrator to have access to the dead man's papers.

'You fellows,' said the old priest, 'are regular resurrectionists. You cannot let the dead rest and bury their histories with them'.

Thinking in silence that it would be 'a tactical mistake to irritate this quaint old man', the narrator says: 'Let's strike a bargain. Every page of this history I shall submit to you for revision, correction or destruction, as seems fit, if you keep me on the right track by giving me as much light as you can'.

That little accidental glimpse of the censorship to come was nothing to be surprised at in the novelist, who, on more important matters, could show prophetic power in *The Graves at Kilmorna*, his moving study of the heroic old Fenian revolutionary living on to be mocked at and stoned in a materialistic time, and in the Gothic pages of the novel about Miriam Lucas, who might have lived on to be the woman Homer sung of. Or Yeats.

But then to be funny or to try to be funny about it, that old priest, a genuine Tiresias, might simply have been foreseeing the gutter-press of the 1980s and 1990s and the tearing away of all privacy from the living and the dead.

Also in that prologue to *Luke Delmege*, Sheehan came out into the open in a most revealing way. 'I am a storyteller,' the narrator says to Luke, 'and you have a story to tell me'. Sheehan is, in a way common enough among novelists and even among more respectable people, talking to himself. And he goes on to make a statement that might have horrified his younger self, Geoffrey Austin, into pages of declamation about the dangers of secular literature:

> Was it not said of Balzac that he dug and dragged every one of his romances straight from the heart of some woman? 'Truth is stranger than

fiction'. No! my dear friend, for all fiction is truth – truth torn up by the roots from bleeding human hearts, and carefully bound with fillets of words to be placed there in vases, of green and gold, on your reading-desk, on your breakfast-table. Horrid? So it is. Irreverent? Well, a little.

Well, now we know that he has accepted the horribleness and the irreverence that must be if novels have to be written at all. Why should they be or why were they ever written? Luke Delmege, from his deathbed, says to the narrator, much as Dr Gray cried out in his blindness: 'Why will novelists increase and aggravate the burdens of the race by such painful analyses of human character and action?'

The narrator answers: 'Do you think that anyone would read a novel if it were not about something painful? – and the more painful, the more entrancing. Men revel in creating and feeling pain. Here is another puzzle'.

But when Delmege is dead, the narrator, or novelist, is allowed to take control and writes: 'He was buried as he desired and his memory is fast vanishing from amongst men; but the instincts of the novelist have overcome my tenderness for that memory, and I give you his life history and experiences. Am I justified in doing so? Time must tell'.

Perhaps a fair number of the graduates of the great seminary of St Patrick's College, Maynooth, as it was at that time, might have thought that P.A. Sheehan was by no means justified in writing down his experiences as a young priest in Ireland or on the English Mission. That one I love: Go out and convert the barbarians. The Hooligans.

It seems that Time also gave him the same negative answer and that he lived to regret the brief moments in the prologue and epilogue to that novel when he played at being his own ghost and described so carefully the predicament of the artist as an Irish parish priest.

'A few days before his death,' Heuser tells us, 'the Canon called his brother and asked him to go over with him his letters and other papers . . . Placing his hand on the memoirs of his own life, he said to his brother: "These might do harm to others; let us destroy them." And then and there the volumes of manuscript were thrown into the open grate, while the dying priest watched the red flames as they crept from sheet to sheet and curled to brown and black, until the glow died down, leaving nothing of the pages but the flaky tinder with its edges of ashy grey'.

That is the most moving passage in Heuser's dull humourless, but valuable book, and I feel from the way it was written that Heuser was as much an accessory after the fact as Canon Sheehan's brother was before. It is tempting, particularly for a layman who once enjoyed the dubious reputation that novelists once had in Ireland, to make too much of what might have been in those memoirs, to hope that they were full of dynamite, that if the flames of Doneraile had not consumed them, we might have been treated to the spectacle of an Irish parish priest taking the lid off and telling the hierarchy where and when to dismount. But there is no reason for supposing that they were burned for any other motive than the wish to preserve Christian charity: '. . . they might do harm to others'. No unfortunate deed was ever done for a better intention. But also: Sheehan had shown how he distrusted self-revelation when he read the letters of George Meredith and said that what Meredith revealed was likely to injure rather than enhance the reputation of the author. By reputation I fear that he meant not Meredith's status as a writer, but that bubble reputation which he as a Christian (and, may I flippantly interpolate, as a Canon) might well have despised.

In his last weak moments, aided and abetted by his innocent brother, he showed how he distrusted his natural instinct as a novelist, just as he would have distrusted any other instinct of the natural man.

Paradoxically he was, it might seem, made a novelist in spite of himself, in spite of the Geoffrey Austin in him, by the intervention of the Irish people, including their priests, and by his mystical love for the land of Ireland. That famous night-ride, described so well in the opening pages of the novel *Glenanaar*, of young William Burke, from Cork to Derrynane and back, to fetch the legal aid of the Liberator for the Doneraile conspiracy prisoners, brought relief not only to those prisoners in the past but to the parish priest of Doneraile, who was writing about them the best part of a century later. The Fenians, who owed so little to the Irish clergy, had, because of their mystic self-sacrifice, their helpless devotion to an ideal that was not material, a faithful champion in the pastor of Doneraile, and like Halpin, the tragic schoolmaster in the novel *The Graves at Kilmorna*, he would have said that no man was 'a true Celt who would not enjoy hiding under a stone wall on the summit of some Irish mountain and watching, for a whole day, the rain blown up in sheets across the heather by the wild wind from the West'.

Sheehan was more severe in his denunciations of the people and the country than the harshest of the realists who were to come. The Irish priest then (perhaps still in some places), because of his training and of the way in which the people looked up to him, thundered from the clouds and knew it; whereas the Irish writer who was merely a writer was never allowed to forget that he was nothing more than a man and, in Ireland, not a very desirable type of humanity.

Sheehan used his sacerdotal privilege, with a heat reminiscent of the old Fenians, to denounce as degenerate so many traits of the poor, plain people of Ireland from their taste for plain porter to their taste (less culti-vated) for imported, popular songs. The young Myles Cogan in *The Graves of Kilmorna* speaks savagely of his own people as 'a race of mendicants'. But the Irish once did take a masochistic pleasure in hearing themselves called names by priests and patriots, and by nobody else: and Canon Sheehan, who made it clear that he thought he was living in a degenerate time, that the old grand people and the high principle were no more, that Romantic Ireland was very much dead and gone, is regarded as a smiling national piety like the coloured label on a box of shamrocks; while Yeats, who lamented the past glory of the Fenians as much as Sheehan did but who told us that if we cast our minds on other days we could, in coming days, still be 'the indomitable Irishry', was at times, and by some, considered no Irishman at all and no better than a naygur and black heathen.

Canon Sheehan had a simple, ascetic ideal for the Irish people. He wanted a hardy race who lived on milk and oatmeal, came in time for Mass and were content with no money in their pockets. Back in the black mountains behind Doneraile was a favourite spot of his, a place called Tooreen, a little green patch against the sombre setting of purple hills. There, he said, dwelt a simple hardy race, leading a kind of monastic life in their solitude, and rarely venturing beyond the seclusion of their valley except to Mass on Sundays or holidays. I had heard of them long before I ever thought I should be their pastor. From far before the famine years, when the population was ten times what it is today, their reputation has come down unbroken as being the very first, Winter and Summer alike, to enter the Church on Sunday morning. They are seven miles away – no roads from the inner fastnesses of the mountains – yet here they are at half-past seven on Sunday morning, eager for the Mass that is to cast its halo of blessings over their labours for the coming week. I tell them that they ought to be holy – they are so near to God'.

That vanishing race of hardy giants commanded his respect and his love. What he felt about them had something to do with his fervent hope that, in spite of the degeneration he thought he saw around him, Ireland would proceed to follow a higher destiny, most appealing to the stricter forms of the clerical mind, and become a second Thebaid. In *The Graves of Kilmorna*, Myles Cogan listens to a monk in the great monastery of Mount Melleray. The good monk is one of those enigmatic Gothic characters Sheehan had an unfortunate habit of dragging up out of nowhere to constipate the narrative by discussing the state of the nation and the world. The monk says: 'The nation will go on: grow fat like Jeshurun and kick. And then it will grow supremely disgusted with itself: It will take its wealth and build a monastery on every hilltop in Ireland. This land will become another Thebaid – and that will be its final destiny'.

The image of Ireland fat and kicking like Jeshurun is still a fairly comic contrast to the state of the nation.

$\smile$ 19 $\smile$

Liam O'Flaherty: From the Stormswept Rock . . .

WHAT TRIBUTE CAN YOU PAY to a great writer on his eightieth birthday except, perhaps, to begin a rereading of what he has written. So I reach for the first book of his that comes to hand. It happens to be a comparatively recent selection of his masterly short stories. And I begin to read:

> It was still dark when Martin Delaney and his wife Mary got up. Martin stood in his shirt by the window a long time looking out, rubbing his eyes and yawning, while Mary raked out the live coals that had lain hidden in the ashes on the hearth all night. Outside, cocks were crowing and a white streak was rising from the ground, as it were, and beginning to scatter the darkness. It was a February morning, dry, cold and starry.

That's one simple way into the world of Liam O'Flaherty, and the devotee or, simply, the admirer of good writing will know it by heart. And, as I turn the page:

> Still, as they walked silently in their rawhide shoes, through the little hamlet, there was not a soul about. Lights were glimmering in the windows of a few cabins. The sky had a big grey crack in it in the east, as if it were going to burst in order to give birth to the sun. Birds were singing somewhere at a distance. Martin and Mary rested their baskets of seeds on a fence outside the village and Martin whispered to Mary proudly: 'We are first, Mary'. And they both looked back at the little cluster of cabins, that was the centre of their world, with throbbing hearts. For the joy of spring had now taken complete hold of them'.

The earth breathed in unison with the people.

Liam O'Flaherty travelled a lot of the world in his time, and in war and peace, and wrote well about his travels. A little before he came to the age of eighty he said, in a newspaper interview, that he had come back to Ireland because it was his country. It certainly was; and in those days he walked the streets of a part of south Dublin city with the soldierly and authoritative stride of a man who knew he possessed the place and had every right to do so.

But he once wrote of his own origins: 'I was born on a stormswept rock and hate the soft growth of sun-baked lands where there is no frost in men's bones. Swift thought and the swift flight of ravenous birds, and the squeal of terror of hunted animals are to me reality. I have seen the leaping salmon fly before the salmon-whale, and I have seen the sated buck horn his mate, and the wanderer leave his wife, in search of fresh bosoms, with the fire of joy in his eye'.

O'Flaherty's contemporary Sean O'Faoláin, in the course of a BBC talk on O'Flaherty's work, once argued that anyone approaching Irish literature should call to mind at once the unconventionality of Irish life. It may be permissible to wonder if it is now as it was all those years ago. 'The basic thing about Ireland,' O'Faoláin then said, 'is that it is a peasant country. What we call "polite society" with its firmly established and clearly defined conventions and rules, amounting or mounting to punctilio, exists in Ireland only in enclaves: little islands of convention besieged by the darkness of the peasant mind'.

Now none of us, as the man said in Séamus O'Kelly's novel *Wet Clay,* wish to be reminded that we are peasants, or the seed, breed and generation of peasants. In other countries, 'peasant' could be accounted a title of honour, but in Ireland it has always been, and still may be, a four-letter word. We are all the spawn of kings and princes, and to talk of peasants, even away back before the Lemass revolution and EEC and all the boys in Brussels, may, even then, have been hazardous. As for the 1990s, and we bloody well running Europe from Dublin Castle, and Bono and U2 sweeping the world with linked sweetness long drawn out . . .

But to come back to what I was talking about.

To find a relationship between that statement by Sean O'Faoláin and the exact truth about life in Ireland would call for a lengthy consideration of the very important work of O'Faoláin. But it can be taken, generally, as truth, as it may have somewhat to do with the work of O'Flaherty. For when O'Flaherty wrote, for some reason or other, a biography of a notable Irish politician who was once, among other things, a witty character in the British House of Commons, he said:

> . . . though Tim Healy was endowed by nature with great gifts and great potentialities, his mind was a plastic mould, a pool of clear water that reflected all the ghoulish figures that stood over it, menacing, murmuring incantations, howling about devils, raising a great noise that was deafening.

Now that might mean that Tim Healy had the mind of the Irish peasant, or of some of our latter-day patriots, with the addition of those great gifts and potentialities.

On one side of the pool of clear water stood the priest and on the other the patriot, menacing and gesturing above the mirror of the water until the present was hopelessly confused with the past. O'Flaherty himself, like a very large number of young Irishmen, including myself, was for a while the gesturing patriot and might easily have developed into the menacing priest. When he was sent off to school, there were some hopes that he might show signs of a vocation for the priesthood. He went through two Catholic colleges and passed on to University College, Dublin. He served in World War I and was invalided out of service in 1918. Then, after four or so years wandering the world, he sat down seriously to write. In 1925, with his novel *The Informer*, he won the James Tait Black Memorial Prize.

He saw himself, and with a good deal of reason, as the realist from that stormswept rock, a man whose god was not the god of Romance, who professed to see the Roman Empire and the British Empire, and Joseph Conrad's attachment to the British Empire, as 'sweet singing on a lower plane'. His own personal preferences were, according to himself, for battle and blood, for Genghis Khan and his herds of camels, hosts of horsemen and jewelled concubines; for the storming of Troy and the war for the Bull of Cuailnge, for 'all the terrible madnesses of men and women crashing their bodies and their minds against the boundary walls of human knowledge'.

A man knows his own heart better than his neighbour can, and O'Flaherty's description of his heart's desire must be accepted. But it is a long way from description to definition: and the concubines, particularly the ones with the jewels, of Genghis Khan, and the men who fought a war at a queen's command for the possession of a brown bull, all live well within the bailiwick of the God of Romance. And there is a resemblance between the way in which Troy was taken and the way in which empires increased and multiplied and filled the earth. Nor is there anybody in the world so hopefully and unreasonably romantic as the man who leaves his wife and sets out on a tour of alien bosoms.

And the man from the stormswept rock, journeying out to visit the world, is blood-brother to the boy who, flying from home, looked back across the valley at sunset, and set off to find the house with the golden windows, and found it, and found himself at home.

O'Flaherty's journey from the stormswept rock to the world resulted in the production of about thirty books. I mention some:

Novels: *Thy Neighbour's Wife* (1923), *The Black Soul* (1924), *The Informer* (1925), *Mr Gilhooley* (1926), *The Assassin* (1928), *Skerrett* (1932), *Famine* (1937), *Land* (1946).

Collections of short stories: *Spring Sowing* (1924), *The Tent* (1926), *The Mountain Tavern* (1929), *Two Lovely Beasts* (1948).

Three volumes of autobiography or itinerary: *Two Years* (1930), *I Went to Russia* (1931), *Shame the Devil* (1934).

Then there was that biography of Timothy Healy and, among other matters, a tragedy written as if meant for the stage. And there was a small book of fantasy called *A Tourist's Guide to Ireland*. Like most good fantasy, it had its connection with the truth. But it should have, like Thackeray's *Book of Snobs*, carried the explanation 'By One of Themselves', for the ideas it contains obviously came to the western islandman when he was on his way from the island to which he belonged to the world he wanted to see, but through another island to which he did not belong. The accident of Ireland's proximity to Inishmore has meant that much of O'Flaherty's comment on, and interpretation of, life has been affected by life, as he saw it lived, when he was a tourist in Ireland.

When he wrote that book on, or biography of, Timothy Healy, O'Flaherty seemed firmly convinced that on his way through Ireland he had made himself unpopular with the Irish people. To prove his worthiness as a biographer, he claimed he had two things in common with Healy: neither had any connection with the whiskey and stout trade; and each in his own time had managed to make himself the most unpopular man in Ireland.

That latter claim was absurdly extravagant. On O'Flaherty's own classification, politicians made up one of the four main divisions of the Irish people. The other three were composed of priests, publicans and peasants. After Sadleir and Keogh, and in the black shadow of the betrayal and fall of Parnell, Tim Healy may have managed for a while to be Ireland's most unpopular politician. But writers and artists could never have aspired to such unpopularity, for the simple reason that the majority of the Irish people did not even know they existed. O'Flaherty came very close to recognizzing that depressing truth, depressing to writers and artists, when he said: 'It is clearly understood among Irish audiences, that when a politician boasts about his services to the people, for the audience to cheer in derision. We laugh at one another in true Greek fashion but, unlike the Greeks, we do not allow our artists to laugh at us'.

Now the minority of the Irish people who were aware, to the extent of attentively reading his books, that a man from the neighbouring island of Inishmore had passed that way could read those words and wonder why Liam O'Flaherty did not laugh if he wanted to laugh, why, at certain terrible moments it looked as if the man had never laughed in his life. The explanation may have been that a shout rather than a laugh went more aptly with the roar of that romantic wind and the sea glorious in anger against the great rocks. Like the artist in his story 'The Child of God', he was discovering that he must be aggressive. Because only aggressiveness could preserve him from the moment he had longed for in distant London when he would see 'these beloved faces once more, to touch those toil-worn hands, to hear these voices, or which he knew every delicate intonation, kiss those lips that murmured when he kissed them, maternal lips that crooned to him as a child'.

When he was a boy at school, he said, the master asked the class to write a story. Little Liam wrote a story about a peasant woman who had the misfortune to be murdered by her husband. At that very early age, the writer in him showed a preference for the decisive gesture, and, after a good hanging, a good murder is as decisive as anything anybody knows. This particular murder was done in the field in which the man was working. And the motive was his natural anger at his wife for bringing him cold tea for his dinner. The large number of people who like their tea hot will see the point immediately.

Anyway, it was with a spade he did it. And when the woman was securely murdered, the husband was confronted with the problem that commonly confronts murderers: he had to dispose of the body. So he tried to bury his late wife in the fosse or furrow between two ridges. 'The point of the story,' O'Flaherty wrote long afterwards, 'was the man's difficulty in getting the woman, who was very large, to fit into the fosse. The school-master was horrified, and thrashed me'.

That delectable little murder story had a Gaelic realism. But the story about the thrashing in the schoolhouse is pure romanticism, in the debased sense in which romanticism can mean either that a man's memory is failing or that he is bending the long bow. The schoolmaster who, appar-ently, had the originality, when imposing topics for essays, to depart from the autobiographies of old boots, or studies of coal mines, or frosty morn-ings, or days in the city, would certainly have welcomed the originality of a pupil who posed not only the problem that faces even the best murderers but also the problem that has been solved only by the very best realists: the problem of how to get rid of the body.

If little Liam was thrashed, and it is most likely that he was, then the reason for that must have been insubordination, or, perhaps, making dirty faces at the backside of the parish priest.

In a play that, for some reason or other, Liam O'Flaherty wrote for the stage (he called it 'Darkness') he created a character called Dark Daniel who, in a wild moment, said: 'I have no Kinship with people. I'm an ungainly lout'. This great writer (and how I used to tremble when I called him anything of the sort) has always had a certain amount of trouble with Dark Daniel intruding himself where, artistically, he is not wanted. O'Fla-herty's novels have never been completely free of the influence of that morose and ungainly man. With, perhaps, the exception of that great novel *Famine*.

Professor Zneimer, who has written a perceptive book on O'Flaherty, disagrees with me about this. But then O'Flaherty disagrees with Professor Zneimer. And disagrees, also, with me. So where does that leave us?

The Dark Daniel side of O'Flaherty's genius had as little kinship with people as the dark side of the mutilated moon. It was even divorced from any sympathetic contact with birds and beasts, with the earth and things growing, and with the sea constantly in motion, and the clouds moving before the wind. His short stories about life on the earth, apart from man, and the passages of pure Franciscan praise, here and there in the novels, can, at times, be on a higher level that most of what he has written about his two-legged fellows. It is not that he has brought men and women down to the level of animals. He has not always managed to raise his men and women to the place where his animals move in fierce and tameless beauty, to make his men and women worthy of the earth.

O'Flaherty's birds and beasts are the perfect children of the earth and, as a rule, the harmony of their movement on the earth is disturbed only by the invasion of man. The earth circling in space, the winds and the sea changing and the seasons changing, can be for O'Flaherty such an absolute harmony that it has the power of drawing almost always with it the birds and beasts and, sometimes, even the men and women. That, roughly, was the theme of the novel *The Black Soul*. In which novel a war-scarred, world-scarred man, Dark Daniel to the tips, or whatever, of his shattered fingernails, returns to the island of Inverara to find peace: 'As soon as he tried to abandon himself to nature his cynical intellect jeered at him . . . "What a cursed thing is intellect," he groaned'.

His cursed intellect and his black soul both submit to the spell of spring in Inverara. Yet it is, perhaps, a pity that the keystone of the submission is an unconvincing intrigue with his landlady. The reader, who is not as utter a romantic as O'Flaherty himself, can only feel a return to the world with the beautiful Little Mary, after the convenient passing of her useless husband, is as final a solution as the reunion at the end of any Hollywood story of that long-ago time. But what Inverara had to offer was something almost on the level of one of the poems of St Francis, with the difference that spring on the island pointed the way to the solution at which the Franciscan canticles, and a poetic treatise by St Robert Bellarmine, had already arrived.

O'Flaherty was aware of all that and could write:

> Life, life, life and the labour of strong hands in Inverara in Spring. From dawn to dark the people hurried, excitedly opening the earth to sow. At dawn they came from their cabins their noses shining with frost, slapping their lean hands under their armpits, their blue eyes hungry with energy. They ran through the smoking dew for their horses. From dawn to dark their horses trotted, neighing, their steel shoes ringing on the smooth stones. Through rain and driven sleet the people worked. Cows

gave birth to calves, and the crooning of women milking in the evening
mingled dreamily with the joyous carolling of the birds. Yellow lambs
staggered by their mothers' sides as they made their first trembling journeys in life. Lean goats were hiding their newborn kids in the crevices
among the crags. Everything moved hungrily for life. Even the grey
limestone crags seemed to move as the sun sucked the dew from their
backs. Smoke rose everywhere, as if nature perspired, conceiving life.

In that, to me, magnificent passage, the aggressive islander recognizes
peace as something far away from his own mood when he damned Conrad
for weaving a cloak of Romance out of Space, and when he shouted out
that some sort of 'brutal denial' was necessary. In the romantic mood of
brutal denial he claimed that what was beautiful in man was that he was
unhappy as a man and wished to be a god: '. . . to be free from death and
the restraint of the earth's balance', to fly into space and loot the universe,
to hanker always after the tree of knowledge, to create gods only in order
to break them, to be constantly in revolt and to find beauty in tragedy.

It all depends on what you mean by Beauty. But even if the story of the
fall of the angels were nothing more than a story, yet the men who told it
were wiser than Liam O'Flaherty and/or John Milton. They knew that
Lucifer was glorious with light only when he sat, without pride, in his
appointed place. After the Fall he was pathetic, as evil can be pathetic, as
exploded pride is always pathetic: as pathetic as the gentleman Raoul St
George is in O'Flaherty's novel *Land*, when he tells his sister that he is a
freethinker, and that she is not to force him to be brutal by interfering with
his conduct in any way:

> You know how cruel and uncompromising men of our family can be,
> when they feel that their authority is being flouted.

The inane Raoul needs only a Gilbertian chorus of priests, peasants,
publicans and politicians to shatter the air with ironic repetition: 'He says
he may be brutal. He says the men of his family have always been cruel
and uncompromising'.

Thomsy Hynes, the most memorable character in the novel *Famine* is
never brutal. He is degenerate and drunken and degraded. On the eighteenth page of the novel he is introduced as a byword all over the Black
Valley where mothers say to naughty children: 'If you carry on like that
you'll be another Thomsy Hynes when you grow'. But in the abjection of
Thomsy, O'Flaherty has laughed the most perfect laughter, as nervous as
the needle of a compass and on the verge of cleansing tears; and in
Thomsy's woeful odyssey, and his final vision, O'Flaherty has sketched
the story of the soul of man.

Thomsy exists on sufferance, having surrendered his rights to the land
his father farmed to Brian Kilmartin, married to Thomsy's sister, Maggie.

Brian's son, in due time, brings his own woman, Mary, under the roof, and Mary decides to clean the house. She procures a new frieze suit for Thomsy and orders him to wash himself before wearing it; and when Mary's man, Martin, forcibly washes Thomsy in hot water, his screams are audible half a mile away.

Judged casually and detached from its context, that might be merely a vulgar incident. But balanced against the apocalyptic power of the whole story, it can stand as symbolic of the cleansing of the never-very-willing soul. Thomsy, like all the other famine-stricken people, will go down before the death of the body, but he will never know despair. When Mary sends him north over the mountains to Mayo to search for Martin, who is in his keeping, he returns from his wandering in a land of desolation, not knowing whether or not he has properly fulfilled his message.

But sheltering in a barn one night, he found hope when he heard a man of Young Ireland talking revolution to a circle of listeners: 'Faith, it was fine talk, and it looked an easy job of work, the way he told it. He said there are millions of the poor and only a few of the rich, and if the poor got together and made themselves into a proper army, with a proper plan . . . they'd make short work of the tyrants . . . Begob I could hold myself no longer in the straw so I up and cried: "More power to you! That's the talk I like to hear."'

But Mary cried quietly as she listened to Thomsy's story and she asked herself: 'What had he brought back? Nothing but a tale told by a stranger man in a barn at night'.

That could be the wisest moment of the many wise moments in the many books of Liam O'Flaherty. It is a vision of raggedness and hunger leaping up to salute liberty or the hope of liberty, of love hungering for love and knowing the hollowness in the heart of hope, and knowing also that in the long chronicle of man on earth no story has ever been told to the end.

Thomsy Hynes, and all that he stands for in the writings of O'Flaherty, is a million times more valuable than all the devils of pride in Raoul Henry St George, or in the man with the black soul, or in MacDara in *The Assassin*. Or in Commandant Dan Gallagher in *The Informer*. Or even in Mr Gilhooley, caught for terrible tragedy in the maze of city streets.

It is unfair, perhaps, to rank Gilhooley with those others, who are so clearly possessed by the devil whose name is Dark Daniel. For the tragedy of Gilhooley in the Dublin streets is as impressive as the tragedy of Skerrett, the rebellious schoolmaster, on the rocks of the island of Nara. Not only are the two men, the schoolmaster who has trampled on all opposition and the retired engineer who has always lived a free life, great tragic figures, but their sombre situations could be paralleled in some of O'Flaherty's stories about animals whose existence has been tampered with to the point of tragedy. Skerrett breaks himself against unyielding obstacles. Gilhooley's tragedy is that of a mild spirit caught helplessly in inextricable toils. They are both worthy of the earth.

For Gilhooley as the worthy child of the earth the words of the drunken poet, Macaward, had significance. In the web of city streets the poet saw only death and corruption, and Gilhooley and himself living in the city were living a lie. For they both belonged, he said, 'only where there are green fields and birds and life, growing and dying, growing and dying, all the year round'. Later on, Gilhooley remembers in vain the wisdom of the proverb-making country people and says: 'But I have strayed a long way from the root. 'Twould be a twisted, twisted path that leads back to it'.

He never did find his way back along that twisted path. And although the young artist in the story 'The Child of God' did follow a similar path to the place he had once called home, he found, when the path ended, that, because he had changed and his people had not changed, home was no longer home. His welcome ended when his people discovered that what he called art, they called dirty pictures and disrespect for the dead.

But when all this appreciative nonsense is said and done, what do you say about a man like Liam O'Flaherty? That he was a legend as I grew up and tried to read, and to write. That he, a man who never, as good writers should not do, talked about books or writers, was gracious enough to offer me his friendship. I was told that once, in my absence, he said: 'Kiely's a good man'. Those words, signed by Liam O'Flaherty, would look well on my headstone.

Sometime, round about 1920, O'Flaherty was summoned to the presence of the great London publisher Jonathan Cape: a man who was for so long famous that when Joseph Tomelty, playwright, actor and novelist, met him for the first time, Tomelty said: 'Mr Cape, I always thought that, like the man in the song, you were your own granda'. What he meant was that it was hard to believe that a man who was as famous as was Jonathan Cape could still, actually, be alive.

The young O'Flaherty, in a ragged trenchcoat and leaking shoes, found it hard to meet the great publisher's eyes and to answer his questions. Having myself stood in Cape's presence when I was short of money, and hoping for the best, I find it not impossible to believe that even The O'Flaherty was daunted. But let him describe the awesome moment:

> I sat down hardly able to meet his eyes or answer his remarks . . . He read me a letter from Edward Garnett advising the acceptance of my manuscript, not because it was likely to sell, but because it was the work of a promising young writer. It is impossible to describe the exalted joy this news gave me. The joy of a lover on realizing that his love is returned is nothing compared to it. I was completely beside my wits. I was convinced that I was already rich, famous, a man of genius. The ten pounds which

the publisher gave me as an advance on royalties seemed an enormous fortune which it was impossible to spend. I wandered through the streets a little astonished that people passed me without recognition of my exalted merit.

Jonathan Cape was never the man to spoil a young author with big advances. On one occasion (to me unforgettable) he told me that Belloc was always a nuisance to his publishers, looking for money for sailing-boats and fine wines, but that 'Ernest' had never bothered him (Jonathan) for money.

At that time Ernest Hemingway was living high and mighty in Havana and I had the hardihood, or the death wish, to say to Mr Cape that, if I was as well-heeled as himself or Mr Hemingway, I wouldn't be at his door with my hat, so to speak, in my hand. Jonathan was, though, as gracious as he was wise, and we remained friends; and I may suppose that back about 1920 even a tenner was better than the blow of a stick.

With that ten-pound-note in his pocket the young O'Flaherty set out to conquer the world. He had already had a good look at it from several viewpoints: from his own stormswept rock, Inishmore; from a college in Ireland where for that brief moment it might have been thought that he was destined for the priesthood; from Caterham Barracks and the Irish Guards and the trenches of World War I from which he emerged, reeling with shellshock at Boesinghe; from the Civil War in Ireland where, at the end of things, he had melted into the crowd and had heard himself described, in no complimentary fashion, by a decent Dublinwoman: 'Did you hear that bloody murderer, Liam O'Flaherty, is killed, thanks be to God . . . thanks be to God. The man that locked the unemployed up in the Rotunda and shot them unless they spat on the holy crucifix. The man that tried to sell Dublin to the Bolsheviks'.

He went at the world and at life, as a writer, with a rush and a shout: something in the style of Genghis Khan, that amiable character whom he had hymned in that most revealing study of Joseph Conrad and again in the book *Shame the Devil*, one of his three efforts at autobiography: 'And there I saw upon the low-tide shore where the sea-bed was a yellow swamp of languid weeds, the hordes of Genghis Khan, laying waste cities because that Lord preferred pastures to a pile of bricks. I saw the shuffle of his skulking camels over the plain, and the mad gallop of his shouting horsemen, putting to the sword philosophers'.

Then he reflected, with the high humour that became characteristic of him in his (almost) venerable age, that he saw all that vision because he had slept well on a Breton island, and the morning sun shone on the sea, and the fermented air was flowing to his lungs. He reckoned that had he arisen with a bile and to look upon a cloudy sky, he might have seen Pythagoras sitting among the yellow weeds and preaching brotherly love.

The result of his headlong approach to life was that ten years after Mr Cape's tenner, O'Flaherty was a deservedly famous writer. And a wild legend. Between hard work and hard living, he had worn himself to a frazzle and thought that he was finished as a man, and as a writer. So he took off from London to find a rest and a cure. But no man was ever more ill-designed to rest, and he took off, you might say, in several directions at the same time: Longchamps, Seville, Toledo, Inishmore, and that Breton island, and a French jailhouse, and New York, N.Y., and a backward glance at Soviet Russia, and a book he wrote about it; and his moods and manners and opinions rising and falling and altering like the billows of the ocean. Tempest was bred into his bones.

He wandered the world without compass, a *seachrán* wrestling with every idea and finding himself in strange places and among strange people, loving them, quarrelling with them, determined to tell the truth, if he could discern it, about himself and everybody and everything else; and so to shame the devil and to offer the extraordinary book he called by that title as a dagger to his enemies. He may have made a few by 1934 when the book appeared, but he approached the whole business with a wild humour, with an ability to laugh at himself, and also with certain misgivings about the future prospects of the universe:

> In a paroxysm of satiric joy, as I smelt my glass of brandy, after the women had left me, I thought of the time when I was impressed by my own importance to humanity: how this most strange of all forms of insanity, the mania of genius, led me to imagine that I mattered in the universal scheme of irresponsible matter. Ho! Ho! My jolly boys! What of the others one has seen? I was always able to laugh at myself, even at my worst: but I never forgot that the universe, in a certain number of millions of years, will have swollen to twice its size and then will burst, annihilating, together with all the various manifestations of man's genius, even the most trifling excrement of the tiniest insect.

Prospero had a somewhat similar idea, or somebody had it for him. That extravagant book *Shame the Devil* is still capable of giving rise to enthusiasms and indignations as strong as itself: so as to set the Sage, Pythagoras O'Flaherty, laughing, wherever he now is. He went, as he said, mooching for Truth and found her a slippery whore.

In the 1980s Seamus Cashman of the Wolfhound Press in Dublin reprinted many O'Flaherty titles and issued, along with *Shame the Devil*, one of his finest novels, *The Black Soul*. The two books complement each other. *The Black Soul* contains that passage I have quoted so often I could damn near whistle it: that hymn in praise of life and the labour of strong hands in Inverara in spring. It is central to O'Flaherty. Not his worst enemy, with or without benefit of dagger, could ever have said that he did not love life.

~~𝓒~~ 20 ~~𝓔~~

The Two Masks
of Gerald Griffin

ABOUT TWENTY YEARS, OR MORE, ago a lady from Limerick heard that I was going to Kilkee in the County Clare, to talk at the Bryan Merriman Summer School about the novelist and poetGerald Griffin (1803–40). She said: 'But is there much to talk about? And what will you say about all that awful poetry?'

An American professor, who had himself written well about Griffin, said about that same time: 'On this rereading, you will, at least, agree with me that *The Collegians* is the great novel of the Irish nineteenth century'. Somewhere in the very wide country between those two opinions is the truth about Gerald Griffin, a strange man, indeed, and a most interesting writer.

Griffin's brother, Daniel, told a curious story about his brother's boyhood. Gerald was fond of the open air, of the Shannonside, the land beside the great river, and of the shooting of wildfowl. In poems and in prose he showed his love for, and his careful observation of, that river and the land along its banks. When we think of his boyhood and youth, we must always remember that we are dealing with a precocious fellow who, at the age of twenty, had written a play that Macready thought it worthwhile to present; that his writing was done between the ages of twenty and thirty-three; that he was dead of typhus at thirty-six, three years younger than was Blaise Pascal when his Lord called him. And Pascal should never be far from the mind when we think of Griffin, although, as far as I can recollect, Griffin never mentioned Pascal's name.

That precocious Limerick fellow, who was later to be so much possessed by death and who had Keatsian forebodings, later to be borne out, of an early death, thought little in his boyhood days of blowing out of the air not only the birds you could eat but also the birds it was supposed to be a pleasure to listen to. Larks and yellowhammers and even sparrows went down before him. He must have been as great a menace to everything in feathers as the French tourist hunters who, about 1970 and in the neighbourhood of Westport, Co. Mayo, drove the local farmers to lock up the barnyard fowl.

Once when Griffin had the gun ready for action, the intended victim began to sing. The boy listened to the song and then shot the bird when the song was done. Daniel Griffin, a devoted but perhaps not too bright brother, saw the incident as an indication of a 'time when the passion for field-sports struggled for empire with the dawning spirit of poetry'. Poetry, and the bird, were the losers. Gerald denied that the incident had happened and, indeed, if it ever did happen, he could easily have subconsciously closed his mind against all recollection of it; just as that tormented young gentleman, Hardress Cregan, is never quite certain about the extent of his guilt in the murder of Eily O'Connor, the rope-maker's daughter. Did Griffin intend Eily for better things when he had her, in the early pages of *The Collegians*, reading Johnson and Addison and becoming, almost, one of Lady Mary Wortley Montagu's lay-nuns until wooed away from quietude by the worldly temptations of Owen's Garden, Garryowen?

The trade followed by Eily's father has, of course, its symbolic significance in the novel. The rope was much in use in the Ireland that Griffin and the brothers John and Michael Banim, and William Carleton, particularly in the blood-red, furnace-red story of 'Wildgoose Lodge', were writing about. So, also, does Griffin give due significance to the coffin-maker's shop and the pesthouse: places of much note in a society continually threatened by famine and pestilence. Thomas Flanagan has said that Maria Edgeworth would never have used a Court of Justice to explain why 'rope-makers thrive at a certain season, why the hangman can endow his daughter so handsomely, and why the science of anatomy is so attainable and so practically understood in Ireland'.

That was a wry (an apt word!) remark, but very true. When, shortly after the surrender of General Humbert and the massacre of his Irish allies, Maria Edgeworth ventured out on a trip to the fatal field of Ballina-muck, she professed herself delighted with the pretty colours of the soldiers' uniforms and with the sight of Highland troops picking black-berries. Not a word in the world about the strange fruit hanging in plenty on trees all the way back, by way of Collooney, to Ballina. Maria's trips out-of-doors to meet the Irish people led her, for educational and improving motives, to the local schoolhouse, or to the writing of an introduction to Mary Leadbetter's improving and salutary little book, *Cottage Dialogues*, later translated into Irish so that no person, God help them all, should lack for ideas about self-and-social improvement. But then she did go out of the house, and all the way to the gate-lodge, to make immortal the noblest of the whole race of slieveens and flunkeys, honest Thady Quirke at Castle Rackrent.

William Carleton said, with painfully obvious irony, of the industrious and well-meaning Mrs S.C. Hall, and her fine husband, that they could not possibly have understood the Irish people because they had never been drunk in their company. The same might, with variegations, be said of Maria Edgeworth and of Gerald Griffin. Yet, if Griffin was never as much at home in the cabins as Carleton was, that could have been because he was never as much at home in the world.

Yet Maria Edgeworth had, and Gerald Griffin too, looked on the people, drunkards and all, with clear and unprejudiced eyes: one of them from the Big House, the other from the reasonable security of the middle class, that is, if that odd phenomenon ever existed in Ireland.

The first fine piece of creative literature to be inspired by the brief life and sordid times of John Scanlan, Lieutenant in the Royal Marines, was the speech made in his defence, and on a charge of murder, by Daniel O'Connell. It was so good, and so well calculated to appeal to that sort of jury at that time, that it almost succeeded in having a man acquitted who, it seems, was guilty as charged. But guilty as charged and guilty in the eyes of God may, for all we know, be two different things; and even though Scanlan seems to have been a callous young scoundrel, his fate and his final asseveration of innocence (which may have been his final infamy) set Gerald Griffin meditating on the nature of guilt and innocence. That was a meditation to which he seemed, anyway, to have a natural inclination.

I am assuming here that most of us are familiar with at least the bare details of the story of the murder-case that Griffin used and altered when he wrote *The Collegians*: that John Scanlan, a young half-mounted gent from the County Limerick, eloped with a teenager by the name of Ellen Hanley, who took with her all the money her uncle, with whom she lived, had saved; that Scanlan went through some form of marriage with her, tired of her shortly, and with the help of his servant, Stephen Sullivan, had her brutally murdered and dumped into the Shannon. That was a sordid and pathetic crime. But the use Gerald Griffin made of it is an exact illustration of what Henry James meant when he said that the art of fiction is not in telling what happened, but what should have happened.

Gerald Griffin was a precociously observant young man who had a lot to say about the Ireland of his time, and of somewhat before his time. He had had an impecunious father who had been a member of that brightly uniformed body of men who, for want of a better, or more accurate, name, we call Grattan's Volunteers. (Would it be fantasy, or a sort of wishful-thinking to see there a faint foreshadowing of the father of a later, and greater, Irish novelist who, notoriously did not, as Griffin did, end up in the Irish Christian Brothers, and whose father despised the crowd and was recorded by his son as having said so? Joyce was the name I was searching for.)

But to come back to the matter in hand. In *The Collegians*, the father of that dull and virtuous young man, Kyrle Daly, had been one of those brightly uniformed men but Griffin, in his own odd style, made Mr Daly Senior a success and not the sort of half-failure that, in the case of his own father, led to emigration to Pennsylvania.

Around that sad little story of murder, transformed into something still tragic but a deal more dignified, if the murder of a hapless girl could ever be so described, Gerald Griffin painted the best picture that we have, outside of William Carleton, of the Ireland of the 1820s. In the characters of the good Kyrle Daly and of the wilful, generous, brilliant, violent, wrong-headed, ill-fated Hardress Cregan, and in the serious, sometimes pedantic, talks between them, Griffin, splitting his own character into fragments, mulled over his own problems: the fear of death, his nerves and melancholia and sense of isolation, the desire for fame, and the taste of ashes that went with fame if the eternal needs of the soul were left unsatisfied. He was the devout son of a devout mother and three of his sisters were to be nuns and, if one excepts a brief moment of wavering when he was in London, he would never have dreamed of delivering the Joycean Non Serviam. His doubts in London were disposed of by a rare combination of Paley's Evidences and the sermons of Massillon. Both in the prudish Kyrle Daly and in the reckless Hardress Cregan, he found some portions of himself. The debates between Hardress and Kyrle, both of whom had been students at Trinity College, Dublin, went on and on in Griffin's mind even after the novel had ended, on and on and on, until he turned his back on the literary fame for which he had worked so hard and suffered so much (particularly during those three lean years in London), on and on until he destroyed all his manuscripts that came to hand, with one exception, and went off to seek his God and say his prayers and teach poor children how to read and write.

One part of Daniel O'Connell's argument in defence of John Scanlan was that by upbringing and training, and by his own choice, Scanlan lived a manly, healthy, out-of-doors life, shooting, fishing and sailing on the Shannon, and that, in the Royal Marines, he had learned habits of discipline and restraint. Was it likely that such a man would commit such a crime?

The Kerry Fox must have laughed to himself when he worked out that line of argument. For who better than he could know that a healthy, out-of-doors type, well used to guns and killing, would possibly be more likely than would have been a sequestered scholar to rummage a country girl or commit a crime of violence. And O'Connell well knew, as did all and sundry, that in the previous thirty years in Ireland, His Majesty's Forces had not made themselves popular or renowned for their discipline and restraint. But he also knew the variety of minds that he would be likely to encounter on a jury in the Ireland of that time. And when he said: 'Find Sullivan [who was on the run] and you will find the murderer,' he was passing the crime along to the person whom the better sort of persons would naturally consider was responsible for all crime in Ireland: the peasant, God help him, even though the word peasant was not acceptable in Ireland, not even to or for or by the peasants. Griffin, who had in him a streak of middle classery as wide as the yard of Dublin Castle, and who had never given much thought to the real reasons for the woeful state of the realm, was easily inclined to follow that argument; and the deplorable Scanlan became the frequently splendid Hardress.

The novelist was more at his ease with a villain like Suil Dubh (or Blackeye), the Coiner in the 'Tales of the Munster Festivals'. He, the novelist, sent Suil Dubh to an end not unlike that dowered on Pinkie by Graham Greene at the end of *Brighton Rock*. Those religious people have no pity for the people they invent. Poor old Suil Dubh, the maker of false coins, was, after all, very much a member of the lower classes and never could have risen high enough to be tormented by Cregan's, or Griffin's, scruples and remorse.

Scanlan on the scaffold made a claim to innocence so well-worded as to make people wonder if he could be guilty: 'May the gates of Paradise be forever shut against me if I had hand or act or part in the crime for which I am now about to suffer. If Sullivan be found, my innocence will appear'. The style of that would be bound to impress any teenager with literary aspirations. Gerald Griffin actually heard those words spoken; he was in the courtroom as a young reporter.

Then the horses that were drawing the cart, and Scanlan, to the place of execution refused to cross the bridge, on the unhappy way, over the Shannon: a striking detail that Griffin could find no place for in his novel because neither he, nor his reading public, could bear to see Hardress Cregan executed. Superstition joined with snobbery to prove that not the sporting gentleman but the brutal peasant servant was the guilty person.

Sullivan, Scanlan's servant, was a straight-backed man. But Griffin made Danny Mann, the servant of Cregan, a hunchback and attributed the deformity to an injury, inflicted in boyhood, and accidentally, by Hardress, and thus, for Hardress, another source of guilt and remorse. That invention of the accident and the hunch as an explanation for the irrational attachment of man to master was a genuine stroke of Gothic genius. It gave visible shape to something unseen and amoral. It gave the dignity of agony to the despicable lack of status of the hanger-on. Straight-backed Sullivan was captured in Scartaglen, where he had been living for a while under an assumed name; a wonderful thing, when you think of it, in days when not even the remotest after-hours pub is secure from the squad-car. A lot of good people hopefully expected that his dying confession would clear Scanlan's name. It did everything but that, and Griffin, when he came to puzzle over his own problems of conscience, in the persons of Hardress Cregan and Kyrle Daly, shrank away from the reality of Scanlan.

But, at any rate, he did deal with Hardress in a serious novel and in the name of conscience in whose power he had a strong old-fashioned belief. For Griffin himself was as tormented as any stainless, scrupulous man with a morbid vision of the blackness of his own peccadilloes. His later adapters and popularizers, Dion Boucicault and Sir Jules Benedict, threw conscience to the dogs and went on blatantly, and for the quite sensible sake of box-office, to prove that Hardress, the dashing gentleman-born, was, like Bonny Prince Charlie, everybody's darling; and, in so doing, they rescued Cregan not only from the gallows but from that sad, and clearly repentant, death on the convict ship, and rescued the Colleen Bawn from the grave. Granted that Griffin did not make as much out of Myles na gCopaleen, Myles of the Ponies from the Reeks of Kerry, as Boucicault and Benedict were to do, or even as Samuel Lover was to do with his noble peasant, Rory O'Moore. Lowry Looby, much superior as the comic and shrewd peasant to Lover's Handy Andy, completely outshines Myles in Griffin's novel. Yet I always feel that it was just that moment in Benedict's *The Lily of Killarney* when Myles na gCopaleen sings twice over that the Colleen Bawn is not dead at all that made Brian O'Nolan decide to use the ponydealer's name for his more zany pen-name, for absurdity could go no further. The taste of the time, no worse we may suspect than that of our own, had finally turned the truth of a sad and sordid story into unconsciously comic opera.

Hardress is Byronic, as it was a fashion of the time for popular heroes to be; there is even a suggestion of the Napoleonic. The Napoleonic delusion has lasted even into our own time and I knew a mild and gentle Irish poet who prided himself on possession of a profile somewhat similar to that of the notorious Corsican.

But four years before Scanlan was hanged, high-born English ladies were melting at the magic of the Napoleonic name in a way that makes one wonder about the state of their minds, or their glands. Worse still, Hardress is Gustavic Adolphean, if such a description be permissible. Griffin introduces him in style:

> It was such a figure as would have at once awakened associations in the
> beholder's mind, of camps and action, of states confounded in their

councils, and nations overrun by sudden conquest. His features were brightened by a lofty and confident enthusiasm, such as the imagination might ascribe to the Royal Adventurer of Sweden, as he drew his sword on his beleaguerers at Belgrade.

Now if Griffin had anything to repent of when he turned more and more to religion, he might well have added that passage to the list of his imagined sins, moral and artistic. The utter absurdity of it was that this demigod, Hardress, was under the thumb of his formidable mother and that, so great was the power of conscience, as Griffin would have thought of it, or so great was Cregan's fear of being found out, he spends a lot of the last third of the novel ranting and drivelling and in the jigs of nerves. Gustavus Adolphus, that man of blood, whom Griffin, writing in a hurry, it must be admitted, seemed for a moment to consider as an admirable model for Hardress, would not so have chickened out. Gustavus would always have been good for another massacre.

Gerald Griffin, grappling with his hero, and half-unwilling that Hardress should be his hero, was still haunted by that dubious ghost of Scanlan, and many varying thoughts about Hardress. Here is Hardress Cregan, the nature-lover, not Scanlan, not Gustavus Adolphus, talking to Kyrle Daly. Is not his the boy who listened to, before he shot, the singing birds?

> As I prefer the works of nature to the work of man, the fresh riverbreeze to the dusty and smoaky zephyr of Capel-street, the bloom on a cottage cheek to the crimson japan that blazes at the Earl of Buckinghamshire's drawing-rooms; as I love a plain beefsteak before a grilled attorney, this excellent whiskey-punch before my mother's confounded currant wine, and any thing else that is pure and natural before any thing else that is adulterated and artificial; so do I love the wild hedge-flower, simplicity before the cold and sapless exotic, fashion; so do I love the voice of affection and of nature before that of finesse and affectation.

Kyrle Daly responds by telling Hardress that his terms are too hard, that elegance of manner is not finesse nor, at all, the opposite of simplicity. So, the two friends go on, Hardress talking magnificently out of character and saying so much that should be said by the virtuous Kyrle, who remains mostly mute or remains, at best, the fall-guy. And all the time it is Griffin talking to, and about, himself.

Griffin, as he grew more and more rigidly moral, or just pitifully prudish, censured Fielding and Smollett and even came down heavily on John Milton whose 'pictures of terrestrial happiness' he found 'often as reprehensible as his images of celestial intercourse are flat and shocking and familiar'. We shall not make any silly jokes or puns about what that good young man knew about intercourse, terrestrial or otherwise. Over the years, words, like all else, change out of all meaning.

To his one terrestrial love, Lydia Fisher, Griffin wrote a most murderous attack on Milton and also one of the oddest passages ever written in a letter to a beloved lady.

Lydia Fisher was a Quaker lady, married, a mother figure, possibly, to Griffin, whose mother had crossed the Atlantic. She was daughter to that Mary Shackleton Leadbetter who had written the puling, improving *Cottage Dialogues*, but who had also written the wonderful *Annals of Ballitore*, and who was, in her turn, daughter to that Shackleton who had been a life-long friend of Edmund Burke and whose father, who founded the school at Ballitore in County Carlow, had been schoolmaster to a young Edmund Burke.

> My brain, such as it is, reels.
> As you were, as the sergeants used to say.

In that letter to Lydia Fisher, Gerald Griffin, a clean young man from Limerick, decidedly and severely condemned Milton's poem on the Siamese twins because it was calculated in the highest degree 'to fan and excite a passion which needs no stimulus whatever among the mass of mankind. A passion which in my poor thought has done more to sow misery on earth than the scourge of war has ever done to mend it'.

A poor thought it was, indeed, and the young man who wrote that confused sentence was as mixed up, in the head, as the preaching-priest who talked of the degrading passion of love. Or as mixed-up as that odd fellow, and he had his fellows, who benevolently considered War to be the answer to the Population Explosion. For many reasons, or un-reasons, that I can never ever attempt to try to understand, War never proved to be anything of the sort.

Yet, in the eyes and in the consideration of all honest men, that young man, Gerald Griffin, has this justification: that he was suffering from the effects of a repressed and hopeless affection, perhaps a passion, for a good woman who may also have loved him but who was married to another man. If Lydia Fisher ever in her most secret heart had had any extravagant or wayward ideas, which seems most unlikely, that sermon would have recalled her, and John Milton, to a sense of propriety.

In spite of his prudishness, though, Griffin had an earlier and easier attitude towards what he knew of the Byronic vices or, at any rate, towards the man who was supposed to have practised them and whose poetry he much admired, as he did the poetry of Goldsmith and of Thomas Moore, that of Moore, at times, to the point of embarrassing imitation. Thomas Moore was friendly with Lord Byron, as Kyrle Daly was with Hardress Cregan, and Moore was, notoriously, all for virtue. Griffin considered that Byron's failings were not so much his own as the result of his education and background. That is a most interesting point, as so and then made by Griffin, for the downfall of Hardress Cregan can then be more mercifully seen against the background of a graceless, drunken, spendthrift, violent society: hard-riding country-gentlemen who would hunt not only animals but men, and would chase poor, hunchbacked Danny Mann along the road for the gentlemanly pleasure of pricking him with their swords. Or who would demand the last hunting-cry from Dalton, the aged, dying huntsman, even though the effort of uttering that cry kills the poor fellow and spatters his deathbed with diseased blood.

Dalton was not the old huntsman, as he has been so often wrongly described. He was a middle-aged man, and middle age was younger then than now, and he was dying of consumption.

Meanwhile the gentlemen, two of whom are crazy duellists, plethoric with a drunken arrogance which is less than pride and which they miscall honour, go on drinking: because as the father of Hardress temperately says: 'I call no man dead drunk while he lies on the high road, with sense enough to roll out of the way when a carriage is driving towards him'.

The rough outline of those events gave Gerald Griffin some of the best pages in the Irish novels of that time. His range and his vision were wide, and he could be every bit as effective in describing a colourful day at the races, or a storm on the wide Shannon river, or in reporting a droll story from Lowry Looby or Dunat O'Leary, the barber. Or again in describing the splendid, patriarchal anger of Mihil O'Connor, the rope-maker, when he learns that his daughter has been stolen. Or the agony of sorrow at the wake of Kyrle Daly's mother where Lowry Looby talks to the unknowing infant whose birth has caused the mother's death:

> The Lord forgive you, you little disciple! . . . 'tis little you know what harm you done this day! Do all you can, grow up as fine as a queen, an' talk like an angel, 'twill set you to fill up the place o' the woman you took away from us this day. Howl your tongue, again, I tell you, 'tis we that have raison to cry, an' not you.

Hardress reproves the drunkards and the duellists to the point of drawing down a lunatic duel on himself. But he reproves them in words that should really have been used by the virtuous Kyrle Daly. Hardress, we may suspect, uses those words simply because, by the way the novel is going, he and not Daly happens to be there. Yet the truth of the matter may be more complicated than that. Griffin, it is said, was fond of quoting the words that Byron was supposed to have used on his deathbed: 'Perhaps I am not so unfit to die as people think'. That could have been a hint to a sensitive, overscrupulous man, as Griffin assuredly was, that the soul and God might have things between them that Society and Society's two-handed engine, the Church and the Law, could never comprehend: that there could be explanations in the case of Hardress and, perhaps, even mysteries in the case of Scanlan. On top of all which, Griffin had scruples within scruples that he was, and his readers would be, giving more admiration to Hardress than to the exemplary Kyrle Daly, who had nothing to recommend him except irreproachable virtue and a stock of platitudes. Kyrle, it is true, once allows himself, or is allowed, to be angry at what he thinks is Hardress's treachery in relation to the lovely young lady, Ann Chute, to whom Hardress is affianced and with whom Kyrle is hopelessly, but not violently, in love. Apart from that anger, Kyrle displays no redeeming vices, and the anger is brief. Of necessity it had to be: not only because Kyrle was so virtuous but because Hardress and Kyrle were, in an odd, intellectual, Damon-and-Pythias way, two portions of the same person: Gerald Griffin.

Griffin had those Keatsian premonitions of an early death:

> In the time of my boyhood I had a strange feeling
> That I was to die in the noon of my day;
> Not quietly into the silent grave stealing
> But torn, like a blasted oak, sudden away.

> My triumphs I viewed from the least to the brightest,
> As gay flowers plucked from the fingers of death.
> And wherever Joy's garments flowed richest and lightest
> I looked for the skeleton lurking beneath.

Woeful verse, in more ways than one. But that was no Byronic posing. It seems to have been genuine black melancholy: and we must take him seriously, too, when he writes of his fears that he would never live to reach 'revered virtue and victorious age', but might perhaps die in youth, 'stained by some sudden crime'. It is most unlikely that he was thinking in terms of (in the Hardress fashion) seducing a country girl and dumping her into the Shannon. But to the spiritually sensitive, any sin may seem a mortal sin. Nor must we ever forget that when Griffin was sixteen, Limerick City saw Scanlan, only a few years older than Griffin, dancing at the end of a rope for a crime that, as the great Daniel O'Connell almost proved, was unthinkable in a young man of good family.

Griffin, when he was struggling in London for literary fame, said that he feared failure worse than death. Another fear was to dominate him, as it has dominated many another: not that of death but of the darkness that might, even-money chance, follow death. The consideration of Scanlan, the murderer, even under the milder mask of Hardress Cregan, could have brought that fear closer to him. With all due regard for, in storytelling, the force of the law of probability, it might seem that Griffin started off to make something tolerable out of Kyrle Daly and that Kyrle was not so much outshone by as absorbed by Hardress. Kyrle, indeed, vanishes after a while like a wax figure in a furnace and, to vary the metaphor, is brought back to life only by his mother's death and at a time when, oddly enough, Hardress is upbraiding his mother as the cause of his misfortunes.

Griffin, who was to be so virtuous in his own life, for once almost allowed evil to take over in his imagination, or could not prevent it attempting to take over. His casuistic compromise was to make Hardress a fine young fellow tormented by remorse and uncertain even about the degree of his own guilt, not an evil man but a rash, impulsive one, reared in a violent society, dominated by a stern mother, dogged by the devil. For all that, there could be for Griffin, the creator, no easy solution. The wages of sin would have to be death. His strict morality, combined with his artistic sense, saved him from the outrages committed by his popularizers, Boucicault and Benedict, and from that melting moment in which the remorseful speech of Hardress to the shade of the murdered Eily ends up like this:

> Once would my heart, with the wildest emotion,
> Throb, dearest Eily, when near me wert thou,
> Now I regard thee with deep, calm devotion.
> Never, bright angel, I loved thee as now.
>
> Though in this world were so cruelly blighted
> All the fond hopes of thy innocent heart,
> Soon in a holier region united,
> Eily Mavourneen, we never shall part.

Scanlan, for sure, could never have sung that verse with much conviction. Eily, according to Benedict's opera, or whatever, 'The Lily of Killarney', was not in any holier region but was alive and well and ready to be loved still more, and to take her bow every night at the final curtain.

Eileen Hanley, in her last moment of life on the Shannon, could never have dreamed of such an apotheosis. Nor that because of Griffin, and of what Boucicault and Benedict had done to or for him, souvenir-hunters would chip away at the gravestone over her sad resting-place. Nor that beauty queens would be selected, in the town of Kilrush, under the name of the Colleen Bawn.

A cynic may feel free to wonder what that beauty queen's first free trip should be. A cruise on the Shannon?

Gerald Griffin made one visit to France but said little or nothing, as far as I know, about why he went or what happened while he was there. It may be that the journey had something to do with an inclination that he felt towards the priesthood which, to judge from a curious sentence in a letter to one of his sisters, he seems to have regarded, finally, as even a more dangerous calling for him than that of being a novelist. He was thinking, we may suppose, of the dangers of spiritual pride. Very few novelists can afford spiritual pride. Did the shadow of Pascal and his particular pride stand on the threshold of the doorway to the priesthood?

When he turned his back on his books and his desire for glory, Griffin went not to the Roman Catholic priesthood but to the Irish Christian Brothers; not through any random choice but, possibly, because the Brothers had, in his own city, proved themselves as Christian heroes in their work for the poor suffering from the deadly cholera. No room in that country for spiritual pride.

When he was a Christian Brother in North Richmond Street, Dublin, that Quaker lady to whom he had, so distraughtly, written about love, called to see him. The message was brought to him. He thought it over and sent back a reply to say that he could not see her. The doubts and scruples of Hardress remained with him to the end.

It is a coincidence, but an interesting one, that in that same street, North Richmond Street, whose houses had, and have, 'brown, imperturbable faces', and behind those faces the consciousness of decent lives, and looking out on that darkness of agony in which man knows himself, 'as a creature driven and derided by vanity', an Irish novelist of a later date was to place the beginning of a story that sent a boy, suffering from first love, all the way to Araby, to find there only disillusion and the sense of loss.

✑ 21 ✑

Orange Lily in a Green Garden:
Shan F. Bullock

WHERE THE CLOGHER VALLEY railway ran westward, and without undue haste, from close to Caledon in County Tyrone, and off in the general direction of Enniskillen, there was, once upon a time, the caretaker of a halt and a level-crossing and he had a wife; and the local people said she was a witch. This was the way she went about her witchery:

> ... and it was said that she boiled quartz stones [presumably with names on them] at the full of the moon. If a stone cracked the heart of the victim would break.

The quartz stones were easy to come by. All the good lady had to do was to pick them up from between the sleepers on the permanent way. Just as a busy lady in the market in Dublin's Moore Street, if she had gone over to witchery, would have found it easiest to boil apples or onions; and the new potatoes. What a woman in a new highprice suburb might boil the Lord, or Satan, only knows.

That gem of a story I came on, a good few years ago, in a book on the Clogher Valley Railway written by Edward M. Patterson, an authority on old railways who had already written two books about those narrow parallel bars of iron that, for the benefit of man and the wonderment of God, used to wind hither and yon through the hills of Donegal. I mean the Donegal Railways.

God be with those days of easy and contented travel when the cynics (who in their dark, secret hearts longed for the Gadarene world we now live in) used to say that a thirsty passenger could hop off a train, milk a cow in a field, drink the milk, put on a spring and overtake the train again. Since my father was a Donegal man, one of the legends I was

215

reared on was about the wild night when the wind blew the train off the viaduct in Barnes Gap.

No such perils were ever encountered in the lush green land that the Clogher Valley Railway ran through. Yet it also had colourful moments:

> The line was generally a quiet one, but perhaps more than in many other places, there were frenzied peaks of traffic, as when every available carriage and not a few wagons were marshalled into the Orangemen's Specials and taken over the one-in-thirty gradients of Tullyvar by three engines, and again when equally lengthy pig-trains headed out after the fairs.

How Myles na gCopaleen would have rejoiced to find out that that railway ran the first articulated diesel railway in Ireland, as well as having a witch (Mad Suibhne's hag) more or less on the staff. The place where the witch lived was Colebrooke which had the distinction of being the stop for the Colebrooke estate where the Brooke family lived. Mr Patterson wrote:

> It was not every halt that had a Prime Minister living beside it. For many years the crossing gates and the buildings were looked after by Maggie Elliott who was officially there as caretaker. When he was chairman of the Railway Committee, Sir Basil would not hear of Miss Elliott being put out because of her advancing years. She was allowed to live on at Colebrooke until infirmity forced her to go to the care of friends, not long before the railway closed.

Maggie Elliott was not, of course, and came long after, the lady who boiled the stones. And the story of latter days is a heart-warming one to hear about Sir Basil, or Lord Brookeborough, about whom there were so many stories.

Through Lord O'Neill, we know that Lord Brookeborough had no desk or that, even if he had had one, he wouldn't have had much time to sit at it. For when he wasn't out shooting, he was off on a ship to the Antipodes. From his own lips we knew that he wouldn't have a papist about the house. Then there was once a profile article in *The Guardian*, written by a polite and clever English journalist who sounded as if he could not credit what he saw or heard and could only put it all down to the Wellsian Time-Machine moving backwards very fast.

There were great stories in that article, some, but not all of them, comic. The one I liked best was about how in the 1920s Sir Basil sat one night up a tree close to his house and waited for the IRA. With the instinct of a good soldier, he reckoned that one shot from the tree would be worth twenty from the house. The only trouble was that the IRA never bothered about him, and all night up a tree, nursing a gun, could have been cold and uncomfortable.

Mad Suibhne, to mention the man again, went up the trees and stayed there because he killed a cleric at some battle or other, was quite properly cursed, and was never the same again until he had the blessing of St Moling by the banks of the Barrow: also a sad fate for an old soldier. Flann O'Brien, who made his own use of Mad Suibhne, would have been overjoyed to hear that story about Basil Brooke. To the *Guardian* article I will return again.

Now a Prime Minister without a desk must feel as bereft as a minister without portfolio, or a priest or nun without a prie-dieu and unable to get the full benefits of the works of Fr Robert Nash. Of course you could argue that to a man who sits up a tree, a desk would be an enncumbrance. And what I really wonder about is if Sir Basil did not, as a prime minister, have a desk, did he have bookshelves? And if he did, what did he have on them? Did he ever, for instance, read the novels of Shan F. Bullock, who knew so much about the people of Fermanagh, Catholic and Protestant.

The only Ulster politician I ever heard mention Shan Bullock was Cahir Healy, who was more than a politician. Indeed it was something or other that Cahir said to me long ago that first interested me in Bullock's novels. Did Cahir ever mention Bullock to Sir Basil? They, Cahir and Basil, met often enough.

It was J.J. Campbell, a great Belfast man, who when he was editing *The Irish Bookman* impelled me to write about Shan Bullock. It was thanks to his carefulness in keeping his files that I was able, the other night, to revisit my mind on what I had to say about Bullock. Doubly impelled now by the news that the murder and savagery destroying the North, and threatening the whole country, had some time ago claimed as victims relatives of the novelist who had had such a clear vision of peace and order.

Shan Bullock was born at Crom in the County Fermanagh in 1865, four years before the death of William Carleton, who had been born not very far away in the Clogher Valley in the County Tyrone. Carleton belonged to the cabins, and the people of his best books are the ancestors of the poor Catholics who were shut out by the wall of Ascendancy from any part in Bullock's boyhood. The Fermanagh novelist belonged to the solid world of the fairly prosperous Protestant farmer, his father being a strong man under the shadow of the Big House of the Earl of Erne. And here and there through the twenty-two books that he wrote, he saw that world as radiantly distinct as an Orange lily in a green garden.

But the humanity of the man, his observing eye and his consciousness as an artist saved him from any spancelling by politics or politico-sectarianism. In the autobiographical volume *After Sixty Years*, published in 1931, he wrote:

> We little Protestants were, I suppose, always better clad and fed, certainly we had the rightful air of superiority becoming an ascendant

class: this notwithstanding, it would always be the barefooted, ragged
Catholic, with his hair through his cap and only a bit of oaten bread in
his pocket, that I was drawn to for play or company.

He was of another breed than ours, had softer ways and speech, better
manners somehow, knew more about the country and its life and the
things that mattered: and supposing him to have a sister – generally he
had five or six – there could be small question about it: Mary Roche with
her raven black hair and wide soft eyes: Rose Healy with her freckles,
and hair the colour of honey, and the smile she had and the quiet chuck-
ling laugh . . .

Bullock's first novel, *The Awkward Squads*, was published in 1893 and
two years later came *By Thrasna River*, the story of two calm years on a
farm by Lough Erne, the complete portrait of the artist as a young farmer.
The closest parallel I can think of in more or less contemporary writing
would be Adrian Bell's trilogy *The Cherry Tree*, *Silver Lea* and *Corduroy*.

Bullock's father had sent him to be educated in Farra School in County
Westmeath: a school later described, and disguised, in his writings under
the name Thalma. From schooldays he went to Dublin to fail an examination and, as a result of that failure, found himself for two years managing
a farm that belonged to his father, living with his younger brother the sort
of life that two young fellows would live when left alone to manage a farm
and do their own housekeeping.

In *By Thrasna River*, and the straight autobiography, *After Sixty Years*,
and in a dozen places here and there throughout his books, that farm
appears under the name of Emo. (When, as a successful author, he found
his place in *Who's Who?*, Bullock's address was given as Emo, York Road,
Cheam, Surrey.) Failing that examination was the best thing that could
have happened to him, for it meant that he found a place to fill his heart, to
provide him with a loved locality, and with the dozens of patient farming
people who live in the pages of his novels.

The boy on the farm by Thrasna River was not worrying his head about
the possibility that he might some day be a man writing books. The little
learning gathered at Thalma was very light on his strong shoulders. A few
nights spent visiting a Dublin theatre with an eccentric relative had possibly helped him towards failure in his examination, and had given him a
hint, slight and elusive, about the existence of a world that was neither a
farm in Fermanagh nor a school in Westmeath.

What he saw in the theatre he described through the mouth of Jan
Farmer in *By Thrasna River*:

A real Irish drama it was, full of people and talk that were familiar to me
. . . true Irishmen in kneebreeches and frieze coats and battered hats . . .
the two old tenants flung out on the snow by a blackguardly bailiff; I saw
the man die and the woman rescued by a gallant band of the boys; I saw
the boys meet in a shebeen and draw lots that one of them might shoot
the black Saxon of a landlord: I saw the hero draw the black bean from

the caubeen and go out with a very white face; I saw the hero shoot the landlord from behind a hedge, then chased by the police, hidden by the heroine, betrayed by the bailiff (who, of course, loved the heroine), tried by a packed jury, led to the scaffold, rescued by his comrades and, with his darlint by his side steal across the stage on his way to America.

That was, as he realized later, all very crude. But it was an attempt to comprehend life in a dramatic way, and down on a farm by Lough Erne he put all that coloured glory behind him, not attempting to comprehend life or to be any more distinct from the place and the people than the grass that grew in the meadows.

He brought some books with him to the house at Emo (not to be confused with that other Emo in County Laois). He piled the books in the corner of a room, felt no anguish while the dust settled and thickened on the undisturbed pile, and for two years he led a life that was in no way consciously mental. Later he wrote of that life:

> You spin no cobwebs; you feel that life can be lived without book or study; you lose your brain, so to speak, and find your limbs and health in the freedom of the fields.
>
> If you climb Rhamushill, mount the castle wall, set your face towards the setting sun, on your right will be Emo and the long glitter of Lough Erne, behind will be Thrasna River and the wilderness of Bilboa, on your left Lackanlough will gleam darkly among the hills. Armoy and its boglands stretch over towards My Lord the Mountain and the pastures of Gorteen spread out below your feet even to the distant whiteness of the ferry road and the rude borders of Drumhill townland.

In his novel *Hetty: The Story of an Ulster Family*, Bullock sent Hetty, her sister, and Hetty's lover on a Sabbath journey across that loughside world:

> Past Lackan Lough, shimmering in its ring of hills, past orchards and fir trees, and white houses showing through poplars and boortrees, past Leemore school and chapel, and forge, through wild Armoy and Gorteen, the land of wisdom; on in sight of my Lord the Mountain stretching its blue length out towards the sea; through flat wastes of heather-brown bogland and through the great loughside country cut into a thousand shapeless plots of pasture, meadow and tillage by high, thick hedges . . .

By gateways, upon the shady ditches, men sat smoking and talking. Groups in their Sunday best trudged homewards from Mass through the dust. And, at intervals, clusters of twos and threes, gay in starched muslins and flowered hats, or sombre in genteel black and rough homespuns, walked leisurely towards Church.

Like jewels in that setting of loughside country, Shan Bullock saw a hundred vivid pictures of the life of Ulster. It could be a picture of the turf-cutters at work in the valley between Emo and Rhamus Hill, squatting at mealtime around their fires, the blue smoke rising thinly to be blown away by the wind, the pungent smell of it filling the valley and making you think about mud walls, soot-blackened rafters, and clacking groups around cottage hearthstones.

Or it could be noonday in harvest, the earth asleep under the sun, only a child playing here and there, or a dog yapping at the sky, or a cart truckling drowsily 'out into that other country', the country away towards the mountain, or out beyond the shining river, or across the crouching hills.

A clerk in a London office, he remembered the place and the people: the crowd at the crossroads, boys and girls from Armoy and Lackan, wild men with red beards and fierce-eyed women from the bogs of Gort, the postman from Bunn in his donkey-cart, the Nolans of Leemore on the road to Bunn with a load of turf. Or the sudden hush at the race-meeting on the hill above Glann when the Angelus bell rang and men stood crossing themselves and praying into their hats, and the thimble-riggers and card-sharpers, the pickpockets, the tramps, those selling drink in the tents, even the policemen and the bookmakers and many of the grand folk in the stand, stood quiet, each solitary in the multitude and for a minute paid homage on the hillside.

One of the Brookes of Colebrooke could easily have been among those grand folk.

Life moved quietly in that world.

The old car-driver, who was the narrator in Bullock's novel *Master John*, summed up in one passage the whole cavalcade of his time:

> We had our share of diversion at times, an election or two, a faction now and then, odd years of famine and distress, doings between the Orange-men and ourselves, raids by the police on the poteen makers, a murder out upon the mountainside, a big fire at the White House, a terrible wind from the sea that nearly blew us off the earth.
>
> Some of the boys in our neighbourhood were drafted to the Crimea, and a few stayed there in a trench. I can remember some, too, fought in the Mutiny. And there was a man came back from fighting the savages in some outlandish part of Africa, and to hear him relate his experiences with gorillas and serpents, and to have his account of people that ate each other, and couldn't count the toes on one foot, you'd call him the greatest liar ever drew a ramrod.

Before the recent horrors got going in style in the Six Counties, and while there were still only warning rumbles in Belfast or Derry City, I spent a sunny day travelling idly through the country that Bullock wrote about: from the pub in Belturbet that was decorated in the style of the Great Wild West, then across the big river before it opens out into yet another length of lake, and on through dreaming country towards Derrylin.

'All quiet here,' said the man in the garage across the bridge. 'You have to go Deep down to get that'.

By 'Deep Down' he meant Belfast and Derry City. By 'that' he meant fighting and destruction. Murder, by bomb and by bullet in the dark, had not then become the fashion.

By the much smaller bridge at Aghalane, the peace and sunshine were beyond description: deep trees, copper beeches glistening over the sallies by the small river. The lovely thatched house a little further on could only have stood at the entrance to Arcadia. A roadside sign with a shamrock on it said: 'Welcome to Northern Ireland'.

On that day, for some reason or no reason, the moorland to the left of the road to Derrylin set me thinking of Bullock. But there was naturally nothing in the smiling landscape to tell me that relatives of his would be touched by the tragedy to come, or that there would be mysterious murder in Derrylin itself. Or that far away in Killeter, in the salient of south-west Tyrone, where nothing ever happened except a ballad and a fair and a funny story, there could be two brutal murders in one week. Faced with horror after horror, it takes a cool mind to remember the failure of governmental and other leadership that has led us to where we are today.

Everywhere in Shan Bullock's country, lake and grass-meadow make love to each other; the intermingling blues and greens must be a headache (or an eye-dazzler) to the cartographer. Little roads go sideways to boat-quays and fishing-stands and names that stay in the memory: Geaglum, Carradiller and a dozen others.

On the road that day under Glenavar, from which you may see all the glory of the Lower Erne, a truckload of trainee policemen had overturned at a tricky corner; scattered around the road were arms enough to fight the Battle of the Bulge.

The Union Jacks were much to be seen on the road to Derrygonnelly where William Carleton once walked through post-Famine loneliness: and afterwards wrote to Gavan Duffy, far away in Australia, about the death of Ireland. Yet he did not believe that that was the end, for on his own deathbed in 1869 he spoke of a future for Irish literature – after twenty-five years.

Duffy, before he left Ireland, had written of the country as of a corpse on the dissecting table. But as a well-known Irish military gentleman once reminded me, the corpse sat up and talked. Can we likewise surface from these present hatreds?

In the evening I talked, in my own native village of Dromore, with a Belfastman, an old friend, a man normally jubilant with talk and great stories. That evening he was gloomy and subdued with foreboding. He talked about fear: 'They're afraid that if we get in, we'll treat them the way they treated us. We're afraid of them because they have the guns and we fear they'll massacre the whole lot of us rather than allow us to get in'.

The sunshine on the intricacies of the Erne seemed very far away.

In a house outside Dromore, almost eighty years ago, and before I was twelve months old, the windows of the room in which I was meditating on the complexities of life, were broken by gunfire. There was a battle or something going on, and the mail train was held up and raided at Dromore Road station. Then one day in 1972 in Omagh Town, the pub around the corner from where my mother then lived was blown to bits. Unavailingly the RUC tried to persuade the old lady to leave her house in case there was another bomb in the vicinity. More than half a century after the bullets broke the windows in Dromore.

As a line in a song she used to sing goes: 'Ireland is Ireland through joy and through tears'. Or as Paddy Kavanagh wrote:

> Shall we be thus forever?
> Shall we be thus forever?

Yet the next line in the song she loved to sing went: 'Hope never dies through the long weary years'.

Fair enough! We'll need it all.

Back now to the blue-and-green pattern of the Upper Erne and the novels of Shan Bullock. For Sir Horace Plunkett, Bullock's writings were important primarily because of their carefully objective description of men and women living on the land, and because of the equally objective account, in *After Sixty Years*, of the way in which, within the memory of Plunkett and Bullock, the power had drained out of the Big House.

That was what Bullock had seen. He had described equally well what he felt in his own soul – the love for the land and the locality, for the people and their quiet lives – and, at the same time, the haunting desire to cross the mountain into a bigger and busier world.

Bullock's case was not the ordinary case of flight from the land. For, although he left the Crom country to work in an office in London, he must always have had deep-down the desire to write something about the people and places he loved. But he was close enough to the common lot to know what the young people felt, to know, also, what the old people felt when watching the eternal restlessness of the young.

Discussing the business of increasing literacy, he made Dan the Driver say in *Master John*:

> Nowadays there's a master in every parish and I hear the children buzzing like bees around him whenever I pass. God be with him and them, I say, but sure it's wonderful how well a man can go through life with his head full of ignorance. So far as I can see, what most of the rising generation learn at school is impudence and the road to America. My father was the best country tailor that ever wore a thimble; he lived

respected and fifteen cars followed his funeral; yet once upon a time when a big wind blew down the signboard from the wall he put it back upside down.

Sir Horace Plunkett was more interested in co-operative creameries than in novels, but he had, naturally, a clear understanding of the actualities and needs of rural Ireland. Prefacing Bullock's short biography of Thomas Andrews, who built and died with *The Titanic*, and whose story was told by Bullock at Plunkett's request, Plunkett wrote:

> While other Irish writers of imagination have used Irish life to express their own temperament, Shan Bullock has devoted his great literary ability almost entirely to the patient, living and sincere study of what Ulster really is in itself as a community of men and women. One feels while reading one of his tales that he loves to look upon a man, especially an Ulsterman.

Possibly that was literary criticism from the point of view of a manager of creameries. But it had validity and discernment. Many years later, in the preface to *After Sixty Years*, Plunkett quoted his own words, went on to praise the objectivity with which Bullock, reared under the shadow of the great house of the Earl of Erne, had described that house and the society that revolved around it.

'In the centre,' Plunkett wrote, 'stands the feudal castle on the slope, not difficult to identify, dominating the country road, amid the mountains, lakes and bogs so characteristic of the Irish scene; a fact, a symbol, beautiful, brave and strong. Elsewhere in the demesne were retainers by the score: a chaplain, a schoolmaster, stewards, engineers, gardeners, carpenters, painters, smiths, masons, a forester, sailors, ferrymen, keepers, workers of all kind and degree'.

Bullock was the last Irish writer to see the Big House functioning efficiently, symbolizing Ascendancy, giving the lowest possible place to the mere Irish (cf. Sir Basil Brooke), not only within the demesne walls but through the whole countryside that the castle or mansion dominated. Certainly within Bullock's lifetime everything the castle symbolized went up as if it had been dynamited – a portent of things to come! – and Bullock knew that. And so did Sir Horace Plunkett. Bullock wrote:

> Well, the influence is done. The old autocrat, God rest him, is lying yonder on the hillside, powerless at last, happily unaware or not caring. The drudges everywhere are free. The State now is their only lord. Like a throne without a kingdom the demesne is there, still splendid, perhaps to some dreamer more desirable now than it ever was; but a centre no more, something now in and for itself, a symbol of lost chances and lost power.

The live novelist may have cared as little as the dead earl. Bullock's father had admired the old earl but had, in the end, preferred independence on his own farm at Emo. Admittedly, the novelist's sympathies were all with the drudges. And as for Sir Horace Plunkett, his chief worry was that the drudges, now liberated, were giving birth to sons ready to abandon, or simply unable to stay on, the land their fathers had sweated blood to gain.

It occurs to me that Shan Bullock would have been fascinated by the spectacle of the rise and fall of Stormont.

The father of Shan F. Bullock had admired, and worked for, that 'old despot' the Earl of Erne, but, in the end, preferred independence on his own Ulster farm. His son left the land and suffered as an office-clerk in London in order, whether at the time he knew it or not, to become a novelist.

Sir Horace Plunkett saw between father and son the same clash between two generations that went on 'in every farmstead in Western Europe, the same pull of the country at the heartstrings, the same drawing to a freer and less laborious life in the town'. Concluding his preface to Bullock's autobiography, *After Sixty Years*, Plunkett wrote: 'No man could have conveyed better what is in truth the tragedy of half the farmers in Europe, when a man who had the passion for the land cannot pass on that devotion to the natural heir of all his toil'.

There was another aspect of that conflict between the generations. It had nothing to do with economics or the decay of rural life. It had a good deal to do with what Samuel Butler had written in *The Way of All Flesh* and Edmund Gosse in *Father and Son*. That Protestant rural society to which Bullock belonged was unusually rich in heavy fathers and, although Bullock's differences with his father seem to have had nothing of the bitterness of the stories of Butler and Gosse, they yet left something in him that reflected itself again and again in his books.

Mark Dell, the father in Bullock's novel *Hetty*, was a man who enjoyed going easy, watching the fields and the cattle, the houses on the hillsides, the people working, the crops growing. But it is not difficult to guess to whom Bullock was really listening when he made Mark Dell say: 'Young men nowadays learn too much at school and learn it badly. They get contempt for the land and contempt for their home. They want to see the world and want to be clerks or something as bad'.

Although much about Mark Dell was as kind as autumn sunshine, the story of the way in which his well-intentioned tyranny drove his son out on the world indicates clearly enough how Bullock felt about heavy fathers. Mark Dell, or the man on whom Mark Dell was modelled, would have reacted interestingly to the discovery in the publisher's list appended to *Hetty* of an advertisement for *Downward: A Slice of Life* by Maud Churton Braby, author of *Modern Marriage and How to Bear It*. Edward Garnet wrote for *Downward* a preface on literary censorship.

It occurs to me, in passing, that there may be an odd notion among people under twenty-five that the Generation Gap came into existence for the first time when students on the campus of the University of California at Berkeley went into revolt over Vietnam and other matters. Give something a catchy name and it becomes more visible. But the Generation Gap is as natural as a Guinness and it has been with us a lot longer. Young people nowadays just have a better opportunity to make themselves heard – and seen.

Everything in a world from which men fly to the moon is accelerated, emphasized, exaggerated. Robert Graves said that young people no longer even knew the songs their parents sang. That may not have been universally true but there was truth in it.

It was no longer necessary, as it was in the days of the old mercenary armies, for the young men of Berkeley to enlist, in order to get a pair of weather-worthy boots, a decent meal, and a better way of living than they had at home. Starve the Irish, Lord Kitchener is reputed to have said, and you'll have an army. And there was that painting by Lady Butler, wife of Sir William who wrote *Red Cloud* and sister of the fe religious poet Alice Meynell, that painting, I say, of the big man following the recruiting officer on wet western roads to join the Connaught Rangers.

If you send a chap to college for a few years and start him thinking (I had almost written 'drinking'), it becomes all the more difficult to persuade him to join an army and be trained to kill. They manage these things better in China. Not all turbulent students, though, seem to be overburdened by thinking. On my last visit to Belfield I was most impressed by the amount of litter left on the floor of the Arts Building at the end of the grinding intellectual day. And the recent exploits of the engineers – from whom though, even in my days, little was expected in the way of civilizzation – were said to have been quite remarkable. And I listen in to the most inspiring conversations in the Belfield bus.

An altered, or earlier, version of the story of father-son conflict as told in the novel *Hetty* appears in the collection *Ring o' Rushes*, under the title 'The Splendid Shilling'. And in several other places Bullock states his disapproval of the weakness that drives men to tyrannize over their children.

Master John, driven from home by a combination of his own wild ways and his father's bad temper, learns so little from his experience that, in later years, he shears the golden hair from his daughter's head as a punishment for disobedience. Human nature being what it is, the young rebels of today may change their manners in time to come.

Hugh Fallon forces his daughter into a marriage with the squireen, Martin Hynes, although Jane had overheard her future husband say, in the course of the bargaining debate on the dowry: 'Make it guineas, and I'll take the heifer'. A dozen Irish writers, with the brutal lack of romanticism that can be part of us, had seen and used the humorous possibilities of the made match. But Bullock was looking at the problems of Jane Fallon as H.G. Wells was looking at the problems of Ann Veronica, with the difference that Ann Veronica's revolt was nervous, with all the hysteria of big cities, and Jane Fallon's acceptance of the inevitable was as level as the incredible patience of the green fields and the everlasting lough.

Anyway, Bullock, driven by restlessness and parental authority and the desire to write, made his way to a clerkship in one of the biggest of the big cities. He even wrote novels with a London background. He wrote *Robert Thorne, the Story of a London Clerk*, of which the London *Standard* said: 'A noteworthy book about the soul-grinding heart-breaking conditions of employment in Somerset House'. A reviewer in *The Lady* said that Mr Shan Bullock had revived. And a reviewer in *The Young Man* said that Bullock had written 'one of the most poignant, haunting tragedies of modern life – the tragedy of a city clerk'. In *The Daily News* G.F.G. Masterman, friend of H.G. Wells, wrote: 'A more accurate and less indignant interpretation of lower middle-class life in London than the novels of George Gissing; a companion to the draper's assistant or scientific student of Mr H.G. Wells'. That was in 1907. Ninety-plus years later, *Robert Thorne* is, for sure, less read than *Born in Exile* or *Kipps* or *Tono-Bungay* or *The New Machiavelli*. And they're not read all that much.

Yet possibly the reviewer who thought the rural novelist had arrived only when he turned to material with which he could never be completely happy, was less to blame than the authorities in the Fermanagh County Library in 1947. In that year Cahir Healy wrote: 'Shan Bullock is not very well-known in his native Fermanagh. I could only find two of his novels in the County Library, and his last – and best – volume *After Sixty Years*.'

Could it be possible that Sir Basil Brooke had never read Shan Bullock?

In *The Barrys* (1911), the background was London for half the book and, for the other half, the Loughshore. And the story when it moved to London degenerated to the level of *East Lynne*. For the writer was as much an exile in London as was the clerk. And with heart returning always to the land by the quiet lake, the eye could never be set steadily on the roaring restlessness of London. Once again, in *Ring o'Rushes* he syllabled the names of the loved places, and then wrote:

> We have made the circuit – our Ring o' Rushes – of that little corner of the earth in which, here and there, the stories that make this book are set. Often, no doubt, you have gone further and fared better; your feet are heavy with Irish clay your eyes weary of Irish rushes, hedges, hills; you have met only heavy-footed peasants by the way, heard only the brogue, and the skirl of the curlews: you say, not without reason, that some great lord of the soil easily might hold our poor Ring o' Rushes in the hollow of his hand; still, strange to say, many worthy souls live happily among

these barren hills, and love them steadfastly: some exiles in this bustling outer world have left their hearts there; and one there is, a poor smoke-dried citizen now, who, as he stands sometimes, blinking across his garden at a sky of fog and a landscape of bricks, has been known to cry out within himself that not all London is worth that hill and valley over which Rhamus Castle keeps watch and ward.

A long sentence, God knows, but a fair picture of the lakeland of Fermanagh.

In the novel *Dan the Dollar*, Shan Bullock brought a significant exile back to Fermanagh. George Fitzmaurice in his play *The Country Dressmaker*, and other writers in other places, realized the comic possibilities of the returned American. Bullock, and, to a lesser extent, Seamus O'Kelly in *Wet Clay*, saw his social significance, his awkward, half-understood strength, his weakness, which was the perplexity of a man caught forever between two worlds.

Dan the Dollar was the son of Felix Ruddy; and Felix and his wife, Sarah, and Phelim and Mary, relatives who had grown up in the Ruddys' farmhouse, were varying aspects of the Ulster to which Dan returned with his strange nasality, and his hard directness and terrifying riches. Here is Felix Ruddy walking to sell apples in the market of Lisnahee: it isn't diffi-cult to substitute the exact Fermanagh place-name.

> A suit of coarse tweeds seemed flung upon his lean, shambling figure; one side of his collar was unbuttoned and had escaped the folds of a rusty black scarf; a corner of his spotted handkerchief hung from one coat pocket and the other pocket bulged with a coil of rope; his trouser bottom was turned up twice, that hung frayed and bedaubed; his brown hat was dented and had no ribbon, his waistcoat was half-open, his boots were not half-laced, and his shirt sleeves flapped wide . . .
>
> In walking he rambled from side to side of the road, now stopping to peer across the hedge, now waving a hand at some neighbour who passed, now calling a friendly word to the pony that drew a box-cart laden with a kitchen table, a stool, a bundle of hay and a creel of apples. Yet he seemed content enough and, seeing his face, you knew he was content.

Felix Ruddy was in no fit state to enter the Common Market, not even in Lisnahee. He didn't sell his apples. He gave them away. While Sarah on the Lisnahee fair-green would not sell the cow because she couldn't get her price. Dan's return from the States was just in time to save them from serious financial difficulties. Yet his arrival, even if it saved them from the local miser and money-lender, was scarcely capable of increasing a contentment that was, anyway, almost complete.

Bullock wrote lyrically about it:

. . . the soft voices, the ready laughter, the constant kindliness, the content; the bright mornings with all their bounty of freshness and beauty flowing from lawn and orchard, the long, slothful days and restful nights; the dim parlour with its smell of musk, the kitchen full of life and sunshine, the kettle singing on the hearth, the dresser shining, the table laid on the red-tiled floor, the morning greetings, the chatter over meals, the evening discussions by the fire; warmth and the breath of flowers coming through the open doorway, and the sound of birds and insects, the cackle of fowl, the lowing of cattle; the yard with Phelim strolling across it, or Mary carrying the milk; the fields bathed in peace and sunshine. Felix basking on a bank, beasts standing in the shade; the great spaces of earth and sky, the languorous air, the infinite and ever-lasting peace.

But Dan the Dollar, remembering the great American city in which he had made his money, was not content with contentment. He wanted movement, to be making and doing, going up in a balloon (he said) and scattering dollar bills over the fields, giving to his own slow people the mighty secret of mastery over the world. When he stepped over the threshold in the first moment of his return, Sarah, knowing him more by instinct than by the use of her eyes, said: 'Is it yourself?'

Dan replied: 'It's what I've made of myself, mother'.

Looking and peering for the thin boy she remembered going lonely out on the world, Sarah saw instead a sturdy man of medium height, about forty years of age, reddish hair streaked with grey, eyes glittering under bushy eyebrows: 'His face was full and strong, clean-shaven, fresh coloured, hard lines upon it and a certain rigid expression of shrewdness – an Irish face materialized'.

Dan, who had learned much and forgotten much in America, looked out from the new soul that America had given him and saw an Ireland badly in need of what he had to give. This, we must remember, was sixty years or more before economic revival, the automobile as it is now, the car-bomb, the Common Market, the affluence of teenagers, and the present price of beef:

'What the Irish need most,' said Dan, 'is backbone. Out of the country they square their shoulders like me and go right through, but here, three out of every four – the fourth being a black Protestant-look as if they were tired to death. That comes a good deal of Saxon ways of government, I suppose, and a good deal is the result of this cursed tea-drinking . . .
'See that woman's face. Do you notice the yellow wizened thing it is? You can see the same face on a Chinaman in the slums of San Francisco, only his is opium and hers is tea'.

Dan may have had in him the makings of a good Mormon. But in the end his effort to revive Ireland, or his own quiet little corner of Ulster, failed. And not through the faults of Felix, Sarah, Mary or Phelim, but because Dan's business-partner in the States failed him. The great American effort collapsed because Dan had to return to his big city to make more money, leaving the loughside country to survive or perish or sleep or be awake as its own soul dictated. Somewhere in that there could be a faint shadowing of one of the (plentiful) tragedies of our time: the erosion of the image of the United States between D-Day and the Marshall Plan, and the Christmas blitz of 1972.

It was illustrative of the divided life of Ulster (of which we tragically know more now than ever we did), and of the universal sympathies of Shan Bullock, that the Ruddy household should be part Catholic and part Protestant. Dan, who had once been a Protestant but who now, according to the local newspaper, preferred to worship at the shrine of nature, lectured Mary severely about the Catholic peasant's indifference to material progress.

He could understand their not caring for money or success but at least, he said, they should keep a good roof over their heads, wear decent clothes, eat nourishing foods, beautify their lives with gardens. Mary could only answer, with much faltering yet with much inner conviction, that it was not principally for eating and drinking we were in the world, that the people were content.

Bullock was certainly more than polite about the detachment of the Catholic peasant. Possibly he was more than severe on his own people when in the novel *The Red Leaguers* he gave this speech to a character called Christy Muldoon, who was by no means an impartial witness: 'In God's world is no creature so narrow and bigoted as your Ulster Protestant. He'll take all and give nothing. Heaven was made for him only, and hell is waiting for all not wearing his black coat. He'd be a good man if somebody'd lead him and he'd be led. But no one will lead him and he'd never follow'.

Bullock's best portrait of the hard, unleadable and unbiddable Ulsterman is in the character of Richard Jebb in the novel *The Loughsiders*, his last novel, published in 1924 when he was fifty-nine years of age. It is his best novel, and one of the best novels that rural Ireland has provoked.

Richard Jebb, sitting in his boat on the Lough, fishing with weapons designed not for sport but for murderous utility, surveys the loughside world, to which he belongs, with a hard black-chinned detachment. He knows the affairs of every household along the green shore. He watches the hay-making, views with disapproval a few girls bathing in a distant corner of the lough. He says to himself: *'It's well to be young. Suppose Rachel had come. We'd both have been put to the blush, even though they have the manners to perform in their shifts'*.

Later Richard proposes to Rachel Nixon and is rejected because, she says, she wants a lover, not another father. Later still, Rachel's father dies, leaving her dowerless. Richard knows that a second proposal would be accepted. Instead, he relentlessly manoeuvres Rachel into marrying another man, manoeuvres her two brothers off to America, and then marries Rachel's widowed mother. His hard mind could, with reservations, admire youth, as he admired the bathing girls, but it had no real place for new ideas or young lives. It was not, though, exclusive to Protestant Ulster. Bullock could be romantic and generous towards the other part of Ulster, and Ireland.

He could also find much colour and whimsical humour in the rigid world of Richard Jebb. He left a lot of his heart in little houses like the house in *Ring o' Rushes*, with 'the old yellow engravings in their wide walnut frames hanging against the damp-streaked walls; the woollen antimacassars worked in orange and blue hanging over the painted chairs; the flaring oleograph of King William over the mantelpiece, flanked on either side by dim old photographs in metal frames; the artificial flowers on the big Bible on the table; the half-open cupboard inside which stood a whiskey bottle among the best crockery ware; the geraniums in the window recess'.

He laughed a lot at characters like Wee James in *By Thrasna River*, who slept always with a loaded gun by his bed in expectation of some papish night of long knives, who looked up for inspiration to an orange-and-blue framed picture of King William that hung in his bedroom:

> D'ye see *himself* up there? That's the boy to put the pluck in ye – that's the lad knew how to scatter all the vermin . . . When I luk up at his face I cud chase fifty men . . .

Sir Basil Brooke took the gun at night with him up the tree and sat there till daybreak to guard the portals of his ancestral home. Terry Coleman, who wrote in *The Guardian*, (26 November, 1971) that most revealing article about the old soldier as Prime Minister, recorded also how, with the 10th Hussars in India in 1911, Sir Basil rode escort to the king-emperor at the Delhi durbar. Sir Basil, or Lord Brookeborough, said: 'About the height of the British Empire. I was there that day'.

Terry Coleman wrote: 'He sat a horse for four hours in a temperature of 100 degrees. He had bought for the occasion a new hussar's tunic of serge and gold lace, and sweated through it. It was ruined'.

All for Empire: a cold backside up a tree at Colebrooke, a scalded one at Delhi: a subject, heaven knows, for any novelist, and on a grander scale than Wee James.

But when the colour faded and the laughter died, the hardness remained, the uneasy feeling, the laughter was at times cracked, hysterically discordant, that the hardness had something to do with social and sectarian division, that some day blood would again be spilled in Ireland.

When, in 1904, Bullock published his novel *The Red Leaguers* he must have felt something like that. He was also meditating on the Boer War and dreading that some day the commandos might ride down through Armoy to burn and murder in Protestant Gurteen. It is not so much a bad novel as an ancestral nightmare. The conscious, creative part of him told the story through the lips of Red Shan, who led out the Red Leaguers to rebellion in Armoy. The subconscious part of him imagined an Irish rising as the papist *jacquerie* that Wee James had provided against by taking to his bed not the wife, that would have symbolized life, but the gun that was the symbol and instrument of hatred and death.

So, in his weakest novel he was yet most revealing about the most fatal characteristic of his own people: that hard suspicion and fear they had built as a wall against the neighbours. But in the light, most lurid, of the murders and burnings of recent years, what can we say? Where can we find the darkest, central cave where evil begins?

22

Dialect and Literature

DIALECT IS A MATTER OF IDIOM and intonation, just as language is, or the chatter of monkeys in the trees, or the carefully balanced dialogues of rooks in a rookery. Or the tumult of starlings in the coigns of an old building. Those who know the language of rooks or monkeys may be able to distinguish localized usages. When a man in Bonniconlon pronounces the placename Shligo, it isn't the name as it would be pronounced by a man in Ballybough or Bunthorpe.

Here in Dublin, where I have spent most of my life, I pass, believe it or not, for having an Ulster accent. Yet once, in my own town in Tyrone, a man told me that I had signs of what he, at that time, called a Free State accent. The ear, as well as the tongue, creates dialect. And although it is not usual to find that anyone who began life with Ulster vowel sounds will ever alter them, or have them altered, except by some major operation that has not yet been invented, yet, because of long residence among Free Staters, Munstermen, Leinstermen, Connachtmen, I found myself using idioms that immediately sounded unfamiliar, even faked, to my fellow Ulstermen.

By way of contrast, I was once, in the state of Virginia, told that I had a southern accent: that is of the Southern States of the USA. And when I asked why that outrageous statement should be made, I was asked to repeat the names of 'God' and of 'Carolina'. The explanation was simply that into the Carolinas, Virginia, Georgia and so on, a lot of people with Ulster vowel sounds had once come, grabbing the land and hunting the red men. The red men are as good as gone. Some of the Ulster vowel sounds remain. There's a county that I've heard of in Alabama where some of the people have, by and large, a Tyrone accent.

To say that dialects and variations within our language make for problems of communication is scarcely to announce any startling discovery. It is also easier for a German to speak to a Polynesian if the German speaks Polynesian or the Polynesian speaks German. Or if the two of them speak Dutch or Hebrew. But in the simple act of talking, dialect presents itself naturally. When it comes to putting dialect down on the printed page, the problems right away multiply. There is an ever-present danger of artificiality. There is the question of some sort of phonetic, as against standard, spelling. Then will the reader be able to understand that spelling. And, further, if he does get to understand it, could he read it out aloud and still make sounds in any way resembling what the author had in his mind or eardrums when he wrote down the words?

As in so many other things, including general history, for an understanding of Ireland, take a look at Scotland. From the earliest relevant time, that would be the time of the Scottish Chaucerians – Henryson, Dunbar and others, the relationship between the English used in Scotland and the language used by the mere English has been of vast interest.

Our own tentative grapplings with the angel of the English language began somewhere in the shadows of the seventeenth century, although it was not, as Seán de Freine has pointed out, until the nineteenth century that English made the conquest to which the material triumph of the people who owned the language entitled it. This is neither to praise nor dispraise the nature of that triumph. But the Scots were more intensely engaged and for a much longer time, and the questions and answers relating to dialect were, in Scotland, much more clearly outlined.

Burns is the most convenient example. The common assumption is that his genius revealed itself at its best when he was writing as he would have spoken to his father or to one of his rural beauties, and not spelling out words as they were spelled out in the academies. The common assumption seems to be the truth, even if there is a lot to be said for the Spenserian pieties of 'The Cotter's Saturday Night', and even as against 'The Jolly Beggars' and 'Tam o' Shanter'. Perhaps the divergence between standard and dialect may be measured by the distance between the cottar on his knees and Tam and the Beggars at their carousing: discipline, devotion and law, in sharp contrast to nature and spontaneity.

But in relation to this island of Ireland, those byart leaves bestrowing the yird, or wavering like the bauchie bird, or that daimen icker in a thrave to which the wee sleekit, cowerin, timorous beastie was as much entitled to as David was to the loaves of sacrifice, meant that Burns became a popular folk-author in Ulster, Catholic and Protestant, as he never was or could have been in any other part of Ireland. He still remained so in my boyhood. And I recall the local ragged rhymester saying to me, with a seriousness at which it was not possible to laugh, that 'Burns was the best of us'.

Yet even Burns, moving at his ease from the way they spoke on the farms to the way they wrote in the academies, and back again, does not fully point up the contrast between polite speech, as we may even yet call it, and dialect. But, at about the same time, John Wilson, an Edinburgh professor, wrote for *Blackwood's Magazine* what today we would call a column, a series of journalistic entertainments under the title 'Noctes Ambrosianae', and under the pen-name of Christopher North. The column took the shape of imaginary conversations in which the two chief participants were Wilson, or North, and James Hogg, the poet, known as the Ettrick Shepherd; he was a sort of Patrick Kavanagh of his period and seems to have spent a lot of his time asleep on a sofa in Walter Scott's Abbotsford.

It is interesting to see, in an amusing volume selected out of that column, North talking in the best standard English, while the poet all the time delivers himself in the broadest of braid Scots. The shepherd has been laid low by the jaundice and North says: 'An obstructed condition of the duodenum, James.' The shepherd replies: 'You begin to hate and be sick o' things that used to be moist delightfu' as the sky, and streams, and hills, and the ee and voice and haun and breast o' woman. You dunner aboot the doors, dour and dowie, and are seen settin' in nycocks and corners, whare there's little licht, no mindin the cobwabs, or the spiders themselves droppin down among your unkempt hair. You canna say that you are unco ill either, but just a wee sickish – tongue furry as if you had been lickin' a muff or a mawkin – and you observe, frae folk starin wee back when you happen to speak to them – which is nae often – that your breath's bad, though a week before it was as caller as clover.'

It is also interesting to note, in the irony of things, that the author of most interest to the time we live in is not Scott, nor Professor Wilson, nor even Burns, but the much-laughed-at Ettrick Shepherd. And for a book in which there is not one word of dialect, a novel *The Justified Sinner* (to abbreviate the title) which startlingly, and even better than Stevenson did when he was meditating on his Jekyll and Hyde, illuminates the double mind of Scots Calvinism; and which has impressed such various writers as André Gide in France and the poet Louis Simpson in the United States.

The homely speech of the Ettrick Shepherd is ordinary in idiom and construction, and only some of the words are odd. Yet my inability to present an exact reading of him, as John Wilson would have had him speak, and as he probably did speak, simply underlines the way in which dialect in literature can create difficulties. And not only to the tongue that is unfamiliar with it, but even to the eye. And the Scots experience is illuminating because it is exact and discernible.

No modern Irish poet has so successfully struggled with two languages, Standard and Lallans, as had the Scots poet Hugh MacDiarmid:

> I amna fou sae muckle as tired – deid dune
> It's gey and hard wark coupin' gless for gless
> Wi' Cruivie and Gilsanguhar and the like,
> And I'm no juist as bauld as aince I was.

> The elback faukles in the coorse o' time,
> The sheckle's no sae souple and the thrapple
> Grows deef and dour: nae langer up and down
> Gleig as a squirrel speils the Adam's apple.

All depending on what part of Ireland, or the neighbouring island, you come from, the drunk man looking at the thistle takes a greater or lesser amount of getting used to. What gives it validity – and this is of general application – is that MacDiarmid does not write this out of any rough, blunt desire for singularity, but because that, for him, is a natural mode of speech. And also, and almost more than anything else, MacDiarmid the socialist seems to fear a linguistic empire, to dread the hopelessness of being entangled in a language endangered by commercialism and the uniformity of what we call the media. For him, dialect is a fortification for the poet, a guarantee of inexhaustible variety.

The echoes of Scotland, of course, have crossed the narrow waters into this island, in dialect, spoken and written, and in other matters:

> 'Tis pretty to be in Baile Liosain,
> 'Tis pretty to be in green Magh Luain,
> But prettier to be in Newtownbreeda,
> Beekin' under the eaves in June.
> The cummers are out wi' their knittin' and spinnin',
> The thrush sings frae the crib on the wa'.
> An' ower the white road, the clachan caddies
> Play at their marlies an' goalin' ba'.

That is Joseph Campbell, the Mountainy Singer, getting the best out of words and phrases of Antrim Scots. Lesser poets, and prose-writers, have with assiduity, sometimes painful to witness, and with varying degrees of success applied themselves to the mixed speech of Ulster. The most effective of them was by no means a major writer but a clerical scholar, a doctor of divinity, and a man who had devoted himself to the study of the survival of older usages, even Elizabethan usages, in the speech of rural Ulster. That was the Rev. W.F. Marshall of Sixmilecross, and it was my honour to have known him.

It may come as a surprise to many people to know that the lament of the womanless mountainy farmer near Carrickmore in the County Tyrone was the work of such a man. It has such a place in popular literature. Here's a portion of the lament of the old man who was livin' in Drumlister and gettin' very oul':

> Wee Margit had no fortune
> But two rosy cheeks wud plaze.
> The farm o' lan' was Bridget's,

But she took the pock disayse.
An' Margit she was very wee,
An' Bridget she was stout,
But her face was like a jail dure
Wi' the bowlts pulled out.

So I swithered back an' forrit
Till Margit got a man.
A fella came from Mullaslin
An' left me just the wan.

I mind the day she went away,
I hid wan strucken hour,
An' cursed the wasp from Cullentra
That made me da so sour . . .

It may not be among the higher flights of lyric poetry, yet it is still immediately obvious that the reverend gentleman has observed his people and listened to them speaking. He had eyes and ears that any writer might be thankful for.

From survival from an older time and, very obviously, from the influence of Irish, even when that influence is hidden and unseen, our English derives. And it retains a richness and colour that modern uniformity has not yet destroyed. Some of that richness may, at times, come between us and lucidity. We are a talkative and adjectival people. And the attitude of any reader towards such superfluity, and towards the exploitation of dialect, will be dictated by the nature of the ancient quarrel between classicism and romanticism, or between Hemingway and Fitzgerald: between whether literature is a matter of leaving out or of putting in.

J. Braidwood in his very valuable study *Ulster and Elizabethan English* applauds the richness. He finds that the first and most striking parallel between Elizabethan English and Anglo-Irish is the sheer delight in language for its own sake. And the Elizabethan period was, linguistically, the most uninhibited in the history of the English language. Why? Because it combined a maximum of art with a minimum of inhibition. And even the greatness of Shakespeare owed much to what Professor Wilcock called his stimulating collaborator, the Elizabethan speaker and listener.

This passage from Braidwood, which I shall quote at some length, may be over-flattering to our national, linguistic pride. That is if you consider that richness, even recklessness, of vocabulary is a good thing. But it is a thoughtful, and thought-provoking passage.

> The Elizabethans (or better, the Tudors) discovered that the hitherto despised vernacular could be used with magnificent rhetorical effect, could even, because a living language of greater flexibility and inventiveness, surpass the traditional Latin. It was, however, during this Tudor period of unparalleled linguistic awareness that certain concepts

began to evolve which, industriously cultivated in the seventeenth and eighteenth centuries with their passion for standardization and authority, made it virtually certain that we will never again reach the heights of Elizabethan speech and literature, for it was this age that first considerably formulated the notion of a Standard Literary English, of a standard of pronunciation, and of a standard spelling.

Today, probably only the Irishman, especially the Southern Irishman, and some Welshmen, work in the Elizabethan linguistic, mastering the language, where the rest of us, with pusillanimous notions of correctness and good taste hammered into us at school, let the language master us. A child's progress along the highway of his native tongue – the byways are prohibited – is impeded by deterrent notices at every step, and he spends far more time on analysis than synthesis, so that he can parse a sentence but not write one. We might occasionally remember that 'the Elizabethans became eloquent before they became grammatical'.

If ever an age had the gift of the gab, that age was the Elizabethan. If ever a nation had the gift of the gab, that nation is the Irish. It is not suggested for a moment that the Irish inherited the gift from the Elizabethans, for the Irish gift is of ancient origin and the nation has long been notorious for loquacity.

That passage is as close to the heart of the matter as makes no difference. But we should use it not merely to lay a flattering injunction to the soul, but to examine the standardization of speech and writing inevitable in our society, pressed on us, as it is, by officialdom, by newspapers, radio and television (to talk of the media may be to use one of the worst of the clichés) and, perhaps, above all by the advertising industry; a standardization that can affect our English and Irish and the variants thereof.

Those young male singers with effeminate voices, coming from Belfast or Derry or where you will, and singing, or trying to sing, with the voices of Afro-Americans from Natchez, or Nashville or New Orleans, may, and generally do, sound absurd. But it seems to me that they may be, if half-unwittingly, in genuine search for a unique idiom, for the phrase flavoured like a nut. Yet it could, perhaps, be argued that they might be better off reading Shakespeare out loud to each other.

Yet in a world so tied up in a tight bundle, language must renew itself from such a variety of sources as was never before available; it must renew itself or die in clichés. But in the long run it is only an inborn taste, afterwards cultivated more by talkative company than by the rules of the academies, that will find the living phrase and record it in writing.

John Synge, as we might expect, did make one of the best, and certainly one of the most succinct, statements on the matter. And, like Professor Braidwood, he was, in his brief preface to *The Playboy of the Western World*, casting his mind back to the Elizabethans: 'In a good play, every speech should be as fully flavoured as a nut or apple, and such speeches cannot be written by anyone who works among people who have shut their lips on poetry'.

The search for the unique phrase must always go along with the search for the theme that is unique and also universal. And Synge's preface to *The Playboy* pairs off in my mind with a celebrated passage from Marcus Antoninus:

> Whatever happens is as common and well-known as a rose in the Spring or an apple in the Autumn. Everywhere up and down, ages and histories, towns and families are full of the same stories.

As deliberately as Wordsworth did, but with none of the unhappy accidents into which Wordsworth's solemnity betrayed him, Synge went searching for the living language of the people, and very deliberately, in remote places where the words of the people had not (as he considered) been debased by schools, cities and newspapers:

> Among certain set apart in a most desolate stony place
> Towards nightfall upon a race, passionate and simple like his heart.

The man, in the judgement of another poet, sought in the flavour and simplicity of that idiom the reflection of himself. He sought life also in the Gaelic idiom and movement that remained with people even in places where the language had died.

The ignorant absurdity, say, of the attack made on the language of Synge by St John Ervine and others, who tried to argue that it was a mode of speech never heard on sea or land, was never so clearly brought home to me as on a day on a road in Tyrone when I heard two countrymen talking in a language as rhythmical and stylized as John Synge ever offered to the stage. And that was not in the west nor south-west, nor in any Gaeltacht, but in English-speaking country and among 'the preaching Luthers of the holy North'.

The advantages that dialect and local usage can bring to the writer is in giving a new sinew to his language, and a variety and a freshness. The disadvantages, in pedantry and eccentricity, can at times be even more obvious.

The Irish novelists of the early nineteenth century found themselves, in that way, in a strange situation. They were caught between two languages, or, you might say, even somewhere in the centre between three: English, Anglo-Irish, and the Irish that was still flowing on the tongues of the people. The occasional efforts made to render the Irish speech in an English phonetic spelling could at times be unhappy. And they persisted right to the end of the century in the efforts made by, say, Jane Barlow to catch in phonetics the speech of Irish people in the villages that she called Lisconnel and Ballyhoy.

She was a woman in the clearest sympathy with the people she wrote about, but she was the daughter of a vice-president of Trinity College,

Dublin. She herself had an academic turn of mind and it was even listed in *Who's Who* that she played the organ as her principal recreation. So with all the pedantry of her background and disposition, she set about to make her Irish people talk real Irish. This could be the result. An old lady called Moggy Goggin is complaining to the lady who owns the animal about the behaviour of a young brindled bull in a meadow called Long Leg:

> I thought I'd just tell you the way he's carrying on. For when he come out first into the field he was paiceable enough. But this last week or so it's outrageous he's been. Time and again he's run at me; and you know, ma'am, I have to be crossin' the strame and the corner of the Mount Field to get to the road gate, and its thereabouts he's keepin' continyal. Bedad, I believe he has his eye on the house, watchin' 'till I come out. Yesterday he had me afeard to stir a step the whole day, and I wantin' to get down to the town wid me few eggs. They're sittin' in the basket yet. Young he is, but he always was a passionate little crathur, and more betoken, I distrust them brundly-coloured bastes.

And so on, in the best or worst style of Kitty the Hare. Which reminds me that I once saw one volume of the plays of Synge that had belonged to Victor O'Donovan Power, the creator of Kitty the Hare. The owner of the book had scrawled on the margins of the pages quite ferocious comments on what he called the Stage Irishness of Synge. It all depends, I suppose, on one's point of view. For what Synge did was to rationalize dialect and idiom with a melodic line, and to enrich an orderly English by the use of dialect. O'Casey did something similar for the speech of Dublin, and all through his autobiographical volumes the rhythms and intonations of Dublin speech are clearly discernible. Yet there is nothing there to halt, by pedantry or affectation, any normal intelligent reader of English.

From Maria Edgeworth onwards, Ireland's writers of the nineteenth century were very conscious that they had a responsibility: they must delineate, as they called it, the Irish people for a readership that knew little about them and that quite often regarded them as ignorant and uncouth savages. Since William Carleton, Gerald Griffin and Michael and John Banim came closer than any others to the heart of the people, they, meritably, saw that responsibility all the more seriously and were the better able to live up to it.

Carleton was almost certainly a native speaker of Irish. His father and mother were, and his father was a story-teller and his mother a renowned folk-singer. There was the famous story that when somebody asked her to sing an English version of 'Bean an Fhir Ruaidh', she refused. She said that the English words and the music were like a man and his wife quarrelling. But that the Irish words melted into the music, like a man and his wife living in harmony. Her words, perhaps, could be taken as a permanent image of the quarrel, or the concord, between standard English and the English spoken by people whose mouths, almost unknown to themselves, had been shaped by Irish.

Her son, who became the first great Irish novelist, made tremendous play with the vagaries of the speech of his countrymen: from the bog-Latin spoken by the voteen of Lough Derg, to the sesquipedalianism, or use of long words, of Mat Kavanagh, the hedge-schoolmaster, or of Denis O'Shaughnessy on that never-ending road to Maynooth. They were a people passionately interested in language. And only from such a people can the continual renewal of language come. The lips must never be closed to poetry.

~ 23 ~

Frank O'Connor and the Long Road to Ummera

RANK O'CONNOR, IN 1966, WENT off along the long road to Ummera as one of his people, an old woman, did in the most moving story of that name. She had made certain that she would rest in death not in Cork city but among her own mountainy people: 'the bleak road over the moors to Ummera, the smooth grey pelts of the hills with the long spider's-web of the fences ridging them, drawing the scarecrow fields awry, and the white-washed cottages between their little scraps of holly bushes, looking this way and that out of the wind'.

O'Connor himself took his rest from storytelling in a place close to Dublin, between the mountains, the sea, and the city. His life's work had been of the utmost importance for storytelling, and for many other matters, in Ireland. His vision of Irish people and places, of which that glimpse of the landscape of one small portion of Munster is a vivid example, is a most important part of our cultural history.

He was the most genial of men: the rich laugh, the handsome head thrown back, the Munster brogue, which could coax the birds off the bushes and which made him superb at the reading out loud of his own stories. He was kindly, and helpful to younger writers. He was also the world's most dogged man at holding on to opinions that could frequently be eccentric. Because of his work, and that of his great contemporary and fellow-Corkonian, Sean O'Faoláin, and of Daniel Corkery, who had his influence on both of them, and of Elizabeth Bowen, Liam O'Flaherty, Mary Lavin, Michael McLaverty, Bryan MacMahon and others, the short story in Irish literature, after George Moore, Yeats and Joyce, has had an extraordinary importance. Perhaps it still has.

There were even those dogged moments when Frank O'Connor came perilously close to arguing that it was the only form that mattered. For him

241

the short story in Ireland, as a modern art form, had had its beginning with George Moore in the collection called, with calm deliberation, *The Untilled Field*. And that was that. The guillotining definition disposed of a certain amount of earlier material, but it is for sure that *The Untilled Field* was the most important collection of short stories made by an Irish writer up to that moment. And it had its influence on O'Connor.

W.B. Yeats said that O'Connor was doing for Ireland what Chekhov had done for Russia. That was not the most original remark the Great Panjandrum ever made. And O'Connor himself might have thought it more accurate if Yeats had mentioned Isaac Babel rather than Chekhov. But the remark did point to the Russian influence which, before O'Connor and O'Faoláin, Daniel Corkery had felt in *The Hounds of Banba* and *A Munster Twilight*. It became a common ploy to pick out Russian and Irish parallels: a brooding quality, earthiness (Corkery was to entitle another collection *Earth Out of Earth*), a dim religious light, an unstable gaiety, a revolution apiece, whiskey here and vodka there.

It was one of the O'Connor crotchets to argue that his contemporary Ireland could produce interesting short-story writers as it could not produce interesting novelists. That was an argument that pleasantly ignored the existence of Kate O'Brien, Samuel Beckett, Brinsley MacNamara, Francis MacManus, Flann O'Brien, Francis Stuart, Peadar O'Donnell, Mervyn Wall, Forrest Reid, and paid no account whatever to the bulk of Elizabeth Bowen, Liam O'Flaherty, three fine novels by Sean O'Faoláin, the satirical romances of Austin Clarke, James Stephens. And so on.

That O'Connor crotchet comically parallels a remark once made by the horrendous Professor William Magennis, Prince of Darkness of the deplorable Irish Board of Censorship of Publications. The learned Professor said that 'these men' (he meant O'Connor and O'Faoláin) had not the makings of novels in them, that they had the stamina only for short stories, which they padded out to novel-length with 'smut' to suit the debased and anti-Irish tastes of London publishers. Good old Magennis. He has long gone to wherever good censors go and, gradually, the deplorable organization he masterminded weakened. Its last holy war may have been against the early novels of Edna O'Brien. Apparently it was not to be tolerated that a young woman educated, as we used to say, at one of the best Irish convent-schools, should come out, even in a fetching County Clare accent, with home truths or sharp statements about what we used to call sex. Percy French's Darling Girl from Clare had, it seemed, up and electrified the local lads sitting on the wall upon a Sunday watching the girls go by, by cycling past in the nude.

All that by the way. Even if the problems raised by that idiotic censorship can, even in retrospect, be irritating to the Irish writer of fiction, short or long, things nowadays are by no means the way they were in the 1940s and 1950s. Now that I remember: Because of a short story of my own, a thing called 'Rich and Rare Were the Gems She Wore', the issue of *Irish Writing* then edited by David Marcus, in which the story first appeared, was withdrawn from the reading-room of Cork City Library, probably at the behest of some blue-nosed old ladies.

The story, a simple idyll, was about an American army officer trying, and failing, to get a prim Irish girl into bed with him in a Dublin hotel. All Irish girls, even in those days of censorship, were not prim, but that one was a credit to the most exalted ideas of Irish female virtue. And the fact that the American failed might have pleased the bluest of blue-nosed ladies.

Pursuing his diverting theories about the short story, Frank O'Connor could almost imply that James Joyce lost his vocation when an idea for a short story got out of hand and ended up as a novel or something by the name of *Ulysses*. Ireland, he would argue, could produce no novels like the novels of C.P. Snow: orderly statements about an organized society. Irish novelists had not lived up to the example of George Moore's *The Lake*. That was an odd argument, and an odd novel in which the naked buttocks of a priest, grey in the moonlight on a Connacht lakeshore, had given evil amusement to James Joyce.

It has been argued that O'Connor's attitude was the result of an unsuccessful love-affair with the novel. That was not to say that *Dutch Interior* and *The Saint and Mary Kate* were not interesting novels. They most certainly were and are. But it may have been that O'Connor himself was not satisfied with them: that they did not finally click shut like a box, as William Yeats said poems could do for him but, as he also said, prose never did. And as his stories certainly must have done for O'Connor to give him the sense of completion, fulfilment, mastery, as in 'Guests of the Nation', 'Uprooted', 'The Bridal Night', or 'The Luceys', a story that he wrote and rewrote to what he did, and we must, consider a final perfection.

His book *The Lonely Voice* has a lot to say about the short story as the voice of submerged minorities. But it never once touched on the mundane consideration of what magazines were or were not, at that time, available to provide springboards for the young writer, who then seemed to me to be well down among the most pathetic of submerged minorities.

Yet the title of that book was, in itself, of interest. For my own part I think of the lonely voice not in relation to the short story but in relation to the folksong. The old Irish songs, as we all know, and even the old country songs in English, were made to be sung without accompaniment, or only with the accompaniment of the wind in the bushes or the waves on the shore. But the old seanachie or storyteller 'between the fire and the wall', did also speak his traditional tale in a sort of splendid isolation. And in his later years O'Connor dwelt a great deal on the short story read out to be heard as much as written to be read. That was because of the radio and the, then emerging, television and also because he himself read his own stories most impressively; and, at that time, Irish sound radio under the beneficent influence of Robert Farren and Francis MacManus had begun to open a market for short stories. There was also the BBC in Belfast and London, and the English and, much more importantly, the American magazine market.

But a young writer will naturally wish to see himself in print in his own country and in Ireland at that time, and as one might expect in a small country with a small population, the opportunities were limited. The cost of producing small magazines, their high mortality rate . . . Well everybody everywhere knows about that.

If crotchety, in a good-humoured way, in his theory, Frank O'Connor was superb in his practice, in his sheer artistry. The last time I saw him alive, we walked along the banks of the Grand Canal in Dublin City. The next day I was leaving for Virginia., USA. He wished me a safe journey and said: 'Another book of stories like *A Journey to the Seven Streams* and you'll be an international figure'.

'Michael,' I said, 'there were a few novels, too'.

At which, head flung back, the grand laughter making music by the quiet canal, he thumped me on the shoulder and went his way. You couldn't argue with him. You could only be grateful to him for what he was and had done, and for the great good fortune of having known him.

He had wandered not as lonely as but as happy as a cloud in his world of what he called the Little Monasteries: the Ireland of the eighth and ninth centuries, a period, or an era, that he found 'probably the most delightful in Irish history'. His heart being in that Ireland, his heart not being here and now, may have accounted for the buoyancy in his step, the high carriage of the handsome head, the good laugh, the affability.

In that happy time he elected to find monks in small wooden monasteries, men not unlike the persons to be found in the fictions of Thomas Love Peacock, or even in those of George Meredith, 'wealthy, worldly, scholarly men, who live in little oases of civilization among the bogs and woods, in comfortable wooden houses with wine cellars and libraries, with clever sons who will become, in their turn, abbots or professors of scripture, and clever daughters who will manage big convents or marry among the ruling classes'.

Frank O'Connor translated well from the Irish poetry of various periods: his most celebrated work in that way being, as we all know, his rendering of Brian Merriman's 'The Midnight Court', that splendid piece of ribaldry and anti-clericalism in which O'Connor found an extension of the delight expressed in his own brief, pungent, delightful 'Self-Portrait', as he modestly called it:

> Last Sunday morning,
> Sitting on the tram,
> I found myself beside a priest,
> A fat and surly man.
> I looked over his shoulder
> And I read 'Namquam'.
> Now I happened to be reading
> 'Les Amours de Madame'.
> And, even though he frowned at me,
> I didn't give a damn.
> And that just shows you
> The sort I am.

When the prudes in the Dublin of those days, the Monkish Moles and the Fearful Firbolgs, decided that O'Connor-Merriman or Merriman-O'Connor were in general tendency indecent or obscene, and that the native language held dark secrets that had nothing to do with the invincible chastity of Mother Erin, O'Connor was to say with rueful humour that the only compliment some of his countrymen had ever paid him was to think that he had written the original poem.

He wrote about these matters in *A Short History of Irish Literature: A Backward Look*. Therein he said that it might be accepted as common ground that 'no Irishman is of much interest until he has lost his faith'. But he made that statement in the humour of that little thumbnail self-portrait, deliberately and delightfully to provoke. Just as in translating Merriman, he got all the delight of swinging an ashplant like the best old-style parish priest of them all, and making fur and feathers fly. Just as when he spoke of Dublin as a provincial hole, how was any innocent visiting American to know that, first and before all, there was a Corkman speaking.

But his mood was very different when he cast the mild nostalgic eye back to those little monasteries and to the men who, as his friend David Greene of Trinity College, Dublin, said, 'wrote like angels'. O'Connor's Munster voice was richer than ever when he spoke of them, as he did most eloquently in the lectures delivered in Trinity not too long before his death. Then *A Short History of Irish Literature* bore a close relationship to those lectures, as to the habits and tastes of a life of careful scholarship; even though he, too easily, would say that he was using merely a storyteller's intuition and not the acumen and perseverance of the trained scholar.

He preferred in his pleasant way to be regarded rather as the friend of scholars, even when he thrawnly disagreed with them: Greene, Binchey, Carney, Flanagan. Two of the scholars, David Greene and Philip Edwards, made it possible for him to mount the rostrum, or the pulpit, in Trinity

College. And a newspaper editor, Hector Legge of the *Sunday Independent* realized how important it was that O'Connor should be back in Dublin. And one of the most intelligent and courageous of Irish priests, Fr Peter Connolly, had him down to lecture in St. Patrick's College, Maynooth: something that would not have been likely to happen in the doldrums of the nineteen forties.

All that meant more to O'Connor than he would readily have cared to admit. In that *Short History* he returned to what he described as the plight of the Irish intellectual in all ages, as expressed in a decree of the so-called Second Synod of Saint Patrick:

> One's own country is to be instructed first, after the example of Our Lord, and later, if this does not succeed, to be abandoned after the example of the Apostle. But he who can succeed, even if he imperil himself, shall teach and show himself everywhere: and he who cannot, let him be silent and depart.

It was not in O'Connor, no more than it was in his great fellow-Corkonian Sean O'Faoláin, to depart forever or, utterly, to be silent. For all that, Ireland has reason to be grateful. His presence along Grafton Street and around St Stephen's Green was one of the many things that kept Dublin from being the 'provincial hole' that the Moles desired. After all, Professor Saintsbury did, and quite according to his lights, describe Ibsen as a provincial.

Thomas Flanagan, who was in Dublin for those lectures, had his own jesting way of referring to the great nineteenth-century trinity of Petrie, O'Donovan and O'Curry as the Ordnance Survey Gang. In Dublin, in that last great year of Frank O'Connor, there was, of a certainty, the Grand Canal Gang: O'Connor, Liam O'Flaherty storming by, Mary Lavin around the corner in Lad Lane, Patrick Kavanagh, equal but separate, asserting his right to his own territory in Baggot Street. There was Flanagan himself slipping scholarly notes under O'Connor's door in the early hours of the morning; in which notes, covertly, and as one of the mere Irishry exiled to the O'Byrne territory in Rathgar, I collaborated; in an effort to save the remains of William Carleton, deceased 1869, from desecration by that rambling Munster man, Donovan or O'Connor or whatever he chose to call himself.

There was, also, in Trinity College, and a pleasant sight to see, the growth of an O'Connor discipleship under the leadership of the (then) young poet and professor, Brendan Kennelly. Alas that all that should have been disturbed by death.

For the purposes of *A Short History of Irish Literature*, Thomas Flanagan almost managed to rescue William Carleton, although it would have been better if Flanagan could have persuaded O'Connor to take seriously a longer novel like *The Emigrants of Ahadarra*.

Maria Edgeworth, the decent woman, Flanagan could do nothing for. According to O'Connor, Maria was didactic (a bad word) and that was that. No point in telling O'Connor that *Castle Rackrent*, viewed against all Maria Edgeworth's work and the circumstances of Time and Place, was a startling escape from didacticism. But on the Irish writers, in English, of that period, as on the Gaelic poets of the previous century, O'Connor wasted little sympathy or understanding. Far from the little monasteries were they reared.

What he had to say about William Butler Yeats was worth volumes of ill-informed, or uninspired, fumbling. Seldom has a great poet been looked on with such a friendly and shrewd eye. What O'Connor had to say about Joyce was frequently twice as perverse as Joyce, a Corkonian on a Dubliner, as perverse as his views on the novel and the short story in *The Lonely Voice*.

But O'Connor himself rightly found the Yeatsian self-epitaph perverse and would have preferred to remember Yeats by those lines from 'The Herne's Egg' that could so easily be applied to his own lovable warm-hearted living, and to his brave going-forth:

> Strong sinew and soft flesh
> Are foliage round the shaft
> Before the arrowsmith
> Has stripped it, and I pray
> That I, all foliage gone,
> May shoot into my joy.

✒ 24 ✒

Memories of the Mountainy Singer

PADRAIC GREGORY WAS A BELFAST architect, a poet and play-wright, a man of gentleness and benevolence: and he was the first man I ever heard talk at length, and with knowledge and enthusiasm, about Joseph Campbell, the poet, the Mountainy Singer, who was many more things even than all that. Campbell was proud of the title that many used as a second name for him, and he dwelt on it several times and in various forms:

> I am the mountainy singer –
> The voice of the peasant's dream,
> The cry of the wind on the wooded hill,
> The leap of the fish in the stream.

In verse as hard and exact as bardic verse he detailed in sixteen lines the matter of his song: the cairn on the crest of the mountain, the girl in the arms of her lover, the child at the mother's breast, the fire on the open hearth, the old woman at the spinning-wheel, the plough in the broken earth, the dark or blind man labouring at his rhymes, the fisherman lost on the lough, the primitive, enigmatic cry at the moment of morn. Then:

> No other life I sing,
> For I am sprung of the stock
> That broke the hilly land for bread,
> And built the nest in the rock!

Yet elsewhere, and beginning with the same opening line, he follows a different stranger road:

> I am the mountainy singer
> And I would sing of the Christ
> Who followed the paths thro' the mountains
> To eat at the people's tryst.
>
> He loved the sun-dark people
> As the young man loves his bride,
> And he moved among their thatches,
> And for them he was crucified. . . .
>
> . . . . .
>
> And they dreamed with him in the mountains
> And they walked with him on the sea,
> And they prayed with him in the garden,
> And bled with him on the tree.

Those images of the sun-dark people and of the dark man making his rhymes for them, that very Celtic and Columban image of Christ on the roads of Ireland and, walking with him, the Gilly of Christ, who might have been Colmcille himself or any of his inheritors, were always much in Campbell's mind:

> I am the gilly of Christ,
> The mate of Mary's Son
> I run the roads at seeding-time,
> And when the harvest's done . . .
>
> . . . . .
>
> No eye has ever seen me,
> But shepherds hear me pass,
> Singing at fall of even
> Along the shadowed grass.

But to return for a moment to Padraic Gregory. In 1934 or 1935 the Omagh Players, under the direction of the late F.J. Nugent, performed with great function in the hometown, and on tour in Derry City, Gregory's verse-play *The Coming of the Magi*. The playwright came to talk to us, for I was, God help us, among the cast, I was even one of the Magi. Gregory was a small, delicately featured man in a long, black overcoat with a Chestertonian cape. He began his talk with Browning's dramatic dialogues and ended with a glowing account of the person and poetry of his friend Joseph Campbell. Already we were familiar with some of the poems and all the songs and, unlike a lot of people who hear them and even sing them, we knew that they had been written by Joseph Campbell.

What Padraic Gregory said on that occasion I cannot exactly remember, but it pleases me now to think that it may have been something similar to the following which I was privileged to read in the centenary year of Joseph Campbell's birth.

> He was born on 15 July 1879.
> Padraic Gregory's memory here is connected with the theatre in the North. He recalled from the early years of the century: 'The Ulster Literary Theatre, then in its infancy, was producing two plays. One was *The Little Cowherd of Slainge* by Joseph Campbell, and the other *Brian of Banba* by Bulmer Hobson, in the Ulster Minor Hall, and I was taken there and give a very important part in connection with the performance. But not on the stage. I was put at the door of the hall to sell tickets and to lift the admission money. Thus began my long money-lifting connection with the Ulster Literary Theatre, and my friendship with Joseph Campbell which lasted until his departure for America.
> 'The first time I saw Campbell', Gregory said, 'he was made up for the name part in the play I have just mentioned. He had a mellow, resonant voice and could declaim heroic verse sonorously. He was a fine actor. I always remember Joseph Campbell dressed in heather-brown Donegal tweed clothes, with brown brogue shoes and brown tie. I am perfectly sure that he had suits *go leór* but, strange as it may seem, I never remember him dressed in anything save brown. He was a genial comrade and a gentle, loveable character and, in my opinion, the most intensely Irish of all the Anglo-Irish poets of his generation'.

That picture of the man and of that enthusiastic period are of interest, and I found it in 1979 in a dissertation by Norah Saunders, Sister Assumpta. The work was written under the direction of poet-professor Seán Lucey of University College, Cork. By the courtesy of the author and of the poet's two sons, and their wives, I was privileged to read the work in the centenary year and thought that as a valuable study of the poet, his life and times, it should appear in book form.

It was good to hear, in due course, that Norah Saunders and another scholarly lady, A.A. Kelly, who had written books on Liam O'Flaherty and Mary Lavin, and who had already been studying Joseph Campbell, were collaborating on a critical biography of Campbell, which later appeared from the Wolfhound Press.

The songs, as I have said, we knew already: 'My Lagan Love', 'The Gartan Mother's Lullaby', 'The Blue Hills of Antrim', 'The Ninepenny Fidil', 'The Spanish Lady', and others. When Robert Farren said that Gaelic verse sang through Campbell's poetry, he went on to insist on the reality of the singing and to point out that many who heard his songs, and, indeed, performed them professionally, paid 'no honour to Joseph Campbell for the greatest song, "My Lagan Love", written by an Irish poet in this century'.

Who that ever heard Michael O'Higgins sing that song will forget the experience? Or heard Michael O'Duffy singing of the blue hills of Antrim, or Cathail O'Beirne, long ago, singing of the ninepenny fidil? All were singers who were honoured to be friends of the poet.

And W.B. Yeats said: 'In Ireland where still lives, almost undisturbed, the last in folk traditions of Western Europe, the songs of Campbell and Colum draw from that tradition their themes, return to it, and are sung to Irish airs by boys and girls who have never heard the names of the authors'.

The last enduring folk-tradition has taken a bad rattling since Yeats wrote those words. But Campbell's songs may still be heard above the cacophonous din and they do, for any boys and girls who still care to read, provide a gateway into a fair field of poetry. Langland's vision, on a May morning on a Malvern hillside, was very much in Campbell's mind when he studied his own folk:

> Shepherd, plougher, pensioner,
> Scholar, priest and labourer,
> Symbols of the god in man
> Since the tale of Time began.

Their field was Ireland and, back of them, were the royal dead, heroes of an older day, a splendid parade out of Celtic mythology, shadowy figures all unseen, except by those who, like the poet himself, looked upon them with eyes 'conscious of the mysteries'. That was a mingling common enough to the poetry of our romantic period at the beginning of the twentieth century. But Campbell saw and felt it all with an intensity of belief that to us now, or at any rate to me, can almost be agonizing.

Nowhere do you as, at times, you do, and perhaps quite unjustly, in the case of AE, get the feeling that this mingling of the man with the mythologies, this talk about the gods returning to the ancient hills, might be a game of suburban make-believe. Or professorial codology, as in the case of Professor Tolkien. Many people may feel that that is unfair to Tolkien. And to AE. With Joseph Campbell, though, there is never any doubt but that the man and the mythologies, the ancient gods and the vision of Christ on the roads of Ireland, meet in a beauty that can too readily become a tortured agony.

In the arrangement of the poems in *The Poems of Joseph Campbell*, edited and introduced by his devoted friend Austin Clarke (Allen Figgis, Dublin: 1963), you can turn from that startling poem 'The Dwarf' to find, on the next page, the poet making his testament of love and beauty. 'The Dwarf' is a long way away from the lilting happiness of 'The Ninepenny Fidil'. The poet sees the dwarf standing by the house of the sad mother who, rumour says, walked across a grave on a black day in spring and gave birth to, in the seventh month, that poor misshapen thing. The doom, as we know, can be spiritual as well as physical. It is said that the dwarf licks cuckoo spittle and eats the dung off the roads. His face is wool-grey and the cast of his eyes is wild and faraway.

Does he see Magh Meala?
Is his breath human breath?
Are his thoughts of the hidden things
Untouched by time and death?

Hanging there by the half-door,
Dangling his devil's foot
Stock-still on the threshold
As if he had taken root.

But to see light beyond that grimacing darkness, turn the page and find the poet finding all love in lowly things, 'no less than in the lusts of Kings'. In lowly things he finds all beauty, shape and comeliness, all valour, strength and gentleness, all genius, wit and holiness. He knows that the flower grows out of corruption, and the corn out of the clay. He cries to the leper to lift his head, to the cripple to dance, to the captive to sing. He knows that the beggar eating his crust is no baser than a king.

In a man of Campbell's strong, honest and irreconcilable temperament there could be no pose about all that. It was the vital knowledge that the successful and victorious may ignore or forget. Then, to vary the intense temperature, those two poems are followed by (happily for me because it has always been one of my favourite Campbell poems) ''Tis Pretty tae be in Baile-liosan'. Those idyllic four verses could forever make a party piece for any good speaker of verse, even if only that they display at its most perfect Campbell's superb knowledge of, and his ability to use, that odd dialect of Ulster Scots. Here is the third verse: a vision of the North as all except the bigots and the madmen (and they are the same people even if their colours vary) would like it to be:

O brave are the haughs o' Baile liosan,
And brave are the halds o' green Magh-luan,
But braver the hames o' Newtownbreeda
Twined about wi' the pinks o' June.
And just as the face is sae kindly withouten,
The heart within is as guid as gold,
Wi' new fair ballants and merry music
And cracks cam doon frae the days of old.

Joseph Campbell came from a strong, and mixed, Ulster origin and was sharply conscious of the songs and stories that came down to him from the days of old in two different streams, you might say, and in three languages: Irish, English, Ulster-Scots. His grandmother used to say: 'Gather round me children. I'm going to count kindred'.

He wrote of one man with whom his work in the North brought him into contact: 'The Corporation Clerk of Works was a unique individual:

Billy Lappin. A loquacious, anything, but a black Orangeman from Loughinisland, County Down. He spoke broad Scots. I filled a notebook with his Obiter Dicta. It has been long lost. If anybody has found it, let him treasure it as the record of a young Ulster poet who hoped to save for posterity the flotsam and jetsam of Ulster's folk-wisdom, swept down by the Flood to the Day of the Mountain'.

Campbell's people were builders, even road-builders, which is a Roman thing to be. And there is a stern, unbending, Roman stance in his attitude towards the qualities, in poetry and politics and in human nature, that he disliked. He was cast in a heroic and, at times, and by his very honesty and irreconcilability, in a tragic mould. He was a man, perhaps, of few but of strong and lasting friendships, and with men of great quality: Padraic Colum, Austin Clarke, Francis Stuart and others. But he was a solitary by inclination and thus subject to loneliness. His devotion to Thoreau was unquestioning, but he went beyond Thoreau when he wrote: 'Night walking – all my best thoughts, I find, come to me that way. Poetry, like devilry, loves darkness'.

His later years were, indeed, years of loneliness and trial. He had a deep, personal grief. For his country, as he saw it, he suffered imprisonment and came out to disillusion. In the United States he lived a straitened but always a generous existence. He would raise money for anybody who seemed poorer than himself, a noble but unprofitable occupation. He laboured there like a slave to set up a centre for Irish culture. There were no easy grants then and no Eoin McKiernan, and writers-in-residence had not been heard of until much later when William Faulkner was invited to Charlottesville and the University of Virginia. On all those matters, and on the nobility with which Campbell faced up to them, the work by Sister Assumpta and A.A. Kelly is most revealing.

For his last few years Campbell returned to the Wicklow hills which he had come to love as well as he loved those black northern hills from which he had taken that other name: The Mountainy Singer. In his prison-cell he thirsted for violins, 'as drunkards thirst for wine'. He hungered for great verse, 'plain-served in ordinaries where poor bards foregather', or 'dished on plates of gold in theatres'. There is in existence a prison journal that awaits publication, perhaps with a collection of his candid and lively comments on poetry and politics, and on life as he found it in Ireland, England and America.

In that prison cell he would have given his living eyes to be able to see the Sphinx, the sun-bleached columns of the Parthenon, the doves about the lion of St Mark, the frescoes of Michelangelo, the canvases of Goya. So he said. But the sights and sounds of prison were otherwise; and, through the black crisscross of his prison-bars, he saw the infant moon cradled in the sombre shadow of the old, a sight of ill omen. In the ballad of Sir Patrick Spens it foretold wreckage and drowning, and Campbell wondered what chance would that conjunction bring to him, what destiny or doom to Ireland.

Sleepless, he hears the city clocks strike midnight. Then a cock crying like the Archangel Michael, from some black midden-heap by the cattle market, lulls his fever and brings him sweet thoughts of home:

> ... the summer peace of Wicklow fields,
> Of mountain liberties, of dew-drenched ewes,
> Of amber rivers, glassing silver birches,
> Of brooding haggards and blue cabin-smoke ...

Francis Stuart remembers Campbell on hunger strike in a prison hut, but amazingly brisk and energetic, and marching up and down the stone floor of the hut with ringing footsteps which annoyed the other prisoners.

But the last word may well be left to the poet Austin Clarke, the man who most closely, in art and in temperament, resembled Campbell. Clarke did not consider Campbell as a solitary but found that he had a laughing contempt for those 'who tried to advance themselves in literature not by the pen but by the tongue. He was steeped in traditional lore. His imaginative, intuitive knowledge of the countryside was profound. This knowledge of Gaelic life and tradition, which Synge merely touched, gave his conversation a fascinating quality. But Campbell was not merely a traditionalist. Paradoxically enough, he was immensely interested in every phase of modern poetry in England, America and elsewhere'.

And this, as Clarke remembered and recorded it, was the first meeting between those two poets:

> The first thing that comes to my mind is his voice. It was strong, vibrant and, at the same time, rich and warm. It was the voice of a man who moved among the hills. When his tall figure loomed in the doorway [of that hillside house in Wicklow] and he said, 'Come in. Come in', his voice with its pleasant Northern burr enveloped one, caught one into its own glow of hospitality, brought one in from the night and the rain to the fire on the hearth. Campbell looked like a maker of sagas rather than a lyric poet with a singularly delicate touch. He was tall, of powerful build, and, to put it romantically, his handsome features were of the eagle type. I think that his most striking characteristic was his independence of mind and character.

But, on further thought, the last words may be left to the man himself.

In a number of striking poems he studied various Irish types, and in his poem 'The Road-Maker' he spoke to his father somewhat as Seamus Heaney did in what I think of as the Spade-and-Pen poem. Campbell wrote:

Road-maker! What other name
Matches thee, O soul of flame?
Father, to whose passion I
Owe my place in destiny.

Did thy knowledge plan the way,
Fix the levels, trench the clay,
Blast the rock and roll the stone
That my feet have travelled on?

I am hardly of the trade
Thou and my forefathers made
Epic of your ancient skill,
Intellect, and iron will.

Yet by that I have from thee:
Prescience and poetry,
I make roads for the feet to tread
To the wonders overhead.

❧ 25 ❧

The Thorn in the Water:
The Stories of Michael McLaverty

THE LAST BUT ONE NOVEL THAT we had from Michael McLaverty was entitled *School for Hope*. In that novel a young woman, a schoolteacher, walking in the County Down countryside in the harvest-time, has around her 'the stooks standing on their shadows and the children's voices carrying far as in the stillness of an evening'. The stream by the roadside tumbles into a chestnut-brown pool, a bramble-branch arches into it and one thorn cuts the water 'with lines as fine as on a snail's back'.

There are many such moments in the novels and stories of Michael McLaverty: intimate moments when the person and the landscape melt into one another. Rathlin Island always had a large place in his world and in his mythology. He spent some of his boyhood there, watched the place with a careful eye, felt it in his heart and never forgot it. The island people in his first novel, *Call My Brother Back* (it appeared in 1939), and the country people in the novels *Lost Fields* and *In This Thy Day*, take with them, into the streets of Belfast, bright and detailed memories of the fields. Here, for instance, is a vision of high summer on Rathlin Island:

> The days were fiercely hot and the blue skies were grained with twirls of cloud. Heat shimmered over the beanfields and wriggled like flame-shadows above the rocks. Cows crushed into the thin shade of the hedges and swished the clegs madly with their tails. Up on the hills the lakes shrunk and left a web of dry mud-cracks on the edges. Grasshop-pers sizzled all day long in the heather. Hens scratched holes at the side of the byre; and Rover panted in the shadow of the heeled-up cart.

Careful observation, exact recording of details, have there advanced to insight, inscape. Forty years ago (a friend reminds me) I wrote, of that passage, that the face of Ireland was therein studied as a lover might study the face of the beloved. At that time I seemed to think that McLaverty showed no suspicion that the soul behind the lovely face might have its problems, as, say, in Brinsley MacNamara's *The Valley of the Squinting Windows* or *Return to Ebontheever*. Or even a suspicion that the heart might be hard, as in the novel *This House Was Mine* of Francis MacManus or in Shan F. Bullock's novel of Fermanagh, *The Loughsiders*.

McLaverty, I then said, and I still think said with a great degree of accuracy, loved the life of rural Ireland simply, poetically, without any reservation, and for its own sake. It was not for him, as it was for Liam O'Flaherty in *The Black Soul*, a place of healing refuge from the things that war and the world could do to the spirit of man. It was the great reality that had been and was and would be, without relation to any other mode of life in any other place: and even when McLaverty's uprooted people found themselves in the streets of Belfast, they brought with them, through poverty and pogrom, the innocence of children examining flowers or speculating on the mysterious flight of birds.

But there is more to it than that. Forty years ago I had not read the novel *School for Hope* for the good and obvious reason that it had not been published. And I had still to be impressed by the significance of that thorn marking the smooth skin of the water. That may seem a trivial detail, yet the merest hint in the McLaverty text can be important. The hint there given sends me back to such gems of the craft of the short story as 'The Game Cock', 'The White Mare' and 'Aunt Suzanne'.

In the first of those stories a Belfast man and his young son bring, after some hazards along the way, a fighting cock to a series of triumphs in Toome. But the day of glory ends with the conquering hero dead in a bag and even when the man says that he'll stuff the cock and keep him, there is no hiding the truth that that sort of immortality is also death.

In 'The White Mare', a stubborn old bachelor on Rathlin Island lives with his two spinster sisters, three of them in the one house and drawing the old-age pension. He says: 'We're a great stock and no mistake; a great pity none of us married!' He insists on defying age and the rheumatism and on ploughing his own field with his beloved white mare. Afterwards, while he is temporarily flat on his back, one of the sisters sells the mare to a mainland dealer: for the old man's good, of course. With supreme skill McLaverty ends the story when the mare is taken away to the mainland in the dealer's boat, and the old man, helpless and hopeless, turns back home. We are left to imagine the decay of mare and man in their separate solitudes.

In 'Aunt Suzanne', a spinster aunt comes to look after the three children of her deceased sister, whose death may have been hastened by drink and, also, to look after the house of her brother-in-law who, not surprisingly, has a thing against drink. Aunt Suzanne sings funny songs, her two nieces love her and sing with her, and her nine-year-old nephew appreciates the pennies she gives him for doing the odd chore. For one foot she has, instead, an iron ring. So right it is that we are never told what did happen to her foot. It is a tantalizing suppression, typical of McLaverty. Any explanation would have strained the fabric of the story.

But Aunt Suzanne, alas, shares her sister's weakness, is detected and sent away in disgrace, leaving behind the two weeping girls and a little boy who never understood, and who is buying chocolate with the penny she gave him before the train pulls out of the station. There are thorns even in the Eden of the children.

In the novel *School for Hope* a young woman, in her idyllic rural and seaside background, has as companion the fear that her family's medical record, a mother and sister dead in a sanatorium, will come between her and marriage. That was in the days when people talked about families as being rotten with consumption and, even if we seem to have moved away from that particular horror, the problem still does not date. If it is not consumption, it will be something else. Mankind is never at a loss for ghosts.

The spinster sister of the man Suzanne loves is bitter about the whole sad business because she has been defeated and driven out by her middle-aged brother's love for a younger and, to her, a frail and, even, a diseased woman. She prophesies: 'You needn't send for me when your troubles come'. The novel ends there. Misunderstanding and stupidity, even hatred, live and flourish in the meadows of peace. Death can have the victory. We know that the loss of the mare will make the old man's last days miserable. We are left to fear that the jealous sister's prophecy may be fulfilled. But, also, to pity her jealousy and her loneliness.

McLaverty has said about himself: 'The background I regard as fundamental and I can never treat it in a casual manner because I feel that character and background should coalesce in such a way that one is unthinkable without the other'.

And again: 'I am not interested in the abnormal or violent – voilent men are usually weak men and those who follow that incline usually lose themselves in a maze of melodrama by an insistent overemphasis. It is the half-said thing that produces intensity of expression'.

And finally: 'Life's experience is the author's raw material but his function is to clarify its night and day, its joy and sorrow and sin and grace, and give them a coherent form. That form is in life's inevitable wintering and summering'.

All three are interesting statements: matter for thought and for argument.

Because of environment, and of choice, Michael McLaverty's concern has always been with man's lot in quiet places, but he was never unaware of Ernest Dowson's aged mariners sitting on the harbour-wall and sadly saying: 'We tell you the truth. There are no fortunate islands'.

ᘓ 26 ᘔ

Green Island, Red South:
Mary Lavin and Flannery O'Connor

THIRTY MILES FROM THE CITY OF Dublin, Ireland, and going
north-west through rich green countryside you come to the town of
Navan and the River Boyne. This is the heart of the ancient county of
Meath, and the valley going eastwards to the Irish Sea at Drogheda is one
of the oldest parts of the country. Before you come to Navan or cross the
River Boyne you have passed, on the left, Tara of the High Kings of
Ireland, a series of rolling mounds of grassland not high but extensive
where bullocks and tourists and archaeologists share, and in varying
degrees disturb, the silence of the ages. A Gaelic quatrain out of a bitter
past once consoled a broken vengeful people with the consideration that
Tara was grass and look at the state of Troy, and the Sasanaigh too, in
God's good time, might come to their day of doom. That was the sort of
apocalyptic statement that Flannery O'Connor, with her Irish name and
her immediate background on the prophetic red clay of the South, might
have appreciated. She would certainly have appreciated the activities of
the hot gospellers of some obscure sect who at regular intervals, and up
until quite recently, dug recklessly into the clay of the Hill of Tara in the
hope of finding there the mislaid Ark of the Covenant.

At Navan the Boyne is joined by the Leinster Blackwater and the two
rivers between them, and their verdant valleys – verdant is a word out of
Thomas Moore's *Melodies*, but there isn't any other, or any better one –
gave Sir William Wilde, father of Oscar, the matter for one of his topo-
graphical, historical, archaeological books, *Beauties of the Boyne and
Blackwater*. Then the river goes on eastwards through one of the oldest
parts of Ireland: under the holy hill of Slane where that dubious man
Patrick did, they say, light the Pascal fire and stole the thunder, or the fire,
or breached the fire-raising copyright, of Laoghaire the High King; or by

the prehistoric burial chambers of Dowth, Knowth and New Grange where George Moore and George Russell went on a pilgrimage that was afterwards remembered in *Hail and Farewell* with something between ridicule and reverence. The valley also holds, in its long shallow green bowl, monastic ruins and ancient crosses, the abbey of Trim, the crosses of Kells, Monasterboice, Mellifont; and the ford at Oldbridge where the Williamites in 1690 crossed the water on the heels of the withdrawing Jacobites; and where the river goes on to the sea by the old cellars and towers of Drogheda, Cromwell conducted one of his most notable biblical burnings, sackings and slaughterings.

The poet F.R. (Fred) Higgins remembered in a poem a walk he was accustomed to take in the company of the late Brinsley MacNamara, the Abbey Theatre playwright and novelist, and R.M. Smyllie of *The Irish Times*, one of the last of the great editors of the British Isles, whom William Yeats, with the supreme effrontery of a man claiming the old man's right to rant, rave and be mad, described as the drunken journalist who had once been the likely lad with a sound flyfisher's wrist. Once when I suggested to Mrs Yeats that her husband had had a damned hard neck to speak thus of Smyllie, she said simply that her husband was human, too, which is a good thing, I thought, to remember about any great poet.

That Higgins poem 'The Boyne Walk' preserves a friendship, and a picture of a green, sunny valley and of a moment when three men recaptured boyhood and had the 'livelong summer day to spend'. I quote one fragment: his memory of following Brinsley, a man of that green country, along the old towing-path between the Boyne and its disused eighteenth-century canal:

> We walked as became two kings outcast
> From plains walled-in by a grass-raising lord,
> Whose saint is the Joker, whose hope is the Past –
> What victuals for bards could that lad afford?
> O none! So off went his dust from our boots,
> But his dust that day was of buttercup gold
> From a slope, with a sight that was, Man alive, grand:
> Just two servant girls spreading blue clothes
> On grass too deep for a crow to land;
> And though they waved to us we kept on our track,
> And though to the banks their own clothes soon toppled,
> We sweltered along – while my thoughts floated back
> Through shy beauty's bathing pool, like an old bottle.

When Higgins was dead and buried at Swift's Laracor and Smyllie was too corpulent to walk so far, and at such a distance, from the Pearl Bar in Dublin, I myself, a much younger man, walked often with Brinsley the eighteen miles, mostly along the Boyne towing-path, from Navan to

Drogheda; and heard from him how a small village in those green quietudes could erupt in murderous fashion, resenting a book in which every villager thought to recognize his or her face. The story of the ructions that in the 1920s, in the village of Delvin in County Westmeath, followed the publication of Brinsley MacNamara's novel *The Valley of the Squinting Windows* is as interesting, and a deal more comical, as the book itself; and Brinsley talking of it would comment something in this fashion:

> Curious thing, you know, the difference between the tempo of life in Dublin City and in Meath and Westmeath, a mere few miles away, where I was reared. Your average Dublin working-man, now, is a noisy fellow, talkative, pugnacious, something out of O'Casey. After his work, he goes to the boozer and drinks one pint of stout, two, three, maybe ten, argues loudly, sings noisily at closing time, goes home arguing or singing and quietly sleeps off his drink. But in the Midlands, in Meath and Westmeath, life isn't lived so noisily. The rivers flow smoothly, the grass grows deep, the cattle graze quietly. Your average working-man there could be a bachelor living in a cottage with his maiden aunt. In the evening after his work he walks or cycles quietly through quiet country-side to a quiet village. In a bar, not talking much, he drinks his pint, or three or four or ten, and walks or cycles quietly home and does for his maiden aunt with a hatchet. A curious thing, you know.

All this by a commodious vicus of recirculation brings me to the stories of Mary Lavin. It is interesting to note, incidentally, that Boyne, as much a goddess-river as the Liffey, does also, like Anna Livia Plurabelle, live and grow along a circling pattern: first flowing west, then curving to the north and again to the east to find the sea, and extinction and renewal.

Mary Lavin's first collection of short stories was called *Tales from Bective Bridge*, and Bective Bridge is on the middle reaches of the Boyne between the towns of Navan and Trim: a lovely place bedded down quietly on a mattress of deep pastureland. Not far away the great houses of the two branches of the Plunkett family, the one that stayed Papist and the one that didn't, still stand over broad acres and outface each other across a narrow road. One branch produced a Beato who, either because he was a bit of a politician or because Ireland, unlike Italy, never had a flourishing Communist Party, has never made it all the way to sainthood. The other branch in much later times produced a nobleman-writer, Lord Dunsany, who encouraged or discovered Mary Lavin as once he had encouraged or discovered the young poet Francis Ledwidge, who wrote sweetly and sentimentally about the Boyne Valley and must have seen it clearly even in the last moments of his life in World War I:

> Somewhere is music from the linnets' bills
> And through the leaden hours the beewings
>   drone,
> And white bells of convolvulus on hills

> Of quiet May make silent ringing, blown
> Hither and thither by the wind of showers,
> And somewhere all the wandering birds have
>   flown
> And the brown breath of Autumn chills the
>   flowers.
> But where are all the loves of yesteryear?
> Oh, little twilight ship blown up the tide,
> Where are the faces laughing in the glow
> Of morning years, the lost ones scattered wide?
> Give me your hand, oh, brother let us go
> Crying about the dark for those that died.

Mary Lavin too had felt all the sad young poet's attraction for the land of Meath. In her story 'A Gentle Soul' she writes at her most lyrical about the coming of summer to those grassy places:

> . . . in our part the summer used to come so suddenly that overnight it would seem to reach full tide, the hedges all in blossom, and the cattle in the pastures wading in through great billows of grass, as if through water, while all at once the meadows were breast high, so high indeed that once, as we went down the lane in the sidecar and saw a man walking down the path through our meadow, it was only when the wind swayed the grasses that it could be seen that by the hand he held a little girl in a pink sunbonnet!
>   Oh, the summers were beautiful; the summers were bountiful; they seemed to be made for lovers.

Nothing could be more idyllic, yet Brinsley MacNamara's hatchet is there ready for murder: if not killing of the body then withering of the spirit, hatred between kin and the long misunderstanding that is as deadly as hatred; and madness and death and the open grave.

The idyllic passage quoted is not spoken by Mary Lavin herself but by a woman called Rose Darker, one of two sisters, the daughters of a rich Meath rancher. Rose has committed the sin, heinous by the standards of her society, of falling in love, even if it is only a miserable, frustrated and unexpressed love, with her father's labouring man, and thereby drawing on her the scorn of her sister, Agatha. In one passage the pathetic Rose remembers that on the day her love died violently, the victim of a rusty runaway mare, she had been standing by the kitchen door looking across the fields, noticing that, although the summer had not yet come, 'here and there, like a spray of foam breaking before its time, far out upon a distant wave, the hawthorn had broken into blossom'. Opulent summer and its blossomy coming is the backcloth for violent death, hopeless love, a petty class consciousness and, for the pitiful Rose, accepting the drilling of her sister and father, and testifying as they dictate at the inquest, in case a family of the labouring class might get uppity notions and claim money compensation from their betters for the death of the young man.

In the end, with the grim tyrannical Agatha gone also to the grave, which under the rich green is so brown-black and wet, Rose is left to think how, when the day ends and twilight begins to descend on the countryside, she would wander across the fields to the old cemetery in which her love had been buried beside his parents and, kneeling down among the cool grasses, whisper to him all the words of love she had never spoken.

In Mary Lavin's vision of that pastoral land, that graveyard is as prominent as the burial mounds of Dowth, Knowth, and New grange are ancient; the grave gapes wide, the earth that grows grass so splendidly seems ravenous for the manure of human bodies; and small houses hold bitter families and there is, with a vengeance, great hatred, little room. It has been said ad nauseam that in Ireland everything begins at a funeral, but it is true that in Mary Lavin's stories a great deal of the action goes on around the grave. One of these stories is called 'The Cemetery in the Desmesne' (there are also, out of Mary Lavin's own selection, 'A Visit to the Cemetery', 'The Widow's Son' and 'A Happy Death') and has as its high moment a meeting and talk between a woman in the demesne gate-lodge (she has an ailing, dying child of whose lack of weight and health she is pathetically proud) and a carter who has come to the place to deliver a load of gravel to the cemetery. The carter is, to begin with, a talkative, affable man, even if he is doomed to live with two unsmiling women, his wife and sister-in-law. It is quite in character that on the way to the cemetery he should have, with an almost equally affable man at a filling-station, a cheery informative talk about varieties of sudden death on the road and elsewhere: some fool might come round a corner on the wrong side of the road and send you to eternity, or even on a straight stretch, a skid or a tyre blowing might fix you, or you could be killed by a slate falling off your own roof; or think of the steeplejack who met his end by eating tainted sardines, or the man who was sitting by his own hearth when the leg of his trousers caught fire and his wife and children could do nothing to extinguish him. This amiable patter leads neatly up to the moment when the woman at the gate-lodge with the still white child in her arms talks so eloquently about the dampness of the graveyard: 'It's an awkward place to be put down in,' she said.

> 'If the river is flooded the open grave gets filled up with water, and they have to lower the coffin down into the water. The people have to stand back, it goes in with such a splash. Sometimes the chief mourners don't like to stand back in case it would look like slighting the dead. They stand there as the coffin is pushed over the edge. The diggers run back from the splashes, but the mourners stand where they are and get it all over them. Your heart would break just to look at the poor creatures, coming out this gate on their way home after it's all over, and their good mourning clothes, that came straight out of the shop, all covered with dirt and their shoes sopping wet.'

In the morning the sister-in-law of the carter said of him: 'He makes me sick. He never stops talking'. But by his return home at nightfall the amiable fellow has been sicklied o'er with the pale cast of thought to such an extent, and is so silent, that she decides there's something wrong with him, something on his mind, and his wife wonders has he eaten something that disagreed with him. He himself is confused and doesn't quite know where his confusion comes from. Academic talk about probable forms of violent death is a fair enough social exercise for a trucker, but that day he has met the keeper of the gate of the house of the dead, the wailing woman with the doomed child; he has seen the graves that are made sodden by the same rain that keeps the grass green; and he has seen a lurking rat in the graveyard's damp grass. He has half-invented and meditated too deeply on the story of the ill-luck that followed a family which had an ailing child cured by a priest reading a gospel over it. His world will never be quite the same again.

The grave's a fine and private place; and Alice and Liddy, two young girls in the story 'A Visit to the Cemetery', going to pray, their young lips moving 'with the quick pecking movements of a bird', at their mother's grave, seem to hold out more hope for the entertainment to be found therein than Marvell was willing to grant himself or his coy mistress. Alice and Liddy are aggrieved that their mother is buried in the old cemetery in the middle of the town, in a cemetery that indeed was older than the town itself, and had once been the site of an old friary 'of which only one stump now remained, sticking up like an old tooth rotted down to its obstinate root'. Small animals, they knew, burrowed in the earth there, and careless digging and refilling of old graves exposed the bones of the past; and, besides, one met nobody there, meaning mainly young men, or on the way to or from that place. The two girls are even more aggrieved that their father will be buried in the same damp ancient clay and not in the new fashionable cemetery outside the town where the air and the view are good, where everything is neat and orderly and where the gravedigger boasts that he'll give five pounds to anyone who finds a bone after him. They console themselves with the reflection that they will not be buried in the old place unless, Alice says archly, they die old maids and are buried in the family plot. Otherwise, and in what they regard as the natural course of events for pretty young girls, they will be buried with the husbands they have not, as yet, achieved, and, at that delicate consideration, Liddy finds herself blushing and is furious with herself until she notices that Alice is blushing a little too. It is very wry humour that can mingle the love dreams of young girls with that vision of flesh finally united in corruption, of passion made perfect in the clay; but Mary Lavin presents all this so skilfully that it is only on long third thoughts that you realize you have been reading about something fairly close to horror.

Liddy and Alice, young and beautiful and unconsciously ghoulish, are at least happy in that they have not yet started to grind each other's spirit to misery as so many of the sisters, and other relatives, held prisoner in houses that seem as confined as graves, do in the Mary Lavin stories: as, for instance, two other sisters, Bedelia and yet another Liddy, do in the story 'Frail Vessel'. Liddy, the younger, makes a foolish marriage with an unsuccessful lawyer. Bedelia, the elder and a half-mother to Liddy since their parents are dead, makes a wise but not what you would call a passionate alliance with Daniel, who had been shopboy to her parents and is now shopboy and bedmate to herself. There is an hilarious picture of the first night of love, with Daniel moving from his bachelor's room to Liddy's room in the same house, his old alarm clock under his arm in case he wouldn't be up betimes to take down the shutters from the shop windows. Bedelia, who would have thought Daniel daft if he had gone on his knees before her in a courtly gesture, as O'Brien the lawyer might do before Liddy in a mingling of sentiment and mockery, is furious and disgusted when poor Liddy, with a dreamy secretive smile, and a tablecloth half-masking her face in a parody of a veiled odalisque of the timeless East, says that she wouldn't mind her feet and O'Brien's feet touching in the bed – after they were married, of course. I am reminded of Brendan Behan's theory that sex in the Abbey Theatre was M.J. Dolan, playing the ageing agricultural father of Michaleen, and slapping the knee of Eileen Crowe, playing the ageing agricultural mother of Nora, and saying: 'Mary Jane, isn't it high time we had Michaleen and Nora settled in life?' Indeed this is not the only occasion on which the quiet sombre humour of Mary Lavin comes to a crossroads with the boisterous humour of Behan to show that we're all Irish under the skin.

The conflict between the sisters intensifies over the very texture and colour of the clothes, bridal white and dark serge, to be worn at their weddings, over the tragic time when the lawyer defaults and Bedelia has the power and the money that could save him and keep Liddy and him together, over the realization – terrifying to Bedelia – that – that Liddy's body is the frail vessel for a life the like of which her body will never nourish, and that her mind can scarcely understand.

Bedelia and Liddy have their strained unhappy fellows in other families and stories: in the mother in the story 'A Cup of Tea', jealous of the father's influence over an only daughter; in the daughter torn between them in an agony in which such a triviality as whether the milk for the tea is boiled or not, can have a lunatic significance – here we are on the road to the monstrous trivialities that blot out the earth and the sun in the novels of Samuel Beckett, and we are further along that road when the daughter in a dream sees that peace will be possible and the world a wonderful place only when people all look and speak and feel and talk and think alike, when, in fact, they all think like herself and her father.

In the story 'The Little Prince', that same indomitable Bedelia drives out from the home a vagrant, spendthrift but lovable brother to make room for the growing prosperity of Daniel and herself, then lives on to know the mercilessness of remorse and of Time's revenges, when the brother vanishes forever into an unforgiving, unanswering silence in a big American city. In the story 'Posy' a woman, who might be a first cousin of Bedelia, dominates a bachelor brother, a sheep of a fellow, to the extent of denying him a happy life with his love, who was of the servant-girl class. In the end the sad parody of a man, accepting the way in which his sister has mutilated his life by his belief that her wordly wisdom saved him from something, because 'young men are very inflammable', feels also in his mean soul that Posy, the woman he loved, might have been the lucky one because she escaped from 'the dungeon of obscurity and petty provincial existence' to the upper air, to some place where the sun shone.

The vision of peace and the world wonderful that the tormented daughter saw in her dream, in the story 'A Cup of Tea', a vision of uniform people at ease in a green land, returns ironically in the opening of the story 'The Will' which, along with 'A Happy Death', adds up, in my opinion, to the second most impressive piece of Mary Lavin's fiction, second that is to the short novel 'The Becker Wives'.

The Conroy family are in a sort of uniform: the unhappy uniform of stiff black mourning clothes. Their mother's will has just been read and the one person passed over is the daughter, Lally, who married beneath her and whom her mother never saw again nor forgave. Her brothers and sisters do their best to pressure her into taking money from them so that, instead of disgracing them by running a lodging-house in Dublin, she could set up in style in a legitimate hotel. She refuses, and in anger her brother Matthew tells her that he sees now that their mother was right when she said that Lally was 'as obstinate as a tree'; and Lally, delighted that her mother had remembered her, even if it was only to accuse her obstinacy, allows her facet to brighten for a moment with the sunlight of youth 'as her mind opened wide in a wilful vision of tall trees, leafy, and glossy with light, against a sky as blue as the feathers in a young girl's hat'.

Afterwards Lally, hurrying to the railway station on her way back to her lodging-house in the city, is tormented with fragmentary memories of the teachings of the school penny-catechism on death and the hereafter: 'Pictures of flames and screaming souls writhing on gridirons rose before her mind'. So she runs for relief not to the brassy burning Jesus of Flannery O'Connor's red-clay land of prophets – there are no mad prophets in Mary Lavin's green wet country – but to a quiet priest in the presbytery, in the hope that the money she give him to say masses may ease the soul of the mother, who, to the last black moment of death, showed her resentment of Lally by leaving her no money in the will. And in that superb story 'A Happy Death' we have the whole long hopeless misery of Lally in her lodging-house: the husband, once a young lover who read poetry, now a weak creature, ailing in health, beaten by life, bullied by Lally, who stubbornly tries to make him live up to the dreams she once had of him and of herself. When all the dreams that had the stuff and colour of life in them are dead, she fastens, with an intensity that comes close to lunacy, on the dream of gaining for her husband the greatest good of all: a happy death, an odd contradiction in terms which means, not that you die roaring with laughter but, as the phrase goes, fortified by the rites of holy church. When he dies in a coma, smiling but not fully and officially blessed, she is taken screaming from the hospital ward.

Mary Lavin has an infinite sympathy for her people, as Chekhov had, but she is also just as mercilessly interested in the truth. Delicately but deliberately she prises open the lid of appearance and displays the quivering, painful emotions. The effect at times trembles nervously on the borders of fantasy, as in what I consider to be her masterpiece 'The Becker Wives'. One of the men of the middle-class Beckers, a family 'conspicuous only by being so very unconspicuous' marries a woman who is different, vivid, talkative, histrionic. The solid conventional women that the Beckers normally marry welcome to their prosaic circle this odd sprite, Flora, and are delighted to discover that by pantomimic gestures she can pretend she is fondling an imaginary green dragon.

> 'Oh, please, please,' Flora. The Becker ladies begged in mercy so much they felt they could not bear to watch anymore. It was exactly – oh but exactly – as if she had a little animal in her arms, cuddling it and talking to it and tickling it, in much the same way that they themselves ... might play with a kitten or a puppy; except – and this was important – that Flora's fingers moved delicately, guardedly, as if her pet had some prohibitive quality, such, as a scaly skin.

Around Flora, the spirit of fantasy, invading a world that is stodgy and commonplace, the prosaic and simple Becker wives make their laughing circle, never suspecting how close the dragon has brought the lovely sprite of a woman to the final fantastic detachment of madness. When she has been duly removed by the keepers, they will retain only a vague meaningless memory of her.

Cormac, one of the Irish High Kings, did, according to the legend, take the cross at Rosnaree, or the Fort of the Kings, by the River Boyne and, when dying, demanded burial in the place where he had seen the light. But his followers, as conventional as the Becker wives, decided to place him in the old pagan burial mound with his peers and predecessors. With his body, shoulder-high, they set out to ford the Boyne, but the river, in spate, swept away the king's body and washed it up at Rosnaree where shepherds in the morning found it and buried it. The legend was celebrated in the nineteenth century in a poem by Sir Samuel Ferguson. That is the only known instance of the Boyne preaching the gospel, that is, if you are not bent upon thinking that the Williamite-Jacobite affair at Oldbridge on 4 July 1690 saved the realm from popery, brass money and wooden shoes. The Boyne is, remember, a holy river, for honest Orangemen used to and may still take its water away in bottles, but the very colourings of that water, black blue and grey or muddy brown, have not the red apocalyptic glory of the southern rivers of Flannery O'Connor. Wasn't it G.K. Chesterton who kept insisting in his fine rolling verse that God made man out of red clay, a rough enough judgement on those of us who are clearly made out of blue clay?

No one could ever speak of the Boyne as the riverside baptist in Flannery O'Connor's story 'The River' speaks of that southern water in which he is as busy as the original John – who according to the schoolboy joke ate locusts and wild honey because he couldn't kep the locusts out of the wild honey. For the baptist's oratorical purpose it is a blessing forever that the river should be red. 'There ain't but one river,' he cries, 'and that's the River of Life, made out of Jesus' blood . . . the rich red river of Jesus' Blood, you people! . . . It's a river full of pain itself, pain itself, moving towards the Kingdom of Christ, to be washed away slow you people, slow as this here old red water river round my feet'. To help keep up the high mortality rate in the works of Flannery O'Connor, that slow ravenous red river devours a child. Or was it the river or that destructive Jesus who, stealing the Adversary's role, runs on the red clay like a lion seeking whom he may devour? What a Jesus this is: compounded out of Irish blood and a little Catholic symbol and the burning imagination of every perfervid Baptist preacher, black or white, who ever wowed a wooden chapel with the tongues of Moses, Paul, Elijah and William Blake. There was that unforgettable Brother Dunwoodie who, in Lillian Smith's 'Strange Fruit', in a moment of fervour added to his stature by climbing the tentpole.

Rayber, the teacher in that extraordinary novel *The Violent Bear It Away*, struggles to preserve his reason against the hereditary contamination of prophecy in his unwise blood, and with his imbecilic son before his eyes, and his nephew, Francis Marion Tarwater, who is irredeemably lost in the unscientific darkness of prophecy, to torment him still further, sees himself 'moving like an avenging angel through the world, gathering up all the children that the Lord, not Herod, had slain'. Tarwater, the nephew, whose face can look like a face in a medieval painting 'where the martyr's limbs are being sawed off and his expression says he is being deprived of nothing essential', knows that he is called to be a prophet and foresees his doom, 'trudging into the distance in the bleeding stinking mad shadow of Jesus' to receive in the end nothing but the miserable reward of a broken fish and a multiplied loaf: the revolting Bread of Life that his mad prophesying old grand-uncle was never done talking about.

The old Irish priest in the short story 'The Displaced Person' studies the peacock's tail, sees it beautiful and full of suns, full of fierce planets, and opines that Christ will come like that; but Mrs McIntyre says to him that, as far as she is concerned, Christ is just another D.P., and that in her logical practical world there are – to make it superior to Europe – no concentration camps, no ovens for burning bodies, no Christ; but in the end the Polish displaced man who works for her is as good as crucified when a resentful local worker sets a tractor going to run over him and break his back.

The Patricide, The Misfit, escaped from prison in the story 'A Good Man is Hard to Find', gives it as his mournful opinion that Jesus has 'thrown everything off balance' by being the first one to raise the dead, an error that The Misfit is not liable to repeat. Walter Sullivan says of him in an essay in *The Hollins Critic* that he represents the plight of man from the beginning of Christian history to the modern age, and he sets forth the dilemma with such blunt clarity that it cannot be misread. Jesus was truly God or he was not: between being God and not being God there is no middle ground. If He were, then all men are free to work out their destinies and the terms of their own happiness for themselves. The Misfit is aware of his own helplessness. Life is a mystery to him: the ways of fate are inscrutable. He denies flatly that he is a good man, and he expects neither human charity nor the mercy of God. He knows only that he does not know, and his awareness is the beginning of all wisdom, the first step towards faith'. That is an interesting passage, even if it does make The Misfit seem like a gentle humanitarian agnostic, for as his second step towards faith he, bringing not peace but the pistol, and his henchmen, murder a whole family including an old granny who had never done any harm except that she had high material notions and talked a lot. I have my serious doubts about The Misfit, feeling, as in the case of Graham Greene's Pinkie Brown in *Brighton Rock*, that the author has dowered a murderous bloody moron with the author's own profound and perverse theological speculations.

But it is in *Wise Blood*, Flannery O'Connor's first and only other novel, that Jesus runs riot over the red clay, and crazy Haxel Motes, possibly the craziest of all her crazy people, is made to affirm by denial, to testify, it seems, to the light even unto the quenching of the light of his own eyes. It is true that a first reading of Sophocles decided her to blind Hazel, but when she remade the novel at the suggestion of Sophocles, it also occurred to her that Jesus had blinded Paul, even if only temporarily. Thomas Huxley once implied that with careful sub-editing he could make a hand-book for unbelievers out of Newman's *Grammar of Assent*; and according to the mood, or point-of-view, or creed, or lack of creed, of the beholder this red clay and corn-patch Jesus is either the truth that burns or a deceptive destructive devil. Old lunatic Grandfather Tarwater held that even the mercy of Jesus burned.

In one of the later stories, 'The Enduring Chill', the Holy Ghost, since an urge for destruction seems to run in the wise blood of the celestial family, is no dove, by heavens, but a killer hawk. Asbury, a staid young prig of a fellow, comes home to die because 'He had failed his god, Art, but he had been a faithful servant and Art was sending him Death'. In conflict with his mother, as sons so frequently are in Flannery O'Connor's fiction – there is an interesting parallel here with Mary Lavin's view of domestic interiors – he has, in spite of her efforts to jolly him up, a death-wish strong enough to get around even the embarrassing revelation that there's nothing more the matter with him than undulant fever, the same, as the coarse country doctor puts it, as bangs in cows. On the wall of his sick room, damp had made a stain the shape of a fierce bird with spread wings and an icicle cross-wise in its beak, as if it were about to descend mysteriously and put the icicle on his head. Because of that death-wish and against the will of his mother and the verdict of the doctor it does descend:'. . . the Holy Ghost emblazoned in ice instead of fire and continued implacably to descend' – and Flannery O'Connor has killed another. Illumination may, of course, follow the icy death. In like manner this Jesus does not save, not even at the Chase Manhattan Bank, and only those of great faith will not have fears that a figure so furiously destructive in this life will be any better company in the next. But Flannery O'Connor shares this quality with her crazy prophets: that, while she drives our reason to revolt, her words and her vision burn, like that dread mercy of God, and make their mark, and we are moved and ruled by things we cannot, or refuse to, understand. She wrote in a most remarkable passage, quoted by Robert Fitzgerald in his introduction to the posthumous collection of stories, *Everything That Rises Must Converge*:

> The serious fiction writer will think that any story that can be entirely explained by the adequate motivation of the characters or by a believable imitation of a way of life or by a proper theology, will not be a large enough story for him to occupy himself with. This is not to say that he doesn't have to be concerned with adequate motivation or accurate reference or a right theology; he does, but he has to be concerned with them only because the meaning of his story does not begin except at a depth where these things have been exhausted. The fiction writer presents mystery through manners, grace through nature, but when he finishes, there always has to be left over that sense of Mystery which cannot be accounted for by any human formula.

Jesus pursues Hazel Motes from the moment his preaching grandfather – in Flannery O'Connor's world damn nearly every grandfather preaches, and age brings no peace, no tolerance, no late evening sunshine – told him that Jesus would never let him forget he was redeemed, that Jesus would have him in the end. Hazel runs from the hunter, or from a hound of heaven that would frighten the living daylights out of most of the faithful who read Francis Thompson: 'he saw Jesus move from tree to tree in the back of his mind, a wild ragged figure motioning him to turn around and come off into the dark where he was not sure of his footing, where he might be walking on the water and not know it and then suddenly know it and drown'. He decides for a while that the best way to avoid Jesus is to avoid sin; later, that the way to the truth is through blasphemy, just as the Misfit is supposed to move towards faith (or does he really?) by way of mass murder; and Hazel's final gospel is that literally there is no gospel, no word of God, no God, no Jesus: so he preaches his new church, the Church of Truth without Jesus Christ crucified, 'where the blind don't see and the lame don't walk and what's dead stays that way', a church that the blood of Jesus don't foul with redemption.

He cries out these words of wisdom in the street, standing on the bonnet of his rat-coloured car, a curious colour and a curious car, and Hazel shows his red-blooded Americanism by giving it the faith and trust that he professes not to give to Jesus. But since wisdom crying out in the street is regarded by no man or woman, a woman coming out of a cinema says to a companion: 'He's a preacher. Let's go' and passes on, leaving him to cry to the air: 'there was no Fall because there was nothing to fall from and no Redemption because there was no Fall and no Judgment because there wasn't the first two. Nothing matters but that Jesus was a liar'. A poster on the roadside rock may make the stones cry out that Jesus saves, but Hazel's response is to say that Jesus is a trick on niggers. And later, speaking not with the tongues of angels but of Jean-Paul Sartre and others, in what Flannery O'Connor may have meant as serio-comic parody, he testifies: 'Where you come from is gone, where you thought you were going to never was there, and where you are is no good unless you can get away from it. Where is there a place for you to be? No place'. He preaches that the only truth behind all the truths is no truth and since, as we all now know, where there is nothing there is God, he makes his final act of faith by blinding himself ('If there's no bottom in your eyes they hold more') and dying triv-ially in a ditch and the back of a police wagon.

His landlady, Mrs Flood – and I feel here that if Flannery O'Connor had been Amanda McKittrick Ross she would have gone the whole way and called Mrs Flood, Dalila Deluge – views the whole lunatic business with the mildly disapproving tolerance of a comfortable daughter of the earth who holds that it is easier to bleed than to sweat. Like the saintly working man of Dublin, Matt Talbot, also still uncanonized – Sean O'Casey called him Mutt Talbot, more than likely because he never paid his dues to the Irish Transport and General Workers' Union – the blinded Hazel has developed stern ascetic habits: gravel in his shoes, strands of barbed wire wrapped around his chest. Mrs Flood says: 'Well, it's not normal. It's like one of them gory stories, it's something that people have quit doing – like boiling oil or being a saint or walling up cats'.

I am reminded that in County Roscommon there's a legend of a virgin saint who had the grievous misfortune to be fallen in love with by a young prince. When she asked him what in her corruptible body he found most worthy of his love, and he said her eyes, she plucked the eyes out and cast them from her. Mrs Flood might have wondered, as I fear I did, what the chaste saint would have done had the prince professed interest in some less detachable portion of the *corp lobhtha* – the rotten body. But that seems to me the sort of grotesquerie that Flannery O'Connor would have found as clay to her fingers and would have found place for it in her own red-clay South, not in a part of green Ireland where, oddly enough, an impressively forbidding cairn marks, it is said, the grave of the mythological Balor of the Evil Eye, who also lost his eye – and he had only the one – violently, and where Loch na Suile, the Lake of the Eye, vanishes and reappears through porous limestone soil. She could have transferred to her South, too, that incident in the life of Matt Talbot when the poor man was prevented by an unseen adversary from entering the Jesuit Church in Gardiner Street, Dublin. Possibly an emanation from the Dominican Church in nearby Granby Lane, where Talbot later dropped dead, and thus, as it is piously held, providentially revealed his good life, his asceticism, and above all the heartening fact that he was a reformed drunkard, for the edification of the faithful. Was it a lingering thirst he struggled with, or the Adversary Himself? Flannery O'Connor could have been interested. She did write in *The Violent Bear It Away*, that amazing study of the growth of the soul's (young Tarwater's soul) converse and intimacy with the whispering persuasive voice, first the voice of a Stranger, then a Friend, then the Foiled Foul Fiend, almost always – and this is to be noted – the voice of something resembling reason. There is nothing that I know of in that style quite as good since James Hogg's *Confessions of a Justified Sinner*. Flannery O'Connor joins indeed with Sartre in making a very rare contribution to modern hagiography, for Hazel Motes, like Genet, is a criminal, is a murderer, even if his victim is only a poor devil of a hired false prophet: ONNIE JAY HOLY, which could be Dublinized as Only Jasus is Holy. His real name is, hilariously, Hoover Shoats. It seems there is no creed so mad or so paltry that cannot draw to itself a scoffer and/or a false prophet.

But in her own South she found all the grotesquerie she needed to gratify her heart and set her imagination soaring, even if the newspaper picture of Roy Rogers' horse going to church in Pasadena made her want to visit California 'for about two minutes' to further her researches. She was most unfair to Roy Rogers, his horse and California. She wrote to Robert Fitzgerald:

> I doubt if the texture of Southern life is any more grotesque than that of
> the rest of the nation but it does seem evident that the Southern writer is

particularly adept at recognizing the grotesque; and to recognize the grotesque you have to have some notion of what is not grotesque and why . . .

Southern culture has fostered a type of imagination that has been influenced by Christianity of a not too orthodox kind and by a strong devotion to the Bible, which has kept our minds attached to the concrete and the living symbol.

The Catholic sacramental view of life is one that maintains and supports at every turn the vision that the storyteller must have if he is going to write fiction of any depth.

There is a lot in that statement that needs qualification and a lot more with the same need in another statement of hers about the advantages and liberties that belong to the writer who belongs to the Catholic Church. One qualification would be that in one country in the world where the Catholic sacramental view of life has had its way, since the passing of the British Empire and the Fenian Brotherhood, it has created a climate hostile to literature and writers: the Irish writer being regarded by the church and the churchgoers as a cross (there's a pun there, if you want a pun) between the village idiot and the socially irresponsible rake who runs away with his neighbour's wife.

There was, though, a time when that seemed to be the thing for Irish writers to do.

It is also quite remarkable how little Flannery O'Connor's symbolism owes to the Catholic creed.

But all that is matter for stale debating societies. It is more interesting to note that when, impelled by the urgings of relatives and by her own tragic ill-health, she went to Lourdes, she dreaded the possibility of a miracle. That dread was a part of her intense vision, and I feel that she might have studied with interest that image of the crippled girl that haunts so much of the strange fiction of Francis Stuart. It is more interesting, too, to turn back to the wild world of her imagination, to that revealing chapter in which Tarwater, after he has drowned Rayber's imbecilic child – the best that struggling reason can bring into or make out of the world , is returning to the forest-clearing where he had once burned the cabin and, as he thinks, also cremated his grand-uncle, whose wish it had been to be buried with a cross over his head so that Jesus would know where to find him on the last day. Tarwater hitches a ride with a truckdriver who is carting automobiles from Detroit and who pretty rapidly comes to the conclusion that Tarwater belongs to the booby hatch: 'You ride through these States,' he says to an unlistening night, 'and you see they all belong in it. I won't see nobody sane again until I get back to Detroit'. He asks Tarwater to talk, or to tell him a joke, so as to keep him awake at the wheel, and Tarwater tells him that, although he did obey his prophet's impulsion by baptizing the imbecile, he did also save his own reason by drowning him; that he had had to prove he wasn't no prophet and he had proved it, that all he has to do now is to mind his own bidnis until he dies, that he doesn't have to baptize or prophesy. 'That don't make sense,' the driver says, 'but make up some more of it. I got to stay awake. I ain't riding you just for a good time'. So Tarwater tells him that when he gets back home, he can sleep in the stall until he builds him back a house, that if he hadn't been a fool he'd have taken his grand-uncle out and burned him outside and wouldn't have burned up the house along with him. 'Live and learn', the driver says, and asks Tarwater has he many sisters, and Tarwater tells him he was born a wreck: meaning he was the bastard child, untimely torn from the womb of a woman who was killed in a car-crash.

When daylight comes and the driver no longer needs the sound of a human voice to keep him awake, he tells Tarwater he doesn't ride nuts in the daytime, and drives on alone, not believing a blessed word the boy has told him. But one feels that realization will dawn on him and, like the truck-driver in Mary Lavin's story, he will never be the same again: for a while he has driven his truckload of autos along the borders of Flannery O'Connor's strange wonderland of symbol and prophecy. Tarwater also goes on alone, but deeper into the gloomy wood to a final conflict with that unseen Stranger who became the Friend and has now become the Adversary, to defilement by a curious pervert who could be the Adversary made visible, to the revelation that the old man has not been burned as reason demanded, but buried, by the coloured people and marked by a cross as he had desired. Tarwater in that moment of discovery has a vision more incredible than anything he talked about to the truck-driver: of his field no longer empty but as full of folk as Langland's field, a multitude, all being fed from one single basket, and he knows that his hunger is so great that he could have eaten all the loaves and fishes after they were multiplied, that nothing earthly can satisfy that hunger which came to him from a line of madmen, going back to Elijah, who would wander in the world 'strangers from that violent country where the silence is never broken except to shout the truth'.

Tarwater and his great-uncle may be mad and murderous, but in that moment of Tarwater's final vision Flannery O'Connor persuades me that even the most reasonable will find identification with them. We are all mad, all murderous and, no matter what the symbols are that have made meaning for us, we all hope for and need a particular and general salvation. This, it could be, is part of the sense of mystery which cannot be accounted for by any human formula.

Index

275